THE FOUNDER'S DILEMMAS

THE FOUNDER'S DILEMMAS

ANTICIPATING AND AVOIDING THE PITFALLS THAT CAN SINK A STARTUP

NOAM **WASSERMAN**

PRINCETON UNIVERSITY PRESS   PRINCETON & OXFORD

In the United Kingdom: Princeton University Press,
6 Oxford Street, Woodstock, Oxfordshire OX20 1TW

press.princeton.edu

Paperback ISBN 978-0-691-15830-3

The Library of Congress has cataloged the cloth edition of this book as follows

Wasserman, Noam, 1969–
   The founder's dilemmas : anticipating and avoiding the pitfalls that can sink a startup /
Noam Wasserman.
      p. cm. — (The Kauffman foundation series on innovation and entrepreneurship)
   Includes bibliographical references and index.
   ISBN 978-0-691-14913-4 (hardcover)
   1. New business enterprises—Management. 2. Entrepreneurship.˜I. Title.
   HD62.5.W375 2012
   658.1'1—dc23
                                                                        2011037954

British Library Cataloging-in-Publication Data is available

Published in collaboration with the Ewing Marion Kauffman Foundation and the Berkley
Center for Entrepreneurial Studies, New York University

This book has been composed in Sabon and Trade Gothic

Printed on acid-free paper. ∞

Printed in the United States of America

20 19 18 17 16 15 14 13

CONTENTS

ILLUSTRATIONS

PART I
INTRODUCTION AND
PRE-FOUNDING

CHAPTER ONE
INTRODUCTION

IT'S UNFORTUNATE BUT TRUE: IF ENTREPRENEURSHIP IS A BATTLE, most casualties stem from friendly fire or self-inflicted wounds. Some four decades ago, sociologist Arthur Stinchcombe attributed much of the "liability of newness"—the particularly high failure rate of new organizations—to problems within a startup's founding team. More recently, venture capitalists in one survey attributed 65% of failures within their portfolio companies to problems within the startup's management team.[1] Another study asked investors to identify problems they thought might occur within their portfolio companies; a full 61% of such problems involved issues within the team.[2]

Researchers have extensively studied the failure rates highlighted by Stinchcombe. Unfortunately, they have focused almost entirely on external causes rather than on the more numerous internal problems Stinchcombe identified.[*] We know amazingly little about the chief perils that beset the entrepreneurial activity we so often acclaim as the very heart and soul of the economy. As researcher Amar Bhide put it, "Entrepreneurs who start and build new businesses are more celebrated than studied."[3]

---

[*] In a classic two-page discourse, Stinchcombe (1965) argued that the liability of newness was due to three internal factors—the needs for the team to develop working relationships, to find their new roles, and to split financial rewards among themselves—and one external factor—the lack of relationships with potential suppliers, customers, and other external parties. The last factor has received vast amounts of attention, the first three very little.

This book scrutinizes those all-important "people problems" that bedevil all founders—even solo founders—and their startups.* These problems often follow predictably from common dilemmas faced by any startup as it grows and evolves—what I call "founding dilemmas." One such dilemma recurs throughout the stages of company development: The need to negotiate a trade-off between wealth and control, between building financial value and maintaining a grip on the steering wheel. Adding further complexity, founders' early choices can have delayed and unexpected but significant effects,[4] sometimes because natural inclinations such as passion, optimism, and conflict avoidance lead to shortsighted decisions. This book delves into the challenges faced or created by each of the main groups of players involved in a typical startup, beginning with the core founder and moving on to his or her cofounders, early hires, and investors.

I've spent over a decade working with hundreds of founders and future founders, and I've collected and analyzed data on nearly 10,000 founders in the technology and life sciences industries. This book will draw on my unique dataset, and we will also follow actual founders as they launch new companies and struggle with dilemmas identified in my research. Most centrally, we explore the experience of Evan Williams, a young entrepreneur who moved from rural Nebraska to the San Francisco area in the mid-1990s, hoping to catch the wave of the Internet boom after working on a failed startup back home. A self-taught Web designer and programmer, Evan recognized the potential of Internet applications, particularly in the exploding area of self-publishing, and created Blogger, one of the first and most popular blogging tools. Later, Evan developed an early podcasting idea, Odeo, which he believed would enable nontechnical people to produce, publish, and share audio content, much as Blogger had done for millions of ordinary people with the written word.

In both startups, and then later when he went on to found and lead Twitter before leaving to work on yet another startup, Evan faced key *dilemmas*—difficult decisions at important forks in the

---

*This is not to say that choice of strategy, business model, and industry segment are not important. We will indeed consider the effects of those choices when appropriate.

road of his entrepreneurial journey—and took steps that would shape the startup's future, affect its value, and help determine his degree of control over it. With Blogger, Evan chose to cofound with his former girlfriend, fighting to retain for himself the CEO title and a majority of the equity. He funded the company using his own money along with money from friends, family, and angel investors, intentionally avoiding venture capitalists (VCs). He hired friends (and later, volunteers) to inexpensively develop the technology. When the dot-com boom ended and Blogger ran low on cash, he received an acquisition offer but refused to sell—a decision that would send his cofounder and his entire staff fleeing for the exits and reduce him to soliciting donations to keep Blogger alive.

Evan eventually sold Blogger to Google and turned next to developing Odeo, partnering with an acquaintance who had experience in online audio. Using some of his proceeds from Blogger, Evan seeded Odeo and let his cofounder take the CEO role. As Evan realized the huge potential for podcasting, he took over as CEO and raised $5 million from VCs, who stepped in to help make significant decisions. With the VC money, Evan hired an experienced and expensive leadership team, hoping to develop Odeo quickly enough to stay ahead of foreseeable and formidable competitors such as Apple and Yahoo.

Evan holds particular interest for us because his very different approaches to founding and running Blogger and Odeo highlight the wide variety of options available to founders. Evan's decisions may seem wildly inconsistent: He takes VC funding in one case and vehemently resists it in another. He hires his pals for next to nothing in one case and pays big bucks for the pros in another. He battles his own ex-girlfriend for the CEO role and finally squeezes her out of the company but then readily turns the reins over to a mere acquaintance in his second startup. Going deep into Evan's story, we will explore both the underlying consistency of his decisions and the powerful motivations and situational factors at work, an exercise that will enable current or would-be founders and others involved in startups to unlock the mystery of their own motivations and dilemmas as they enter the battle that is entrepreneurship.

CORE CONCEPTS AND ARGUMENTS

Founding a startup can seem like a fragmented, even chaotic, way of life. Perhaps no business pursuit is messier than creating an organization from scratch. Founders themselves are an extremely varied group, and academic research on entrepreneurs is fragmented, with different researchers looking at different stages of the founding process, turning different disciplinary or functional lenses on the issues they study, and developing findings with little apparent consistency. Meant for entrepreneurial scholars, educators, and mentors of entrepreneurs as well as entrepreneurs themselves, *The Founder's Dilemmas* highlights the consistent, coherent, and systematic patterns and trade-offs involved in the most critical founding decisions, from the dreamer's decision of whether or not to found in the first place through the founder's decision to exit the company he or she has created.

Before we can get started, we must define some core concepts and arguments. I focus the discussion on the founding of *high-potential startups*; that is, startups (often technology- or science-based) with the potential to become large and valuable, even though their founders may subsequently make decisions that limit their growth. Where necessary, I integrate relevant findings from research on high-potential startups with the larger literature on founding small businesses, careful to note differences between the founding of high-potential startups and the founding of small businesses that are designed to remain small and owner-operated.*

Founders, as I speak of them, are individuals who start new organizations to pursue opportunities, as scholar Howard Stevenson put

---

* Carland et al. (1984:354) state, "[A]lthough there is overlap between entrepreneurial firms and small business firms, they are different entities." Aldrich et al. (2006) differentiate between the small businesses on which they focus and "high technology" startups, such as those studied in the Stanford Project on Emerging Companies (SPEC). Yet, many of SPEC's startups were outside traditional "technology" industries, as is the case with the life sciences startups in my dataset, necessitating the use of a broader term for such organizations. (Thus, I use "high-potential startups.") Schumpeter (1934) provides us with another way to differentiate between small businesses and "entrepreneurial" businesses. He characterizes new entrepreneurial businesses as being geared toward introducing new goods, introducing new methods of production, opening new markets, and/or opening new supply sources. See Carland et al. (1984) for further discussion of these characteristics and differences.

it, "without regard to the resources they currently control."[5] They make the early decisions that shape the startup and its growth, an influence that begins even before the founding itself and that can extend through all stages of the startup's development.* This book's central message is that these founding decisions need to be made *by design*, not by default. Each decision requires the founder to assess multiple options; there are more critical decisions—and more options within each decision—than many founders realize. Often, the "right" decision is by no means obvious, and may even be counter-intuitive. In addition, it can come with a burdensome cost, making the decision gut-wrenching and requiring the founder to face stark trade-offs. Meanwhile, the most common decisions—cofounding with friends, splitting equity equally among cofounders, etc.—are often the most fraught with peril. That's why I refer to the decisions discussed in this book as *dilemmas*. Founders who feel they have gained everything and lost nothing by an early decision that felt like a no-brainer may be in for a nasty surprise later on, when they find out what trade-off they should actually have been considering.

The major parts of *The Founder's Dilemmas* explore the dilemmas founders face by progressively introducing new players whose involvement in a startup provokes difficult decisions that significantly affect the startup's direction and outcomes. We begin with the core founder, then add cofounders, and end with hires and investors. In each unfolding part, we examine the impact of these players on the startup's outcomes—most centrally, on the stability of the founding team, the valuation of the startup, and the founders' abilities to keep control of the board of directors and the CEO position. An appendix to Chapter 11 also delves into exit dilemmas, which come long after founding but are faced by founders lucky enough to make it to that point, and which involve many of the same underlying factors.

The primary founding dilemmas we'll explore, and the questions a potential founder should ask about them, break down into the following:

---

* Stevenson's definition of entrepreneurship has also been applied to people who did not start their organizations but are "acting entrepreneurially" in building those organizations. In contrast, "founders" are the people who *start* their organizations.

1. **Pre-founding: Career Dilemmas**—When in my career should I launch a startup? If I am passionate about an idea, but haven't accumulated the right career experiences yet, or the market is not yet receptive to my idea, or my personal situation is unfavorable, should I make the leap anyway?

2. **Founding Team Dilemmas**—Deciding to launch a startup introduces many more dilemmas regarding the startup's founders.

   a. **The Solo-versus-Team Dilemma**—Should I launch the business myself or try to attract cofounders?

   b. **Relationship Dilemmas**—Whom should I try to attract as cofounders: Friends? Family? Acquaintances? Strangers? Prior coworkers?

   c. **Role Dilemmas**—What positions should each of us take within the startup? Which decisions can we make alone, and which should we make as a team? How should we make those decisions?

   d. **Reward Dilemmas**—How should we divide equity and other financial rewards among the founding team?

3. **Beyond the Founding Team**—Both the startup's growth and lingering gaps in the founding team's abilities or resources often require founders to consider adding nonfounders and their resources. This introduces further dilemmas.

   a. **Hiring Dilemmas**—What types of people should I hire at different stages of growth? What challenges will my early hires face as the startup grows? Should I compensate early hires differently from later hires?

   b. **Investor Dilemmas**—What types of investors should I target at different stages of growth? What challenges will these investors introduce?

   c. **Founder-CEO Succession**—Why and how are founders replaced as CEOs of the startups they founded? How can founders exert more control over the process? What happens to the founder and to the startup after he or she is replaced by a hired "professional CEO"?

Figure 1.1. Sequence of Founding Dilemmas

Figure 1.1 is a high-level summary of these dilemmas and a road-map to which we will return regularly.

These dilemmas do not necessarily occur in the clear sequence implied by the book's structure. The founding process is often chaotic and nonlinear,[6] with founders improvising rather than following a script to build their startups.[7] For example, core founders often get an idea—the proverbial light bulb goes off—and then face the question of whether to pursue it alone or attract cofounders. This is the "idea-then-team" approach to building a startup, exemplified in this book by Tim Westergren (of Pandora Radio) and others. But it can also happen that a team decides to work together on a startup, *then* hunts for an idea. This is the "team-then-idea" approach, exemplified by Janet Kraus and Kathy Sherbrooke, who met at Stanford Business School, formed a close working relationship through joint leadership roles, and decided that they would eventually try to find an idea with which to found a company. That startup later became the corporate-concierge company Circles. Given such differences in sequence, I've written this book so that people who want to learn about founding dilemmas in sequence can read the chapters in order while people interested in specific dilemmas can go straight to the chapters that most interest them.

More important than the sequence is what the dilemmas have in common: They are all difficult but necessary decision points, each with a number of often-unrecognized options that, in turn, have important consequences for the founder(s) and the startup. They each call for careful and rational decision making—sometimes by a lone founder and sometimes by a founding team. Finally, the dilemmas examined in this book all hold in common their tendency to manifest the following three major themes.

Short-term versus Long-term Consequences

An "easy" short-term decision may introduce long-term problems; a "hard" short-term decision may often be best in the long run. *Conflict avoidance* often leads founders to make easy short-term decisions; they succumb to the temptation to sidestep or postpone acknowledging—not to mention resolving—these dilemmas, especially if coming to a decision would require difficult conversations about what could go wrong. Let's suppose you have started a company and made your brother the chief financial officer, as did one of the founders we will study. What if your brother turns out not to be very good at it? The only thing more awkward and awful than talking about that in advance would be dealing with it once it's happening. Founding a startup is akin to a wedding, a declaration of mutual devotion. It seems inappropriate and even counterproductive to plan for a breakup, yet in entrepreneurship, failing to make the prenup part of the wedding vows, so to speak, can prove disastrous.

To make matters worse, entrepreneurs usually find it much harder and more costly to undo an early founding mistake than to make the right decision to begin with. Sequences of decisions are also often *path dependent*; early decisions tend to close off future options that the founder would otherwise have regarded as attractive. We will examine costly mistakes that should be avoided and, where possible, explore ways to undo such mistakes.

Members of the entrepreneurial community often say that the founding process is "a marathon made up of a series of 100-yard dashes." Every 100 yards, the runner/founder faces a key decision with long-term consequences. Unless you have a clear picture of the path to the finish line, decisions made during any specific dash can throw you off course or put you out of the race altogether.

Natural Biases: The Perils of Passion, Optimism, and Instinct

Founders tend to pride themselves on being action-oriented and optimistic—necessary traits, indeed. A founder's passion is essential to launching a startup, but it can become deadly at almost every step.

Likewise, founders' natural biases—toward optimism over realism, toward instinct over systematic planning, toward strong attachment to their ideas, their startups, and their employees over dispassionate reasoning—often turn on them.

Take optimism. Excessive confidence and optimism in the start-up's prospects can lead entrepreneurs to involve family and friends both as employees and as investors, imperiling both the relationships and the startup. Optimism leads founders to make overly rosy predictions about their own chances of success in comparison to their competitors' chances,[8] to overestimate their own abilities and knowledge,[9] to underestimate their initial resource requirements, and to fail to plan for foreseeable problems. As a result, founders often fail to attract the resources they will actually need, increasing their chances of failure.[10] Too much hubris, confidence, and passion can hinder a founder from exploring alternative approaches and making necessary adjustments.[11] In addition, the entrepreneurial environment itself can exacerbate a founder's vulnerability to his or her own overconfidence. Many entrepreneurs work in highly uncertain and "noisy" environments in which feedback is ambiguous and based on uncertain evidence. Such environments render people especially susceptible to cognitive biases and errors, including overconfidence,[12] and to following their instincts, the one "input" that does seem clear.

As we will find in each chapter, founders need to see past their instincts and their natural propensity for wishful thinking to grasp the full range of options and consequences. They need to expect the best while preparing for the worst and to make decisions strategically rather than reactively. Founders may repeatedly find that simply following their instincts will prevent them from thinking hard enough about their decisions and the consequences of particular paths of action.

Divergences among Can, Do, and Should

Thanks to conflict avoidance, path dependence, natural biases, and ignorance of the long-term consequences of their decisions, founders often take actions that diverge considerably from what they *should* do. In each chapter, we will explore the range of available options (what founders *can* do) and how often founders choose each option (what they *do*). Whenever possible, we will examine how decisions affect important outcomes, such as the startup's growth, the founding team's stability, and the founder's long-term control; this will offer insight into what founders *should* do. Each chapter will close with prescriptive recommendations: how founders can make better decisions.

First-time founders will likely not know about the dilemmas we will examine. They may not understand the full range of options available to them, and they may not appreciate their decisions' long-term and often cumulative consequences. (They may not even realize they are making an important decision!) But even experienced founders can blunder, especially if their experience has afforded a vivid but limited picture of the founding dilemmas.

WEALTH VERSUS CONTROL: A CLOSER LOOK

Now that we've introduced the key concepts and arguments relating to founders' dilemmas, let's probe deeper into the most common and difficult dilemma of them all. Founders may misunderstand not only the rules and moves of the game, but also their goals in playing it. Many admire founders who built and still run their companies, startup founders who became rich and powerful CEOs. They remember Bill Gates, the geeky teenager who became the fearsome CEO of one of the world's biggest and most aggressive companies, not to mention the world's richest person. Yet it is the rare founder who achieves this "entrepreneurial ideal" of building a business, running it, and getting rich from it. In fact, a dirty little secret of entrepreneurship is that many decisions along the entrepreneurial journey—even unquestionably "right" decisions—tend to push that ideal a little farther out of reach by forcing the founder to choose between building the company's value and maintaining his or her own control over it.* Evan Williams faced these trade-offs with each

---

* Parts of this trade-off have parallels in at least two other academic literatures. First, the finance literature has looked at the "private benefits of control," using such measures as

step he took building Blogger and Odeo. The very different decisions he made in each case brought about very different outcomes precisely because he had struck different trade-offs.

Although the desires for wealth and control seem complementary, as entrepreneurial motivations they turn out to exist in perpetual tension with one another. This counterintuitive clash results from the central challenge entrepreneurs face—the "resource-dependence" challenge.[13] Founders need to attract outside resources—people, information, and money—in order to pursue opportunities and build the greatest value.[14] But acquiring these resources typically requires that founders cede more and more control. Cofounders and key employees want equity. Skilled and experienced employees want to call some of their own shots. Investors want to protect their investments, typically by means of a strong presence on the startup's board and by other terms of the deal structure.

With a wide range of possible options, how can entrepreneurs choose the best one? The key is to know what they want to accomplish with any given decision. Similarly, when founders must choose over and over again between profiting from their hard work and keeping control of their own creation, the best way for them to know what to do is to know their own motivations—why are they there in the first place? An individual's motivations are almost always complex and rarely transparent to anyone—including the individual himself or herself. Still, research shows that founders' two most common motivations are (a) building wealth and (b) driving and controlling the growth of their startups.[15] Founders who consistently make decisions that build wealth are more likely to achieve what I call a "Rich" outcome (greater financial gains, lesser control), while founders who consistently make decisions that enable them to

---

the difference in the prices of securities that are identical except for their voting rights, and found that people are willing to give up economic gains to gain control or voting rights (e.g., Grossman et al., 1988; Lease et al., 1983). Second, the negotiations literature (e.g., Walton et al., 1965) has examined some elements of the theoretical tension between value claiming and value creation.

maintain control of the startup are more likely to achieve what I call a "King" outcome (greater control, lesser financial gains).*

Multiple studies have confirmed that these two motivations are the most common. In the Kauffman Foundation's study of 549 founders of American technology startups, 75% of the respondents said that building wealth was a very important motivation for becoming an entrepreneur and 64% said the same of wanting to own their own businesses.[16] Likewise, the Panel Study of Entrepreneurial Dynamics asked 1,214 respondents about their motives for starting a business. The top six motivations were control motivations, such as freedom to take one's own approach to work and fulfilling a personal vision, and wealth-building motivations, such as gaining financial security and building great wealth.[17] The CareerLeader database, which includes more than 2,000 entrepreneurs (and 27,000 executives in total) worldwide, found that for male entrepreneurs in their 20s and 30s, the top four motivators all amounted to forms of control or wealth gain.† Other motivations, such as intellectual challenge, altruism, and prestige, can prove important, but across entrepreneurs as a whole, wealth and control compose the big two, and are also the two that repeatedly come into conflict with each other.‡

A founder who knows whether wealth or control is his or her primary motivation will have an easier time making decisions and can make *consistent* decisions that increase the chances of reaching

* This is one of the areas in which owner-operated small businesses differ significantly from high-potential startups, which require significant resources to reach their full potential.

† The very extensive CareerLeader survey, which was developed by psychologists and psychometricians Dr. Tim Butler and Dr. James Waldroop, also evaluates a person's core interests, the kind of organizational culture he or she most enjoys and succeeds in, his or her strengths and weaknesses, and the characteristics that may limit his or her success. Chapter 2 lists the 13 potential motivators and details the breakdown of motivators by entrepreneur/non-entrepreneur, gender, and age group.

‡ Founders often talk broadly about starting a business because they want to "have an impact." Yet what they mean by "impact" can vary widely. Control-motivated founders might dream of bringing to market a product that fully realizes their uncompromised vision, even if it means that fewer people will buy it. Wealth-motivated founders might dream of getting a product into as many hands as possible, even if the founder wound up having little influence over the product's characteristics and features. Diverging ideas about impact can—and should—lead founders to make very different decisions and take very different actions.

the desired outcome—Rich or King. Figure 1.2 summarizes the core wealth-versus-control dilemmas we will examine throughout Parts II and III and that we will revisit in the book's concluding chapter. (In Chapter 11, we will also explore the potential advantages and risks of making deliberately inconsistent decisions and of trying to maximize both wealth and control.) Yet the motivations themselves do not necessarily remain fixed. Founders must also watch for changes in their own motivations; we will consider the factors that cause such changes and how they should affect a founder's subsequent decisions.

UNSOLVED PUZZLES

One test of any new framework or model is whether it can explain unanswered questions or unsolved "puzzles." This book will tackle puzzles about entrepreneurs, including the puzzle of "the missing private-equity premium" and the notion that founders aren't as powerful within their companies as we commonly assume.

Most economists assume that entrepreneurs are out to make a lot of money. According to one researcher, "That the entrepreneur aims at maximizing his profits is one of the most fundamental assumptions of economic theory."[18] One recent study supports the notion that entrepreneurs want to build personal wealth by owning equity in a valuable startup,[19] finding that many founders of high-technology startups believe they stand a much greater chance of becoming wealthy by launching a startup than by ordinary employment.[20]

If many founders really do believe this, it appears they are largely wrong. On average, entrepreneurs earn no more by founding startups than they would have earned by investing in public equity—less, in fact, from a risk-return perspective.[21] One large study of startups suggested that, on average, it would not make sense for potential entrepreneurs with a normal amount of risk aversion and a moderate amount of savings to become founders of venture-backed startups.[22] Likewise, for the self-employed, initial earnings are lower and earnings growth significantly slower than for those engaged in paid

Potential Participants in the Startup	Decision Area	Decisions Oriented toward Maintaining Control	Decisions Oriented toward Maximizing Wealth
Cofounders	Solo vs. team	Remain solo founder (or attract weak cofounders)	Build founding team; attract best cofounders
	Relationships	First look to immediate circle for "comfortable" cofounders	Tap strong and weak ties to find the best (and complementary) cofounders
	Roles	Keep strong control of decision making; build hierarchy	Give decision-making control to cofounders with expertise in specific areas
	Rewards	Maintain most or all equity ownership	Share equity to attract and/or motivate cofounders
Hires	Relationships	Hire within close personal network (friends, family, and others) as required	Aggressively tap broader network (unfamiliar candidates) to find the best hires
	Roles	Keep control of key decisions	Delegate decision making to appropriate expert
	Rewards	Hire less expensive junior employees	Hire experienced employees and incent them with cash and equity
Investors	Self-fund vs. take outside capital	Self-fund; "bootstrap"	Take outside capital
	Sources of capital	Friends and family or money-only angels; tap alternative sources (e.g., customer prepayments or debt) if possible	Target experienced angels or venture capitalists

	Terms	Resist investor-friendly terms (e.g., refuse any supermajority rights)	Be open to terms necessary to attract best investors (e.g., supermajority rights)
	Board of directors	Avoid building official board; when built, control composition and makeup	Be open to losing control of board if necessary to get best investors and directors
Successors	Trigger of succession	Avoid succession issue until forced	Be open to initiating succession when next stage of startup is outside one's own expertise
	Openness to succession	Resist giving up the CEO position	Be open to giving up CEO position to better CEO
	Desired role after succession	Prefer to leave than to remain "prince"	Want to remain executive in position that matches skills and preferences
Other factors	Preferred rate of startup growth	Gradual to moderate	Fast to explosive
	Capital intensity	Low capital intensity	High capital intensity
	Core founder's "capitals"	Well equipped to launch and build startup without much help	Important gaps that should be filled by involving others
Most likely outcome		Maintain control; build less value	Build financial value; imperil control

Figure 1.2. Wealth-versus-Control Dilemmas

employment, a finding that has been confirmed in a variety of industries and using a variety of earnings metrics.[23] All told, entrepreneurs earned 35% less over a 10-year period than they could have earned in a "paid job."[24] The authors of these studies therefore wondered why so many intelligent people would wish to play this game if there is indeed no "private-equity premium."[25] In Chapters 2 through 10, we will find pieces of the answer, while Chapter 11 offers a comprehensive answer: Founders face decision after decision in which they must choose between increasing their wealth and maintaining control. Founders who choose to remain King should indeed end up less Rich.

Turning to the question of founder power, academic studies have assumed that the founder of a startup—the person who conceived the idea and assembled the people and resources—looms as a powerful person within that startup.[*] How could the "revered founder" not be?[26] Yet once again, the evidence described here belies a fundamental assumption. My quantitative research found that a high percentage of founder-CEOs are replaced as CEO, most often against their wills.[27] The public thinks of business eminences such as Bill Gates, Richard Branson, Anita Roddick, and Michael Dell—wealthy and powerful CEOs of the companies they created—but these are the very rare exceptions. Far more common is the founder-CEO who is replaced before his or her startup gets anywhere near the public markets. How can we explain this? And why is it that founders receive, on average, significantly *lower* compensation than nonfounders?[28] Again, these seemingly puzzling facts will make sense by the time we revisit them in Chapter 11.

In much of the academic literature, wealth and power go hand in hand. In C. Wright Mills's classic analysis of the "power elite," for instance, the corporate power and economic wealth of top executives reinforce each other, with corporate positions serving as

---

[*] For instance, in his seminal study of the dimensions of executive power, Finkelstein (1992:509) posits that founders not only are powerful figures within the startup team itself, but "may gain power through their often long-term interaction with the board, as they translate their unique positions to implicit control over board members." The power of the founder is assumed to be so strong that it even enhances the power of the founder's relatives who are involved in the startup.

the source of wealth while "money provides power."[29] However, my research has found that wealth and power are decoupled for entrepreneurs and, indeed, in active conflict. As a result, few founders of high-potential startups can achieve both wealth and power; most choose between one or the other and often end up with neither. Even a seemingly reasonable strategy for achieving high levels of both wealth and power, rather than maximizing one over the other, is actually more likely to put them both out of reach. We will see why this frustrating condition occurs.

10,000 FOUNDERS STRONG

To paint a rich but rigorous picture of the most important decisions made by founders and the outcomes that founders experience, *The Founder's Dilemmas* marries deep case studies with analyses of a unique large-scale database.* Given the lack of comprehensive public data sources about startups, I collected my own data from across the United States by performing annual surveys of private high-potential startups. The survey included questions about each startup's founders, nonfounding executives, compensation and equity holdings, financing history, board of directors, and other dimensions of organizational life. I conducted these surveys for 10 consecutive years, from 2000 through 2009, creating a unique dataset that includes 9,900 founders—and more than 19,000 executives in total—from 3,607 startups. These data are more representative of high-potential startups in the United States than any other dataset of comparable size and richness. The decade covered in the surveys spanned all stages of the business cycle, from the heights of exuberance in Internet startups to the depths of despair and pessimism, and back. As such, it forms the quantitative backbone for every chapter of this book. Appendix A provides detailed breakdowns of the startups that

---

* For a discussion of when "hybrid" methods (those that integrate qualitative and quantitative methods) are appropriate for domains in which our knowledge of a phenomenon is still developing, see Edmondson et al. (2007).

participated in the surveys as well as the survey questions posed to entrepreneurs.

The dataset and case studies both focus on the two most central industries for high-potential startups, technology and life sciences.* Together, these industries dominate every measure of young startup employment and funding. Of the initial public offerings (IPOs) during the decade (2000–2009), 48% came from those two industries, and no other industry accounted for more than 12%.[30] Furthermore, of the angel capital invested during the decade, 74% went to those two industries,[31] as did 71% of venture capital.[32] Many more low-tech "small businesses" (themselves the subject of a growing literature) start up each year than high-potential startups, but most of those small businesses lack employees and do not intend to grow or innovate.[33] This leaves high-potential startups as the core of the economic growth associated with entrepreneurship.

My focus on technology and life sciences startups in the United States allows us to examine the tensions between wealth and control, particularly potent in these startups because of their intense need for outside resources and because of the terms under which entrepreneurs typically acquire those resources. Including large numbers of both technology and life sciences startups enables us to compare the data and dynamics from those very different industries and assess which patterns are industry-specific.[†] Where we find patterns common to both industries, we can feel more confident that they generalize to startups outside these two industries. On the other hand, the degree to which the patterns described here apply outside the United States is an open question that deserves empirical attention. A lack of financing options in many other countries may preclude founders from considering some of the investor-related

---

* I will usually focus on the commonalities across these two industries, but at times I will also use the technology startups as a baseline against which to observe differences between them and life-sciences startups (e.g., in the preponderance of solo founders and in the amounts of capital they raise from investors).

† But even for patterns that are common to both information technology startups and life sciences startups, we cannot conclude that they are universal without further cross-industry analysis.

decisions described in Chapter 9, while a lack of experienced executives might preclude some of the hiring dilemmas described in Chapter 8. In other industries, such as those that are not capital-intensive or those that can attract customer revenues before they incur expenses (such as those in which subscription-based business models proliferate), founders may not have to consider outside financing options because they can fund their startups themselves. The applicability to those industries of the dilemmas described here is likewise an open question, one taken up in detail in Chapter 11.

INTRODUCTION TO THE PRINCIPAL CASE STUDIES

Of the more than three dozen case studies of founders of high-potential startups we'll examine, I chose to highlight seven across multiple chapters, both for the insights gained from the dilemmas faced by the founders and for the window these case studies collectively open on a wide range of circumstances, dilemmas, decisions, trade-offs, and outcomes. Figure 1.3 summarizes these seven startups in terms of their founders' backgrounds, their founding teams, and their hiring and investor decisions.[*] Let's briefly meet these six entrepreneurs (in addition to Evan Williams, whom we've already met) and introduce the dilemmas they faced in starting and running their businesses.

Pandora Radio's Tim Westergren is as unlikely a founder as you could imagine. He studied piano and political science at Stanford, then worked as a nanny, ran an admissions office at Stanford, and started a rock band, touring with it for nearly a decade before deciding to move on to freelance composing. During his composing years, Tim had the idea to create a music database (which he called the "music genome project") that categorized music based on a long list of attributes and that suggested to users new artists and songs that fit their tastes. In 1999, Tim met Jon Kraft, a Silicon Valley

---

[*] Full-length Harvard Business School case studies are available from HBS Publishing for each of the principal case studies below and for most of the other cases discussed in this book. Appendix B provides full citations for those cases.

Startup (Core Founder)	First-Time Founder?	Solo Founder?	Prior Relationship with Cofounders	Hiring	Investors
Pandora Radio (Tim Westergren)	Yes	No	Acquaintances	Friends	Friends
Masergy (Barry Nalls)	Yes	Yes	N/A	Young, replace as startup scales	Top partners from top VC firms
Smartix (Vivek Khuller)	Yes	No	Classmates (and one prior coworker)	Pre-hiring	Pre-funding
Sittercity (Genevieve Thiers)	Yes	Yes	"Couple-preneur"	Young, replace as startup scales	Angel investors
Ockham Technologies (Jim Triandiflou)	Yes	No	Prior coworkers	N/A	Deciding on angel vs. VC
Blogger/Odeo (Evan Williams)	Serial founder	No	Various	Various	Various
FeedBurner (Dick Costolo)	Serial founding team	No	Prior coworkers	Various	Various

Figure 1.3. Principal Case Studies

entrepreneur. The two decided to pursue Tim's idea and formed Pandora (originally called Savage Beast), adding Will Glaser, a talented software engineer, as the third cofounder and CTO. The team split the equity equally, adopted a clear division of labor that matched their very different areas of expertise, and gave each founder autonomy to make hiring and business decisions within his own function. However, as the company burned through its dwindling cash and had to defer founder and employee salaries, these early decisions about roles and team structure heightened tensions within the team and exacerbated personal problems, leading Jon to leave and causing problems for the remaining founders.

Masergy's Barry Nalls also had an intriguing background. Some in the entrepreneurship world might call him a late bloomer—something he acknowledges but regrets. Barry joined GTE, a large telecommunications company, right out of school and over the next 25 years steadily climbed the ranks, gaining deep sales experience, profit-and-loss responsibility, and other executive skills. When GTE announced merger plans, he left to work for a couple of young companies. He finally took the leap himself and founded a telecom service provider called Masergy. A self-described "solo guy," Barry decided to be the sole founder and CEO of Masergy and used a six-month severance from his last employer to fund his startup until finally raising millions of dollars from VCs. Although his startup benefitted from his wealth of prior work experience, it was only after taking the founder's leap that Barry learned key lessons about hiring a team for a fast-growing startup, managing a board of directors, and negotiating the tensions between sales and operations.

Vivek Khuller of Smartix, our next founder, struggled with the other side of the problem faced by Barry: Would a young MBA student be able to revolutionize an industry about which he knew next to nothing? While Vivek was working as a summer intern at an investment bank, he conceived the idea of using electronic-ticketing technology to allow sports and entertainment venues to issue and process their own tickets, thus eliminating intermediary ticketing agencies such as Ticketmaster. Vivek decided to advertise for co-founders within his MBA program, choosing two bright classmates with backgrounds similar to his own. Through his business school contacts, Vivek was able to pitch his idea to several high-profile venues, which were interested in partnering with Smartix, and to several top-tier VC firms, one of which issued a term sheet. However, his early founding decisions soon came back to haunt him.

For **Genevieve Thiers, founder of Sittercity,** the biggest dilemma was also highly personal: Her most important coworker was also her fiancé, Dan. What would happen to the business if she and Dan broke up? And what would happen to her relationship with Dan if their business relationship soured? The epiphany behind Sittercity had come to Genevieve as she was helping a pregnant woman post fliers for a babysitter. Reaching back to her own experiences as a professional babysitter, Genevieve realized that a website allowing parents to quickly access babysitters could be a winning idea. After graduation, she worked as a technical writer at IBM and pursued her avocation as an opera singer, developing Sittercity in her spare time. When IBM shut down her division, Genevieve focused on Sittercity full-time. As the startup grew, she enlisted Dan as a technical advisor, and the two worked closely to build the business. Dan eventually became COO, but Genevieve was nervous about the arrangement. She needed to find creative and essential ways to erect "firewalls" to protect herself from the inherent dangers of her early choice of a coworker.

By contrast, **Jim Triandiflou of Ockham Technologies** experienced a dilemma that most entrepreneurs would envy: choosing from a number of interested investors. Jim suspected that the decision would deeply affect the company's future and his own role in it. Should he choose the angel investor who came with few strings attached or the VC firms that expected more control but would provide needed resources? Jim was the son of schoolteachers; his father was risk-averse, having worked in the same classroom for 33 years, and Jim saw himself in the same mold. With a degree in marketing and an MBA, Jim had been working at a consulting firm and not even thinking of taking the plunge as an entrepreneur. But after talking to his colleague Ken about Ken's idea for a sales-management software startup, Jim decided to give it a try. Jim and Ken recruited Mike, who had worked for Jim at the consulting firm, as the third cofounder of Ockham Technologies. The arrival of his first child convinced Ken not to quit his job to join Ockham after all, leaving Jim and Mike to proceed on their own. In short order, they landed IBM as a customer and used an outsourcing company to develop their software. As CEO, Jim was successful at pitching the concept to investors, but each investor's offer would hold significant implications for Ockham's growth and development.

The book's final primary case study focuses on **Dick Costolo, founder of FeedBurner and three prior startups and, subsequently, CEO of Twitter.** After collaborating on several startups, Dick and his "serial founding team" seemed to have developed a winning formula for low-tension, high-value cofounding. Before embarking on his business career, Dick had been a Chicago stand-up comedian. After a few years working as an engineer at Andersen Consulting, he became frustrated by Andersen's lack of interest in pursuing Internet technologies and left with a colleague to start a website consulting company. In their early startups, the team ran into problems with poorly chosen hires, with investors, and with each other. But the founding team stuck together, in the process losing one cofounder while adding three others. In their fourth attempt, FeedBurner, they seemed to hit on all cylinders as they applied lessons from their prior startups. They were within striking distance of the Promised Land when they learned that even a smoothly functioning team can fall into disagreement as it nears the finish line. After solving those dilemmas, Dick went on to become part of one of the highest-profile founder-CEO succession events ever, taking the helm at Twitter.

These founders appear throughout the book. Other founders, such as a husband-and-wife team who founded a life sciences startup, play important roles in individual chapters. As a group, these founders are extremely varied, with very different personalities, styles, backgrounds, and abilities. Yet, as we'll see, the dilemmas they face are surprisingly similar. All must decide when to make the leap into founderhood, whether and how to cofound with others, when and how to hire nonfounding employees, and whether to self-fund or raise outside capital. At each fork in the road, the wrong decision can send the startup over a cliff or bring about the founder's replacement as leader of the expedition. Less dramatically, each outcome also heightens the startup's chances of success or failure.

Founders embarking on their entrepreneurial journey have had no roadmap to follow, no way to anticipate the forks, potholes, and ditches they may encounter. By arming entrepreneurs with a founders' roadmap, I want to point out common pitfalls, improve the stability and effectiveness of their teams, and help them reach their desired destinations. Our three dozen case studies will map the terrain, and our data on 10,000 founders will show us how often each decision is made and with what implications. Founders who gain insights into their core motivations for embarking on this perilous startup journey should also gain understanding of the trade-offs they will have to make each step of the way and which choices will help them reach their destination.

The first fork in the road is the pre-founding decision about whether and when to embark on the journey. As I will argue, when three factors—career factors, market factors, and personal factors—are all favorable, the decision is easy. However, potential founders who encounter one or more unfavorable factors grapple with real dilemmas about when to found, potentially imperiling the startup, their family situations, or their ability to embark on an entrepreneurial journey in the first place. These three factors, and the ways in which they should affect the decision to found a company, are the focus of Chapter 2.

CHAPTER TWO

CAREER DILEMMAS

POTENTIAL FOUNDERS FACE A VARIETY OF PITFALLS WHEN DECIDING whether, when, and how to found a startup. They may dive into launching a startup without thinking about whether they have the skills and motivations necessary to succeed; they may focus on business issues without considering their personal situations and how those situations may undermine their success (or be undermined by it); or they may fall in love with the idea of founderhood and enthusiastically latch onto an exciting idea without dispassionately evaluating it. Founders who dive in too early may doom themselves to destructive failure. Those who wait too long may find themselves handcuffed by a high-priced lifestyle and a steady paycheck, then look back at the end of their careers and regret having never made the leap.

To help us understand the wide range of career options, let's meet two potential founders who faced very different circumstances and made very different decisions.

Humphrey Chen was a potential early-career founder. Although he came from a traditional Taiwanese family that strongly encouraged him to pursue a career in medicine, he was drawn instead to startups and cutting-edge technology; he loved the "excitement and uncertainty" of rapid-growth industries and businesses. While still in the second year of an MBA program, Humphrey and a classmate developed a new technology to enable a listener to identify and purchase music that was playing on the radio. "The idea just lit up in

my head," said Humphrey.[1] By dialing a phone number and input-
ting the station number while the song was still playing, listeners
could immediately order the song. Humphrey was so excited by his
idea that he filed a patent, developed a basic technology demo, and
incorporated a company he called ConneXus to monetize the idea.

Meanwhile, a top consulting firm had offered Humphrey a lucrative job working on innovative media and communications projects
in Manhattan. The job fit nicely with his interests and background.
Adding to his dilemma, Humphrey was getting married in a few
months to Cecilia, who was working toward her pharmacy degree
and not earning a salary yet. Cecilia explained, "I'm not as bold
as Humphrey . . . I am more of a stable person. The consulting job
would offer security and I would definitely feel comfortable with
that."[2] Humphrey, however, did not want to turn away from his
startup idea and began negotiations with investors, torn about
whether to pursue launching ConneXus full-time or to take the consulting job.

In contrast, Barry Nalls waited much longer before considering
whether to make the leap. Barry came from a long line of small-
business owners in Texas and had been, as he said, "surrounded by
entrepreneurs and small businesses my entire life." But instead of
following in his father's and grandfather's footsteps, Barry earned
a two-year technical degree and then went to work for GTE, one
of the largest companies in Texas. Over the next 25 years, Barry
climbed GTE's corporate ladder, tackling increasingly more responsible positions. But when GTE announced in 1999 that it would be
merging with Bell Atlantic, Barry's worries about what the merger
might mean for him spurred him to think more deeply about starting his own business. He was married with two school-aged children, but his wife encouraged him to make the leap and was even
willing to move to make the transition easier. After first working for
two startups and gaining knowledge of what that kind of life was
like, he found his wife still supportive of his becoming a founder
himself and began looking around for an idea with which to start a
company of his own.

Do most founders start at a young age, like Humphrey, or are
they later bloomers like Barry? Neither. Stage of life does not seem

to be a strong factor in starting one's own business. In my dataset of thousands of first-time founders of technology and life sciences startups, there was wide variation in the stage of life during which founders decided to make the leap; there was no "sweet spot" of founding ages.[3] On average, founders had worked for 14.0 years before making the leap, but with a large standard of deviation of 9.8 years. Technology founders averaged 13.1 years of prior work experience and life sciences founders averaged 15.9 years. A full 35% of founders had worked 20 years or more before founding, including 47% of life sciences founders, but a distinct subset founded with only 0 to 4 years of work experience.[4] Humphrey would fall at the very low end of this age distribution and Barry at the high end.[5] But while they were quite different regarding the ages at which they had the urge to found a company, the factors they considered when deciding whether and when to act on that urge were remarkably similar.

Before following their passions, potential founders should step back to answer the pre-founding questions we will tackle in this chapter:

1. Should I become an entrepreneur?
2. If so, when should I make the leap into founderhood—early in my career or after I accumulate more career experiences?
3. How can I dispassionately evaluate my idea?

These questions are particularly complex because they mix personal issues ("Will my spouse be supportive when things get tough? Is my family situation conducive to founding a startup?"), career issues ("Have I accumulated skills and experiences that prepare me to found a company?"), and market issues ("Is my idea good enough, or is my passion for it misleading me?"). Each founder's answers to these questions will have important repercussions for all of the subsequent dilemmas he or she will face. Early-career founders, for example, will need to consider adding cofounders and experienced hires to make up for their own missing skills. Late-career founders who accumulate relevant pre-founding experiences, on the other hand, may be in a better position to consider solo founding and hiring less-experienced people.

SHOULD I FOUND?

At almost any age, potential founders may be struck by a high level
of passion, whether for a business idea itself or for the idea of becoming a founder or for the chance to change an industry. That
passion is often a critical source of entrepreneurial motivation,[6] and
it is common to all the founders discussed in this chapter. That said,
the founders examined here differ in almost every other way: age,
experience, childhood influences, personality, marital and family
status, economic status, and where their ideas came from. Are there
patterns in the way people decide to become founders?

Despite the popular conception of entrepreneurs as risk takers, risk
aversion does not seem to affect the decision to become an entrepreneur. Academic studies testing for a significant difference in risk aversion between entrepreneurs and non-entrepreneur managers have
produced conflicting results or suffered from methodological problems.[7] However, as detailed below, studies have suggested that two
other factors may separate entrepreneurs from non-entrepreneurs.
First, early influences can have a powerful effect on people who are
considering becoming founders, pushing some toward founderhood
and pushing others away from it. Second, these influences can be re-
inforced by people's natural motivations and the rewards they value.

Early Influences

A founder is greatly influenced by the family and culture in which
he or she grew up and, in some cases, by specific role models. Dr.
Tim Butler, who has studied entrepreneurial career issues for more
than two decades, says that the most powerful, though often un-
noticed, influences may come from the early messages sent by the
words and actions of older relatives or by the culture in which a
person grew up: "We receive very powerful messages about what's
important, what success is, what failure is, what counts for achievement and what doesn't. In many cultures, that includes messages
about the value of owning your own business versus being an employee, which shapes our career decisions." Those messages can

push strongly against becoming an entrepreneur. Humphrey Chen, for example, grew up in a family that did not value entrepreneurs. "My parents have always been against my career choices. My dad's a doctor and both of my brothers are doctors. In Taiwan, you go into business only if you have failed at becoming a doctor [or lawyer or another professional] . . . it was a different class. . . . I was the black sheep in my family."[8] This negative message weighed heavily in Humphrey's thinking about whether to become an entrepreneur or to follow a more traditional path.

In contrast, people whose parents, close friends, or neighbors had been self-employed are more likely than others to become entrepreneurs.[9] Barry Nalls learned to appreciate business ownership from the entrepreneurs in his family. "My father owned gas stations and a gun company. My grandfather sold antiques, bought and sold land, and owned a wrecking yard. My uncle owned a bulldozer company. So I was surrounded by entrepreneurs my entire life," commented Barry. One of his earliest memories was attending a flea market with his grandfather: "I was barely high enough to see over a table when my grandfather took me to a First Monday Trades day. He put six items on the table: a lantern, a cook stove, an antique gun, and other stuff. He said, 'Ask this price. If the buyer asks you to take a lower price, then you can take this much.' He'd go off making trades and I would stand there making deals. . . . Having grown up in this environment, I saw the whole makeup of how you get an idea, how you move forward with it, how you get customers to care about what you're doing, how you treat customers." Even after working for a large company for more than two decades, Barry's long-ago experiences at the flea market still exerted a powerful influence on his inclination to become an entrepreneur at some point during his career.

Although many founders lack such strong early influences, people who reflect on their early family and cultural influences often gain insight into why they are attracted to or shy away from starting a new company. When such influences are combined with analyses of the person's core motivations, a more complete picture emerges of whether or not the person should become a founder sometime in his or her career.

Founder Motivations: The Centrality of Wealth and Control Motivations

Chapter 1 described the CareerLeader data that capture the most common motivations for thousands of people worldwide. For each survey participant, CareerLeader analysis rank-orders 13 possible motivations, or "work reward values": affiliation, altruism, autonomy, financial gain, intellectual challenge, lifestyle, managing people, positioning, power and influence, prestige, recognition, security, and variety.[10]

Working with Dr. Tim Butler, the cocreator of CareerLeader, I separated the 27,000 surveys in the CareerLeader database by gender, age cohort (people in their 20s, 30s, or 40s and older), and entrepreneurial status (entrepreneur or non-entrepreneur).[11] The differences in motivation between entrepreneurs and non-entrepreneurs were striking, but there were fewer differences between the genders (we will focus on gender differences later in this book) and even fewer differences among age cohorts (especially for entrepreneurs, whose motivations were more stable over the decades).

The top four motivations for males in their 20s are shown below. For the entrepreneurs in this category, the list is dominated by control-related items (power and influence, autonomy, and managing people) and financial gain.* Interestingly, with the exception of financial gain, the top-ranked motivations for entrepreneurs were much lower ranked for non-entrepreneurs and vice versa.

The founders we will study span this spectrum of entrepreneurial motivations. For instance, at Blogger, Evan Williams certainly felt that having power and autonomy was important, even justifying his refusal of a multi-million-dollar acquisition offer. "After four years of pouring my heart into Blogger, I saw a lot of risk in

---

* As described in Chapter 1, the centrality of wealth and control choices is echoed by the (very different) Kauffman and Panel Study of Entrepreneurial Dynamics datasets. I emphasize the CareerLeader dataset because (a) it is much larger (its 27,000 executives and entrepreneurs dwarf past datasets that were used to examine entrepreneurial motivations), (b) it enables separate analyses for each gender, stage of life, and entrepreneurial status, and (c) it is based on rich underlying psychological research that uses multiple approaches to evaluate motivations.

Table 2.1
Top Four Motivations for Males in Their 20s

Rank	Male Entrepreneurs in 20s (Rank for Male Non-entrepreneurs)	Male Non-entrepreneurs in 20s (Rank for Male Entrepreneurs)
#1.	Power & influence (#10)	Security (tie) (#13)
#2.	Autonomy (#13)	Prestige (tie) (#6)
#3.	Managing people (#9)	Financial gain (#4)
#4.	Financial gain (#3)	Affiliation (#11)

giving up control," he explained. In contrast, by the time founder-CEO Dick Costolo got acquisition offers for FeedBurner, he was motivated by money: "I'm not an engineer any more. To me, best price wins." Frank Addante, too, explained that his motivation for launching StrongMail was financial: "I thought about it from the perspective of, 'What's going to keep me motivated to stick with it and run this for a period of time?' A big enough equity piece will keep me motivated to stay." Each of these founders aspired to build a high-impact startup, but "impact" meant very different things to each; to the financially motivated, it tended to mean a large gain in wealth, but to the control motivated, it tended to mean that the startup would bring to the world the product or service they envisioned.

The top four motivations for females in their 20s are shown below. Once again, with one exception (altruism), the top-ranked motivations for entrepreneurs were much lower ranked for non-entrepreneurs and vice versa. (Mirroring results for the males, control motivations also dominate the list for female entrepreneurs, but financial gain ranks much lower than it does for their male counterparts.) Genevieve Theirs, who founded the online babysitting company Sittercity while in her 20s, noted that autonomy and influence were among her motivations: "I felt very disassociated [working for IBM], like I was part of a big machine in which I had no idea where I was going. I realized that I needed to understand the big picture to be motivated. . . . [At Sittercity], I was on a mission to do something big and beautiful."

Table 2.2
Top Four Motivations for Females in Their 20s

Rank	Female Entrepreneurs in 20s (Rank for Female Non-entrepreneurs)	Female Non-entrepreneurs in 20s (Rank for Female Entrepreneurs)
#1.	Autonomy *(#12)*	Recognition *(#10)*
#2.	Power & influence *(#13)*	Affiliation *(#12)*
#3.	Managing people *(#10)*	Security *(#13)*
#4.	Altruism *(#5)*	Lifestyle *(#11)*

The data show that these motivations are relatively stable throughout life, with most of the top-ranked motivations for people in their 20s persisting into their 30s and 40s and beyond. The table below shows, for each category (in alphabetical order), which of the top-four motivations from the 20s age cohort remained top-four motivations in the 30s age cohort and which new motivations emerged. For female entrepreneurs, variety becomes a top-four motivation once they reach their 30s, but entrepreneurs of both genders experienced no other changes in their top-four motivations. In contrast, the motivations for non-entrepreneurs seem to be less stable, with half of the top-four motivations changing for each gender.

As shown below, the motivations for male entrepreneurs change noticeably as they enter their 40s and beyond. Two of the motivations (autonomy and power & influence) persist throughout their 20s, 30s, and 40s, but in their 40s, male entrepreneurs also become motivated by altruism and variety. (Male entrepreneurs lag female entrepreneurs by a decade when it comes to prizing variety and by two decades when it comes to altruism.) For non-entrepreneurs, once again, two top-four motivations carry over from the prior decade and two new top-four motivations emerge. The motivations for all groups become more similar in their 40s, with autonomy and altruism appearing in all four top-four lists and variety appearing in three.

When Major League Baseball pitcher Curt Schilling began to contemplate life after baseball, he named altruism as his top motivation

Table 2.3
Top Four Motivations for the 30s Age Cohort

30s Age Cohort	Male Entrepreneurs	Female Entrepreneurs	Male Non-entrepreneurs	Female Non-entrepreneurs
Top 4 motivations carried over from the 20s	Autonomy Financial gain Managing people Power & influence	Autonomy Altruism Power & influence	Prestige Security	Recognition Security
New top 4 motivations		Variety	Positioning Recognition	Altruism Variety

Table 2.4
Top Four Motivations for the 40s-plus Age Cohort

40s-plus Age Cohort	Male Entrepreneurs	Female Entrepreneurs	Male Non-entrepreneurs	Female Non-entrepreneurs
Top 4 motivations carried over from the 30s	Autonomy Power & influence	Autonomy Altruism Variety	Recognition Security	Altruism Variety
New top 4 motivations	Altruism Variety	Intellectual challenge	Altruism Autonomy	Affiliation Autonomy

for starting a company. Schilling's philanthropic work on behalf of ALS ("Lou Gehrig's disease") had motivated him to "philanthropically change the world." One of Schilling's model philanthropists was Bill Gates, who had made billions of dollars in the business world and then used much of that money to found a high-impact philanthropic foundation. As a result, Schilling decided to found 38 Studios, a massively multiplayer online gaming (MMOG) startup, with the hopes that gains from it could be used for philanthropic causes.

The picture that emerges is that entrepreneurs and non-entrepreneurs are motivated by very different rewards, especially early in their careers. Potential founders whose highest-ranked motivations overlap with those of either entrepreneurs or non-entrepreneurs can get a good idea of whether they should consider founding a company at some point in their careers. For the people whose motivations are similar to those of entrepreneurs, the next question becomes: When in my career should I found?

WHEN SHOULD I FOUND?

For those who are entrepreneurially inclined, it is extremely tempting to become a founder as soon as possible. However, given the challenges of trying to build an organization from scratch, would-be founders should look before they leap. In particular, they should look at whether their career experiences have prepared them for the leap into founderhood. However, there is another side to this coin. The chance to become better prepared often leads potential founders to wait before founding, but waiting until late in one's career can introduce its own perils. Working for other organizations can, in itself, make it harder to eventually found one's own startup. Figure 2.1 summarizes the factors that pull in each direction. Below, we will delve into each of these competing factors.

Reasons to Wait

People who wait to become founders can use their pre-founding career experiences to prepare themselves for the extreme challenges of founding. A well-planned pre-founding career can arm a potential founder with the human capital, social capital, and financial capital appropriate to a startup.

Building Human Capital

As potential founders progress through their careers, they accumulate more and more of the human capital needed to found a startup. In this context, *human capital* refers to the skills, knowledge, and expertise needed to launch and build the startup. It includes both

Found early in career... ⟵——————————⟶ **Wait to found until...**

- ...before golden handcuffs get too strong
- ...before family handcuffs get too strong
- ...before becoming too specialized
- ...before becoming too reliant on employer resources

- ...build more human capital
- ...build more social capital
- ...build more financial capital

Figure 2.1. Factors Affecting the "When to Found" Decision

general human capital that is widely applicable (e.g., leadership ability or the ability to speak and write clearly) and specific human capital that is tied to a specific organization or context (e.g., knowing how a particular product is manufactured). Looked at a different way, human capital includes formal human capital acquired through schooling (e.g., getting a degree in biomedical engineering or computer science) and tacit human capital acquired through work and life experiences (e.g., knowing how to negotiate with equipment sales reps).[12]

As founders accumulate experiences, they also develop mental models (or schemata)—ways of categorizing and making sense of information.[13] A doctor and a marketing expert—each of whom wants to found a medical software company—will each look at the same information and make sense of it in different ways, considering different details to be more important and to have different implications for the planned startup, because each brings a different mental model to bear. Founders' approaches to building their startups are powerfully shaped by the mental models they bring to those startups.[14] Accumulating more experience is far less valuable if that experience does not shape the mental model in relevant ways (or, worse, if it shapes the mental model in counterproductive ways).

Work and School

Before attending business school, Humphrey Chen had spent about a year each at a wide variety of employers—Price Waterhouse, Morgan Stanley, a marketing consultancy, and an Internet-based music retailer—gaining some breadth of business knowledge. A broad range of work and educational experiences is indeed associated with a significantly higher willingness to become self-employed.[15] However, Humphrey's breadth came at the expense of specific deep experience or skills that could enable him to fully understand the scope or the value proposition of his bright idea for ConneXus. In contrast, Vivek Khuller, another young founder, had worked as an engineer for Bell Atlantic for five years before enrolling in business school. He understood much more deeply how a world-class organization operated and had a much deeper view of the technologies relevant to his startup, which enabled him to develop a technical prototype much more quickly. At the same time, Vivek's background did not include experience in the entertainment venues that were his intended market. As we will see below, the lack of one or more "capitals" can create a hole that must be filled when building a successful startup.

While Humphrey lacked an extended career in a corporate setting, he did invest time and financial resources in schooling. He had expended considerable effort and had achieved success pursuing a technical degree and an MBA at top-rated universities. Attending a targeted program, such as a focused business-function program, or earning an industry-specific credential can be a shortcut to the kind of human capital that others, such as Barry Nalls, amass through years on the job. More years of schooling is indeed linked to a greater likelihood of becoming a founder; after surveying a wide range of evidence, Professor Scott Shane concludes, "Including professional school, getting more education *increases* the likelihood that a person will start his own business."[16]

Managerial Experience

Unlike Vivek and Humphrey, Barry had only a two-year degree. But he had more than a decade of experience as a manager of large and small teams and had had profit-and-loss responsibility for a large organization where he was a general manager who had to knit diverse functions into a coherent whole. As a merger-and-acquisition manager at GTE, Barry had regularly analyzed startup technologies and was practiced at identifying the strengths and weaknesses in new companies' business plans. Working through several boom-and-bust business cycles had given him the ability to maintain a strategic long-term view in the midst of uncertainty.

Barry credits his prior managerial experience (and an MBA earned years later) with providing him with the tools to build and lead a team at his startup, Masergy. When his board differed with him about whom to hire for his executive team, Barry's experience gave him the confidence to stand his ground. "Less-experienced CEOs would have had a hard time pushing back against the board and the board's industrial psychologists, but I felt comfortable doing so," he explained. However, such pre-founding experience is relatively rare. Among the founders in my dataset, only 18% had management experience before founding their startups, including 19% of technology founders and 15% of life sciences founders.[17] (This is consistent with another study that found that technical founders tend to lack prior managerial experience and may even lack interest in developing managerial skills.[18] Among the *Inc. 500* list of the fastest-growing private companies, "the founders also often lack deep management or business experience."[19])

Functional Backgrounds

Founding a startup requires the knitting together of all of the functions required to make an organization run effectively, from product development to marketing to sales to finance to human resources. Having prior experience in those functions arms the founder with the ability to understand how each one operates on its own and as part of the larger whole. Founders who lack experience in a function either will be blind to key aspects of how it contributes to the whole or will have to spend valuable time learning about it rather than building the startup. One challenge for young founders is that it takes many years to accumulate multifunction or general management experience. For Barry Nalls, it took many years of working at GTE to accumulate that type of experience, even though he was a high-performing employee there.

Founders who have gaps in their functional backgrounds can be blindsided by problems in those areas. When Jim Triandiflou and his cofounder, Mike Meisenheimer, founded Ockham Technologies to offer a sales-force-optimization software product, both had strong sales and consulting experience. They understood their customers and the value proposition of their product, but lacked any background in software design and development. Jim recalled, "We had no idea the level of detail that you needed to write software. No idea. . . . We used to joke that we'd have to take classes at DeVry to learn how to code software, because we don't [know how]." This inexperience caused serious delays and missteps with product development and prototype demonstrations. "Although consulting was brainpower-intensive, software was operationally [i.e., execution] intensive. In consulting, you do not get into nearly the level of detail that a real operation does. . . . I look back now at some of my ideas and say I didn't have a clue. I was so unrealistic about what really gets done and how hard it is to get these things done," explained Jim. Barry, too, found that his sales and product management background put him on a different timetable than his operations staff, making him impatient for faster progress.

An executive's functional background can also have a powerful effect on the company's strategy and focus. In particular, when company executives have backgrounds in "output functions" such as marketing, sales, and R&D, the company tends to emphasize product innovation, related diversification, and advertising. Conversely, when company executives have backgrounds in "throughput functions" such as production and process engineering, the company tends to emphasize automation, up-to-date plants and equipment, and backward integration.[20]

Industry Knowledge

How well the founder understands the startup's industry can make a big difference in the challenges he or she faces; specific knowledge of an industry can help a founder avoid potentially fatal problems. Even before Barry Nalls came up with the idea on which Masergy was based, his deep industry experience helped him play to his strengths. With his 25 years of relevant experience, he had developed enough human capital in the industry he chose for his startup to be his own in-house expert on potential target customers, what those customers would find desirable, and what his value proposition could entail. "As I started to build a new business plan, my planning was very similar to building a business plan for a product rollout at GTE. I asked myself a series of basic questions: 'What do I know?' I know telecom, so the business should be in that. 'Whom do I know?' Enterprise clients. 'What do these enterprise clients care about when it comes to telecom? What are they willing to pay for?'" Barry knew how to answer these questions and he built a solid business plan around those answers.

Vivek Khuller, on the other hand, had an industry-changing idea for online ticketing, but knew very little about the venues and events that would use such technology. "We were engineers who had never worked in this area. I've been to the Fleet Center [a Boston arena] just once. I have never been to Foxboro Stadium [a New England football stadium] to see a game and I've never entered [New York's] Madison Square Garden in my life. . . . [We're] not sports fans or anything of that sort." When Vivek first met with the operations manager of a large stadium, he realized he was woefully unprepared. "I had no idea how these venues were organized. . . . [T]his guy was concerned about how much more operational risk would he have to undertake by adopting this new technology. . . . We had done very little research on that. We had very few answers to his questions."

According to Professor Scott Shane's survey of the research on small businesses, "More than half (55 percent) of entrepreneurs start businesses in industries other than those in which they had previously been working."[21] Many of those founders like to believe that ignorance of the industry in which they are founding is a benefit because it leaves an opening for fresh thinking.[22] This can be true, but the advantages of ignorance are often easily outweighed by the disadvantages of inexperience. Past research has suggested that founders who launch startups in industries in which they haven't worked raise less capital, have lower employment growth, and have a higher rate of failure than founders with prior industry experience.[23] This should be particularly true when the mental models developed in one industry do not transfer smoothly to the new industry. For potential founders who have worked for a long time in one industry, and may even have had a lot of success in that industry, switching industries often requires substantially adjusting their mental models. Even when they do realize that they will have to adjust their models, they can be blindsided by parts of their models that unexpectedly cause problems or by industry-specific assumptions they didn't even realize they were making.

For instance, Curt Schilling, a prominent former professional baseball player, would seem to have had tremendous advantages as an entrepreneur. One would expect that his status as a baseball star would open doors closed to others; that people would line up to work for him, advise him, and fund his company; that the financial capital he had accumulated during his baseball career would help launch his company; and that his work ethic and leadership abilities would be of great value in the business world. Some of those advantages did benefit Curt when he launched his MMOG startup, 38 Studios. In other areas, however, he was in for a rude awakening, despite having spent some time observing the employees at a large gaming company. "There were so many things I didn't understand," he admitted.

Some of those disconnects were to be expected for any first-time founder, especially one who hadn't yet worked full-time in the industry, but many could also be traced to the "career imprint"[24] Curt had taken from his career in baseball and the mental model he had developed of how organizations work and how people are motivated. For example, he was initially mystified as to why people couldn't work 14 days straight and did not understand why they would need weekends off, or even regularly scheduled time away from the business. He had to adjust to how people were motivated and how teams were constructed in business. Baseball players are paid salaries and do not receive equity stakes in their teams, but employees in the MMOG industry expect to receive both salary and equity. Even seemingly innocuous terms he had taken for granted took on opposite meanings. Finding himself confused during a meeting, he finally realized that when businesspeople use the term "burn rate," they are referring to the amount of cash being used up and they want to keep it to a minimum. For a baseball pitcher, "burn rate" is the speed at which you can throw the ball—the higher the burn rate, the better. After grappling with each confusion, Curt struggled to figure out his disconnect and begin adjusting his mental model, only to find further disconnects between his old mental model and his new industry.

Working in Small versus Big Companies

Working for someone else's startup helps you develop tacit knowledge about entrepreneurship that increases the likelihood of becoming a founder yourself.[25] People with more entrepreneurial experience have more ways to recognize and evaluate potential opportunities—more cognitive rules of thumb for knowing what to try and how to try it.[26] Because of the division of labor in society, every person has different prior knowledge. To discover entrepreneurial opportunities, entrepreneurs must combine their prior knowledge with the right new knowledge, then figure out the correct combinations of means and ends with which to make the most of the opportunity.[27]*

The origin of Smartix is an example of such a combination. Vivek had a degree in electrical engineering and went on to work in a technical job for five years before entering business school. During his business school internship, he came in contact with a company that had developed electronic access cards. The internship, in conjunction with his prior education and experience, sparked a new idea:

---

*Experienced entrepreneurs seem to be more likely to use "effectual reasoning," wherein they start with a given set of means—their personal strengths and the resources they already have at hand—rather than a predetermined goal, and then allow opportunities to emerge to which they can react. In contrast, non-entrepreneurial executives tend to use causal reasoning, in which they set a goal and then seek the best ways to achieve it. For more details, see Sarasvathy (2008).

Vivek realized immediately how keycard technology could trans-form ticketing, allowing venues to ticket their own events. He was able to tap multiple elements of his background in order to recognize the technology as a particular kind of business opportunity.

Learning about relevant patterns and causal relationships may be more likely to occur while working in entrepreneurial organizations. Employees of small companies are indeed more likely than employees of large companies to leave and become founders of their own companies.[28] Also, companies that were once VC-backed were 20% more likely to spawn at least one startup than were companies that had never received VC funding. Another study found that half of all founders came from companies with fewer than 25 employees and 64% came from companies with fewer than 100 employees, more than three times as much as would be expected since those companies account for less than 20% of all employees.[29] One possible explanation for these results is that larger organizations may be better at incorporating their employees' innovative ideas and thus keeping those employees within the organization.[30] Another possible explanation is that younger organizations may attract more employees who are entrepreneurially inclined. However, career expert Dr. Tim Butler cautions against gaining work experience in *too immature* a startup: "A more developed startup is a better training ground than two guys in a garage. A startup that is more mature, and has brought in experienced executives who will be good mentors, will prepare you better. This moment in the development of a company is a 'sweet spot' for [someone] who wants both a startup environment and access to talented manager-mentors with proven track records ... [along with opportunities for] working closely with a truly seasoned manager as tough day to day decisions are made."

Still, some large companies can provide "entrepreneurial career imprints" that prepare future founders to make the leap. For instance, people who worked at Baxter, a global healthcare company, in the 1970s were well prepared to help found and build biotech startups because Baxter provided high-potential employees with "mini-CEO jobs" that helped them develop the capabilities, connections, confidence, and cognition required to found.[31] Indeed, almost one-quarter of the biotech startups that went public from 1979 to 1996 had a team member who had worked at Baxter. In contrast, people working at Baxter's competitor, Abbott Labs, worked in more specialized roles and developed a "functional career imprint" that was much less relevant to founding a biotech startup. Former Abbott employees were much less frequently found on the teams of biotech startups that went public. In other large companies, roles in new-product development or in launching offices in new countries can also provide solid preparation for future founders.

Although GTE did afford Barry some Baxter-like entrepreneurial experiences, the fact that he had worked for such a large company for so long resulted in a few blind spots he had to overcome when founding his own business. His challenges stemmed from the disconnect between his big-company experiences and the core demands of a startup: to attract outside funding, to manage a board of directors, and to manage the distinct challenges of hypergrowth. Sensing that there would be a gap between his GTE experiences and the cognitive capital he would need to become a successful founder, he first spent short stints in two startups, but those experiences were not enough to fill the gap. "With investors, I didn't understand the funding options," Barry explained. "I didn't know any way to go about funding other than VCs." When he presented to VCs, Barry found that his business plan, which mirrored the ones he had prepared at GTE, was too detailed, failed to highlight the most important handful of milestones, and lacked focus on the management team. Whereas the GTE name and reputation had been the focus before, Barry eventually learned that, in startups, "[investors] really care about, number one, the team," requiring him to devote the biggest segment of his presentation to a discussion of the individuals involved.

Once he obtained funding, Barry struggled with how to manage his newly formed VC-led board, an entity he had not encountered during his time at GTE. One surprise was the amount of time required to prepare for his initial monthly board meetings: a full 25% of each month. He said, "I knew that VCs had to see what was going on in the company and I figured they would need much more than what a governing body at GTE needed, but I didn't know what they would be looking for."

At first, Barry thought of his board as a boss and spent hours following through on their directives. Later, he realized that he had much more autonomy than a boss/employee relationship would imply. "From a governance standpoint, board members give you suggestions and ideas, but don't have responsibility to make sure you do them," explained Barry. "Their suggestions don't have any weight if you don't agree." Barry also didn't immediately understand which things he should delegate and which he should not; like many other founders, he had a hard time delegating and giving up control of decisions. After presenting a real estate report at one board meeting, one of his board members said, "We need you to do other things. If you ever come back in here knowing so many details, we're going to fire you!" Barry recalled. "That was a key message about their expectation of the CEO and what I should be doing as CEO. I was used to working hard, but it made me stop and think about how much to delegate versus how much I should take on myself."

Barry also came to understand that the pace of growth in a startup created different management issues than the ones he had faced at GTE. "Prioritization is even more important [in a startup] than in a stable business," said Barry. "I realized that I needed people to not only prioritize what to do, I needed them to create *not*-to-do lists. It was easy for people to find new products for us to bring to market, new pieces to add, new customer segments to go after. . . . When you're smaller, if you go after something, it takes precious resources. You're also moving a lot faster, so you can harm the organization. . . . There's much more at risk, much more damage you can do."

Harnessing Nontraditional Experiences

We typically focus on schooling and work experiences as sources of human capital. However, founders can also gain relevant human capital outside of school and work, often in ways they did not anticipate. For instance, Tim Westergren's experience leading a rock band taught him leadership and management skills that he put to use founding the pioneer online radio service Pandora Radio. Tim's efforts as a composer had given him invaluable sales experience and had taught him to persist through the ups and downs of searching for success, which proved to be a valuable commodity after he became a founder. Dick Costolo, the founder-CEO of FeedBurner, was a standup "improv" comedian before he started his first IT company. Such a career path wouldn't seem particularly helpful for a budding entrepreneur, but in fact Dick learned quite a bit about human nature and team construction from his years on the stage. Reflecting on his improv comedy years, Dick said, "My biggest team lesson was that you can't build [an improv] team from parts that look like they'll make a good team. We had a show with three people, all of them all-stars. Individually, they were hilarious and some have gone on to greatness. . . . But everyone could see they weren't working well together. . . . [I learned] the fit between personalities was so much more important," a lesson he then applied when building his startup teams.

Building Social and Financial Capital

While people are building relevant human capital, they are often also building the social capital they hope to leverage as founders. In this context, *social capital* is the durable network of social and professional relationships through which founders can identify and access resources.[32] Here, as with human capital, youth is often at a disadvantage. Barry, for example, spent years building connections with potential employees, customers, advisors, and investors before he started Masergy. That deep reservoir of resources enabled him to meet his ambitious deadline of six months to make Masergy viable. Compared to Barry, Vivek and Humphrey had narrow social fields. Vivek, however, was able to tap his past work contacts and school connections to build Smartix; his software developer was a former coworker at Bell Atlantic, and he recruited cofounders and advisors from his classmates and professors at business school. His school connections led to potential customers (Fleet Center, Madison Square Garden), which in turn built cachet to attract venture funding. All the same, he lacked the industry-specific connections necessary to fill the biggest hole on his team—the lack of an industry veteran. Barry's years at GTE had provided him with a wealth of exactly those types of connections.

Financial capital is another area in which Barry had an advantage over Humphrey and Vivek. Many future founders, while still working as employees, try to accumulate a cash cushion that will keep them going after leaving to work on the startup. The size of this cushion can largely determine the amount of time the founder is able to give the startup, the amount of stress and urgency he or she feels to become cash-flow positive, and the decisions he or she makes to build the startup. One founder described how he first had to attain a "walk-away" level of savings—enough to feel secure walking away from his current job to found a startup. Barry left his last company not only with his own savings but also with a six-month severance package, a cash cushion that both Humphrey and Vivek lacked but that gave Barry time to get Masergy off the ground. In contrast to Barry and others who have accumulated financial capital, Humphrey and Cecilia had to live with his parents after their wedding in order to keep their expenses low enough to pursue ConneXus, causing considerable stress in their relationship and putting pressure on the startup to succeed quickly. Even so, Humphrey was more fortunate than many potential founders, who aren't able to make the leap at all for lack of financial capital.[33] One study found that 51.3% of people who had seriously considered becoming entrepreneurs could not do so because they lacked the necessary financial capital.[34]

The accumulation of one type of capital can spark a virtuous cycle. Research has shown that people who accumulate more social capital before founding are able to attract more human capital (such as cofounders) and financial capital (such as seed capital) with which to launch the startup,[35] and to do so more quickly.[36]

The Perils of Waiting

Although it is tempting to tell potential founders that they should work a long time so they can build the capitals needed to increase the chances of becoming successful founders, there are dangers in taking this route. First, it may not be a good idea to continually accumulate more human and social capital. Not only are there diminishing returns, but it may also be counterproductive to building a successful startup. According to one study, startups survive the longest when founded by people with midrange prior work experience, estimated at 25 years.[37] Founders with more than 25 years of work experience faced higher probabilities of startup failure than did founders with approximately 25 years of experience.[38] Second, by working for a long time, founders may get handcuffed to their pre-founding positions and may also become less fit to become founders.

Stronger Career Handcuffs

If people accumulate relevant capitals as they gain more work experience, they should become more likely to found a startup the longer they work. But as we saw at the beginning of the chapter, this isn't so. The likelihood of founding a startup does not increase with age or years of work experience.

A major reason is that waiting to found introduces its own challenges. Working for many years can strengthen the handcuffs tying the potential founder to his or her employer. These include psychological handcuffs, such as the social status of an impressive title or well-known employer, and "golden" handcuffs, such as a high salary or a vesting schedule that requires one to keep working in order to earn stock awards. One founder vividly admitted, "I had to get off the heroin drip of a salary." All of these handcuffs reduce the likelihood of becoming a founder by raising the opportunity costs of leaving the employer, lowering the relative attractiveness of launching a startup, and reinforcing the inertia of remaining an employee.

There may also be legal handcuffs, such as a noncompete agreement preventing the employee from competing with the employer (these tend to be particularly relevant to key senior employees) or an employer's claims on intellectual property developed by the employee while working for the employer. Such agreements made Jim Triandiflou, founder-CEO of Ockham Technologies, think twice about leaving his consulting job with The Alexander Group (TAG). Having become part of the senior management team, Jim found the appeal of going off on his own was somewhat darkened by noncompete and nonhire agreements that would prevent him from using a strategy similar to TAG's and even from taking on independent consulting projects to generate cash flow for the startup.

Lower "Fitness to Found"

Working as an employee for a long time can decrease not only a person's willingness to become a founder but also his or her fitness to do so. As people rise in their organizations and in their careers, they tend to develop specialties in which they have deep knowledge and contacts. As described above, depth of knowledge is important, but people who have depth without breadth do not become the sort of jack-of-all-trades that a founder needs to be.[39] At GTE, Barry Nalls avoided becoming specialized by working in a variety of positions, spending an average of less than two years in each position. Also, given the division of labor within formalized organizations, employees get used to relying on organizational infrastructure, processes, and support functions, making the most efficient use of their own time but diminishing their own self-reliance. On both of these dimensions, a founder is the antithesis of the experienced executive and the transition to founderhood is made harder by the habits and mindsets that the experienced executive has developed.

The when-to-leap decision can certainly be affected by the would-be founder's perception of the risks involved and how that perception changes over time. For instance, Vivek Khuller reflected on his decision to found Smartix: "We were all young and if, for any reason, it didn't work out, we each had lots of other options. . . . At the same time, as you get older, you start getting a lot more cautious, prudent, maybe gun-shy. With the amount of energy it takes, you cannot do more than a few startups well. It just tires you. The amount of energy it takes from you, once you have a family and everything else, you don't want to deal with it."

Stronger Family Handcuffs

Single, childless founders are much less constrained in their founding decisions; the "family handcuffs" often tighten as spouses or children enter the picture. At Ockham Technologies, although it was Ken Burows who had come up with the idea for the startup, he was hesitant to join full-time after the birth of his first child. "When push came to shove, Ken . . . decided he didn't want to quit his job," explained cofounder Jim Triandiflou. "He had his first child. He just said it wasn't the right time for him. Which was the irony of all ironies, because he was the entrepreneur of the group."[40]

Even potential founders with older children may be constrained in their founding decisions. For Barry Nalls, both his emotional attachment to Texas, his home state, and the practical considerations of having a special-needs child led him to focus on founding in North Texas instead of heading to a more promising area for an entrepreneur. He said, "I absolutely did not want to move out of Texas. That was my limiting factor. I love Texas, Texas is home. It's where all my family is. I would move if I had to, but I really didn't want to. . . . [Also,] I had significant pressures to stay in North Texas because of all of the resources there for my autistic son: schools, therapists, doctors. Instead of trying to change that . . . I made the decision that I was going to stay put and try to make things work in North Texas. I wouldn't do anything that would detract from our ability to support his requirements."

Worried about having support at home, Barry and Vivek negotiated time frames with their spouses before starting their businesses; Barry received a commitment of six months and Vivek and his wife agreed to a year. While these constraints were challenging, the blessings and commitments of the spouses were crucial. "What they don't teach you in business school is to make sure your life partner is in sync with what you're doing," Vivek explained. "You can divide your 24-hour day into three parts: eight hours work, eight hours personal, eight hours sleep. If your eight personal is not in sync with your eight work, then your eight sleep will suffer."

In contrast, as Humphrey desperately tried to secure funding for ConneXus, his wife and parents hoped he would soon leave the startup and pursue a more secure job. Their lack of support made an already difficult situation even harder. He explained, "You have to make sure that your family and your spouse, all the people you love and care about, are supportive of what you are doing. There is always a temptation to abandon the idea, to jump ship. If you don't have the support around you, it's much harder to resist. If you don't have 100% support, wait until you do, and [start a company] then."

Part of the problem that Cecilia, Humphrey's wife, had with ConneXus was Humphrey's unrealistic timeline, which she realized only in retrospect. Originally, he told her that he would secure funding by the time they were married in October. But by the end of the year, the couple was still living with his parents and the startup had not yet received the promised funding. If Humphrey had painted a more conservative—or at least realistic—scenario for Cecilia, rather than trying to "sell" her on letting him found ConneXus, she might have been prepared for the uncertainties of the startup process and the down parts of the entrepreneurial roller coaster. But as another founder said, "My wife doesn't know that it will probably take twice the time I expect and cost twice as much as I expect. If I tell her that, will she even let me try?"

An entrepreneur may also be constrained by his or her personal financial situation—the mortgage, college loans, credit card debt, and so on. A working spouse can be crucial. When Tim Westergren got the idea to start Pandora, he was entering his 30s and knew he wanted more financial stability. The fact that his wife's salary provided them with a financial buffer enabled him to go ahead with his startup. A survey of founders of high-growth businesses found that 70% were married when they founded their startups and that 60% had at least one child.[41] For these founders, a nonworking spouse makes the challenges particularly acute; research has shown that people whose spouses were not employed were less likely to become entrepreneurs.[42]

Developments That Release the Handcuffs

Although career handcuffs, golden handcuffs, and family handcuffs tend to get stronger as time passes, other developments can release these handcuffs and make it more possible for the potential founder to launch a startup. These developments, which are summarized in Figure 2.2, include the following:

An Employer's Slowing Growth

Employees tend to leave companies to become founders when their employers' growth rates begin to fall, reducing the attractiveness of staying there and the opportunity costs of becoming founders.[43] The likelihood of an employee leaving to become a founder has also been linked to the employee's own performance. Employees whose performance was in the middle of the distribution were the least likely to leave; the most likely were the poor-performing employees (the "slugs" whose pay wasn't high and who had the least to lose by leaving to found a startup) and the high-performing employees (the "stars" who had the potential to earn high wages by becoming self-employed).[44] Although high-paid employees may be less likely than lower-paid employees to walk away from their salaries, if they have saved a high percentage of their earnings over the years, that nest egg may make them more likely to make the leap than if they hadn't saved.

An Employer's Change in Strategy

The employer's acquisition or change of strategy may spark the potential founder's leap. Barry Nalls's work at GTE was consistently interesting enough to keep him there, his startup dream deferred, until the firm announced its impending merger with Bell Atlantic, another large telecom company. Barry explained why the merger pushed him to leave: "GTE had a lot of freedom; we could do a lot of innovative things. But when we started the merger discussions with Bell Atlantic, it was apparent that we were so different in culture, in the degree of innovation, and in the ways we worked. And there was the probability that my job would be moving to the Northeast, which I didn't want to happen."

Employment Shocks

For founders, probably the most drastic career trigger is the loss of a job. Genevieve Thiers was working for the Lotus division of IBM

Handcuffs	Developments That Can Release the Handcuffs
Career handcuffs	Employer's growth slows Employer changes strategy or is acquired Being laid off or fired
Golden handcuffs	Severance payment from layoff Inheritance or large gift
Family handcuffs	Spouse starts working Children grow up Emigrate to country (or region) that fosters entrepreneurship

Figure 2.2. Developments That Release Each Type of Handcuff

while developing her babysitting website, Sittercity, on the side. She had been planning to leave IBM eventually to work full-time on Sittercity, but in 2002 the economic downturn caused IBM to lay off the entire Lotus division with a six-month severance payment. As Dan Ratner, Thiers's husband and early employee, explained, "The biggest inflection point for an entrepreneur is when to quit the day job. Genevieve was fortunate enough to have the decision made for her."

Financial Shocks

Triggers can also be positive. Unexpected personal windfalls, for example, can spark the decision to leap; people who receive an inheritance or a large gift are more likely to found businesses.[45] (Negative financial shocks can also alter the founding equation, but usually by precluding or delaying the decision to found.)

Family Developments

Although Humphrey Chen's family developments hindered his leap, family developments can also trigger a leap. These triggers can range from marrying someone whose paycheck can support a leap into founderhood to having one's children become more independent. For Robin Chase, founder of car-sharing company Zipcar, having her young children start school offered the freedom to launch her startup.[46] Moving to a country or region that is more supportive of entrepreneurship may also release the potential founder from familial or cultural handcuffs.

HOW CAN I DISPASSIONATELY EVALUATE MY IDEA?

To ensure that the best decisions are being made about whether and when to launch their startups, potential founders should also be evaluating as objectively as possible the potential ideas on which they might base them. However, a founder's natural passion and confidence can prevent an objective evaluation and set up the founder to fail.

Evaluating Ideas

A study of fast-growing startups found that, for 71% of them, the founder got the idea while working at a regular job.[47] Tim Westergren's idea for Pandora Radio was sparked by his work as a musician and composer. For other founders, the idea for a startup may feel like it came out of the blue, while actually being grounded in some aspect of his or her past. For instance, when Genevieve Thiers happened to encounter a pregnant woman looking for a reputable babysitter, an inspiration hit her: "Wouldn't it be interesting to put a listing of all of the babysitters in the country in one place?" In fact, her own experience as a teenage babysitter helped spark that business idea and gave her an instinctive sense that it would fill a broad and important need. (Similarly, Vivek Khuller's encounter with a company that had developed electronic access cards inspired his business idea, but this idea was also sparked by his experience as an electrical engineer.)

Other founders are more like Barry Nalls, who had to work to discover an opportunity. As described above, Barry had to take a top-down approach to finding an appropriate industry segment, specific target customers within that segment, and then the services for which they would be willing to pay. In going through that process, Barry's years of experience both selling to customers and learning the telecom industry were the foundations on which he could build the idea for Masergy.

Regardless of how the idea was generated, a key step in the decision to leap into founderhood is the evaluation of the idea's potential—whether the "market window of opportunity" is favorable. Academic research has emphasized the value of market analysis by establishing connections between industry characteristics and startup success. Volumes have been written about how to analyze the attractiveness of industry and market opportunities and readers who plan to do such an analysis are referred to those volumes.[48] The following are some of the questions that potential founders ask about the market window of opportunity and how some of the academic research provides guidance:

Market potential: Are customers willing to pay for such a product or service? How big is the market? Is it growing? Startups with a broader potential reach (e.g., they can target a national market instead of a local or regional one) have higher survival chances.[49] Startups with products that "disrupt" the market by introducing a new architecture or component are more likely to succeed than those whose products are more "sustaining" and thus compete head-to-head with those of established competitors.[50] But startups with disruptive products may also have to plan for more development time than would be needed for sustaining products, for which a market already exists. When Vivek Khuller gave himself one year to establish a viable company, he did not realize that, for an innovative, industry-changing product like Smartix's, one year was probably not enough.

Competitive landscape: Is it favorable? Are many companies competing for scarce resources? When a groundbreaking company is founded and creates a new niche in the market, it does not have to compete with other players for resources and customers. But as more companies enter that niche, the competition increases rapidly until the population of companies outgrows its market niche and disbanding rates become greater than founding rates. The result is an S-shaped pattern of growth within the industry niche, with the early stages of growth being much more attractive competitively than the later stages.[51] At the points on the curve where the niche is more "munificent" with plentiful resources available to companies, organizational birth rates are highest.[52] Startups in highly competitive environments have lower survival chances than in lower-competition environments.[53]

"Ticking clock": Is there a ticking clock that requires me to move quickly to pursue my idea? Is the window of opportunity about to close? Ticking-clock industries include (a) those in which products and services are quickly derived from and just as quickly outdated by technological or scientific advances, (b) those with strong "network effects"—that is, the value of the product increases as more people use it,[54] and (c) those with significant economies of scale. Such industries tend to have stronger first-mover advantages, while in other industries, late entrants have a decent chance or may even have an advantage—a chance to outdo the first movers by learning from their mistakes and allowing them to develop customer awareness and a supply chain.

For the eventual founders of Proteus Biomedical, a developer of miniature computers and sensors for life science applications, understanding whether or not they were facing a ticking clock was critical. In 1989, Andrew Thompson and George Savage, who had degrees in engineering and medicine, respectively, and had met at Stanford Business School, saw an article in *Time* magazine that described micro-electrical mechanical systems (MEMS). Andrew envisioned these as "little scissors that one day would float around in your bloodstream, gobbling up cholesterol" and the duo was intrigued by the possibility of a startup. They concluded, however, that "while applications like these were potentially interesting, they couldn't be built yet. We shelved the idea, but periodically asked ourselves, is it time?" George said, "Healthcare generally isn't a good place to try out revolutionary technology that hasn't been proven elsewhere."[55] A decade later, however, Andrew and George decided that the technology to develop MEMS had matured to the point where the market for it might emerge quickly, sparking their founding of Proteus Biomedical.

Startup ideas must also be evaluated in light of the specific person's capabilities and skills. The same telecom opportunity would be seen in a very different light if it were being pursued by Tim Westergren instead of Barry Nalls, or even by an early-career Barry Nalls instead of a late-career one. A potential founder who has accumulated the right capitals should have very different answers about whether and when to leap than one who has not done such a good job preparing for the leap. For instance, a well-prepared founder should have more confidence in his or her ability to quickly create and deliver a product worth paying for and to identify and convince potential customers.

Clouding Judgment: Passion and Optimism

Passionate founders who have evaluated all of these dimensions of the opportunity must still guard against their natural overconfidence and optimism, which may have skewed their evaluation. Founders tend to be highly confident in their own abilities, in the potential of their ideas, and in the prospects of their startups. In a survey asking entrepreneurs to compare the prospects of their startups to those of similar startups, 95% of the respondents believed that their own startups had a better than 50% chance of succeeding, but only 78% believed that a similar startup had the same chance of succeeding. A full one-third of the entrepreneurs believed that their startups had a 100% chance of success.[56] The authors of that study concluded that entrepreneurs tend to be overconfident in their prospects. In another study, entrepreneurs were found to be 20% more overconfident about their ability to answer factual questions about medical issues than were non-entrepreneur managers. Such overconfidence may encourage entrepreneurs to take action sooner than they should have or to have overly rosy views of their prospects.[57]

   Is optimism an advantage or a disadvantage for a potential entrepreneur? On the one hand, optimism may spark more innovation and less of a tendency to "follow the herd."[58] Founders who are optimistic tend to act more quickly and to launch faster-growing businesses.[59] However, optimistic founders also tend to create unrealistic business plans based on rosy projections and to underestimate their competition.[60] They are more likely to overcommit to the initial idea instead of flexibly adjusting it and to underestimate the resources they will need to build the startup, thus increasing their chances of failure.[61]

Multiple studies have found entrepreneurs to be more optimistic about the future than non-entrepreneurs.[62] For serial entrepreneurs, that can actually be a disadvantage, leading them to discount negative information, to be more susceptible to confirmation biases,* and to repeat their past actions rather than question whether those actions apply to the current opportunity. As a result, higher-optimism entrepreneurs have 20% lower revenue growth and 25% lower employment growth than lower-optimism entrepreneurs, who would be less susceptible to the perils of optimism.[63]

In short, optimism is often a double-edged sword. Venture capitalist Guy Kawasaki, in his blog "How to Change the World," lists the "top ten lies of entrepreneurs." Most of these lies have to do with founders' oversized confidence and naïve expectations, from their projections of revenue and market size to their "proven" management team to their lack of competition. When an entrepreneur says he or she will make $50 million in four years, explained Guy, "I add one year to delivery time and multiply [the revenue] by .1."[64]

Founder optimism can also affect the decision about when to leap, leading some to leap sooner than they should and others to leap when they shouldn't at all. As we will see throughout this book, overconfidence and optimism also play a role in many subsequent founding dilemmas, from the decision about whether to found alone or seek the help of cofounders, to the financial terms a founder is willing to accept from investors, to a founder's expectations about how long to remain CEO of his or her own startup.

CLOSING REMARKS

One hears a lot about "following your passion." Potential founders should avoid the mistake of thinking that their passion excuses them from a rational assessment of their circumstances. The French

---

*A *confirmation bias* is a tendency to favor information that confirms preconceptions, regardless of whether the information is true. It may be caused by wishful thinking or by bounded rationality (i.e., limitations on people's abilities to process information) and often contributes to overconfidence.

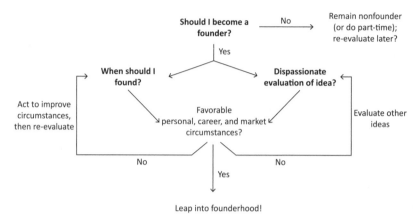

Figure 2.3. Three Big Career Questions

author François de La Rochefoucauld observed that "[t]he heart is forever making the head its fool," and Steve Jobs, cofounder of Apple Computer, was fond of saying, "Follow your heart, but listen to your head." Sometimes the head is right and the heart is wrong, at least for the time being, and especially for passionate overconfident founders. To make sure that "the head" is part of the decision, potential founders need to first ask the three big career questions examined in this chapter and summarized in Figure 2.3.

Humphrey's and Barry's decisions about whether, when, and what to found were powerfully affected, in very different ways, by where they were in their careers, by the characteristics of their start-ups, and by their personal situations. Figure 2.4 shows the three recurring factors we have examined—career factors, personal factors, and market factors—that affect the three questions outlined in Figure 2.3.

When founders see all three factors as being favorable—that is, if the situation falls into the small black "bull's-eye" region at the center of Figure 2.4, where the founder's career experiences provide a solid foundation on which to build the startup, his or her personal situation is conducive to becoming a founder, and the market is favorable—then it's time to follow the heart and make the leap!

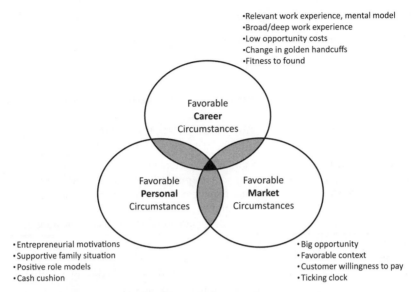

•Relevant work experience, mental model
•Broad/deep work experience
•Low opportunity costs
•Change in golden handcuffs
•Fitness to found

Favorable
Career
Circumstances

Favorable
Personal
Circumstances

Favorable
Market
Circumstances

• Entrepreneurial motivations
• Supportive family situation
• Positive role models
• Cash cushion

• Big opportunity
• Favorable context
• Customer willingness to pay
• Ticking clock

Figure 2.4. Career, Personal, and Market Circumstances

However, many founders suggest that such a perfect alignment of all three factors is rarely, if ever, encountered; there is no "perfect time" to become a founder. Potential founders who keep waiting for perfect alignment may come to the end of a long career regretting that they never made the leap. Nevertheless, founders who are overly optimistic or who misread their circumstances as being more favorable than they truly are will be taking unnecessary risks by leaping into founderhood when the three factors are really not favorable. Like those who waited for the perfect moment that never came, these overconfident potential founders may also end their careers with remorse, feeling that they squandered too soon the resources that might have made for a more successful leap later on. A better way to proceed when the factors are clearly not favorable is to dispassionately evaluate which circumstances need improvement and then to act to improve them prior to launching the startup.

Thus, the toughest dilemmas are the much more common situations in which the potential founder is passionate about becoming an entrepreneur but only two of the three factors are favorable. If

"Gray-Area" Obstacles	*Potential Solutions for Getting to the "Bull's-Eye"*
"I have everything but an idea."	Top-down evaluation of potential markets, customers, and business models Find "idea founder" whose own holes match your strengths Participate in other startups as an advisor or seed investor Attend conferences and read journals and blogs in your area of interest/expertise
"But I'm not armed for battle yet" (especially early-career founders).	Find job to fill functional or industry hole Attend entrepreneurial-networking events Find complementary cofounders, advisors, or mentors Fill hole by attending targeted class or program
"But I'm going to hurt my family."	Probe spouse's fears and openly explore ways to address them Agree on *realistic* timelines and resources that will be committed to the startup Explore whether part-time founding is feasible
"My handcuffs have gotten too strong" (especially late-career founders).	Save money to supply cash cushion and seed capital Maintain low "personal burn rate" Resist accumulating redundant or irrelevant human capital and social capital Seek broad range of assignments in various functions Scrutinize all noncompetes and other agreements before signing

Figure 2.5. Obstacles and Potential Solutions for Gray-Area Potential Founders

perfection is never to be expected, how close is close enough? These situations are represented by the three gray regions in Figure 2.4. Each region poses its own challenges for the potential founder, but each challenge comes with its own set of possible solutions, summarized in Figure 2.5 below. However, as potential "gray-region" founders tackle the remaining area of weakness in an effort to move into the bull's-eye, they need to remember that they are aiming at a moving target and to make sure that other factors have not become unfavorable. Let's examine each gray region:

"I Have Everything But an Idea!"

When Barry Nalls decided to quit his job and start a new company, he was comfortable with his personal and career positions. Professionally, he felt he had gained the skills, contacts, and experience he needed—both from GTE and from his time at various early-stage companies—to create his own startup. On the personal front, his wife was fully supportive. But Barry, unlike many of our other entrepreneurs, had never had an idea hit him, even though he had a broad idea of the business segment in which he might find an idea. Without an idea, he had no "market circumstance" to even evaluate, let alone pursue as a startup. To solve this problem—two favorable factors but no idea—Barry sat down and very systematically developed his business concept using the process described earlier in this chapter, then built a business plan to take advantage of his abundant human and social capital.

Another option for potential founders who lack an idea is to seek a cofounder who does have an idea but lacks something else that the idea-less founder can provide. For instance, James Malmo had business savvy and multiple ideas for high-tech products but lacked the engineering skills to implement them. He began attending meetings of the MIT Entrepreneurship Club, where he met Javier Pascal, an MIT engineer in search of an idea, and the two eventually became cofounders of Lynx Solutions. Other sources of complementary "idea founders" include coworkers—as was the case for the founders of Ockham Technologies, who were coworkers at The Alexander Group—and school, where the Smartix cofounders met as classmates.

"But I'm Not Armed for Battle Yet!"

Tim Westergren had a supportive spouse and had already had an epiphany that led to his idea for Pandora, an online radio station; his personal and market circumstances were favorable and beckoning. However, Tim was reluctant to leap because he felt he lacked the professional skills and experience to tackle a startup. As a former musician and composer, Tim had no idea where to begin. "It was a complete mystery to me how you start a company. I still had not had a real job. I didn't even know the basics."

This is often the situation for early-career founders. When planning their startups, such founders should assume that they are missing important skills and contacts and then carefully diagnose the gaps in their human capital, social capital, and financial capital. By attending a class or by finding a job that provides the professional skills that are lacking, inexperienced potential founders can try to develop the specific kinds of expertise they need. To fill social capital gaps, they can search out—and force themselves to regularly attend—local networking events, making sure to follow up with new contacts. Over time, regular networking can yield a much stronger set of contacts.

Along the way, potential early-career founders should also be searching for potential cofounders, hires, and investors/advisors. The involvement of one or more of those players can help fill in the gaps in the various categories of capital, can provide the objective perspectives necessary to counter the founder's natural passion and optimism, and can provide guidance about decisions and patterns that aren't yet a part of the potential founder's mental model. For example, it wasn't until Tim Westergren's wife introduced him to Jon Kraft, who had founded a high-tech company in Silicon Valley and had the business skills Tim lacked, that Tim was able to fill his career holes and found Pandora. (However, as described in Parts II and III, founders should carefully weigh these benefits against the challenges introduced by involving other players in the startup.)

"But I'm Going to Hurt My Family!"

Although Tim and Barry eventually entered the bull's-eye region of Figure 2.4—Barry by using his own reservoir of knowledge to come up with an idea and Tim by partnering with a key cofounder to gain the professional capabilities to start a company—Humphrey Chen's experience suggests that the most insurmountable obstacle to founding may be unfavorable personal circumstances. One

cannot alter them so easily by taking purposeful action or by seeking the help of others. Humphrey's market and career circumstances
were favorable and he was passionate about building ConneXus.
But his personal circumstance was quite unfavorable—although he
didn't fully realize it—and about to get worse. His new wife craved
stability and was risk-averse; both she and his parents favored his
full-time consulting offer. When Cecilia became pregnant with their
first child, Humphrey decided to take a secure job with Microsoft.

The challenges of balancing startup demands and family demands
can be particularly acute. While reflecting on his own experiences
trying to achieve that balance, serial entrepreneur Steve Blank came
up with "four big lies entrepreneurs tell themselves about work and
family."[65] Those lies were "I'm only doing it for my family," "My
spouse 'understands,'" "All I need is one startup to 'hit' and then I
can slow down or retire," and "I'll make it up by spending 'quality
time' with my wife/kids." He concluded that, for him, "None of these
were true." Because of that, "Over time I began to recognize and
regret the trade-offs I had made between work and relationships."

A possible solution to an unfavorable family situation is to work
on the startup part-time—after hours or on weekends—either as a
long-term approach or as a transitional phase with the option of
leaping full-time later. Proposing or agreeing to such an option may
help persuade a spouse to support the entrepreneurial endeavor.
However, in some situations, agreeing to go the "safe" part-time
route can reintroduce the career handcuffs and can actually increase
risks, slowing down progress and letting the market window slam
shut. Vivek Khuller observed, "My wife could have been strict. She
could have said, 'Go ahead with Smartix, but also have a part-time
job so you can pay your share.' If she'd done that . . . I would have
gotten another job and would not have had the time or energy to
do Smartix."

In industries where competitive pressures force founders to
move quickly, it is indeed advisable to try to dive into founderhood
full-time. Where there is less rush to build the startup, founders
can often manage their personal risks and gain buy-in from their
families if they take a more gradual approach to founding. However,

cofounders or potential funders may force the founder to make a full-time leap sooner than planned. Jim Triandiflou was still working at The Alexander Group and working on Ockham Technologies part-time when a potential angel investor, Bobby Crews, pushed him and his cofounders to quit their day jobs. As Jim recalled, "Crews said, 'We are interested in doing it, but you've got no customers, you haven't even quit your dang jobs yet, and you have nothing for a product. . . . Right now, you're playing both sides where you got a job and you're making money. We've got to see substance and we've got to see commitment.'" As a result, a month later, both Jim and his cofounder, Mike Meisenheimer, quit their jobs.

"My Handcuffs Have Gotten Too Strong!"

Potential late-career founders have to guard against the perils of waiting. They should avoid the trap of continually accumulating more human and social capital. They should also maintain a low "personal burn rate" so they don't get used to the handcuffs of a high-priced lifestyle and so they can accumulate seed capital for their eventual startup.

In retrospect, many late-career founders regret not having made the leap sooner. Four years after founding Masergy, Barry Nalls lamented, "Boy, I wish I had become an entrepreneur long ago! Why did I wait so long?" A year after founding a startup that provides customer-behavior analytics services, founder-CEO David Wellman reflected on his decision to leap:[66]

> Well today is my birthday, 40. And I am just finishing year 1 of my own venture. I have professional investment backing. A product in its infancy. Two large clients and a dozen smaller ones and a lot in the pipe.
>
> So that means I have that CEO title, and I was sweeping floors this morning. It's 3:30AM and I am still at work, for the second all-nighter this week. I don't have enough people, time, or energy to deal with all the daily problems—like making a Costco run to get more printer paper.

Yes, the hours are arduous, [and] my customers [are] more demanding than the most incompetent boss I have ever had. My pay is paltry and I sometime need to give it back. The work environment is less desirable than my college dorm room.

But the second half of my career looks so good from here!

Resolving the career dilemma in favor of making the leap is a big and exciting step, but it leads directly to many more dilemmas, each with the potential to smother a young startup in its cradle. In the coming chapters, we will examine some of the most important—and most interesting—of those founding dilemmas, many of which are directly tied to the pre-founding career decisions discussed in this chapter. Founders who make the leap early in their careers should be more inclined to look for help from complementary cofounders, hires, or investors and should be more willing to give up the equity, decision-making control, and compensation required to attract them. In contrast, late-career founders who already possess much of the capitals needed to launch the startup should be able to consider the option of being a solo founder and should also be able to attract complementary players by offering less attractive packages. Each of these career paths thus leads to very different potential outcomes.

PART II
FOUNDING TEAM
DILEMMAS

INTRODUCTION

The light bulb has gone off; a new business idea has sparked the decision to launch a startup, and the founder now faces a myriad of decisions. In this part of the book, I first focus on the dilemmas faced by the "core founder," the person who had the idea to launch the startup and is driving the initial stages of building it.[*] The first of these dilemmas is the solo-versus-team dilemma: Do I begin the startup by myself or do I attract cofounders to help me start it?

The decision to attract cofounders introduces further critical decisions about whom to attract, what role each cofounder should

[*] As described in Chapter 1 regarding the Circles team, it is possible for a founding team to have more than one core founder. The dilemmas described in this part also apply—and sometimes apply even more strongly—to such teams, for these core founders must also decide how to manage the challenges introduced by their prior relationships, how to split the roles and decision making, and how to split the financial rewards among themselves.

play, and how to split the equity among the cofounders. I call these three core dilemmas "the Three Rs"—relationships, roles, and rewards. In Chapters 4 through 7, I use the Three Rs framework to examine how founding teams can, do, and should make these decisions; how these decisions are interconnected; and how they will affect the outcomes of team stability, company valuation, and control.

OVERVIEW OF CHAPTERS

The first chapter in this part will focus on the initial solo-versus-team dilemma. The subsequent chapters focus on team issues, with a chapter devoted to each of the Three Rs, followed by a chapter examining the linkages among them. A brief overview of the chapters in this part follows:

Chapter 3: **Solo-versus-Team Dilemma**—Founding solo can help avoid the relationship, role, and reward dilemmas described below but introduces its own challenges and risks, such as a lack of human, social, or financial capital and a lack of emotional and psychological support during the toughest parts of the entrepreneurial roller-coaster ride.

Chapter 4: **Relationship Dilemmas**—The cofounders' previous shared experience—or lack of it—affects the team's ability to tackle tough issues together, its diversity of skills and perspectives, and its stability, sometimes in surprising ways.

Chapter 5: **Role Dilemmas**—The division of labor within a founding team can be a major source of tension if cofounders are fighting over titles, if they have overlapping roles, if the collective decision making fosters gridlock or interpersonal conflict, or if the division of labor cannot be adjusted as the startup evolves.

Chapter 6: **Reward Dilemmas**—The division of equity and the allocation of financial benefits can cause problems within teams if members feel they are not being compensated fairly for their contributions to the startup. Compensation arrangements that align interests and protect against negative surprises are hard, yet critical, to accomplish.

Chapter 7: **The Three Rs System**—When founding-team decisions are aligned across all three dimensions, the team is more likely to be stable and experience lower turnover. Conversely, misalignment is likely to lead to greater intrateam tension and higher turnover. Thus, to fully understand the factors that lead teams to splinter, it is critical to examine not only each R on its own but also their mutual alignment or misalignment.

In these chapters, I describe each dilemma in detail, survey the relevant research, and discuss case studies of founders and founding teams to illustrate the interpersonal tensions and dynamics and to provide examples of best practices. Where possible, we will examine how two main outcomes, the founding team's stability and the growth in startup valuation, are affected by early decisions about relationships, roles, and rewards. Although we will examine each set of dilemmas separately, the dilemmas are interdependent and may be encountered in different sequences, a theme to which we return in Chapter 7.

In each chapter, I will present data that show the pervasiveness of the patterns described in the field cases. In 2006, I enriched the founding-team section of my annual survey; thus, for this part of the book, I make extensive use of the data collected since then (i.e., a dataset that combines the 2006, 2007, 2008, and 2009 surveys). This dataset includes 4,232 founders from 1,542 private startups in technology and the life sciences. Of the startups in this combined dataset, 88% were founded between 1998 and 2008. Appendix A provides further details on the survey and the dataset.

The data are complemented by case studies of founders who faced these dilemmas, sometimes successfully but often not. For instance, we will examine the decisions of Evan Williams, a serial entrepreneur who took a variety of approaches across his startups, often learning from his prior outcomes. In each chapter, we will meet Evan and several other founders from whom we will have much to learn.

CHAPTER THREE

THE SOLO-VERSUS-TEAM DILEMMA

AS WE SAW IN CHAPTER 2, CAREER, MARKET, AND PERSONAL FACTORS play a powerful role in the decision to become a founder. They also play a central role in one of the first and most important decisions faced by a founder: whether to "go solo" or to form a founding team. People who have thought carefully about whether to become founders and have considered the issues raised in Chapter 2 gain insights that also prove useful for the solo-versus-team decision. In contrast, people who go solo when they shouldn't will increase their risk of failure, while people who bring on cofounders when they should have gone solo will usually face team tensions they could have avoided.

As shown in Figure 3.1, in my dataset of high-potential startups, only 16.1% were solo-founded, with a high of 17.5% in the technology industry and a low of 11.7% in life sciences. More than one-third of the startups had two founders and one-quarter had three. What separates the minority of solo founders in these startups from those who build founding teams?

REASONS TO GO SOLO

There are a number of reasons why a founder might choose to go solo. For instance, the founder may already have many of the resources needed to found the startup, or there may be little need for

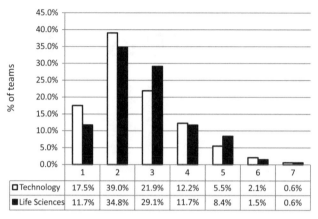

Figure 3.1. Sizes of Founding Teams for Technology and Life Sciences Startups

the startup to grow quickly. The startup may not be expected to grow big enough to support multiple founders. The founder may want to keep all the equity and control of all decision making, which would be particularly true for control-motivated founders. The founder may also be tempted to keep things simple in the early stages and thus dodge the coordination problems that come with bringing cofounders on board. Here, the founder's instinct (or prior experience) is backed up by Arthur Stinchcombe's groundbreaking article on what makes new organizations especially prone to failure.[1] Three of the four factors he identified were repercussions of forming a founding team: Cofounders were often challenged—and often undone—by the need to (a) learn new roles within the founding team, (b) negotiate the distribution of economic rewards among themselves, and (c) form trusting relationships with strangers (i.e., each other).

With one or more of these reasons in mind, a founder might conclude that this is something he or she can do without cofounders, so why ask for trouble? Barry Nalls, for example, founded Masergy, an enterprise telecom company, on his own, convinced that he had the resources he needed and that he was better off making all his own decisions. He had worked at GTE for 25 years, starting off with only a two-year technical degree and working his way up the ranks (earning an MBA along the way), gaining valuable experience managing teams, spearheading new programs, and running sales and marketing groups. In the mid-1980s, he had taken a break from GTE to start a small business, but it stagnated without adequate funding. After returning to GTE as a product manager for new technologies for several more years, Nalls had again tested the entrepreneurial waters by joining a small startup in Texas, but soon left that startup after a disagreement with the CEO. By the time Nalls decided to found Masergy, he felt he had the broad range of skills he would need. He had sales and operating skills, deep knowledge of the industry, contacts with potential customers, and a cash cushion to provide living expenses while he developed the business plan. He could wait to hire and involve other people, and in the meantime saw little to gain by adding a cofounder. Going solo made sense. Barry was not alone in thinking so: The core founders in my dataset were 26% more likely to go solo if they had pre-founding management experience than if they lacked it.[2]

Going solo also fit with Barry's style of work. He explained:

> I realized that throughout my career, I've been a solo guy. I pull together teams, but from a peer standpoint, I've always figured things out myself. With my years of experience at GTE, I could do the technology, marketing, and administrative pieces myself, so I never considered pulling in other founders. Also, I learned from my grandfather and dad that partnerships never work. They always were sole proprietors. I learned that leadership is all about taking in information and making a decision—shared information but not shared decisions. Make decisions yourself and live with them. Another key is speed. I want a single decision maker, even below me. If I have a VP of operations, he makes the call about operations.

The decision to be a solo founder may not always be made for such efficiency reasons. Core founders may have such a strong preference for control that the decision to go solo doesn't even feel like a decision. Dr. Kevin Stone, for example, inventor of the first ready-to-drink glucosamine supplement and founder-CEO of Joint Juice, states emphatically, "Maniacal drive by a benevolent founder is a *solo* activity!"[3] Founders who want to retain 100% of the equity for themselves, or who plan to launch the startup on their own and later hire employees to fill their holes, are also more likely to

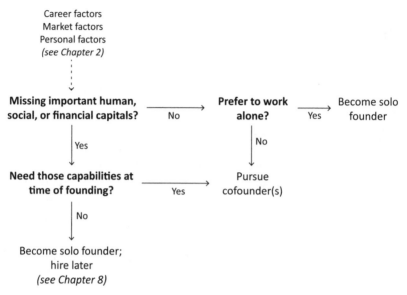

Career factors
Market factors
Personal factors
(see Chapter 2)

Missing important human, ⟶ **Prefer to work** ⟶ Become solo
social, or financial capitals?   No   **alone?**   Yes   founder

Yes   No

Need those capabilities at ⟶ Pursue
time of founding?   Yes   cofounder(s)

No

Become solo founder;
hire later
(see Chapter 8)

Figure 3.2. Central "Solo versus Team" Questions

fly solo. Figure 3.2 presents a decision chart that captures many of these considerations.

Going solo is, like most decisions we will discuss in this book, a decision with a set of short-term consequences and a different set of long-term consequences. In the short run, solo founding may seem like the easy choice, but not all solo founders with Barry Nalls's determination also have his wide range of skills and experience.[4] By remaining solo founders, they take a much greater risk than he did that their startup will either fail to reach its full potential or just fail outright. For example, they may prioritize a need for control over growing a more valuable company, or, in their overconfidence and their passion for the idea, they may underestimate the need for help.

THE ARGUMENT FOR COFOUNDERS

While there are many valid reasons for founding a startup alone, a large percentage of founders decide to build a team of cofounders.[*]

---

[*] Other core founders try in vain to attract cofounders, and decide either to go solo or to defer founding the startup (Ruef, 2010).

Their reasons are both tangible and intangible. The tangible needs that could be met by adding a cofounder include three kinds of capital. In Chapter 2, we looked at how each type of capital can and should affect the decision to become an entrepreneur, but similar considerations affect cofounder decisions:

- *Human capital.* Human capital includes the explicit knowledge derived from formal education and the tacit skills derived from prior experience. It is a rare founder who already has all the skills and knowledge needed to build a new organization from nothing. For instance, founders with deep technical backgrounds are often unable to tackle the early tasks that require sales, marketing, business development, and financial knowledge. Founders who lack industry experience may get blindsided by problems that could have been anticipated by an industry veteran. Cofounders with those complementary skills will maximize the startup's chance of anticipating or dealing with such problems.
- *Social capital.* Social capital refers to the benefits derived from one's place in information and communication networks. New startups need to reach out to recruit employees, establish relationships with potential partners, meet potential investors, and gain access to many other outside resources. Unless the core founder has a particularly rich set of relevant contacts, the startup will benefit from cofounders' contacts and social capital.
- *Financial capital.* Financial capital refers to the money or other tangible resources that can be used in the founding process. The founder of a capital-intensive business, or any founder who has not accumulated the necessary financial capital, can benefit from cofounders who have their own financial capital to invest in the startup.

A founder taking this "capital-based approach" to the solo-versus-team decision needs to assess the human, social, and financial capital required to build the startup; compare it to the human, social, and financial capital he or she already possesses; see how much is missing; and then decide whether to build a founding team or remain a solo founder. A startup facing a very diverse set of challenges—for example, designing a complex medical device, developing and testing it (and securing enough venture capital to engage in such a lengthy and risky process), securing patents, complying with complex federal regulations, creating a marketing and sales plan, navigating among tough and successful competitors, convincing hospital administrators to use the device and insurers to cover it, supporting the product, preparing for legal liabilities, upgrading the product, and so on—probably needs multiple cofounders, while a solo founder may be enough to start a medical-device distribution company. Industries with high levels of competition, and ones in which early entrants have an advantage over late entrants, may also increase the need for cofounders. These are some of the reasons why solo founders account for about half of the businesses in the Panel Study of Entrepreneurial Dynamics (PSED) small-business dataset but fewer than 20% in my dataset of technology and life sciences startups.[5] In that latter dataset, more than one-third of the core founders attracted one cofounder and about 10% of founding teams even included five or more founders, as shown in Figure 3.1.[6]

Tim Westergren took such a capital-based approach to founding Pandora Radio. In 1999, he came up with the idea to construct a database of the musical attributes of songs and use it to make recommendations to customers (via online music retailers) based on their descriptions of what kind of music they liked. Tim had a political science degree from Stanford and had spent the previous 11 years as a film-score composer and member of a rock band, which had given him substantial expertise in music, some sales and management acumen from managing his band and selling his composing services to filmmakers, a small cash cushion, and broad contacts with musicians who could help him catalog the music. But he had never held a "real job." Well aware that he lacked substantive knowledge of the complex technologies his idea required and that he had never even worked in a business, never mind founded one, he knew he would need help. He decided not to move forward until he had secured cofounders who had the human capital to fill in his technology and business holes, the social capital to get to potential nonmusician hires and potential investors, and additional financial capital.

Even if a core founder has all the requisite skills, contacts, and seed capital, he or she may nevertheless decide there is too much for one person to do (or do well) and therefore seek a cofounder. Core founders may be tempted to do everything themselves, but this is probably not as efficient as it sounds. Founding a startup is almost guaranteed to be more work than its founder imagines; the founder's having a full plate right from the start leaves no room for the unexpected tasks—whether emergencies or opportunities—that are sure to arise. In any case, working full-tilt all the time sounds heroic but is not very efficient. If crucial decisions are being made by people who are worn out or burned out, the startup will suffer. Jim Triandiflou recalled the early days at his startup, Ockham Technologies, trying to design an entire product suite for IBM with only his partner, Mike, and a team of consultants: "We spent Saturday and Sunday in [the consultants'] office in a conference room, trying to cram through what the requirements were going to be for the whole [product] suite. We were trying to boil the ocean. We were going to have six modules done in six months."

At the same time, the personal preferences and psychological needs that lead core founders to choose cofounders can outweigh the tangible factors:

- *Task preferences*—A core founder who has all the requisite skills, contacts, and seed capital but dislikes carrying out one or more of the critical early-stage tasks may look for a cofounder to take on those tasks. For example, Vivek Khuller had worked for Bell Atlantic for several years, including two years as a software programmer and analyst, developing software for new services and systems. Vivek had the skills to create the software for his online ticketing idea, but he had long since moved on from programming, had held a series of management jobs, and was currently enrolled in an MBA program. Instead of taking on the programming task himself, Vivek chose to add a cofounder, a prior coworker from Bell Atlantic, to develop the ticketing system. This left Vivek free to focus on business development and finding funding for the startup.

- *Collaborative style*—Sharing the idea with a potential co-founder can help the founder articulate and enhance it. When Vivek Khuller took on Saurabh Mittal, a fellow MBA student, as a cofounder, their discussions helped Vivek refine and change his business proposition. During late-night sessions from 10 p.m. to 4 a.m., Vivek and Saurabh honed the Smartix revenue and pricing models, and developed plans for how much capital to raise and how to use it. Such collaboration was Vivek's preferred working style.
- *Support and validation*—A core founder who has a strong need for affiliation, validation, or psychological support may seek cofounders, even if they add little capital to the startup. One founder admitted he was "anxious to get somebody on board," even though there was no clear hole that a cofounder would fill. Another founder said, "If I can't even convince one friend to join me, how good could my idea be?" Brian Scudamore started out building Rubbish Boys, a residential rubbish-hauling company, by himself, but quickly decided to add a friend as an equal partner: "I didn't put much thought into it, didn't think about what holes he could fill or the marriage of skills. I just liked the guy and figured we'd have fun doing this together. I figured it might be more fun if I had someone to do this with. I needed the camaraderie, the support, the confidence-building of having someone else."

It can take time for some of these psychological needs to become evident. Even a core founder who can handle all of the tasks may find the ups and downs of the "founder roller coaster" taking a psychological toll and may decide it's time to look for some cofounders. Lew Cirne, the founder of enterprise-software startup Wily Technology, worked alone for a year, developing the core technology for his startup's first product: "It was a critical year, and a real test of my inner fortitude. There were a lot of sleepless nights, from work, excitement, fear, and anxiety, wondering whether it had any commercial value." Instead of waiting so long to involve others, Lew could have gained valuable moral and emotional support to help get through those tough early days. Given the natural tendency for passionate founders to expect the best, if they doubt their ability to withstand the pressures, they should seriously consider attracting cofounders who can both provide support and enhance the team's capabilities.

HOW MANY COFOUNDERS?

Once the core founder has decided to add cofounders, he or she has to decide how many cofounders to add. Each new cofounder increases coordination costs and inefficiency. As highlighted by Stinchcombe, the larger the team, the greater the coordination costs and the higher the risk that roles will overlap and cause conflict within the team.[7] For example, in FeedBurner's four-person team, two of the founders were happy to focus on their own functions, but Dick and Steve, who shared many of the high-level decisions, experienced time-consuming conflict over roles and responsibilities until the startup grew large enough to enable Steve to focus full-time on business development. The core founder's motivation can also play a powerful role in the decision of whether to add each cofounder: A desire for control might lead the core founder to add fewer cofounders, while a desire to build the startup's value might lead to a bigger founding team.

Each additional person also adds more nodes to the communication network, slows things down, and weakens incentives.[8] Thus, each new cofounder should add important elements to the team—for example, filling in gaps in human capital or having the ability to reduce a key area of task overload for the other founders—that bring more value than is lost by adding the new cofounder. In the case of UpDown, a social-networking site for small investors, core founder Michael Reich added MBA classmates to his team, but their skills, experience, and networks were similar to his, which meant that the three-person team still needed to add a programmer, Phuc Truong, to build the product. The resulting stress about roles and equity splits could have been reduced if Michael had invited only Phuc—the one person he truly needed to realize his idea—to join the team.

As Michael's experience at UpDown illustrates, founders tend to underestimate the costs and complications added by each new cofounder; they don't realize that, as one serial entrepreneur observed, "Complexity increases exponentially with more cofounders." Like Michael, many founders also tend to overestimate the value that will be added by redundant cofounders who might not add new capabilities. As a result, they end up with larger teams than they should, a problem that could be avoided by taking a more disciplined approach to evaluating each potential cofounder's marginal costs and value. In addition, core founders need to understand the potential risks and problems introduced by adding cofounders, which we will detail in Chapters 4 to 7.

THE BROADER CONTEXT

The broader environment in which the startup operates may also affect the solo-versus-team decision. Solo founding may fit with some environmental contexts while other environments may require a founding team. In particular, some industries are highly competitive or strongly favor first movers. An industry with powerful network effects, for example, will provoke a "ticking clock" race to develop the initial product and to attract and lock in customers.[9] In such an industry, the core founder faces a more urgent need for cofounders to fill in the holes in each area of capital. He or she may also have a greater need to fill in the psychological holes when setting out on what is likely be a very stressful roller-coaster ride.

The more complex the environmental contingencies faced by the startup, the more need for additional founders.[10] Teams dealing with complex environments need to process more information; larger teams are better able to do so. The turbulent environments in which startups operate are marked by rapid technological discontinuities and unstable success factors.[11] Such environments increase the team's information-processing needs by creating opportunities and crises that require the organization to adapt its strategy and structure. Larger groups are better at solving problems because they can (a) absorb and recall more items of information, (b) correct more errors in inference and analysis, (c) consider more potential solutions, and (d) bring a broader range of perspectives to bear on the problem.[12] Thus, larger founding teams,

Solo-found when . . .	*Build a founding team when . . .*
• Founder has deep human capital and social capital (and sufficient financial capital) that is relevant to the startup's industry • Founder has a strong preference for maintaining full control of all decisions • Founder does not have a strong need for support or validation • The business is small and in a slow-moving industry	• Founder has important holes in human capital, social capital, and/or financial capital • Founder prefers not to do some tasks required in the early days of the startup • Founder prefers a collaborative style • Founder has a strong desire for support or validation • The business is in a fast-moving industry, especially if there are first-mover advantages or network effects

Figure 3.3. When to Solo-Found versus Build a Founding Team

which arm the organization with additional resources, have higher organizational growth rates and rates of survival.[13]

These differences in context further reinforce why solo founding is the exception in my dataset of technology and life sciences start-ups, but tends to be relatively common in predominantly low-tech small businesses.[14]

In summary, as shown in Figure 3.3, solo founding should be pursued by founders whose backgrounds, goals, and startups meet the following criteria: The founder has deep, relevant experience; the founder is driven to keep control of the key decisions; the industry does not demand fast growth; and the idea and its implementation are relatively simple. The opposite decision should be made by inexperienced founders, those who are willing to give up some control in order to attract an excellent cofounder, those founding startups in challenging or fast-growing industries, and those whose startup ideas are complex.

SYMBOLIC FOUNDERS VERSUS HIRES

We tend to think of "founder" as an objective status that applies to a person who was a full-time participant in the startup when it was founded, took part in originating or developing the idea on which it was based, and played a central role in getting it off the ground. This view suggests that all so-called founders joined the startup at about the same time. But in many instances, people considered to be founders joined the startup months after the core founder began it.[15] Thus, "founder" can actually be a very subjective—even symbolic—status. For instance, when I asked the founder-CEO of an email startup about the widely differing start dates and equity stakes of his cofounders, he told me, "To me, the 'founder' title is symbolic of their playing a key role in building a new function for me. Even if someone was employee number ten, if he was the first hire for his function, I'll call him a founder. Bestowing the 'founder' title is also a way for me to sweeten a job offer without having to give up scarce equity or cash."

Yet, there are dangers to granting "founder" status too easily. The founder title brings higher status in the startup and may make the person feel more entitled to have and keep a senior position. However, as captured by founder and investor Jeff Bussgang's "jungle, dirt road, and highway" metaphor, startups go through dramatic changes, first needing people who can find their way through a wild jungle, then people who can create and traverse a dirt road, then people who can pave and drive down a highway.[16] As we will see, startups can have major problems when early "jungle stage" employees later prove ineffective on dirt roads or highways and have to be sidelined or fired. When that person carries the founder title, these problems have even deeper, sometimes unanticipated, impacts on the startup's culture and employees.

Even a team of "actual" founders can find themselves having to decide whether or not to give later hires the status of founder. The founding team of UpDown wrestled with just this issue. Michael got the idea for the startup in his first year of business school and almost immediately involved two classmates, Warren and Georg. Warren's interest soon waned. Georg and Michael, however, were still committed and knew they needed to involve a software developer to create the site. They placed advertisements for a chief technology officer and found Phuc, an experienced technologist. Although Michael and Georg could have hired Phuc as an employee, they decided to give him the title of founder and share the equity with him, even though he had contributed no seed equity and had not been involved until months after the founding. Giving Phuc the title of founder helped solidify his commitment at a time when Michael and Georg didn't have the resources to pay him a salary. On the other hand, although Warren was involved at the inception of the company, Michael felt strongly that Warren should not be deemed a founder because Warren would not be playing a central role in the startup, was not fully committed to it, and would not be receiving more than a sliver of equity in the startup.

Empirically, we can use multiple indicators to assess which people are truly founders of their startups.* When all indicators for a given founder point in the same direction, we can be more confident that he or she was a core or "real" founder. When the indicators are mixed, as in the email startup above, we can be more confident that the founder title is closer to symbolic.

CLOSING REMARKS

Excessive optimism can blind many founders to their startup's critical needs, so they must be particularly vigilant about identifying the gaps in their skills, knowledge, and contacts and evaluating whether and when those gaps should be filled by a cofounder. Underestimating the need for a cofounder heightens the risk of failure.

An immediate and critical need that cannot be filled by the founder's own human and social capitals does not *necessarily* require a cofounder. Other options may include outsourcing, finding

---

*The indicators used in my analyses were the following:
- Is each founder's start date the same as the startup's founding date, or are some later?
- Was each founder at least partly responsible for the idea or intellectual property on which the startup was founded?
- What was each founder's initial role in the startup? For example, did each founder begin with a C-level title? Were some founders on the board of directors from the board's inception while others were not?
- Which people are explicitly labeled as founders of the startup?
- What was each founder's equity stake?

advisors, or partnering with complementary companies. But often these are not enough.

Well-prepared, multitalented founders who do not need a co-founder to meet any of the startup's immediate needs may want one anyway because they prefer the camaraderie of working in a team. But as Brian Scudamore learned the hard way, this can be very risky. A core founder might think, I know I can get along without this cofounder if I need to, so what have I got to lose? Plenty. Cofounders can slow down decision making and introduce tensions, the more so if they aren't really fulfilling any essential need. Nonessential cofounders also take up equity stakes that could be used more productively to attract hires, investors, or other important players. As we will see in Chapter 6, it is extremely difficult and costly to undo a bad cofounder decision, as it was for Brian. Before exposing the startup to these hazards, a founder should be reasonably sure that a potential cofounder will add an important piece to the startup puzzle.

Sometimes a founder knows that he or she is alright for now but is going to be missing a critical piece later on; for example, he or she has the deep technical background and skills to develop a prototype product but not the sales and administrative skills to attract and enroll beta-testers after the prototype is finished. As suggested in Figure 3.2 earlier in this chapter, such a core founder can found solo, develop the prototype, and then hire employees to fill the gaps as the needs (and financing) arise. This strategy lets the core founder keep more control over the early decisions—to stay king longer.

However, the wisdom of this go-solo-and-hire-as-necessary strategy depends on the circumstances. When the startup's industry is growing quickly or if there are other challenges that place a premium on speed, even a founder who is self-sufficient at present may need a cofounder from the start because (a) the need for that cofounder will come soon and it may be hard to find the right person quickly enough and (b) a well-chosen cofounder can help build the startup more quickly than the core founder could do solo.

Figure 3.4 summarizes the advantages and disadvantages of remaining solo versus building a founding team and suggests ways to mitigate the disadvantages.

Option	Advantages	Disadvantages	Potential Ways to Mitigate Disadvantages
Going solo	• Retain all of the equity • Maintain decision-making control • Avoid communication, coordination, and incentive problems	• Have to rely exclusively on the founder to fill gaps in human capital, social capital, and financial capital, either slowing the startup's launch while the founder becomes prepared or exposing the startup to potential failure if the founder moves forward without the requisite capitals or a critical competency • Less ability to gather and process complex information • Slower response rate • Lack of collaboration/support; lonely	• Postpone or extend decision to found; systematically fill holes by gaining relevant experience • Find experienced advisors and mentors to fill holes, at least temporarily • Find complementary corporate partners or outsource some tasks • As needs arise, use equity to attract hires and investors to fill holes (see Chapters 8 and 9, respectively) • Found in a slower-moving, less complex industry
Building a founding team	• Fill holes in human capital, social capital, and financial capital • Increased ability to gather and process information • Faster response rate • Gain support/ collaboration • Have more fun (for the right personality mix)	• Sacrifice equity • Sacrifice decision-making control • Communication, coordination, and incentive problems	• Carefully evaluate the marginal utility of each new cofounder; only add cofounders whose marginal benefits are more than the added costs • Proactively develop process for decision making within the team (see Chapter 5) • "Try before you buy"; invest time in getting to know prospective team members and their working styles

Figure 3.4. Advantages and Disadvantages of Going Solo versus Building a Founding Team

Even when bringing on cofounders is the right decision, it is almost never an easy one in the longer run. It immediately adds complexity to the startup and sows the seeds for a myriad of future dilemmas and challenges, many of them underappreciated or unanticipated when the initial decision is made. Understanding those challenges *before* making that initial decision is crucial for making the right founding-team decisions. In particular, there are three recurring categories of founding-team decisions—relationships, roles, and rewards—each involving trade-offs and tensions. These "Three Rs" are the subject of the rest of this part of the book.

CHAPTER FOUR

RELATIONSHIP DILEMMAS: FLOCKING TOGETHER AND PLAYING WITH FIRE

Founders who decide to form a founding team must now decide whom to choose as cofounders. As shown in Figure 4.1, the prior relationships within the founding team introduce one of three major sets of dilemmas with which founders have to deal, and which we examine in the remainder of this part of the book.

Core founders have many options for where to look for cofounders, which can be envisioned as a series of three concentric circles. The inner circle includes people with whom the core founder is in *direct contact* because they already have a relationship that ranges from old neighborhood friends to husbands and wives. The middle circle includes people met through *indirect contact* or *indirect networking*; that is, through a mutual acquaintance. The outer circle includes people met through an *impersonal search* process; that is, strangers who are identified for having particular traits or abilities—or sometimes just because the founder takes a liking to a new acquaintance.

The case of Evan Williams illustrates both the range of options available to cofounders and some of the possible short-term and long-term consequences of their decisions. To found his first two startups, Evan chose people who were socially close to him. The first startup, a direct-marketing firm, was cofounded with his father and also involved his then-girlfriend, his brother, and several college

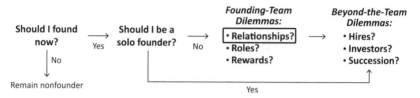

Figure 4.1. Relationship Dilemmas, in the Context of the Broader Set of Founding Dilemmas

friends. The team avoided discussing tough issues, such as how to deal with conflicting roles, and never developed an effective working relationship. After three years, Evan shut down the startup: "It was a mess with our relationships and the failed projects. . . . It was a train wreck management-wise." His second startup, which turned into Blogger, an early pioneer in the blogging segment, was cofounded with Meg Hourihan, a technology consultant whom he had been dating. The problems and pains that Evan experienced when cofounding with his relatives, friends, and girlfriends—experiences that we will discuss below—led him to take a very different approach in his third startup, a podcasting company called Odeo. This time, he decided to cofound with Noah Glass, an acquaintance who had prior experience in the online-audio industry but whom he did not know well. As we will see, at Odeo he avoided some of his previous risks, but encountered others.

In this chapter, I focus on two issues in particular: (a) whether the founding team should be homogeneous or diverse and (b) whether to found a startup with family or close friends, which has high benefits but underappreciated risks, or to found with other types of people. I examine the core dilemmas, describe the quantitative implications for team stability, and outline ways to manage the risks while getting the benefits of each option.

FOUNDING-TEAM HOMOGENEITY VERSUS DIVERSITY

Proverbial wisdom states that "birds of a feather flock together." Sociologists call this natural tendency *homophily* and have shown in small businesses that people of the same gender or race and people of similar geographic origins, educational backgrounds, and functional experience are disproportionately likely to found companies together. Excluding spousal teams, all-male or all-female founding teams have been found to be five times more likely to occur than would be expected by chance, and teams are remarkably homogeneous with regard to skills and functional backgrounds.[1] (Also, ethnically homogeneous teams were found to be 46 times more likely, and, even after controlling for the possibility that ethnic homogeneity is the result of family ties among the team, ethnically homogeneous teams occurred 27 times more often than would be expected by chance.) Thus, homophily has powerful effects on the homogeneity within founding teams.

We can get a sense of how powerfully homophily affects the formation of founding teams by considering how the teams in my dataset vary in terms of work experience. One might expect, for example, that the greater the team's average years of work experience, the more variation there would be within the team due to young people with exciting ideas recruiting experienced cofounders to help them build the startup, or to older founders recruiting young cofounders who are more in tune with the latest technology, social trends, and so on. However, except for the least-experienced teams, there seems to be a consistent threshold—in my dataset, about a decade of difference in prior experience—beyond which teams resist adding people who are much more or much less experienced than they are, no matter how experienced the team. Whether the teams average 10 years of prior experience or 29 years, they tend to include people who are similar in the length of their work experience.

Short-term Benefits of Homogeneity

Homogeneity has important benefits, perhaps the most immediate of which is speed. For the founder scrambling to meet the challenges of a growing startup, choosing cofounders from among people with whom he or she probably has important things in common is often the quickest and easiest solution.[2]

Not only does it generally take less time to find people who are like you in some important way, but it also generally takes less time to develop effective working relationships with people who are like you. When founders share a background, they share a common language that facilitates communication. They have higher confidence that they will be able to develop the deep level of trust necessary to become an effective founding team. To some extent, they already understand each other and can skip over part of the learning curve that would absorb the energies of people with very different backgrounds. It is also easier to access people who are similar to you. Having a team of well-acquainted individuals with similar backgrounds can facilitate the early process of constructing an organizational identity with clear borders between members and non-members,[3] and may enable teams to consider alternative viewpoints without splintering.[4] Increasing homogeneity may therefore be a particularly tempting—and, in some ways, a particularly wise—approach for novice founders heading into unfamiliar territory.

Indeed, studies have found that the greater the heterogeneity among executive team members, the greater the risk of interpersonal and affective conflict[5] and the lower the group-level integration.[6] Heterogeneous cofounders may run into early problems if their differences result in incompatible working and communication styles and if they have trouble appreciating the value that the other person brings to the startup. Michael Reich, for example, cofounded UpDown with Georg Ludviksson, an MBA classmate, and Phuc Truong, a software programmer whom he had recruited through an ad placed on the Harvard Alumni Start-ups mailing list (a classic example of impersonal search). Michael took the lead in business development and financing, Georg focused on product management, and Phuc was the CTO whose job was to build the software to run the site. As Michael worked on the business plan and on securing funding for the startup, he became increasingly unhappy with the relative amount of contribution by his cofounders, and created a revised equity agreement that increased his own equity in the startup. This angered Phuc, who felt that his contribution would eventually be the most important and time-intensive part of the startup phase and was being severely underrated. Phuc also felt that Michael, not being a programmer, could not understand the time and effort it took to create a software program. Michael, on the other hand, felt that other programmers could do what Phuc was doing, whereas his own contributions were irreplaceable. The dichotomy in the two founders' backgrounds created an impasse where neither understood the other's point of view, sparking a crisis within the team.

Longer-term Risks of Homogeneity

As tempting as it is to go with the "comfortable" and "easy" decision to found with similar cofounders, founders may be causing long-term problems by doing so. As we saw in Chapter 3, teams with a broad range of relevant functional skills may be able to build more valuable startups. Conversely, homogeneous teams tend to have overlapping human capital, making it more likely that the team will have redundant strengths and be missing critical skills. Although we saw above that heterogeneous teams were more prone to internal conflict than homogeneous teams, teams with homogeneous functional experience have been found in multiple related contexts to be less stable than their heterogeneous counterparts.[7] To find the broad range of hard skills needed in the startup, founders have to fight their homophilic tendencies by taking a structured approach to defining the startup's needs for human, social, and financial capital, assessing the gaps, and seeking cofounders who can fill them, even if those cofounders are not similar in background. In addition, as explored in the next chapter on roles within the team, cofounders who have similar skills will also gravitate to similar, overlapping roles and thus tend to experience greater conflict than when there is a clear division of labor between them.

   If the homogeneous team is also a relational one, made up of prior close ties, the problems can multiply. One experienced founder commented, "I have seen several startups where star salespeople figure they can use their experience to cofound a successful company. . . . At first, sales take off, and the friendship continues. Down the road, they find out their best friends all share the same business skills and—unfortunately—the same weaknesses. Sales are great, but other areas, such as managing inventory or supply chain or personnel issues, necessarily suffer."

Diversity in the functional backgrounds of team members is especially important in turbulent contexts—exactly what entrepreneurs are likely to face—because it enables teams to quickly adapt to changes.[8] It also affects strategic creativity. A longitudinal study of high-tech firms from Silicon Valley found that cofounders coming from diverse prior companies were more likely to adopt an "exploration" strategy (developing an innovative product that increased variance within the population of organizations and generated intraindustry variety), while founding teams with shared work experience at a prior company were more likely to use an "exploitation" strategy (i.e., a product that decreases variance in outcomes, increases routinization of processes, and increases efficiency of use).[9] One founder said that this was consistent with her experiences: "A founding friend relationship can have too much stability, not enough change to grow the company or to grow with the company. The psychology of a family unit can really create an impasse in the growth of a company. Friendships can also suffer, though to a lesser degree, as people try to balance being nice and being business."

To the extent that they think about diversity, founders tend to focus on diversity in skill sets. However, diversity in networks also deserves attention. Teams with diverse networks are often more creative and innovative, have better access to a range of potential investors and corporate partners, and are able to tap into a wider range of potential employees.[10] Thus, core founders should seek cofounders who have social networks that both differ from their own networks and are not overweighted with one type of social contact. For example, a core founder who has deep contacts with Silicon Valley engineers should seek a cofounder who has few engineering contacts but lots of contacts in other relevant areas, such as business development, sales, and the investment community. Individuals with more variety in their social networks are better suited to entrepreneurship; a study of founders in Germany found that people who had a relatively uniform portfolio of social contacts (dominated by many contacts of one type) were 14% less willing to become entrepreneurs.[11] Founders should consciously counter the powerful draw of homophily by watching for potential teammates who can add not only complementary skills but also complementary networks and strong relationships with a diverse set of contacts.

The contrasts between two founding teams highlight the effects of homophily on team homogeneity. The team that founded Smartix, an online ticketing startup, was a group of business school class-mates with similar backgrounds, networks, skills, and knowledge.[12] Vivek Khuller, who conceived of Smartix, had graduated with distinction in electrical engineering from a university in India and had held engineering and management positions at two large American companies before coming to business school and interning at an investment bank. On the lookout for a cofounder, Vivek was attracted to a classmate who had graduated at the top of his class in electrical engineering at a university in India, had worked as an engineer at a large American company (though outside the United States), and had interned at an investment bank. But, by coming together on the basis of having so much in common, this team failed to fill a very large hole—the need for deep knowledge of the ticketing indus-try. Vivek had a potential cofounder within his grasp—an industry insider with deep knowledge and extensive contacts—but did not appreciate how important such a person's contributions would be and did not try to draw him into the team. Only later did Vivek realize how his own lack of industry knowledge affected pitching the idea to stadiums: "Since I did not have any experience in this industry, I had no idea how these venues were organized." He found he wasn't able to answer basic questions about how the online tick-eting would work operationally.

In contrast, Tim Westergren of Pandora Radio did not limit him-self to people with whom he had a lot in common. Tim understood that, while his business would have to do with music, what it had to *be* was a business; specifically, a business-to-business technology provider to the online music industry. He understood that he lacked the skills such a startup would need and that a merry band of fellow musicians would lack them, too. Therefore, he looked farther afield to find business and technical expertise, tapping weak ties (e.g., friends of friends) to find a serial entrepreneur to be CEO and an experienced technical lead to be CTO. As it happened, Tim's wife had a friend whose husband, Jon Kraft, had recently founded and sold an enterprise database startup and had experience with venture capitalists. After discussing Tim's idea, they decided to form a startup and recruit the engineering expertise they both lacked. Jon had good Silicon Valley contacts and was able to recruit Will Glaser, an outstanding engineer with triple degrees from Cornell whom he had met through a mutual contact. Jon even joked to Tim that, with Will on board, "our company just became worth $10 million." Although forming the Pandora team took longer and required more effort than if Tim had simply formed a team of his musician friends, his team of relative strangers was highly diverse and had the key skills needed to monetize Tim's idea. If the context is not time-sensitive, taking more time at the beginning can sometimes yield longer-term benefits for the team.

Tangible versus Intangible Differences

You can often tell from a resume or by asking a few questions where a person comes from and what he or she has done. But there are types of similarity and difference that are not so easy to pick out. A potential cofounder's resume may not tell you much about his or her risk tolerance, personality, time horizon, commitment level, and value system. Founders tend to neglect these "soft" factors because they are harder to assess than skill compatibility and functional backgrounds, but they can become serious problems for even the most well-matched teams. Assessing soft factors usually requires a lot of time (and skill), often in the form of talking frankly to people with whom your potential cofounder has worked and, even more importantly, "trying before buying"—getting to know each other in actual work settings or preliminary projects before committing to working together.

For example, a founding team is most likely to keep functioning effectively over time if the cofounders are personally compatible and have similar (or at least not conflicting) values and work styles. Founders talk about the parallels between cofounding and getting married; in either case, it is very hard to assess compatibility without having already spent a lot of time together. Likewise, risk tolerance is hard to measure, but incompatibilities in risk tolerance can be stressful or even fatal in anything as inherently risky as founding a startup.

Differences in soft factors can build over time. Steve Wozniak and Steve Jobs, cofounders of Apple Computer, not only were best friends beforehand but also had complementary skills, with one serving as the clear technical leader and the other as the external salesperson. However, their partnership frayed because of differing values (most centrally, ethical steadfastness versus business expediency) and motivations (Wozniak's focus on technical prowess versus Jobs's focus on monetary rewards). Wozniak, for example, had fond memories of working in a mall as an *Alice in Wonderland* character because it was enjoyable, while Jobs thought the job was horrible because it paid so little.[13] Wozniak's code of ethics was, "Extreme honesty, extreme ethics, really. . . . I never lie even to this day," but Jobs was willing to cut ethical corners, sometimes at his cofounder's expense.[14] This stark divergence in values and motivations would eventually erode the trust the two had shared in their friendship and early working relationship.

In short, founders need to be aware of the decisions they are making with respect to very different kinds of similarity. Figure 4.2 highlights that a founding team whose members are similar in various objective ways (their human capital and social capital) can deprive the startup of necessary diversity. However, a founding team whose members are too dissimilar in terms of "soft factors" (commitment, opportunity costs, risk preferences, etc.) can be setting itself up for early and disruptive tensions. Those tensions are most likely to flare up when the team is facing decisions that could make or break the business (e.g., how to split the equity among themselves, which founder should be CEO, whether and how to raise outside capital, whether to hire a new CEO, whether to sell the business, and other issues examined in subsequent chapters). Ultimately, as described above, cofounders

		Benefits of a Homogeneous Team	Risks of a Homogeneous Team
Tangible factors	Human capital	Cofounders with similar human capital often can communicate more quickly and easily about issues.	Overlapping functional backgrounds increase the likelihood that the team will be missing critical skills.
	Social capital	Cofounders with similar contacts may have higher confidence that their mutual obligations are more enforceable.	Overlapping social networks reduce the diversity of information received by the team; limit its contacts with potential customers, hires, and investors; and may decrease innovation.
Intangible factors	Decision-making style (e.g., hierarchical vs. consensus)	Cofounders with similar styles will often make decisions more quickly and easily.	Cofounders with similar styles often do not act as effective counterbalances to each other's natural styles.
	Risk tolerance (e.g., risk-seeking vs. risk-averse)	Cofounders with similar risk tolerances may be more stable partners.	Cofounders with similar risk tolerances will not counterbalance each other's tendencies to shoot from the hip or to be overhesitant.
	Commitment level (commitment of time, capital, etc.)	Cofounders with similar levels of commitment will be more likely to appreciate each other's efforts.	Cofounders who are all moderately committed may not be able to sustain the startup. Cofounders who are all intensely committed might burn out, leaving no one to pick up the slack.
	Value system	Cofounders with similar values will be more aligned regarding their priorities and preferences.	Cofounders who all have similar value systems may not be able to counterbalance each other. For example, founding teams who all believe in taking care of their employees at all costs might not be able to take necessary actions to prune the work force as the startup's needs change.

Figure 4.2. Effects of Homogeneity within the Founding Team

with complementary skills but similar value systems can form a more effective whole. However, homogenization and the need for diversity continually conflict,[15] requiring founders to proactively assess and regularly discuss and manage the resulting tensions.

A Recurring Metaphor

Founders of startups often reach for metaphors from family life. They refer to dating potential cofounders before getting married. Then, of course, comes the honeymoon, during which "founders approach their business much like a fresh romance," as one founder put it. A founder's attachment to his or her startup is often compared to a parent's love for a child; founders themselves continually refer to their startups as "my baby." Cofounder tensions are compared to fights between spouses, founder agreements to prenuptial agreements, and founder breakups to divorce.

We can learn something valuable by looking at founding teams in light of the first marriage described in the Bible. When God considers the ideal relationship between Adam, whom He has just created, and the spouse He is about to create, the phrase in the original Hebrew is *Eizer K'negdo*, "a helper against him."[16] While this seems self-contradictory, it captures a crucial aspect both of marriage and of cofounding a startup: the development of a cohesive working relationship that includes opposition and the tension that arises from partners with different skills, experiences, responsibilities, and motivations. Founding teams should consider whether their early decisions about whom to include in the team, how to structure it, and how to split the rewards will stir up unproductive tensions that cause the team to underperform, fail, or splinter, or whether those early decisions will enable the team to achieve the "helper against him" ideal that will increase their chances of success.

FOUNDING-TEAM OUTCOMES: FRIENDS AND FAMILY ARE LESS STABLE

In building their founding teams, the founders of ordinary small businesses tend to rely more on trust and familiarity than on functional competence and functional diversity.[17] Likewise, in high-potential startups, founding with friends and family ("relational teams") is a very common—though often not very well-thought-out—decision. In my quantitative dataset, I found that 40.0% of the founding teams included at least one set of cofounders who had a prior social relationship without having shared a prior professional relationship (i.e., "founding with friends") and 17.3% of teams included at least one set of cofounders who were related to each other ("founding with family").

Many of the same factors that lead to homogeneous teams also lead to relational teams: ease of access, speed of formation, and high comfort level with people who have shared experiences and communication styles. But in addition, cofounders with whom the founder is already close can provide the emotional support required to deal with the stress of beginning a startup. For instance, serial entrepreneur Dick Costolo says, "There are *always* points in the startup's life when things are going very, very badly, and the stress can be unbearable. Knowing the other people in the boat with you can be very helpful in navigating the rough waters."

Although it is clear from the data that relational founding teams are common, the hazards of close relational teams can outweigh their benefits and imperil the stability of the founding team. Paul McManus, a member of a Boston venture capital firm, reflected on his experiences with founding teams of friends: "In my opinion, those who found companies with friends will (a) lose the company, (b) lose their friends, or (c) lose both. I strongly advise against it and shy away from deals where the teams are too tightly knit on the personal side. Blood [family relationships] is almost always a show-stopper."

Why is founding a startup with close friends or family so risky? For one thing, tapping only the inner circle of potential cofounders may result in a weaker team that builds less value. One founder observed, "In a startup you need highly motivated people who don't need constant direction and who bring much more than the job requirements. In an average group of friends and associates there may be one in ten people who fits this description. So the chance that a candidate from this group will succeed is small." A venture capitalist suggested that this may be even more of an issue with relatives: "I would question whether the two perfect cofounders for a business could really come from the same family."

A study of nearly 400 startups, conducted by my colleague Matt Marx and myself, supports McManus's observation; we found that prior *social* relationships (friends or family) and prior *professional* relationships (prior coworkers) differed demonstrably in their impact on a founding team's stability.[18] Categorizing the founders' prior relationships along the spectrum of strong to weak ties—family, friends, prior coworkers, and strangers/acquaintances—we found that, controlling for a wide range of other characteristics, the type of prior relationship had a significant impact on team turnover. For example, each additional social relationship (i.e., a preexisting relationship not involving shared work experience) within the team increased the hazard rate—that is, the likelihood—of cofounder departure by 28.6%. Teams of prior coworkers were significantly more stable than both teams who had a prior social relationship and teams of strangers. It is particularly striking that turnover was higher for teams of friends, as those teams would be expected to put a high premium on team stability and harmonious relationships. Most surprising, teams with prior social relationships were even less stable than teams of strangers. As we will see below, it seems that a prior social relationship can be an obstacle to building something superficially similar but essentially very different—an effective professional relationship.

This is *not* to say that friends and family members should never found a startup together, but that they should make sure that they proactively analyze the potential consequences of their prior relationship and take the steps described below to reduce the inherent risks. However, the picture that emerges from the data is that founding with coworkers can be beneficial, while founding with friends or family is a high-risk, "high-variance" proposition. (The complexities can multiply when a team includes a mix of these prior relationships.) A family/friends team could turn out to be either the best or the worst of both worlds. At best, the team is in perfect sync, a high-performing whole greater than the sum of its parts. At worst, the cofounders make suboptimal business decisions in order to protect their social relationships, but as the business suffers from those poor decisions, tension rises and the social relationships suffer, too. The best-case scenario is much more likely in teams that understand the "relationship risk" and proactively act to reduce that risk, as described later in this chapter.*

Cofounding with Past Coworkers: Less Endearing but More Enduring

The most appropriate professional structure within a startup is often at odds with the structure of the cofounders' established social relationships. A boss-subordinate relationship, for example, may make perfect organizational sense but will not suit a pair of best friends very well; nor will positions of equal authority suit a father and son. Unlike actual strangers, friends and relatives have to undo a prior relationship (at least while on the job) in order to build something very different and even contrary—a professional relationship. Many either choose not to do so or never even consider doing so. One study of high-technology startups found that the vast majority of firms in which family or friends of the founders were listed as key partners adopted an employee-relations model based on informal communication and the decentralization of authority rather than more structured and explicit approaches.[19] One founder observed,

---

*It should be noted that turnover within a founding team is not always detrimental. If a cofounder did not fit to begin with, or if that founder is not scaling with the startup and is refusing to take a lesser role, then his or her departure may decrease tensions within the team. On the one hand, in a sample of small businesses in the United Kingdom, turnover was higher in founding teams that had some founders with prior founding experience and some without prior founding experience (and lower in teams with more similarity in prior founding experience), possibly because of a dysfunctional power dynamic within the team. On the other hand, studies have also shown that teams that have spent more time together have entrenched "standard operating procedures" that hinder creativity; the "diversity shock" when a homogeneous team member is replaced by someone new can help kick-start the creative process. But whether founder turnover is beneficial or detrimental to the team, it will almost certainly be painful. As one founder observed about his experiences cofounding with friends compared to his experiences cofounding with acquaintances, "The highs are higher, but the lows are much lower." In upcoming chapters, we will see other causes of turnover, some beneficial but many detrimental.

"Reframing a profound friendship as a business relationship is difficult and sometimes painful." Teams of friends may start off strong and enthusiastic, but as the realities of life in the workplace begin to settle in, professional issues can creep into cherished personal relationships. It is instructive that my work with Matt Marx shows that, during the first six months of the startup's life, there is no statistical difference in the stability of teams with and without prior social relationships, but after that honeymoon period, teams with prior social relationships are significantly less stable.

For all of these reasons, the transition from a previous professional relationship to a new professional relationship should be easier and longer lasting than the transition from a purely social relationship to a professional one.[*] Across a variety of entrepreneurial contexts, research has shown that teams with greater shared work experience have higher growth rates, higher levels of social integration within the group, and lower risk of company dissolution.[20] Comparing the founding teams of Apple Computer and Ockham Technologies highlights the very different dynamics among cofounders who had been friends before founding a startup and those who had already been coworkers before founding a startup. Jobs and Wozniak were best friends first before becoming cofounders; their friendship hindered their ability to avoid conflicts in advance or at least to resolve them before they became unresolvable and the friendship itself became damaged beyond repair. For the cofounders of Ockham, the prior relationship had been not only professional but also hierarchical; founder-CEO Jim Triandiflou had been the supervisor of one of his cofounders. Ockham's cofounders were able to tackle tough issues, such as equity splits, that Apple's cofounders had felt the need to evade.[†]

---

[*] At the same time, attorney Bill Schnoor points out that there may be legal obstacles to founding with prior coworkers (or even hiring them as nonfounding employees), especially if a potential cofounder has a noncompete or nonsolicitation agreement with the prior employer or if the employer may have a claim to the intellectual property on which the startup is based. Before deciding to cofound (or hire), each founder should make sure he or she is familiar with the other's agreements and the potential problems they may pose.

[†] Although it is less common, when the prior professional relationship conflicts with the one adopted within the founding team, the transition is usually much rockier than Ockham's. For instance, if the former boss now reports to the former subordinate, the team has to work extra hard to effect a smooth transition.

The picture can be complicated by the fact that cofounders often develop very close relationships as their startup evolves; this happened with the Ockham team. But such "cofounders-then-friends" relationships are usually quite different from relationships where friends later become cofounders, and do not face as much business risk. Venture capitalist Tim Connors observes, "The best situations I've seen are founder teams who have worked together in the past, especially if that work was relevant to the new venture. . . . They're friends, but the friendships developed out of mutual admiration for their commitment, capabilities, and expertise. They can trust each other. Each one knows how the others think and work. So the whole 'cultural fit' question is taken care of right from the start." Business historian Richard Tedlow, paraphrasing John D. Rockefeller, puts it succinctly: "A friendship built on business can be glorious, while a business built on friendship can be murder."

Where do classmates fall? In many ways, they are very similar to friends. The initial basis for their relationship is social, they face strong homophily pressures, and they are more likely to overlap in their skills than to complement each other. They may be impressed by each other's comments during a case discussion but not realize the gap between that and the ability to contribute constructively to building a startup. On the other hand, school can provide low-risk opportunities to work together on projects or on entries in business plan competitions, efforts through which they can gauge compatibility before they have to make long-term commitments to cofounding together. For instance, Janet Kraus and Kathy Sherbrooke, who later cofounded corporate-concierge company Circles, met at Stanford Business School. They spent much of their time at Stanford coleading activities—for example, the student show during their first year of the MBA program and the alumni gift campaign during their second year—and figuring out if they were an effective team. Janet recalled another formative experience:

> The last thing we did upon graduation was to drive cross-country for five days and talk about what it would take for us to start a business together. What would be our hopes and aspirations, what kind of business would we start, what were our financial risk profiles, what

would we be proud of, what things did we like to do, what did we not like to do, what were our greatest strengths and greatest weaknesses, what were our pet peeves, what we wished we could change about ourselves, what we feared, what would make us quit trying, what kind of people would we hire and what would we expect of them, would we consider another founder for skills we did not have (no), what would our values for the company be? We were really trying to make sure that we would be good as partners.

Classmates who neglect such opportunities to work together, but assume that being classmates ensures their compatibility, face the heightened risks that Janet and Kathy were able to mitigate during their time as classmates.

TAKING RELATIONSHIP RISKS VERSUS CREATING FIREWALLS

However risky it is to found a startup with friends or family, the lure is great, and we can assume that the practice will remain very common. If there is no way to reduce the lure, at least it may be possible to reduce the risk by understanding the factors that increase or decrease it.

The Playing-with-Fire Gap: Damage versus Avoidance

Two factors in particular affect the stability of the founding team and depend on whether the cofounders are closely related (family or friends), have prior relationships as coworkers, or are acquaintances. Clarifying these factors will highlight the reasons why founders should try to avoid founding with friends or family, but also help us come up with approaches to reducing the risks of doing so.

Damage If the Social Relationship Blows Up

The closer the prior relationship, the greater the damage if tension from the business spills over into the relationship. There is no shortage of firsthand testimony to the prevalence and seriousness of this risk. As one founder who had been burned by such problems commented, "I don't mix friendship and business anymore. It's turned out very uncomfortable in the past. It's very hard to maintain a friendship after the business relationship turns sour."

Evan Williams recalled the price he paid when disagreements over strategy and control of Blogger, along with its financial difficulties, caused unresolvable tension between himself and his cofounder, Meg Hourihan, who had been his girlfriend when the startup began. Many of his closest friends also worked for the startup.

> When everything fell apart, it was especially hard for me because my social life was wrapped up with my work and so I didn't really have a support network of friends to fall back on or find comfort in, because they were all gone with my work, with my employees. Things even got tense with my roommate, who was now dating Meg. My roommate didn't work for [Blogger], but his brother did, and his brother was actually the first guy to quit. It was just very awkward because I felt like all these people very close to me, in sort of this intertwined circle, were all against me, all of a sudden, as well as their extended community of friends who we would socialize with. Because there were more of them than there were of me, it just seemed like I was rejected from my entire social circle.

Another founder elaborated, "I personally find that it is a double-edged sword. Working with loved ones, family, or friends can allow for better communication, and more trust—they probably want you to do well, as well as wanting the best for their own future. But when there are conflicts, it is hard to leave them in the office. It becomes personal, and the other edge of the sword can cut in." An experienced investor reminds us of the worst-case scenario: "I've heard some successes here, but if you think having a friendship fail out of business failure is bad, imagine the implications if this is family—you only have one of those."

Avoiding the "Elephant in the Room"

At some point, there is bound to be an important problem that at least some of the cofounders will find uncomfortable to talk about—the elephant in the room. Cofounders with prior professional relationships, who are used to working through such tough business issues together, are the most likely to bring up problems like this, followed by cofounders who were strangers and realize that, because they don't know each other, they have to work through such issues. Cofounders with prior social relationships are often the least likely to deal with the elephants in the room.

Unsurprisingly, they tend to avoid difficult discussions and confrontations in order to maintain their relationship. They tend to worry that raising thorny issues between friends (or family) would signal distrust of that friend (or relative). If a business decision makes business sense but might damage the social relationship, founders naturally try to avoid making the business decision in the hope that the problem will pass. For instance, if one cofounder's ability to contribute is not growing as the startup grows, relatives or friends on the founding team may be very reluctant to reassign him or her to a different (often lower-level) role and may just wait, hoping either that the person in question will somehow rise to the occasion or that the occasion itself will somehow pass. Instead, avoidance often exacerbates the problem to the point where the startup suffers and the cofounder who was being sheltered is squeezed out altogether. As one cofounder put it, "I sometimes feel that if I continue to push to make this business work, unless my partner begins to match my energy—and soon—then both the business and friendship will be over. If I walk away, I may lose my once-in-a-lifetime opportunity to kick-start an effort that will really make a difference in transforming this planet . . . as well as losing what has been a valued friendship." After the splintering of another team, a cofounder recalled a key moment when the team could have recovered: "No one wanted to be the fall guy who raises the issue and tries to make the team stronger."

In such cases, concern for the social relationship interferes with making the right business decisions and the startup will either fail to reach its full potential or else fail altogether. Bei Guo, a serial entrepreneur from China, said about cofounders who were friends, "Because they are your most trusted friends, you can be almost 99%

open with them. But somehow there is 1% out there you think you will risk hurting them if you say it. It is exactly this 1% that makes all the difference."

Cofounders who have a prior social relationship also assume that "we know each other well" and thus don't need to discuss the "elephants." But their new professional relationship is quite different from their prior social relationship; in this sense, they need to think of each other as "strangers," which is very hard to do. The dangers may begin even before the founding, for the prospect of cofounding a startup with friends or family may cloud the judgment of a potential cofounder trying to decide whether to go ahead with it. You might join a good friend in a startup that you would never join otherwise, but the reasons why you wouldn't join that startup with a stranger are probably just as valid as in the case of your friend. Mutual affection may blind the team to what is missing from the idea, the business plan, or the team itself. As one founder pointed out, "We trust our friends too much at times; founding with a stranger will force a person to critically assess both the idea behind the startup and what their own personal role will be. The startup will be viewed not so much as an exciting fun project with a bunch of old coworkers and friends, but as a business proposal with significant career risks." The founder went on to explain that judgment may also be clouded in ways that exacerbate the downsides of homophily: "I think you're much better off founding with and hiring strangers; they're easier to part with, easier to be 'all business' with, and, whether you like it or not, will bring a lot more diversity to the company than family and friends."

Steve Wozniak and Steve Jobs again provide a good example. For Wozniak, his friendship with Jobs was a critical element in favor of starting Apple Computer. "I was excited to think about us like that. To be two best friends starting a company. Wow. I knew right then that I'd do it. How could I not?"[21] But later in their working relationship, Wozniak and Jobs failed to discuss crucial issues about roles and rewards that were too uncomfortable for best friends to broach. For example, Jobs felt that his employee number ("number two" versus Wozniak's "number one") indicated that the company did not value his role; he wanted to be assigned "employee number zero." Wozniak, on the other hand, felt that Apple's later treatment of Jobs's Lisa product-development team relegated Wozniak and his Apple II team to second-class status. Neither Jobs nor Wozniak seemed to truly understand each other's contributions to the company. For Jobs, technology was secondary to the monetary value of the product; for Wozniak, the monetary value of a new technology was almost beside the point. These issues festered unresolved during their entire working relationship. In such teams, things are often very calm on the surface, but tensions rise underneath as tough conversations are avoided.[22]

Wozniak also disagreed with Apple's reward system, particularly in the way the company awarded stock options to some employees but not others. But instead of coming to an agreement with Jobs about how to change the system, he created the "Woz Plan," selling his own shares to employees at an extremely low price. His relationship with Jobs prevented him from acknowledging, even to himself, what may have been the largest elephant in the room—his increasing disappointment in Jobs's moral code. Wozniak recalled learning of Jobs's duplicity regarding the financial rewards from a project building a circuit board for an Atari game: "He got paid one amount, he told me he got paid another. He wasn't honest with me, and I was hurt. . . . But you know . . . he was my best friend, and I feel extremely linked to him."[23] As they continued to avoid talking about sensitive issues, the tensions continued to rise between the former best friends, and they eventually parted ways.

The Playing-with-Fire Gap

Figure 4.3 shows how these two factors—"damage if relationship blows up" and "likelihood of discussing 'elephants'"—vary with the type of prior relationship the cofounders have. For each type of relationship, the greater the distance between the two factors, the more the cofounders are "playing with fire." The Playing-with-Fire Gap is greatest for cofounders with a prior social relationship. They are the least likely to deal with the elephants in the room and will suffer the

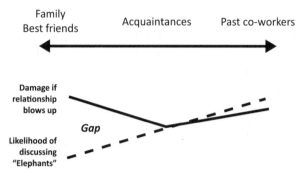

Figure 4.3. The Playing-with-Fire Gap

most damage if business tensions undo their social relationships; yet their failure to deal with the elephants makes such business tensions all the more likely. They are, indeed, playing with fire.

Past coworkers face a moderate level of damage—a higher level of damage than acquaintances—if the relationship blows up, but this is counterbalanced by a high likelihood of discussing the elephants in the room. These cofounders face little or no Playing-with-Fire Gap.* For acquaintances or strangers, there is relatively low damage if the relationship blows up, and also some likelihood of discussing the elephants in the room; because they are unfamiliar with each other, they tend to discuss those tough issues before agreeing to cofound or early in their cofounding relationship.

Reducing the Gap: Forcing Sensitive Discussions and Creating Firewalls

Some founding teams take deliberate steps to reduce the Playing-with-Fire Gap. For instance, Sittercity, a pioneering online service for matching parents with babysitters, was built by a young first-time entrepreneur, Genevieve Thiers, and her boyfriend, Dan Ratner, a serial entrepreneur. Dan explained what happened when he

---

* In fact, as shown in the figure, past coworkers may even have a "negative gap" given their high likelihood of discussing elephants while facing only moderate potential damage if there's a blowup.

became his girlfriend's subordinate within the startup: "The transition was harder for Genevieve than for me. There are three parts to your life: family, friends, and business. Genevieve was risking two of those while I was only risking one." They tried to minimize the risk by actively working on both sides of the Playing-with-Fire Gap. While things were still calm, they agreed on a framework for speaking openly about whatever elephants were in the room (including the fact that they were risking their own romantic relationship by working together). Dan's family had worked together for at least two generations and Dan himself had worked with his sister in a prior startup, so he was used to tackling sensitive issues. Genevieve explained that "running Sittercity has gotten me used to discussing things in a calm and professional manner with Dan," who had become her most important coworker. She described how the duo had proactively crafted a "Geneva Convention" to prevent professional disagreements from becoming personal: "When we have a disagreement, we have to write it up and copy the entire executive team. That forces us to get other people involved and to stay focused on the issues at hand rather than on each other." This helped them tackle issues head-on rather than avoiding issues on which they might disagree.

Addressing the other side of the gap, Genevieve and Dan constructed "firewalls" that would reduce the damage should their relationship dissolve. Initially, Dan said, "When we fought about something at work, it carried over into our personal life, which was draining at times. . . . Sometimes it was hard to figure out what level of familiarity to bring to the office; familiarity that would be fine at a personal level doesn't work at a business level. I'd say something to her that frankly would not be appropriate for me to say to her in her capacity as my boss." To avoid such problems, they erected firewalls that included an explicit "Disaster Plan" calling for Dan to leave the startup were there to be any irreconcilable disagreements. (These disaster plans for the business culminated in a prenuptial agreement, the ultimate in tough discussions, which covered both personal and business issues.) This had the effect of pushing downward the "damage if relationship blows up" line in Figure 4.3 and therefore decreasing the gap (and the risk). In addition, Dan delayed joining the startup full-time until there was a clear need for his expertise. He also understood his role to be secondary to Genevieve's ("This is Genevieve's business, and I'm here to help her") and he worked hard to establish relationships with the startup's initial employees so as to be genuinely part of the company and not just the boss's boyfriend. Over time, Dan's and Genevieve's decisions and actions reduced their Playing-with-Fire Gap dramatically by minimizing the distance between the two lines in Figure 4.3. As Genevieve explained, "Eventually, Dan integrated into the company, after which it didn't seem odd that he was with Sittercity full-time. We needed time to learn to trust one another in our new roles. After a difficult beginning, we were on our way to becoming a 'two-headed monster' where we would finish one another's sentences."

Other teams have found additional ways to reduce the Playing-with-Fire Gap. For instance, a founder who brought in his mother to help create a marketing plan asked her to report to his cofounder in an attempt to "compartmentalize" their two relationships and limit the impact of work tensions on their family relationship. Other teams that include friends or family try to involve an outside, experienced party whom both cofounders respect and who forces discussions about sensitive issues, plays the role of "objective mediator," and can play a tie-breaking role in an impasse. There may well be other important mechanisms for managing the Playing-with-Fire Gap by crafting creative firewalls; researchers would do well to seek them out for study.

CLOSING REMARKS

Founders have to guard against many natural inclinations to follow the "easy" path. One of those is the tendency to build homogeneous founding teams. Doing so makes sense—one expects that people who are like each other will get along easily and be able to understand and trust each other—but there are fatal flaws. Teams in which the cofounders have similar backgrounds tend to lack some necessary skills, to have more conflict over roles (as we will see in Chapter 5), and to have a comparably limited range of useful contacts. Such teams will thus tend to build less valuable startups than do teams whose skills and contacts match the startup's needs rather than the cofounders' comfort zones. Instead of defaulting to the easy option of finding similar cofounders, core founders should consciously analyze and decide which capabilities they need and then actively pursue people with those skills and abilities.

On the other hand—and making life more complicated—core founders who do aim for diversity in human capital and social capital should also aim for *similarity* in "softer" areas such as values, commitment, and risk tolerance. Of course these are harder to evaluate, but they are the areas in which similarity helps reduce founding-team tensions. This isn't just a matter of comfort versus aggravation; it's often a matter of whether the startup survives at all and, if it does, how much value it creates for its founders and investors. The best way to evaluate such compatibility is often to "try before you buy" by finding self-contained work tasks on which to collaborate before committing to be cofounders—a commitment that is very unpleasant to reverse.

A natural place to look for cofounders is among family and friends. Think twice! Founding with family or friends involves the risk of homogeneity *plus* two other much higher risks.

First, it is natural but wrong to assume that trust and relationships developed in the social realm will transfer easily to the professional realm. Social and professional relationships have very different foundations and operate in very different, often conflicting, ways. For instance, social relationships place a premium on fairness and equality while professional relationships place a premium on equity and merit, and, in many situations, equality and equity can conflict. It makes sense for a diverse group of siblings to divide a family inheritance evenly; it does not necessarily make sense for those same siblings to apportion a startup's executive responsibilities, compensation, or equity evenly. The mistaken assumption that friends and relatives will be able to make a smooth transition to a cofounding relationship can be very dangerous if it leads the cofounders to *avoid tackling sensitive issues up front*. My analyses show that friends-and-family teams are not only more unstable than teams of prior coworkers (which we might expect) but even more unstable than teams of strangers. This is because strangers usually realize that they have little or no idea how their potential cofounders operate in a work environment and will therefore engage in tough discussions to hammer out expectations *before* they commit to the startup. Friends and family, who already have so much (social) experience with each other, tend to feel there is no need for such uncomfortable conversations. The irony is that friends and family risk much more—a treasured relationship—than strangers do, yet typically take much less care to mitigate that risk.

Second, it is extremely difficult to keep the new cofounding relationship from affecting the underlying social or family relationship. The extreme ups and downs of startup life can cause *major ripple effects in social relationships*, potentially setting up a vicious cycle that can sink the startup and strain, damage, or even destroy the original social relationship. When the best professional decision—say, demoting or firing an underperforming CFO—conflicts with what is best for the social relationship—say, that CFO is your brother—the hard decision is typically either avoided, thus damaging the startup, or taken, thus damaging the relationship. In many cases, both the startup and the relationship are dearly damaged.

Founders who decide to mix business and social relationships despite these dangers should at least take proactive steps to protect themselves and the startup:

- **Compartmentalize relationships.** If the team's size allows, avoid having cofounders report to their relative or close friend. Instead, have the cofounder report to another senior executive, keeping the private and professional relationships separate.
- **Envision negative scenarios.** Think about the obstacles—such as family issues, medical crises, and legal problems—that could affect a cofounder's ability to work on the startup. Resist the natural inclination of many founders to "stay positive," focusing on only desirable or "expected" scenarios.

- **Create a disaster plan.** Put in writing a plan of action for the worst-case scenarios, such as an irresolvable business conflict or a breakup in the social relationship. Also, make it clear who has the final say in an impasse. Sign an exit contract that will apply if a worst-case scenario develops.
- **Force sensitive discussions.** Make a long-term policy of being open and honest about every personal issue that arises in the process of working together. Increasing the likelihood of discussing sensitive issues—by establishing a mechanism for it—can reduce (though certainly not eliminate) the Playing-with-Fire Gap. Resist the natural inclination to put off or avoid discussions of difficult issues in the hope that they will solve themselves.
- **Involve a referee.** In order to prevent a professional disagreement from getting personal, write up a memo on the issue at hand and copy the entire executive team, as Sittercity's team would do in accordance with its "Geneva Convention." This forces others to get involved and puts the emphasis on the issue itself rather than on the people advancing the issue. Or, use a mutual mentor or impartial advisor to mediate.[*]

The data described in this chapter support venture capitalist Paul McManus's suggestion that "[t]he ideal [lowest-risk] founding team is a team made up of former coworkers. By working together in the past, these teams have developed and worked out critical professional/interpersonal relationships that will be critical to their success and, most importantly, they have proven they can work together and get things done." Even so, *prior coworkers* thinking about becoming cofounders should evaluate any disconnects between their prior professional relationships and their upcoming cofounder relationships. For instance, if one founder used to be the other's boss and now they are going to be equals, those cofounders could have a rocky adjustment period. It is particularly

---

[*] Venture capitalist Jeff Bussgang points out that, to encourage full candor, this impartial mediator should ideally *not* be an investor or board member.

important that they agree on a code of behavior and a conflict-resolution procedure.

Cofounding with *classmates* may seem much like founding with former coworkers, but it can be a lot more complicated. This decision can counterbalance the strengths of cofounding with coworkers with the dangers of cofounding with friends. If the classmates know each other only socially and have not really "worked" together, they may face both sides of the Playing-with-Fire Gap, for they assume they know each other well and thus don't need to surface sensitive issues, and they also risk blowing up their social relationships if things go sour within the startup. Such founders also need to "try before they buy" or else to erect the firewalls described above. In contrast, if the classmates have already collaborated—or create an opportunity to collaborate—on substantive work, such as class projects or leadership in campus organizations, they may bring to the startup the strengths of cofounding with prior coworkers.

CHAPTER FIVE

ROLE DILEMMAS: POSITIONS AND DECISION MAKING

FIGHTS OVER WHO SHOULD BE CEO, GRIDLOCK OVER CRITICAL decisions, and company-endangering tensions: Evan Williams's experiences with two of his startups, Blogger and Odeo, illustrate the various ways roles and decision-making dilemmas affect startups. In Blogger's early days, Evan insisted on being CEO. Cofounder Meg Hourihan eventually agreed and took the vice-president title. But in fact, they made decisions by consensus, took turns freelancing for Hewlett-Packard to fund the startup while developing the product, and sat together on a three-person board with their first investor. It sounds ideal, but the results—ambiguity about who was really in charge and tension over how to divide the tasks that both of them wanted to lead—caused disagreements that culminated in a serious conflict over Blogger's direction. Meg wanted to pursue a pragmatic focus on large enterprises, while Evan fought to retain his democratic vision of Blogger as a gateway to the Internet for anyone who wanted to publish his or her thoughts online. The company's employees, wanting a steady revenue stream, sided with Meg. Meanwhile, Meg argued that Evan's leadership had put Blogger in jeopardy and that she should now take over as CEO. While Meg and Evan argued over direction and who should lead, the company could not secure additional funding and eventually had to lay off all its employees. Unable to convince Evan to let her take over as CEO, Meg also left the startup, leaving Evan alone with his vision.

When Evan finally was able to resuscitate the startup, he realized that he wanted to be "completely free to do what [he] wanted with Blogger." This time, he deliberately avoided adding partners, instead hiring employees on short-term contracts and refusing to grant equity in lieu of salary. After selling the company to Google for $10 million in stock, Evan invested some of that money in Odeo, a podcasting startup he was founding with an acquaintance, Noah Glass. The two of them, anxious to avoid the ambiguity that had characterized the early days of Blogger, worked out clear roles and titles. Noah was to be a full-time CEO, while Evan would act as an advisor. But when Odeo began to take off, Evan committed to full-time involvement, sparking another struggle over who would be CEO.

Evan is hardly the only serial entrepreneur to find himself wrestling, from one startup to the next, with the role arrangements, title assignments, and decision-making approaches within a founding team. Of all the dilemmas we will cover in this book, role dilemmas show the widest variety of approaches, themselves affected by the widest variety of factors. There are so many different ways for cofounders' roles to go right or wrong—and so many different reasons why they do. Evan's own experiences touch opposite ends of a spectrum. At Blogger, he and Meg had different titles but equal decision-making power. As a result, decisions that required someone to have the final say led to a conflict that blew up the founding team. During the early days of Odeo, Noah was clearly the lead decision maker. However, as we will see below, even this arrangement can cause problems as a startup evolves.

In this chapter, we will look in detail at the dilemmas faced by founders when structuring proper roles for themselves. Once again, we will focus on what founders can do (their range of options), what they actually do (how often each option is chosen), and what they should do (the implications of their decisions). Multiple metrics will help us see how the different approaches are used and how frequently. These metrics include the official executive titles adopted within the founding teams at the time of founding and the extent to which the team's decision-making structure is hierarchical or egalitarian. I build on the existing literature on role dilemmas within teams while using my own data and case studies to show how each approach affects the founding teams that adopt it.

EXECUTIVE TITLES: WHO WANTS THEM?

How much do titles matter? Founders often insist, "I don't care about my official title." But at Blogger and Odeo, the jockeying between Evan and his cofounders for the title of CEO—not at all unusual—highlights how seriously many founders do take their executive titles. In fact, they should. Titles are imbued with a symbolic significance and can translate into real authority.[1] (They also speak volumes to outsiders, who often interpret them quite differently than the cofounders themselves do.) Which cofounder receives which title—especially the CEO title—is usually one of the toughest early negotiations between cofounders, and rightly so because it is a very important one.

Some founders shun the CEO title. For instance, a scientific founder may aspire to be chief scientific officer (CSO) or a technically oriented founder to be chief technology officer (CTO) rather than CEO. However, founders commonly complain, "Everyone wants to be CEO." One founder admitted, "I have noticed that we are all trying to jockey for the leader role." After the negotiation, non-CEO founders often complain, "I feel like the lesser of the founders." Frank Addante recalls that when he started Zondigo, "I wanted to start something on my own; this time, be 'The Guy' instead of 'The Guy Behind The Guy.' Prove to myself that I can take on a challenge like that and lead the charge, that I could do it on my own. I thought, 'I'm going to lead the army and go after that market and conquer it.' It was personal motivation more than anything else." Had he not received the CEO title, Frank would have been far less motivated to build Zondigo and may even have even decided not to cofound it at all. As we will see below, "idea people" frequently grab the CEO title.

Because founders usually want senior titles, startups tend to create C-level positions first, whether or not these executives have

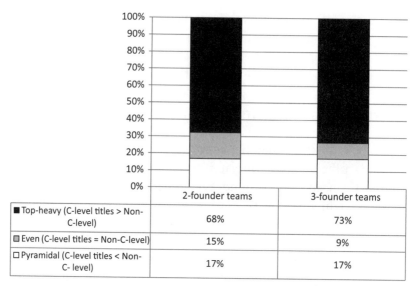

	2-founder teams	3-founder teams
■ Top-heavy (C-level titles > Non-C-level)	68%	73%
▣ Even (C-level titles = Non-C-level)	15%	9%
☐ Pyramidal (C-level titles < Non-C- level)	17%	17%

Figure 5.1. Degree of Top-Heaviness in Two-Founder and Three-Founder Teams, at Time of Founding

anyone reporting to them, any products or services to sell, any customers or clients to serve, or any budgets to spend. In my sample of technology and life sciences startups, 89% of the multifounder teams had at least one founder with a C-level title; 79% had a CEO, 45% had a CTO or CSO, 14% had a chief operating officer (COO), and 8% had a chief financial officer (CFO). Of the teams, 18% also had a non-CEO chairman.

Larger, mature companies almost always have a "pyramidal" structure with a single decision maker at the top, a layer of people reporting to that chief executive, and a larger group at each subsequent level.[2] In contrast, 74% of the startups in my sample had adopted "top-heavy" or "even" structures at the time of founding; 67% had more C-level founders than sub-C-level founders, and 7% had as many C-level as sub-C-level founders. Figure 5.1 shows that this top-heaviness existed in both two-founder and three-founder startups. Even more extreme, in 36% of the startups in my sample, all founders received a C-level title, possibly as a way to resolve the jockeying over who would be CEO. This was particularly pronounced for two-founder teams, 60% of which consisted of two C-level officers.

As we will see in Chapter 8, "Hiring Dilemmas," such early "title inflation" can come back to haunt teams who have to replace or demote those founders or early employees who were given senior titles but are having trouble scaling with the startup's growth and challenges. Startups with a top-heavy structure are most at risk for this particular heartache.

A founding team's top-heaviness is, in itself, an indication of the founders' high level of confidence in themselves and their startup, which can, in turn, render them less likely to consider that such problems will occur and less prepared to deal with them when they do. Thus, such solutions to the immediate problem of "who's going to call the shots" can have severe long-term implications for the company.

EXECUTIVE TITLES: WHO GETS THEM?

How do teams assign their top positions? My quantitative analyses suggest that three major factors are (a) each founder's level of commitment, (b) which founders are the *idea people* who had the original idea or developed the intellectual property on which the startup was founded, and (c) each founder's human, social, and financial capital.

Founders who quit their jobs or academic pursuits to make a full-time commitment to the startup are more likely to receive senior titles. In turn, a founder's title may affect his or her level of commitment; a founder who is unhappy with his or her initial position may be less motivated to fully commit to the startup. At Ockham Technologies, Ken Burows ended up with the COO title, while his cofounder, Jim Triandiflou, took the CEO title, primarily because Jim excelled at sales and Ken was more of a nuts-and-bolts person. While Jim's commitment to the startup grew with each milestone they passed, Ken became less committed (and also began devoting more attention to family life). Ken finally opted out completely when Jim began urging him to quit his job in order to work full-time on the startup.

Regarding the impact of idea people and the founders' human, social, and financial capital, economist Thomas Hellmann and I analyzed my founding-titles data to see which factors predicted which founder would receive each of the three most common founding titles: CEO, CTO, and chairman. In addition to whether each founder was an idea person (of which there could be more than one on a team), we focused on three other characteristics that indicated whether or not the founder was bringing valuable human, social, and financial capital to the startup: whether the founder had founded a prior startup (i.e., was a serial entrepreneur), the founder's years of prior work experience (in any context), and the amount of seed capital that the founder had invested in the startup. We found that all four factors had an impact on founding titles, but in different ways.

Most centrally, our regressions showed that idea people were far more likely than non-idea people to become CEOs. As shown in Figure 5.2, 47% of the idea founders but only 12% of the non-idea founders became CEOs.[3] Many idea people assume that they deserve to be CEO, regardless of whether they are true CEO material. One said, "Of course the startup idea's creator will act as a CEO and have veto on everything and approve the other's visions." Another idea person argued vehemently, "When you take an idea and then spend 18 months with no salary, living and breathing the idea, raising $150,000 from friends and family, putting together an executive team, etc., you have one driven CEO. No one is going to care about the company more than the idea guy, no one will be driven more than the idea guy, and no one will be able to make the tough decisions and shape the direction of the company like the idea guy. When you go through what most idea guy/entrepreneurs go through to make their idea a success, their idea becomes like a child to them and no one will love their child more than a parent."

Idea people often believe that they have the best market knowledge and insight on the team, that they should be shaping the startup's culture, that they will be the best people to shape and realize their vision, and that they can best do so from the CEO position. (In addition, as we will see in Chapter 6, idea people and founder-CEOs often get a larger equity stake than other founders.) Even non-idea

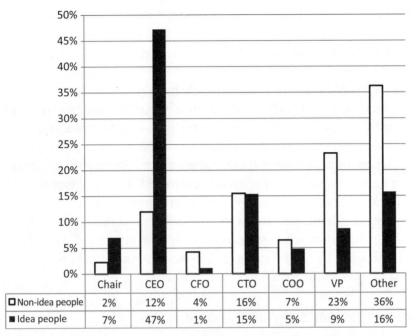

	Chair	CEO	CFO	CTO	COO	VP	Other
☐ Non-idea people	2%	12%	4%	16%	7%	23%	36%
■ Idea people	7%	47%	1%	15%	5%	9%	16%

Figure 5.2. Percentages of "Idea" and "Non-idea" Founders Who Received Formal Titles at Time of Founding

founders can see why idea people would make the best CEOs: "I feel the successful assignment of the CEO, especially in the early stages, also needs to take into account who is the most passionate about the venture. In most cases, that passionate person is the idea person. I have seen quite a few teams willing to sacrifice some of the mainstream skills of a CEO for the passion and drive that an 'idea person' can bring to the table." All the same, as we will examine in depth in Chapter 10, "Founder-CEO Succession," the idea person's fit with the CEO position, as good as it might be in the early stages of the startup, often weakens considerably as the startup matures, introducing its own difficult transition issues. Inertial tendencies and a founder-CEO's natural resistance to giving up the CEO title can make matters even worse.

Being the idea person doesn't only increase the chances of becoming CEO; it also can help buffer a founder from receiving a much lower-level title within the organization. As shown by the two right-most sets of bars in Figure 5.2 (and verified by regression analyses), idea people were significantly less likely to receive a VP-level title or a lower title, with 59% of non-idea people receiving such titles but only 25% of idea people receiving them.

Looking at the other background variables, Hellmann and I found that, even after controlling for who had the idea and other factors, prior founding experience had a significant positive impact on who would be named CEO and who would be named chairman, but had no impact on who would be named CTO. The years of prior work experience had a significant positive impact on who would be named chairman, but not on who would be named CEO or CTO. Finally, founders who invested more seed capital were more likely to be named CEO or chairman; CTOs were more likely to have invested less capital than had other founders.

OVERLAPPING ROLES VERSUS DIVISION OF LABOR

Title assignment is much easier when the founders have very different skills. The Apple team of Jobs and Wozniak is a classic example: Wozniak was the technological guru who invented the early personal computer, while Jobs was the marketing visionary who understood how to monetize Wozniak's invention. Jobs and Wozniak had perfectly complementary skills and ambitions—Jobs wanted to build the company, while Wozniak wanted to build the product—leading to a natural division of labor. In contrast, when founders have very similar backgrounds or are flexible jacks-of-all-trades, they tend to adopt overlapping day-to-day tasks. During the early stages of a startup, when there are too many things to do and not enough people and time to do them, when the startup is cash-poor, and when the strategy and business model may have to turn on a dime, having an organization with flexible and overlapping roles—changeable as needed—can be a big advantage. Figure 5.3 lists some of the strengths and weaknesses of adopting overlapping roles versus a division of labor. But, as we will see below, this advantage can become a liability.

	Strengths	*Weaknesses*
Overlapping roles	• Offers flexibility appropriate to early-stage startups • Team members can pitch in wherever needed • Taps collective knowledge of all team members	• Diffused responsibility may weaken incentives • Overloaded startups should be trying to minimize redundant responsibilities • May increase tension as founders step on each other's toes • As the startup evolves and becomes more differentiated, team members may resist having to focus on specific functions or areas, also increasing tension
Division of labor	• Enables assignment of titles, tasks, and responsibilities • Provides better accountability • In heterogeneous teams, enables the team to fit role assignments to founder strengths	• May be hard to get individual functions to collaborate on cross-cutting tasks • In homogeneous teams, may cause early, suboptimal role assignments • Failure to evolve can lead to disconnects between organizational structure and task demands

Figure 5.3. Strengths and Weaknesses of Overlapping Roles versus Division of Labor

Two contrasting cases offer insights into the benefits and drawbacks of teams of people with general skills and overlapping job tasks, as compared to teams of specialists with a clearly defined division of labor.

The Smartix team adopted an overlapping approach. All three cofounders were highly educated engineers, had work experience in top-flight organizations, and were MBA students at the time. Being so similar in background and skills, they gravitated toward overlapping roles in the startup. (They had brought in a fourth, "silent" partner to develop the software for the product, leaving the three cofounders to work on the business plan and fund-raising.) They worked together without clear separation of tasks or roles, although Vivek Khuller, the founder who had had the original idea and was financing the startup, acted as the de facto leader.

Because Vivek gave himself only a year to test his smart-ticketing concept (due to the family pressures discussed in Chapter 2), the Smartix team did not last long enough for this arrangement to become a problem. However, overlapping teams can run into trouble as the startup evolves and becomes more differentiated. One founder in such a team described the situation: "Two of my college friends [and I] are invested into a business we came up with. As it stands right now, my personal feeling is that it will go sour soon. Dividing workloads is tough, especially when we all have the same talents. The ability to stay open-minded about each other's work and what will be best for the client has been a frustrating one. A lot of butting heads as to 'which one is better' or 'I feel mine is better than yours.' This last one isn't openly said but we all know it is there by our critiques. I feel that this business would be better served if we each had our own strong talents. Because we would all know what needs to be done and we would leave the other jobs for the person to complete." Another founder described how his founding team had evolved overlapping roles: "When all three founders cannot meet with a client, the person who does meet the client takes responsibility for fulfilling the client's needs." For that team, however, flexibility came with a cost: "The other two don't shoulder the responsibility as much."

Closer to the other extreme, the Pandora Radio team adopted a clearly defined division of labor. Jon Kraft had experience developing startups and had connections with Silicon Valley engineers and VCs, Will Glaser had extensive skill and experience as a software engineer, and Tim Westergren had a decade of experience in the music industry and a broad network of musicians and recording engineers. The founders could quickly develop an unambiguous delineation of roles and responsibilities: Jon, the "business guy," would be responsible for managing finances, business development, and administrative details; Tim, the "idea guy," would be in charge of crafting and articulating the vision of the music tool's capabilities; Will, the "engineering guy," would be in charge of building the prototype. Within his domain, each founder had almost absolute power over decision making and complete control over hiring. In this model, the goal is minimal overlap. As one founder described her startup's founding team, "Each person is a dictator in their own task, outlined via 'contract' beforehand. If you're in charge of it, you get final say."

With a clear division of labor comes clear accountability: Everyone (initially the cofounders, later the board of directors) can see who is responsible for each success and each failure, at least for those tasks or milestones that clearly fit into a particular domain. At Pandora Radio, each technical success or missed deadline could be traced to Will and each new partnership agreement or administrative mistake could be traced to Jon. When there is a breakdown within one of his tasks, each "dictator in his own task" finds it harder to blame others.

The experiences of the FeedBurner team highlight both a hybrid possibility and the dynamic characteristics of the division of labor. FeedBurner's founding team was made up of two specialists and two generalists. Dick Costolo was a computer science major who had worked on systems integration and development projects at Andersen Consulting, where he had managed large teams and worked directly with clients, and where he had met his future cofounders. At Andersen, Matt Shobe was working as an interface designer, and Eric Lunt and Steve Olechowski were both recent college graduates working on software architecture. As Dick explained, "We had very complementary competencies. For example, Eric was a solid architect, but didn't like to do user-interface work [which Matt did so well]." When they cofounded a startup, neither Matt nor Eric wanted to pursue the "business stuff" that interested Dick and Steve. Consequently, they adopted a mixed structure, where the two specialist founders (Matt and Eric) focused on specific roles while the other two (Dick and Steve) moved across the remaining tasks. As Dick described it, "Steve and I can hop around a lot and do a lot of different things well—we're what you might call 'best athletes.' Steve and I could switch roles—he could run product management and I could run business development—and we'd be just as good. Eric and Matt are a different story. Eric is a software architect through and through; he couldn't manage a project any more than he could build a spaceship and fly to the moon. He has no interest in dealing with people and managing them. Matt is a user-interface designer, period."

Dick and Steve greatly enhanced the flexibility and responsiveness of their startup by switching roles as needed, but their overlapping skills and ambitions caused problems. Dick explained how the roles within the team evolved over time: "During the proto-stages, some of our roles just fell into a natural form: Eric was the lead software architect and de facto CTO and I played the role of fundraising and running the company. But Steve wanted to have a more senior role, so Steve and I began sharing some of my tasks and we had to figure out who was doing what. . . . It was contentious at times. I would think I should be doing something, and he thought he should. So I just said, 'Any product work related to a partner, you take it, Steve.' It was very organic, a result of contentious discussions rather than our consciously mapping out territory." Finally, Steve's role evolved into business development. As Costolo said, "His role took two years to evolve, but it gave Steve a significant piece of the company to run, and it allowed me to focus on product and operations." Thus, over time, the FeedBurner team developed a more effective and lower-tension division of labor.

This is not to say that tense discussions are to be avoided within founding teams. Discussions that are contentious because of personal friction (also known as "affective conflict") tend to signal a lack of trust and can cause destructive tension and frustration within the team.[4] Conflicts about ideas or about tasks ("cognitive conflict"), however, can often improve the team's decision making, intensify and enhance the relationships, and increase satisfaction. Specifically for the nonroutine tasks on which founders have to collaborate, such as setting strategy and resolving management issues, cognitive conflict is positively related to performance.

However, a startup's evolution can cause problems for even the most elegant early division of labor, if that division of labor fails to evolve. For instance, Pandora's task-oriented model, which seemed unassailable, failed to keep pace with the needs of the growing business. The division of labor became very rigid, which became problematic when the startup needed to adapt its strategy.

Resolving issues and decisions that crossed the domains of two of the founders—such as fund-raising—introduced added tension, slowed down decision making, and distracted them from big-picture issues. In addition, as Tim's leadership skills developed and his ability to fund-raise grew, his role increasingly overlapped with Jon's. Eventually this situation added to pressures on Jon that caused him to leave the startup.

DECISION-MAKING APPROACHES:
EGALITARIAN VERSUS HIERARCHICAL

Founding teams have to balance a wide variety of trade-offs when deciding *how* to make major decisions, balancing dynamism in decision making with clarity of direction and balancing collective decision making with accountability and efficiency. Even if the team is not thinking about such trade-offs, it is still making them and will face the consequences. The decisions teams make are often ad hoc but sometimes derive from the founders' backgrounds or from their official roles within the startup (a common unintended consequence of how titles are assigned to the cofounders in the first place).

To bring some order to this variety, I focus first on two contrasting ideal types, then consider some mixed cases.[5] The first ideal type is the *egalitarian* or *consensus* approach. The members of an egalitarian team ignore their official titles (in rare cases, they don't even give themselves titles), make decisions collectively by coming to a complete consensus, and act as peers rather than superiors and subordinates. The second ideal type is the *hierarchical* or *autocratic* approach. Hierarchical teams have a formal process for making decisions and a clear hierarchy, with a single person responsible for final decisions.[6] These opposing approaches each have important strengths and weaknesses. Each can work well if it is aligned with the founders' abilities and preferences and with the startup's needs. Even so, as the startup's needs evolve, the decision-making approach also needs to evolve, and early decisions—even decisions that were good at the time—often delay or derail subsequent adjustments on which the startup's success depends.

The Benefits of Egalitarianism

Some teams prioritize team cohesion and early trust building and believe that these will be facilitated by a collective decision-making approach. Other teams see collective decision making as the best way to avoid mistakes. In the dynamic, high-velocity environments faced by high-tech entrepreneurs, dominant, autocratic CEOs are likely to be less successful than their less dominant counterparts. In a study of 26 large firms in the innovation-intensive computer industry, CEO dominance was associated with a 19% decrease in firm performance.[7] Similarly, a study of eight firms in the microcomputer industry found that greater centralization of power, in which the CEO makes key strategic decisions, was associated with the formation of competing political factions within the top management team, as well as with poor firm performance.[8]

Perhaps in turbulent environments such as high tech, the complexity of the information cannot be processed effectively by even the most talented autocratic CEO, but instead should be handled by a broader team of decision makers.[9] An experienced VC observed, "While dictators can move resources quickly behind an idea, they can also move resources quickly behind bad ideas and can ignore feedback." Having multiple decision makers can help avoid this problem, acting as a check on the so-called dictator. One founder highlighted the trade-off between decision quality and the speed of decision making by saying, "We had a very good experience as a triumvirate of founders. The mix of points of view probably slowed down our decision-making process but we felt that the decisions that emerged from the collaborative approach were worth the added overhead."

When Are Founders Likely to Choose Egalitarianism?

Egalitarian approaches are particularly likely to emerge in two situations: when the founders have similar backgrounds and when the team does not name an official CEO. It seems fairly natural that founders with similar backgrounds would be more likely to assume overlapping roles and treat each other as equal decision makers, but in startups that choose not to choose a CEO, egalitarianism may be a consequence rather than a cause of that choice. Recall that 21% of the teams in our sample avoided naming a CEO when they first assigned themselves titles. In some cases, this may not reflect a commitment to egalitarianism but rather may have been a way to sidestep divisive negotiation over titles, which might occur when multiple cofounders are very control-motivated.

If so, this may show either weakness or wisdom. On the one hand, not choosing a CEO might indicate that the founding team has trouble resolving tough issues, of which the "CEO" negotiation will be only one of many. Avoiding naming a CEO, as we have seen, also tends to compromise the clarity of the decision-making structure. On the other hand, venture capitalist Tim Connors points out that premature assignment of a CEO—as might have been the case at Odeo with the early crowning of Noah Glass as CEO—can also be problematic. This is particularly true if none of the founders legitimately has the skills to be CEO: "If there isn't an obvious quarterback [who can call plays for the team], it is dangerous to choose one of the founders as the quarterback. If there isn't a capable quarterback on the founding team, it should tell you that there is a hole in the founding team. I had a friend who founded a company with three other engineers and they arbitrarily declared one of the engineers as the quarterback. That founder had no experience managing a team and he started making bad decisions. That team would have been better off making collective decisions until they found the right quarterback, either as another cofounder or as a hired CEO."

Another way of not choosing a CEO is to choose two. An official co-CEO arrangement is rare[*]—only 1% of the startups in my

---

[*] Even iconic founding teams who are commonly believed to have been co-CEOs often adopted hierarchical titles within the early team. For instance, when Hewlett-Packard incorporated, David Packard was president while Bill Hewlett was vice president. During the early days of Google, Larry Page was CEO while Sergey Brin was CTO. Even at ice cream company Ben and Jerry's, where both founders "had their name on the door" and on every pint of ice cream, Jerry Greenfield was president.

dataset had founders sharing the CEO title—and if a team is using such an arrangement to avoid a tough negotiation over titles, it can be a signal of future trouble. Two kings fighting over a throne can leave the kingdom devastated. But if complementary cofounders are indeed operating as joint chief executives, and if they arrived at the arrangement after frank discussions about the potential pitfalls and mechanisms for avoiding those pitfalls, it can be an effective arrangement. For instance, at online entertainment pioneer iWon, founders Bill Daugherty and Jonas Steinman held the "co-CEO" titles from founding to exit, leveraging their divergent perspectives to achieve better decisions than they could have achieved on their own. At the time, Daugherty reflected, "We've had very few issues where we've had differences. Where we did, the one who's been most passionate about his position has carried the day."*

Founders may also leave the CEO position vacant to signal their openness to bringing in an experienced CEO. But for whatever reason the CEO position is left vacant, that choice leaves the decision making ambiguous and often encourages an egalitarian approach within the team. (As described in Chapter 7, teams that split the equity equally may also be more likely to adopt an egalitarian approach.)

The Problems of Egalitarianism

Building consensus takes time and careful deliberation, which may help decision makers take into account the various, far-reaching consequences of important strategic decisions. But founders of high-potential startups often have no time to waste considering all the possible courses of action, as fleeting opportunities for growth must be seized to keep cash-poor startups afloat. Professor Kathleen Eisenhardt found that consensus-based teams make decisions too

---

* Perhaps the most famous co-CEOs in the technology industry today are Michael Lazaridis and James Balsillie at Research in Motion Ltd, which makes the BlackBerry. Commonly believed to have cofounded RIM, Balsillie was actually hired by founder Lazaridis in 1992, eight years after the founding.

slowly for startups operating in "high-velocity" environments, those in which there is such rapid and discontinuous change (in demand, competitors, technology, or regulation) that information is often inaccurate, unavailable, or obsolete.[10] Other researchers reached a similar conclusion: "Consensus is a worthy goal, but as a decision-making standard, it can be an obstacle to action or a recipe for lowest-common-denominator compromise."[11]

At Pandora Radio, although each of the three founders had almost absolute power over decision making within his domain, the team required a unanimous consensus to make decisions affecting the company as a whole. Even a 2–1 split on an issue would result in additional debate to convince the holdout. Tim stated, "If one person disagreed, we had to make sure we weren't missing something, to give that person's opinion a full airing." The founder of another startup warned against this sort of decision making: "I'd rather have a decisive dictator who makes the occasional mistake (and learns from it) than an indecisive committee of founders that can't make a timely decision. Even a lame-duck CEO is better than [egalitarian] management. . . . [Egalitarian] is inherently less decisive because every move must be discussed and analyzed until a consensus is reached. A dictator has the power to make any decision without discussion or consensus building. Startup management *must* be decisive." In a panel discussion among four serial entrepreneurs, the one area of consensus was that "a startup has to be a dictatorship." One participant said, "Either I have to be making the final decisions or I have to be working under my cofounder who is. 'Co-CEOs' just doesn't work."[12]

This seems to be a lesson many entrepreneurs have to learn for themselves.* Although most veteran entrepreneurs warn against egalitarian approaches, most founding teams choose them during the early stages of their startups.[13]

---

* Interestingly, the "lean startup" philosophy for building startups abhors bureaucracy and shuns hierarchy, yet places a premium on being able to "pivot" quickly; an experienced high-tech serial entrepreneur points out that "pivoting is very hard to do without a strong CEO in charge."

Egalitarian	←——————————→	Hierarchical

Advantages:
- Can help build trust among groups of strangers
- For teams of friends, affirms expectations of equal treatment

Disadvantages:
- Consensus-building often takes too much time; this may be particularly problematic for high-velocity entrepreneurial environments.
- Accountability is less clear

Advantages:
- Decision-makers can quickly mobilize resources behind a new initiative.
- Clear accountability

Disadvantage:
- Complex environments cannot be processed by one person; input from multiple people with specialized knowledge usually leads to better decisions.

Figure 5.4. Egalitarian versus Hierarchical Decision Making

Figure 5.4 summarizes the advantages and disadvantages of egalitarian versus hierarchical approaches to decision making.

Rocky Transitions from Egalitarianism to Hierarchy

As we have seen from the experience of these founders, the startup's stage of development has a powerful impact on the effectiveness of egalitarian versus hierarchical models. Even when teams begin with a clear and effective egalitarian structure, they usually have to adopt a more hierarchical structure later on, which is often a painful and difficult process.[14] Failure to do so, however, can be even more painful and costly.

The two founders of Ockham Technologies began with a formal reporting relationship: Mike, the director of product management, reported to Jim, the CEO. In practice, however, they developed a "co-CEO" decision-making structure. Prior to landing their first customer, Mike and Jim met with the software developers, wrote product specifications, came up with a blueprint for how to manage the company, and toured the country together to sell the idea, even sharing a hotel room. Once they signed a million-dollar contract with IBM, however, Mike's job was supposed to narrow to managing the product development, while Jim would run the company, sell the product, and secure funding. Jim felt that the close collaboration he and Mike had at the beginning seriously hindered their ability to make this transition. As Jim explained, "We've gone through our first growth spurt and I think we need to divide and conquer. We need to become a real company. We need to split things up instead of both being involved in everything. That means that Mike can't be involved in all decisions." However, Mike's prior involvement in key decisions hindered his ability and willingness to reduce his involvement in those decisions.

At another startup, it took the company's imminent demise for the team to be willing to name an official CEO and transition to a hierarchy. The team of three cofounders had been making decisions collectively since founding. They had been pushed several times by advisors to improve decision making, efficiency, and accountability by moving to a more formal and hierarchical structure, but had resisted all such changes. Only when the investor-led board threatened not to fund the startup's upcoming round of financing—in essence, to shut it down—did the founding team name a CEO and relegate the other cofounders to secondary roles and then to nonexecutive consulting roles.

Indeed, although only 79% of the teams in my dataset began their startups having named a CEO, 94% had named a CEO by the time they had raised their first rounds of financing, a change that presumably brought more clarity to their decision making. (Such "professionalization" is often one of the major changes driven by outside investors.)[15]

Expanding on these dynamics, the founder of another startup said, "My chief regret is that we didn't adjust our management structure and style quickly enough to adapt to the changing situation. My view now is that, as an early startup where the imperative is avoiding making the big mistake, having a group of [equal] partners with divergent views is a good thing. At that point, you're all very polite and respectful anyway. When the time comes that your business is working and you need to act fast and make decisions quickly to grow and seize opportunities, the best thing is to have a dictatorship. Making the transition at the right time is the elusive challenge here."

Balancing the Best of Egalitarianism and Hierarchy

While it may be the path of wisdom for founding teams to evolve from egalitarianism to hierarchy, there is always the risk of going too far in that direction. We have already mentioned that, in a high-velocity environment, an overly autocratic CEO runs the risk of being unable to process the flood of information well enough on his or her own and the risk that his or her leadership will provoke political factions within the executive team. Kathleen Eisenhardt, also noting that autocratic CEOs may fail to achieve buy-in for key decisions, describes a two-step "consensus-with-qualifications" approach, balancing the efficiency of an autocratic approach with the buy-in of an egalitarian approach. First, the team attempts to reach a full consensus. If consensus is not forthcoming, the CEO and relevant functional VP make their decision, but only after getting input from everybody in a public forum.[16] Describing a different model for balancing the risks and benefits of each approach, venture capitalist Tim Connors says, "It is important for someone to be the 'quarterback,' as you need one person calling plays on the field. A quarterback needs to call a play, you go run the play, then everyone comes back to the huddle and shares info, and another play is called. If the quarterback isn't listening to the inputs and adjusting the play calling, the team loses and a different quarterback is selected."

DUOS VERSUS TRIOS

If a team adopts a model with multiple decision makers of equal power (whatever their titles), how many should there be? There are important differences between groups of two founders and groups of three. In general, larger teams have more cognitive conflict; that is, different people know or believe different things and there are more views the group needs to at least keep track of, if not reconcile. This naturally makes group cohesion and communication harder, which in turn invites more interpersonal misunderstanding and conflict.[17] In addition, a complementary duo in which each cofounder has a clear domain—most commonly, an inside/outside duo or a technology/business duo—may find it easier to agree on goals and to be aligned with each other than if there were three cofounders who had to be aligned.

At the same time, the experience of the cofounders at Lynx opens a window into the evolution of a team that went from an egalitarian trio to a contentious duo when one of their team moved on. Although the team of James Milmo, Javier Pascal, and Doug Curtis had each taken formal titles (Javier as CTO, James as president/chairman, and Doug as CEO), they initially formed what James called "a triumvirate making decisions. We were a threesome: We could see when two of us agreed and the other would relinquish the point, which helped mitigate many problems."

When Doug left the team, they hired Clark Evans as an interim CEO. In addition to adding executive experience to the team, Clark served as the tiebreaker and buffer between James and Javier. As James recounted, "Javier and I would have intense debates with each other all the time, and the only thing that kept us from going crazy was having Clark around to break it up." After Clark phased out of his position, James and Javier could not find a suitable replacement and were left as dual (and dueling) decision makers, a configuration that was fraught with conflict, tension, and frustration. When they were in the midst of that stage, James explained, "[N]ow, we're extremely tired of living by consensus. Without Clark around to mediate, we work through differences endlessly and seek a consensus on everything, no matter how long we have to debate an issue. Forcing consensus is exhausting! Not only do we have to manage the business, but we also have to manage each other. Clark had been the third leg of the stool, but without that third leg now, it has become really uncomfortable. We have no structural way of resolving our problems and our decision making is breaking down."

James and Javier fought over nearly everything: how to manage the company, whether to grow aggressively or conservatively, and whether they should allocate money toward market testing. The constant discord finally forced James to give Javier control over the day-to-day management. As James recalled, "Eventually, we had to divide the responsibilities super-clearly just so we could function. We decided that it was better to make wrong decisions fast than no decision, especially when coming to a consensus was getting harder and harder. I finally relinquished control and said to Javier, 'You go where you want, and I'll stop reaching over and taking the wheel or pushing the gas pedal when you want the brake. I'll sit on my hands when we disagree.'. . . Frankly, it was a relief."

Echoing this metaphor—and highlighting the trouble that duos have resolving a split (1–1) vote—one founder said, "One thing I am clear about now: Two people at the wheel is the worst way to drive. You end up going straight when either a right or a left would be better." Another founder said that tensions between him and his cofounder harmed both the startup's exit value and their personal relationship. "We finally managed to get an exit for the company, but it cost us a lot in our personal relationship and, worse, the outcome of the company to which we devoted years of our lives. Arguably the exit was substantially less than it might have been had we been of one mind or had we 'fallen into line' with one of us being dictator sooner."

ONE FOUNDER ON THE BOARD VERSUS MULTIPLE FOUNDERS

In addition to serving as members of the executive team, many founders also serve as members of the startup's board of directors. It is tempting for a founder-CEO to fight to have a cofounder, presumably more supportive than outside directors, on the board. Indeed, across all of the startups in my 2006–2009 dataset, 67% had at least one founder on the board of directors. Among those startups that had not yet raised a round of outside financing—that is, startups in which the decision of whom to put on the board still belonged to the founders—34% of the boards included two or more founders and 40% included one founder. But among startups that had raised their third round of financing (the "C-round"), things had changed: Only 18% of the boards included more than one founder (42% included a single founder). But on what grounds were the decisions made and with what consequences?

Most startups begin with an informal "founders' board" that includes all of the founders and takes part in major decisions. However, once the founders begin to involve outside parties, such as investors, an official board is formed and board seats become more of a zero-sum game, wherein one founder's remaining on the board means that another has to leave it. (See Chapter 9, "Investor Dilemmas," for more details on the formalization of the board and other effects of investor involvement.) During each round of professional financing, a fixed number of seats are allocated to founders, non-founding executives, investors, and other outsiders. The number of founder board seats is often smaller than the number of founders and shrinks with each progressive round, forcing the founders to negotiate among themselves who will serve on the board and very likely creating or increasing tensions between them. Sometimes—for example, when one founder is the CEO—it is clear which founder should remain on the board. But if, for example, multiple (but not all) founders can serve on the board, or if a nonfounder is CEO and the founders hold other C-level positions, the negotiations about board membership can be contentious. For a founder, becoming a director has strong attractions but also high costs. Many founders seek the additional decision-making control that comes from serving on the board and feel a deeper affinity to the startup if they can remain a director. But serving on the board requires a founder to put in more hours and to play a more complex fiduciary role than nondirector founders do.

After FeedBurner's first round of financing, there were two board seats available for the four founders. The team agreed that Dick Costolo, the founder-CEO, should receive one of those seats, but had trouble assigning the other. In the end, the team decided that Steve should sit on the board along with Dick, mainly because of Steve's involvement in business development and legal issues. At Lynx Solutions, all three founders managed to stay on the board through the first two rounds of financing. But during the third round, the VCs, wanting to avoid a board that was too big to be effective, negotiated with the founding team to reduce the number of founder-directors to two, forcing the founders into a difficult negotiation. As founder James Milmo explained, "We were very concerned about maintaining the balance of power within the group, not destabilizing things." Rather than leave one founder off the board entirely, all three founders continued to attend the board meetings. Although they had only two voting seats, they tried to circumvent this constraint by making joint decisions and voting as a block. Although this reduced the initial tension over who would be represented on the board, it did introduce another recurring source of tension whenever the team disagreed about how to vote on the board.

Even when there seems to be clarity within the executive hierarchy, this clarity can be compromised when non-CEO founders serve on the board of directors. If one founder is CEO but other founders are on the board, it is less clear that the CEO has the final say within the executive team. Similarly, if the CEO has a subordinate who is also on the board to which the CEO reports, their power relationship can be unclear. Having a non-CEO founder on the board can even interfere with the board's effectiveness. For instance, if a founder-CEO who is facing challenging cofounder issues wants to get the board's advice, a sensitive situation can become even more complicated if the cofounder also serves on the board. And when a board wants to give negative feedback to the founder-CEO, can it do so effectively—and without causing problems within the executive team—if the CEO's cofounder-subordinate is present?

In the case of Ockham Technologies, even though Mike reported to Jim, both founders served on the board, which led Mike to assume that he was an equal when it came to high-level decision making. As Jim later recounted, "In hindsight, I would never again put another executive from the company, other than the CEO, on the board, because you're inevitably going to get into very sensitive discussions about how you are going to grow and how you are going to split responsibilities. I would have liked to have had those conversations without Mike being a part of that [decision-making process]"—even at the expense of losing his most natural ally on the board, his cofounder, and at the risk of imperiling their mutual trust. Other founder-CEOs have struck a different balance by having a cofounder serve on the board in a limited role. For instance, the board may conduct separate sessions that are not attended by non-CEO executives of the company. Alternatively, non-CEO cofounders may be given one-year terms on the board or may serve as "observers" who can attend meetings but do not vote.

ROLES AND WEALTH-VERSUS-CONTROL MOTIVATIONS

We have seen that founders can base their decisions about title assignment, division of labor, and decision-making approach on such relatively objective criteria as who has what skills, contacts, or passion, who are the idea people, and how all these forms of human capital overlap. However, a major factor in role assignment—harder to assess, but often more powerful than the more objective criteria—is each founder's motivation for launching the startup. Core founders should examine the motivations of their potential cofounders to see if they are compatible with their own motivations. Looking at two broad sets of motivations—control and wealth—we can see configurations that are compatible and others that are likely to be disruptive.

In a two-founder team, for example, both founders can be control motivated, both can be wealth motivated, or there can be one of each. Conceptually, a team of two control-motivated founders should be less stable than the others; both will want to be CEO, both will want to serve on the board, and both will want final say over important decisions. Much of what undid Blogger in its first incarnation was the fact that both cofounders, Evan Williams and Meg Hourihan, wanted control but each wanted to go in a very different direction. Even an early hierarchical arrangement can be unstable if the cofounders share a control motivation. In the early days of Odeo, Evan agreed to give the CEO title to cofounder Noah Glass, but later asserted his control and replaced Noah as CEO in order to be able to pilot the startup the way he wanted.

When both founders are wealth-motivated, they are more likely to be aligned. Their decisions regarding roles and decision making should favor whichever arrangements will build the greatest value for the startup, regardless of the control implications. At FeedBurner, the cofounders shared the goal of a lucrative sale, which helped align their interests at each stage of the startup's growth and increased the chances of their getting to the Rich outcome they desired.

A wealth-motivated founder and a control-motivated founder can be very well aligned as long as the wealth-motivated founder has confidence that the control-motivated founder can build the startup's value.

Potential cofounders need to assess this type of compatibility *before* deciding whether or not to begin a startup together. Motivational compatibility does not guarantee success, but incompatibility is asking for trouble. Founders who launch their startup and only later realize that their motivations are misaligned will encounter higher tensions within the team at almost every stage of decision making. These tensions will be particularly severe regarding the role dilemmas described in this chapter, for control of the startup is intimately tied to how titles are assigned and how decisions are made within the founding team. However, control is also strongly affected by how much equity is owned by each founder, an issue examined in our next chapter. As we will see, high-tension negotiations over the splitting of roles are often matched by high-tension negotiations over the splitting of financial rewards.

CLOSING REMARKS

In assigning roles to cofounders, just as in choosing those cofounders in the first place, there is a set of natural inclinations— "easy paths"—that founders need to guard against:

Avoiding Conflict

When more than one founder wants to be CEO, teams often try to avoid a confrontation by crowning multiple decision makers. This is a recipe for delay, lack of accountability, and ineffective decision making, especially as the startup grows. While ducking the original conflict may seem to have saved the startup from an early implosion, it actually causes longer-term conflict, endangering the startup's future.

Underestimating "Title Inertia"

It is surprisingly easy to dismiss as inconsequential the decision about who will be CEO or to acquiesce without a fuss when someone (the idea person, or even the founder with the loudest voice) crowns himself or herself CEO. In the early stages, everyone is working so hard to make the startup succeed that it hardly seems to matter who has which title. However, the CEO has considerable symbolic and substantive power and, presumably, the startup won't always be so small and cozily egalitarian. The founding team as a group should determine who would be the best initial CEO and understand that inertial tendencies will make their decision hard to reverse without major disruption if that person cannot keep up with the changing demands of the position or if another founder later proves to be the better choice. Most CEOs are reluctant to relinquish their status and power.

These challenges are particularly acute when, as is often the case, the idea person wants to be CEO. Although idea people often seem a natural choice because they possess the passion and vision necessary for an early-stage CEO, founding teams should carefully assess whether the idea person is the best candidate to be CEO on all counts—not just passion and vision—or whether he or she might better fit another role requiring those two traits, such as chairman, chief technology officer, or chief scientific officer.

Inflating Titles

The dangers of inertia likewise apply to non-CEO founders who take C-level titles. Once the startup has grown much bigger, many of those founders will not be the best people to fill those senior positions. Yet, demoting or replacing "overtitled" founders can be quite disruptive. Given these long-term dangers, teams should be more hesitant to assign C-level titles to themselves without consciously weighing the pros and cons.

Wanting Allies on the Board

When boards of directors are being formed or modified, it is tempting for founder-CEOs to want to have allies on the board. Their cofounders are often the first choice. But having more than one founder on the board can have long-term costs that outweigh the immediate benefits. For example, having a non-CEO founder on the board tends to cause role confusion within the executive team, to hinder some board discussions, and to cause even more challenges for the founder-CEO.

Ignoring Incompatible Motivations

Founder motivations can have a powerful effect on role tensions within the team. If two founders are strongly control-motivated, for example, both are likely to want to be CEO, as was the case with Evan and Meg at Blogger. Solving this by appointing co-CEOs or creating an ambiguous power structure sets up the problems described above in "Avoiding Conflict." In contrast, teams should be more stable either when both founders are wealth-motivated (and thus more aligned in their decision making) or when a wealth-motivated founder has joined forces with a control-motivated founder whose skills and capabilities are up to the challenge of being CEO. Before founding together, potential cofounders should assess each other's motivations to understand the potential sources of role conflict.

In Chapter 7, we examine other founding-team problems that are caused by the combination of these natural but often misguided inclinations in making decisions about relationships, roles, and rewards.

CHAPTER SIX

REWARD DILEMMAS: EQUITY SPLITS AND CASH COMPENSATION

SPLITTING THE OWNERSHIP OF A STARTUP IS OFTEN EVEN MORE contentious—and may have even more dramatic implications— than splitting the roles and titles. For many founders, the main financial motivation is the large potential equity upside rather than the paycheck, which is often smaller in their cash-poor startups than what they could earn elsewhere.[1] Unfortunately, many of our natural inclinations about equity splits are wrong or counterproductive, destined to cause problems in the long run even when they seem eminently fair, wise, and peaceful in the short run. Therefore, the bulk of this chapter focuses on equity splits, examining the various types of splits, the criteria used when splitting, and the central issue of static versus dynamic splits. At the end of the chapter, we will also delve into founders' cash compensation, looking at the team-level issue of salary equality and the insights we gain into founders' attachment to their startups by examining the "founder discount."

"WAR" OVER EQUITY SPLITS

In late 1999, as he was getting Blogger off the ground, Evan Williams negotiated a 60/40 equity split with his partner Meg Hourihan. He recalled, "Her expectation was that the equity would be 50/50, but I proposed an equity split of 60/40 in my favor; that was the key thing to making it work. I had brought the idea and had the more relevant experience and felt that that justified my having a bigger percentage. I wanted to get that up-front. I wasn't confident enough to make an argument for 70/30, but really wanted 60/40." Meg and Evan settled on 60/40 with a handshake agreement; it wasn't until the spring of 2000, when raising a small angel-investor round, that they made the agreement formal and added four-year retroactive vesting terms.* Evan said, "The fund-raising also made everything more official . . . the founders' stock agreements became official for the first time; it was the first time we paid for lawyers." In the meantime, Evan cared relatively little about receiving a paycheck: "I had about $10,000 in the bank when we started. I put some of it in the company. I wasn't taking a salary." Eventually, Evan would invest all of his own money, max out his credit cards, and work for months without pay in order to keep Blogger alive.

In his next startup, Odeo, Evan agreed to give Noah Glass 70% because Noah had been more responsible for the idea and would be serving as full-time CEO while Evan would be working only part-time. Evan recalled, "I sort of thought of myself as a 'half' co-founder." Having had more experience with startups at this point, Evan involved "good lawyers" and formalized the equity split earlier than he had at Blogger.

From afar, splitting equity can seem like it should be a very rational process in which each founder's value to the startup is matched to his or her equity stake. Evan's approaches to the equity splits for Blogger and Odeo seem logical and straightforward, yet both splits burdened the startups with agreements that couldn't stand the test of time. Both Meg and Noah left within two years of those splits. The break with Meg was particularly painful and hard to resolve. She left Blogger at the end of 2000, after about half of her shares

---

* As described in detail below, "vesting" refers to the requirement that a person earn his or her equity stake over time or by achieving certain milestones. It can, and usually should, play a central role in equity incentives.

should have vested, and three months later Evan moved to reclaim her unvested shares. After six months of legal wrangling, Evan finally settled with Meg. "I just decided I needed to be practical and get it over with because it was killing us," he recalled. It was "a huge distraction at the worst possible time." He marveled, "I spent more on lawyers in 2001 than I paid myself!"

The problems are visible not only in hindsight. The equity-split negotiation can be among the most emotional and visceral events in the development of a founding team, with feelings overwhelming rational considerations. Founders often describe their equity-split negotiations as a "war," "exasperating," or "stressful," even when they don't end up experiencing Evan's legal fisticuffs. The founders' abilities to fight such battles constructively often foreshadow how well they will be able to handle other upcoming sensitive issues.

WHEN TO SPLIT

Founders can choose to split the equity either at the time of founding or later.* In my dataset, 73% of teams split the equity within a month of founding, a striking number given the big uncertainties early in the life of any startup. The founders of UpDown, for example, split early in the life of the startup, before they knew each other well and could judge each other's abilities and commitment. In fact, their initial split severely underestimated one founder's contributions and overestimated another's. Such mistakes can be very painful to correct. Researchers have shown that initial psychological "anchors" have a powerful effect on subsequent negotiations and final outcomes, making it hard for even experts to overcome the inertial effects of anchors.[2] The anchoring effect (and legally binding nature) of UpDown's early one-page equity-split agreement caused major tension within the team when one of the founders wanted to renegotiate the split a few months later.

---

*Founders usually cannot split any later than the closing of the initial round of outside financing.

In contrast, putting off the split for several months or more can give the cofounders a chance to learn whose skills and connections will contribute the most to the startup, how those contributions change as the startup's strategy and business model change, how well each founder gets along with the others, how committed each founder is to the startup, and more. Founder-CEO Vivek Khuller, for example, pushed his Smartix team to wait as long as possible—until they were forced to split while raising their first round of financing. "You shouldn't exercise an option until you need to," he explained. "There's always more you can learn about the venture and your team and that might change how much equity each person should get." Holding off on the split may also provide a strong incentive for the founders of a young startup to contribute and to prove themselves, rather than free riding* once the split has been determined.[3]

In founding a startup, almost every benefit comes with a risk. Holding off on the equity split in order to be more informed and to keep the cofounders motivated can also cost the team an opportunity to attract another cofounder. The Smartix team, for example, was seriously disadvantaged by the cofounders' ignorance about how sports venues worked and a lack of industry contacts. Early in the evolution of the team, though, they had within their grasp a potential cofounder, David, who had deep industry experience and whose contacts had yielded some important early meetings for them. But David ended up pursuing a more attractive job opportunity. Vivek later concluded that by deferring the equity-split negotiation, he lost the chance to offer David a large stake to join the team.†

Furthermore, equity-split negotiations are usually much calmer when done before the stakes become very high, which generally

---

* A *free rider* is a person who benefits from a collective effort while contributing little or nothing to it. In this context, it refers to a founder who owns equity but contributes less than his or her share of the value creation, at least in part because this lack of contribution will not jeopardize his or her equity stake.

† By not offering any equity to David and to other people who contributed to developing the business plan but were no longer involved in the company, the Smartix team also took a risk that those early "forgotten founders" would later assert ownership rights. For more on the potentially severe problems that can be caused by forgotten founders, see Bagley et al. (2003).

Split earlier  **Split later**

Split earlier	Split later
• Attract key players who need equity incentive • If already worked extensively with cofounders in another startup • Negotiate calmly before you're under pressure to split	• Learn about cofounders' contributions • Solidify startup's strategy and business model • Solidify roles • Learn about cofounders' commitment; strengthen incentives • Avoid continual renegotiations as things change

Figure 6.1. Reasons to Split Earlier versus Later

means before any financing has been secured and an objective valuation has thus been placed on the startup. Negotiating when millions of dollars of financing are on the line leads to very different dynamics and can make it very hard for the cofounders to agree.*

Figure 6.1 summarizes the factors weighing in favor of splitting early versus late.

The cofounders themselves may differ about when to split. Founders whose major contributions come early in the life of the startup, such as the founder who had the idea or the founder who contributed the most seed capital, may want to split earlier than those whose major contributions are yet to come, such as the technical lead who will develop the product once the other founders have developed the product specifications. Ideally, the equity split will approximate each founder's long-term level of contribution, but judgments about those levels of contribution will naturally be affected by the founders' early experience with each other. During the ups and downs of the startup's evolution, it is inevitable that the importance of each founder's contributions will wax and wane, and so may their idea of the best time for the equity split. (When founders disagree about whether to split early or late, they might be able to resolve the disagreement by using the dynamic approach discussed later in this chapter.)

---

* There are also tax consequences to waiting to split the equity, including having a higher "basis" for the stock and a later start for the long-term capital gains tax clock. For more details, see Wasserman et al. (2009).

Sometimes a founder can use these fluctuations in the team members' relative importance to improve his or her negotiating position. For example, when Frank Addante and John Bohan started L90— a merger between Frank's company, ReaXions, and John's much more valuable company, Adnet—John offered to give Frank half a million shares, out of 15.5 million shares outstanding, reflecting the fact that Frank was also far less experienced than John was. But Frank was hesitant to make a firm decision about ownership at that early point: "What I said was, 'Why don't we see how this thing goes, and we can have the discussion six months from now.' So we didn't decide what the equity breakout would be up-front. I decided to wait until later to see what kind of value I [would] add and what kind of value [John and the other employees would] add." Six months later, an angel investor offered to invest $2 million for 20% of the company, for the first time placing a value on the startup ($10 million), and Frank took that opportunity to carve out his share. He asked for and received 1 million shares out of a total of 20 million shares outstanding. In this case, waiting earned Frank paper gains of about $250,000.[*] Likewise, a junior cofounder who is confident in his or her own skills may benefit disproportionately from delaying the split.

CRITERIA FOR EQUITY SPLITS

If cofounders have decided to negotiate the split, what are the criteria they should (and often do) consider? On the one hand, there are no "right" answers and no objective criteria that can be used; the outcome is fully subject to negotiation between the founders. On the other hand, from my quantitative analyses and in-depth examination of actual equity splits, at least four sets of criteria emerge that can help sharpen the negotiation and increase the chances of crafting a sustainable agreement. Those criteria are past contributions

---

[*] Frank ended up with 500,000 more shares than he would have had he accepted John's initial offer; each share was worth $0.50 ($10 million valuation/20 million outstanding shares).

to the startup, opportunity cost, future contributions to the startup, and founder motivations.

Past Contributions

First, each founder's equity stake is often based, at least in part, on how much—relative to the other founders—he or she has contributed to building the value of the startup so far. (Outside of questions of fairness, the team's ongoing relationship often benefits from rewarding such "bygones.") The extent of a founder's contribution can depend on when the team decides to do the splitting—at the time of founding or several months later—but even very early on, many founders have contributed at least an idea or intellectual property on which the startup is based and/or seed money to fund the startup.

The Idea Premium

All other things being equal, do idea people deserve an *idea premium*—a greater equity stake than other founders? Many academics and non-idea founders argue that "ideas are cheap; execution is dear." However, we saw that Evan Williams certainly placed a value on either having the idea, as he did for Blogger, or helping to shape it, as he did for Odeo. In my field research on founders, I have come across many who share Evan's attitude toward the importance—even the sanctity—of the idea. Frank Addante demanded more equity in Zondigo, his fourth startup and his first as founder-CEO, in part because he had provided the idea. Frank explained how his three-founder team had agreed to give him most of the equity: "I had realized in past ventures that the value I was contributing wasn't matching my equity amount. I had gotten advice from other folks that there should be a premium for the idea. . . . My cofounders agreed. Based on my research and advice from others, I offered them 5% each. . . . They were fine with that." Phuc Truong described how the team for his first startup, Crimson Solutions, thought about equity: "We had a short discussion about splitting the equity and we decided to split it 50–25–25. Seth and I both thought that Wellie deserved more because he had the idea and had organized everything. . . . Without him there would be nothing. So it felt right that he'd get much more than us." In UpDown, Phuc's next startup, the team negotiated an early agreement in which they awarded Michael, the idea person, a 5% premium.

Other founders, like James Milmo, believe that their ideas should be rewarded not with more equity, but with more *immediate* equity. James explained that he agreed to split the equity in Lynx equally with his cofounder, but, "I told him, 'I want you to [have to] vest, but I don't want to [have to] vest. It was my idea and I invited you to join the company. I already earned my stake—my invention and patent are worth a lot—but you have to earn yours by working for two years.'"

Not all ideas are equally mature or valuable. Some ideas identify a market need but are far from proposing a solid solution; cofounders are needed to refine and develop it. Other ideas are backed by patents, years of research, and a solid business model. One can also draw a distinction between an idea and an idea for making money from that idea. For example, Steve Wozniak's father felt that Steve Jobs shouldn't receive equity because "he hadn't done anything,"[4] whereas Wozniak had actually invented the personal computer on which the startup was built. On the other hand, Jobs sometimes indicated that he believed he deserved more equity than Wozniak since without Jobs's insistence on starting the company, Wozniak would probably still be an engineer toiling at Hewlett-Packard.

Across this spectrum of "ideas," is there an idea premium, and, if so, how large is it? Is Crimson Solutions's 25% typical, or is UpDown's 5% more the norm? To examine this quantitatively, I included a survey question that would identify which cofounders were the idea people,[5] along with other detailed questions about the founding team's characteristics, and created regression models to analyze whether idea people received an idea premium.[6] My analyses showed that there is indeed a statistically significant idea premium: All other things being equal, idea people receive 10 to 15 more percentage points of equity than do non-idea people.[7] In addition to rewarding this past contribution, the idea premium may also be a recognition that the idea person might be more likely to contribute important additional ideas in the future and to make other contributions that are linked to having been the idea person.

For teams where it is clear which founder had the idea and that the idea is valuable, the team may be risking resentment if it does not award at least a small idea premium to its idea person. Even if the idea person is initially willing to forgo the premium in order to avoid putting sand under the saddles of the non-idea cofounders, it may be at the cost of putting sand under the idea person's saddle— i.e., introducing friction that grows over time. This sand will continue to chafe as the idea person's resentment grows over not being rewarded for having had the idea, thus creating another source of tension within the team.

Capital Contribution

Figure 6.2 shows the distribution of capital contributed by each founder in my dataset. Of the founders, 41% did not contribute any capital. Of the other 59%, the majority contributed between $1 and $25,000, but 11% contributed more than $100,000. At the team level, in 42% of ventures, all founders on the team contributed some amount of capital.

In 38% of teams, the amounts of founder capital differed within the team. My regression analyses showed that the more capital a founder had contributed, the larger that founder's equity stake.[8] Ockham's founding team actually used the differing amounts of seed capital as the sole determinant of equity stakes. Founder-CEO Jim Triandiflou recalled that, at first, the idea was that each founder would contribute one-third of $150,000, but neither of his cofounders wanted to give that much, so "I said . . . put in whatever you want, I'll make up the difference. . . . In the end, I had about 50%, Mike had about 30%, and Ken had about 20%. That's how [the equity split] ended up—simply because of the dollars."

At one level, founder capital is a very tangible contribution to the startup, allowing the team to rent an office, pay the phone bill,

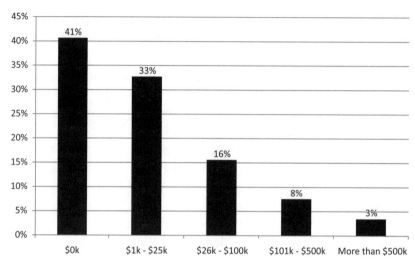

Figure 6.2. Founders' Capital Contributions

and make presentations around the country. Yet, differences in the financial capital contributed by each founder may simply reflect the differing ability of each founder to contribute money. However, at a deeper level, a founder's capital contribution may also indicate his or her commitment to and confidence in the startup. It may thus foreshadow which founders will make the biggest contributions to the startup, all other things being equal. In Ockham's case, although Ken had generated the idea and had worked with Jim even before they added Mike as a cofounder, when it came time to actually commit money to the startup, Ken was the least enthusiastic and contributed the least capital. This decision anticipated his ultimate departure from the startup; when Jim and Mike quit their jobs to commit full-time to Ockham, Ken admitted he enjoyed his consulting job and, with the birth of his first child, was unwilling to make the leap.

Opportunity Cost

Some founders are involuntarily unemployed when they begin discussions about joining a founding team. Others, such as Ken Burows at Ockham, are fully employed in high-level positions which they enjoy and which give them a financial security they find hard to forgo. For the first group, the opportunity cost of joining the startup is low, but for the others, the opportunity cost is high and the rest of the team may have to make the startup opportunity more attractive to entice the potential cofounder. Sometimes, the attraction is the chance to be a founder, to get a more senior title, or to play a more central role. Other times, it may be the chance to earn a large equity stake.

In forming the Smartix team, Vivek Khuller identified Saurabh Mittal, one of his classmates, as someone who could contribute greatly to the startup. Vivek explained, "During our discussions, I learned that Saurabh was already working on two other high-potential startup ideas. But he expressed interest in the Smartix concept so I decided to get him involved." Vivek and his team conducted a lengthy equity-split negotiation that culminated in Saurabh receiving the most equity (27%) after Vivek (35%), in large part to attract him away from his other potentially lucrative options and to compensate him for working without a salary.

Similarly, when Phuc Truong joined UpDown, he had already worked on a successful startup and had several lucrative software development jobs. When the team discussed equity splits, Phuc's point of view was that, whereas the other cofounders "would only be giving up a social life at business school," he would sustain a tangible—even quantifiable—loss in income by joining UpDown full-time. He would therefore need either a substantial salary or more of the equity as compensation.

Future Contributions

A founder's future contributions, although often the hardest factors to evaluate, are in many ways the most important for determining equity stakes. "Remember," warns one entrepreneur, "when the pie is split, 95% of the work required for success remains in the future." Often, a founder's potential to contribute to the startup can be estimated by considering his or her background in combination with his or her commitment level.

Researchers have already observed that specific founding experience is more valuable for startup growth than are overall work experience and educational human capital.[9] Serial entrepreneurs are commonly expected to have stronger human and social capital (and possibly even greater financial capital) and are therefore expected to contribute more to building the startup's value. My quantitative analyses with Thomas Hellmann found that a prior founding experience was associated with a *serial premium* of 7 to 9 percentage points more of an equity stake. Yet, after controlling for prior founding experience, status as an idea person, and capital investment, a founder's greater overall prior work experience—any work in any company—did not lead to a larger equity stake. Thus, specific founding experience is indeed much more important for equity splits than is general human capital. (As discussed in Chapter 7, different founding roles and titles are also associated with greater equity stakes.)

The level of future contribution is also presumed to depend on how much time a founder can or will commit to the startup. Full-time founders tend to receive larger equity stakes than part-time founders. For instance, in her third startup, serial entrepreneur Tracy Burman wanted to cut back on her workload to spend more time with her young children. She therefore negotiated two terms with her cofounders. First, rather than be the CEO, as she had been in the past, she would be the COO, reporting to the CEO. Second, she would work 80% of the time that her cofounders would work, receive 80% of the equity stake that she would normally have received, and earn 80% of the other founders' salaries.

Founder Motivations and Preferences

As with most of the dilemmas examined in this book, the founders' motivations play a central role in the equity split. Founders with strong wealth motivations will place a high premium on maximizing their financial gains from the startup. As described in Chapter 7, other motivations will lead other founders to prioritize a particular role, title, or lifestyle flexibility.

Related factors that may influence a founding team's equity split are as follows:

- A founder's degree of risk aversion, confidence in his or her own abilities, and confidence in the startup's prospects will affect how much priority he or she places on gaining every additional percentage of equity versus gaining additional cash compensation from the startup.[*]
- Tolerance for conflict will affect a founder's willingness to engage in tension-filled negotiations over each type of financial reward.
- Prior relationships among the founders may influence the split, as described in Chapter 7, "The Three Rs System."

Figure 6.3 summarizes the core factors that should affect equity splits as well as some of my research findings about how much of a difference each factor actually makes. All of these factors deserve further study by researchers and careful attention from founding teams.

EQUAL VERSUS UNEQUAL SPLITS

It seems unlikely that any two founders could be making *exactly* equal contributions to the value of the startup, have the same opportunity costs, and have equal motivations. Thus, it would follow logically that if equity splits are meant to reflect the founders' relative contributions and value to the startup, equal splits should be rare or nonexistent. Such is not at all the case. As shown in Figure 6.4, 33% of the teams in my dataset split equity equally.[†] Why did they make this decision? Was it a good decision? Did it make the team more stable? Is it associated with higher or lower valuations when raising outside financing?

---

[*] The macroeconomic environment may also be an influence, though in uncertain and maybe conflicting ways. For instance, in boom times, founders may be more likely than in downturns to fight for each percentage point of equity because they believe that an IPO or other successful exit is likely. During downturns, on the other hand, when there is no rising tide to raise all boats, founders may be more likely than in boom times to fight for every last percentage of whatever equity they manage to create. Future research could examine whether either of these—or other—conflicting effects predominates.

[†] Founding teams are even more likely to split equally in small businesses, where 70% of teams do so (Ruef, 2009).

1. **Past Contributions:** How much has the founder contributed to building the value of the startup so far?

   a. **Idea Premium:** Founders who contribute the original idea on which the startup is based have made a unique contribution to the venture.[*]
   b. **Capital Contribution:** Founders who have made larger contributions to the startup's seed capital should see a proportionate increase in their equity ownership.[10]

2. **Opportunity Cost:** What are the founders sacrificing in order to pursue the startup?

3. **Future Contributions:** Most of the work required for the startup to be successful will come in the future, but these contributions can be hard to anticipate. How much can each founder be expected to contribute to the value of the startup down the road?

   a. **Serial Founders:** Members of the founding team who have previously led a startup to a successful exit can be expected to contribute more human and social capital down the road.[†]
   b. **Level of Commitment:** Founders who are committed full-time to the venture can be expected to contribute more value.
   c. **Titles:** The official positions of the members of the founding team have been shown to influence equity splits, with CEOs receiving a substantial equity premium.[‡]

4. **Founder Motivations and Preferences**

   a. **Wealth Motivations** should lead founders to prioritize larger equity stakes.
   b. **Risk Aversion** and **Optimism** will affect how much priority a founder places on gaining equity versus cash compensation.
   c. **Tolerance for Conflict** will affect a founder's willingness to engage in negotiations.
   d. **Prior Relationships** can affect expectations about equity splits (see Chapter 7).

---

[*] As described earlier in the chapter, quantitative analyses of my dataset revealed an "idea premium" of 10 to 15 percentage points of extra equity.

[†] As described earlier in the chapter, quantitative analyses of my dataset revealed a "serial premium" of 7 to 9 percentage points of extra equity.

[‡] As described in Chapter 7, quantitative analyses of my dataset revealed a "CEO premium" of 14 to 20 percentage points of extra equity.

Figure 6.3. Factors for Determining Equity Splits

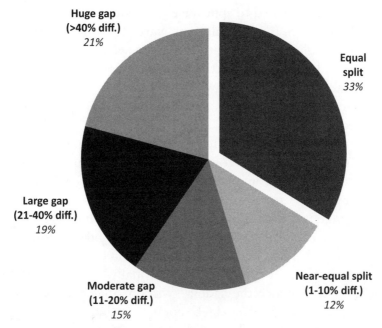

Figure 6.4. Difference in Equity Stakes between Founder with Largest Stake and Founder with Smallest Stake

A Threshold of Psychological Pain versus Financial Gain

Thomas Hellmann and I analyzed my data to assess possible explanations for the prevalence of equal equity splits.[11] Assuming that negotiating an equity split is inherently tense, so that most people would have a strong motivation to avoid it if that could be justified, we wondered whether there was a *threshold of intrateam difference* that separated equal-split from unequal-split teams. That is, if cofounders differ enough in the value of what they bring to the startup—be it experience, ideas, investment capital, or fire in the belly—the team will be willing to engage in a tension-filled negotiation over equity, because a simple equal split would seem too inequitable. Below a threshold, however, the gains from engaging in such a negotiation would not be worth the problems introduced, and the team would be inclined to split the equity equally. Tim Westergren of Pandora Radio, for example, was warned that negotiating over equity, rather than simply splitting equally, would "introduce sand under the saddle," causing friction within the team. After pondering that advice, Tim decided that whatever extra equity stake he might be able to insist on wouldn't be worth the potential problems, and he agreed to split equally.

Hellmann and I gauged how similar or dissimilar a team's founders were in value by comparing two aspects of the founders' backgrounds—prior founding experience (i.e., he or she was a serial entrepreneur) and prior years of work experience—and two of their early contributions to the startup—ideas or intellectual property and seed capital.[12] Our quantitative results indeed showed that "close to equal" founding teams tended to split equally, while more heterogeneous teams tended to split unequally.[13] This is consistent with the "sand under the saddle" wisdom that causing friction within close-to-equal teams can be counterproductive, leading such teams to split equally and avoid the high-tension negotiation. Our finding is also consistent with the fact that roughly equal contributions are cognitively difficult for the founders to distinguish, so that close-to-equal teams will find that an equal equity split feels more sensible.

"We're a Team"

Some founders argue that an equal split sends a good signal to everyone on the team. One founder explained that it showed that "we were more concerned with the success of the enterprise than our own personal wealth accumulation; that we had the presence of mind to realize the success of the first would ensure the latter. . . . We're all starting from the beginning, we're all taking the same risk, we're a team. If we're successful we'll all 'get enough' without trying to jockey for equity position this early in the game. Jockeying for position this early in the game does nothing for the effectiveness of teamwork." Of course, showing unity and avoiding conflict can be overlapping motives.

Financing Outcomes: Quick Handshakes versus Thoughtful Equal Splits

Some teams arrive at an equal split after carefully concluding that the founders have similar backgrounds, resources, or levels of commitment and can therefore be expected to contribute similar amounts to the startup. It is a very different matter, though, when the team prefers to avoid negotiating the split and defaults to a quick handshake and an equal split. Indeed, we found that equal splitters tended to spend much less time negotiating the split than did unequal splitters. Of the equal splitters, 60% of the teams spent a day or less negotiating the equity split, while only 39% of the unequal splitters made their decision that quickly.

We categorized the equal-split teams who had spent a day or less negotiating their split as "quick-equal" teams and those who had spent more time on the negotiation as "slow-equal" teams. Interviews with founders suggested that there were qualitative differences between quick-equal and slow-equal teams. For instance, one serial entrepreneur observed that "a quick-equal split is a symptom of a founding team that doesn't have any experience or methodology for making the founder split so they just say screw it and do 1/N."[*] Another founder echoed that "a quick handshake is a symptom of inexperience and/or lack of real preparation, or real glue to the idea, before going on the 'tough journey.'" We'll see examples later in this chapter of founders who regretted making an equal split.

To assess quantitatively whether quick-equal teams and slow-equal teams fared differently (due to underlying differences between such teams, rather than due directly to how they split the equity), Thomas Hellmann and I focused on the first round of financing.[14] Our analyses showed that, controlling for a wide variety of differences across teams and startups, quick-equal teams received significantly lower valuations than slow-equal teams and unequal-split teams, lending credence to anecdotal evidence that there is a real difference between teams who engage in a serious dialogue about

---

[*] That is, the members of a two-founder team each receive 1/2 of the equity, the members of a three-founder team each receive 1/3 of the equity, and so on.

the split and those who avoid such a discussion and rely on a quick handshake. The handshake, for all its cultural resonance as a symbol of trustworthiness and echoes of a golden age "when you could do business with a handshake," is often a symptom of a founding team's weakness. Many VCs report that they do examine the team's equity split before investing and that a problematic split could have important consequences. One explained, "We spend time during our diligence process understanding how the split came to be" (e.g., whether it had resulted from a quick handshake); whether the split had "led to suboptimal behavior," indicated weaknesses within the team, or introduced additional tensions within it; and whether those issues should affect the startup's valuation.

51% versus 50%

Some founders, particularly in a two-founder team, will argue for a 51% equity stake, and sometimes the other partner is quite willing to go along with that. In one of his earliest startups, serial entrepreneur Frank Addante agreed to such a split. When he and his cofounder, Cary, started ReaXions, Cary funded the startup but was otherwise a silent partner, while Frank was to receive a salary for his full-time work. Cary insisted on receiving 51% of the equity; since he was putting up the money, he wanted control over how that money was spent. As Frank explained, "49% versus 51% meant we had a similar amount of equity, but if a major decision needed to be made, it was his." Thus, the additional 1% of equity can have a substantial impact on decision-making control.

Frank was willing to give Cary 51%, but in many founding teams, that additional 1% can cause major problems. It may suggest that one cofounder is overly focused on control instead of on crafting an effective partnership, or it may foreshadow a dysfunctional team dynamic. The 51% share can also provoke resentment. One founder complained, "My partner, who came up with the idea, controls 51% of the company, based on an early conversation we held. However, I am providing the initial funding and have done most of the work as of late and I feel a 50–50 split is plenty fair." (This example also makes a good case for the kind of dynamic splits described later in this chapter.)

Founders should realize, though, that even the "absolute control" seemingly granted by a 51% equity stake is not absolute and may not last. For one thing, a 51% equity stake does not guarantee direct control of all decisions. The most important decisions, such as sale of the corporation's assets, are left to a vote of shareholders; here, the founder with a 51% share does have absolute control. But the next tier of important decisions is in the hands of the board, which is elected by the equity holders (who may also have seats themselves). As the number of directors increases, the equity stake necessary to elect a director decreases. Most importantly, the board elects the CEO, who controls the third tier of decisions, including oversight of day-to-day operations.[15]

In any case, for teams planning to raise at least one round of outside financing, the power of 51% equity will be only temporary. As soon as the team takes some outside financing, the 51% stake will shrink to less than 50% and that founder will have to build a coalition with other shareholders to have his or her way.[*] (In addition, as described in Chapter 9, investors often receive securities that have more rights than does the simple "common equity" received by founders.) Nike cofounders Phil Knight and Bill Bowerman, for example, originally split the equity 51%–49% in Knight's favor and Knight resisted giving up equity, even to a crucial early employee, in order to keep control of the firm. By 1971, however, Knight was desperate for funding and accepted $200,000 from a private offering. In return, he agreed to give up 35% of the company and with it his controlling interest.[16]

FORMAL VERSUS INFORMAL SPLITS

When the founders split the equity, they can either keep the agreement informal or commit it to writing. As shown in Figure 6.5, the

---

[*] In fact, even in 60%–40% splits, the holder of the larger stake will be diluted to below 50% in the typical financing round.

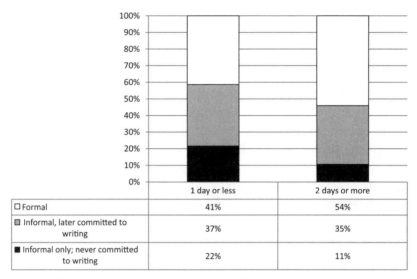

Figure 6.5. Time Spent Negotiating the Split versus Formality of the Agreement

longer the cofounders negotiate to reach agreement on the split, the more likely they are to commit the agreement to writing, either on their own or with a lawyer. Teams who split quickly (within one day) are much more likely to stick with a verbal agreement (22% of the teams, compared to 11% for the teams who spend longer negotiating) and less likely, if they do formalize the agreement at all, to do so right away (41% versus 54% of longer-negotiating teams).[17]

Two factors might affect this linkage between negotiation length and formal agreement. First, when the agreement is straightforward—with no complex or subjective contingencies and no intellectual property issues—the team is more likely to be able to agree quickly and less likely to feel the need to capture the details of the agreement in writing. (On the flip side, teams who are in a rush to get to an agreement may craft simpler agreements.) Second, teams who try to avoid the tension of negotiating the split (by doing so as quickly as possible) may also be more likely to try to avoid the tension of committing the agreement to writing, which can involve reopening some of the issues.

While the advantages of a formal agreement are obvious, there can also be disadvantages. For instance, overly rigid contracts can lock parties into arrangements that don't allow for adjustments as circumstances change, and overly detailed contracts can undermine trust by preventing spontaneous displays of good intentions.[18] When formalizing the agreement, founders should also anticipate future tax or legal issues that could be avoided if handled appropriately.*

STATIC VERSUS DYNAMIC SPLITS: THE PERILS OF SETTING THINGS IN STONE

Setting the early equity split in stone, without allowing for changes, is one of the biggest mistakes founders can make. With their confidence in their startup and themselves, their passion for their work and their mission, and their desire not to harm the fragile dynamic within the nascent founding team, cofounders tend to plan for the best that can happen. They assume that their early, high levels of commitment will last long into the future, rather than waning as the challenges of founding begin to sap their passion for the idea and for each other. They assume that no adverse events will change the composition of the team. They also tend to take a very short-term view of the factors that should affect equity splits. They assume that the tasks that they are performing during the early stage of startup development are the same tasks that will be performed during the next and very different stages. They assume that their skills will remain as valuable to the startup as they are right now. They overestimate the amount of value that they will build in the first months compared to the value they hope to build over the subsequent years, and thus overweight their past contributions compared to the future contributions that will be required of them. Each founder places more value on his or her own contributions than on the contributions of the other cofounders,

---

*For instance, when handling intellectual property issues, founders must take into account Section 351 of the Internal Revenue Code, and need to make timely and valid Section 83(b) elections if they are adopting vesting as part of the equity split. For more details, see Wasserman et al. (2009).

knowing the cost and extent of his or own efforts in a way that he or she cannot know the cost and extent of others' efforts.

But such a best-case approach is hazardous. Uncertainties abound. At the company level, founders learn about the flaws in their initial plans and adjust the startup's strategy, business plan, and business model. Professor Scott Shane reports that "almost half (49.6 percent) of new firm founders indicated that their business ideas [had] changed between the time they first identified them and the time when they were surveyed about them."[19] Such adjustments can cause major changes in the obstacles that the startup faces, the skills needed to address those obstacles, and thus the roles that each founder (or perhaps a new founder or a nonfounder) will have to play in building the startup.

At the individual level, as the strategy and business model shift, the skills of some founders become more important than the skills of others and roles often shift. As each founder learns about the demands of building a startup, reflects on his or her motivations, and sees how well his or her abilities address the startup's needs, his or her commitment to the startup may change. The founders also come to understand each other's abilities and commitment at a far deeper level than was possible at the beginning. Yet founders tend to overestimate how much value they will build during those early days, which can cause even bigger problems when a cofounder's contributions wane later on.

A founder's personal life may also affect his or her commitment and contributions. At Ockham, all of the founders were aware of the imminent arrival of Ken's first child. However, even Ken was unsure how this would affect his willingness to quit his full-time job and focus on building Ockham. Extreme and unexpected health problems can catch all parties by surprise. For instance, while Microsoft was still a private company, cofounder Paul Allen was diagnosed with Hodgkin's lymphoma, which caused him to quit the company, leaving Bill Gates as the sole active founder during the crucial three years before it became a public company.*

---

* Gates and Allen apparently had no mechanism for adjusting their equity holdings in accordance with such events, despite the asymmetry in the founders' contributions to pre-IPO

In such ways, even the most comfortable equity split can be thrown into disarray. For instance, when Robin Chase and her partner, Antje, founded the car-sharing startup Zipcar, they agreed with a quick handshake to split the equity 50–50. The team believed it had avoided destructive tension over the equity split and could now focus on building the startup. "We shook across the table, 50–50," Robin recalls, "and I thought 'great.'" Robin had heard about other teams that had faltered because of tough equity-split negotiations, and she breathed a sigh of relief that she and Antje had avoided such problems. Robin poured her heart and soul into the startup, making major contributions to its growth, and was fully expecting Antje to do the same. Antje, however, remained at her full-time job and, by the summer, was expecting her second child. Robin wondered when her partner would be able to become more involved, but, in the end, Antje never joined full-time. Knowing that Antje still owned the same percentage as she did ate away at Robin, who later reflected, "That was a really stupid handshake, because who knows what skill sets and what milestones and what achievements are going to be valuable as you move ahead. That first handshake caused a huge amount of angst over the next year and a half."[20] Eventually Antje left the company altogether while continuing as a shareholder.

The cost to fix such problems can be very high, ranging from Robin Chase's "angst" to more tangible financial costs. At govWorks.com, founders Kaleil and Tom had a cofounder, Chieh, who put up $19,000, worked "after hours" for five months (he had kept his day job instead of joining govWorks full-time), and

---

Microsoft. They initially split the equity 64%–36% in Gates's favor; Gates's stake was 1.8 times that of Allen's. Even though Allen had been absent for the three crucial years before Microsoft went public, examination of Microsoft's S-1 prospectus shows that, at the time of Microsoft's IPO, Gates's equity stake was still 1.8 times that of Allen's stake (45%–25%). Allen's recent book (Allen 2011) describes Gates's extreme plan to readjust their equity split, a plan that was foiled by Allen. It is hard for the heart to bleed for Bill Gates, who despite having gotten the short end of the stick ended up becoming the world's richest man, but all founders should learn the importance of incorporating dynamic elements into equity splits, as we will discuss below.

then dropped out. When the remaining cofounders were about to close their first round of financing, their potential funder, Mayfield, was not willing to close until Kaleil and Tom bought Chieh out and reclaimed his equity. The VCs were willing to do a $410,000 "sweetheart deal" to facilitate the buyout. However, Chieh wanted $800,000. Amid the pressure to close the round, Kaleil and Tom ended up settling with Chieh for $700,000, making up the $290,000 out of their own pockets.[21] Kaleil felt he was "being extorted." Although the risks of this kind of outcome are real, teams often fail to address them proactively. In my dataset, half of the teams had neglected to include any dynamic elements (vesting, buyout terms, and the like) in their equity agreements, sentencing themselves to the same risks faced by the Zipcar and govWorks.com teams.

A Template for Founders

How should founders deal with such developments? In short, by assuming when they do the initial split that things *will* change, even if the specific changes cannot be foreseen, and therefore structuring a *dynamic equity split* rather than the static splits used at Zipcar, govWorks, and many other startups. As important as it is to *get* the initial equity split right—by matching it as closely as possible the founders' past contributions, opportunity costs, future contributions, and motivations—it is equally important to *keep* it right; that is, to be able to adjust the split as circumstances change.

The UpDown team provides a good example of the need for a dynamic agreement and a template for discussing forward-looking issues. They first split the equity in November 2006. Up to that point, all four founders (one of whom, Warren, had become a dropout cofounder who would no longer be contributing to the startup) had worked only sporadically on the business plan and there was no funding in sight. The three remaining cofounders therefore decided to ignore past contributions (with the exception of a small idea premium for Michael), assume that they would make equal future contributions to the startup, and split the equity equally except for Michael's 5% idea premium.

A month after the team had made this agreement, Michael entered talks with an interested angel investor and was motivated to increase his work effort dramatically. At the same time, Phuc was busy with his own consulting jobs and Georg was still on an extended vacation with his wife and two young children. After a few weeks, Michael worried that his team members' current motivation and contribution levels might foreshadow their future contributions and thus set out to develop what he felt would be a more accurate template to use for a new equity split, one that would award him more equity for building more value. A simplified version of the template is shown in Figure 6.6.

Overall, with the addition of the dynamic elements described below, Michael's template can provide a model for other teams grappling with how to split their equity. It breaks down the qualitatively different stages of startup development into separate phases, provides a structured way to discuss and weight the importance of each phase for building the startup's value, and provides an opportunity to plan and evaluate the various tasks that are being or will be performed by each founder. Michael's cofounders disagreed vehemently with several details in his template (e.g., the overweighting of Phase I, the list of contributions by Phuc, and changes to the Phase III contributions), but the template provided a structured approach to discussing a variety of complex factors, thereby facilitating the team's renegotiation.

A structured approach can also serve as a check on the natural tendency to overemphasize tangible factors at the expense of intangible factors which may have more impact on team dynamics and the success of the startup. For founders—and for researchers!—past contributions are usually easier to assess than future contributions, cash contributions are easier to assess than contributions to honing the idea, and skills are usually easier to assess than commitment and motivation, but teams should seek mechanisms that enable them to discuss and balance this wide variety of factors. By developing the template together, a founding team may also be able to shift its focus away from wrangling over specific numbers and toward a more productive process for agreeing on criteria, arriving at weightings, and negotiating tasks and responsibilities.

Weighting	Phase I: Oct 2006–Jan 2007 40%		Phase II: Feb–May 2007 30%		Phase III: Jun–Jul 2007 30%		Total Weighted Equity Stake
Founder	Contribution	Equity	Contribution	Equity	Contribution	Equity	
Michael	Identification of opportunity; define business strategy, fund-raising	60%	Investor management	33¹/₃%	Same	33¹/₃%	45%
Georg	Define business, market strategy, etc.	28%	Marketing, product management	33¹/₃%	Same	33¹/₃%	28%
Phuc	Initial mock site; define business strategy	10%	Site improvement	33¹/₃%	Same	33¹/₃%	26%
Warren	Define business strategy; financial plan	2%					1%
Total		100%		100%		100%	100%

Figure 6.6. UpDown's Template for Splitting Equity

Recall that the UpDown team negotiated its equity split twice in order to account for the varying contributions of each founder over time and also used the template to do some forward-looking planning, but even that wasn't enough. After the team had agreed on a new split in February 2007 and had worked through the summer, both Georg and Michael applied for work visas, which would enable them to quit school and work full-time on UpDown. In the 50–50 visa lottery, Michael was granted a visa but Georg was not, making it impossible for Georg to be involved in the startup full-time. They hadn't thought of this during their equity-split renegotiations and now had to work out the equity split one more time, again heightening the tension within the team. Anticipating such changes, in the ways discussed below, would have helped them avoid further tensions by structuring the initial agreement to adjust to those changes.

Terms, Contingencies, and Trust

Dynamic equity agreements can make use of a number of approaches, such as buyout terms (in which a founder's stake might be bought on prenegotiated terms by the startup or by other founders) and vesting schedules. At their core, however, all of these structures are geared to deal with the uncertainties inherent in startups.

Inspired by a famous quote from former U.S. Secretary of Defense Donald Rumsfeld, my colleague Deepak Malhotra has developed a general way to categorize the different types of uncertainty involved in contracts as "knowns" (whose outcomes are already known or are ensured), "known-unknowns" (scenarios for which one can anticipate the occurrence but not the outcome), and "unknown-unknowns" (whatever complete surprises the future holds in store).[22] These three types of uncertainty can be addressed by terms, contingencies, and trust, respectively.

Founders' equity splits involve knowns, such as how much capital each founder has contributed and who owns the patents, which can be addressed using standard contractual terms. For example, Zondigo and Crimson Solutions dealt with the fact the one of the founders had had the original idea by giving him a larger share of equity; Lynx handled the same known by means of a vesting arrangement. Ockham dealt with its founders' differing cash contributions by splitting the equity in like proportions.

Known-unknowns can be addressed by using contingent provisions that outline how the equity split should change for various worst-case, expected-case, and best-case scenarios. The Ockham team, for example, did not know what Ken would do once his new child was born; Ken himself didn't know. But they all knew the possibilities—he would either join the startup full-time, join part-time, or leave—and therefore dealt with this known-unknown by crafting a buyout agreement that carefully laid out the rules and price for buying back founder shares should a founder cease to participate in the startup. The agreement specifically mentioned the possibility that Ken would not be working for the startup: "In the event Burows is not a full-time employee of the Company by April 19, 2000, the other Founding Shareholders shall have the right . . . to purchase fifty percent (50%) of the Shares owned by Burows."

But in the high-uncertainty world of startups, an awful lot can fall into the category of unknown-unknowns. The first step in dealing with them is to work hard to identify as many as possible and discuss how things should change if such an event occurs; that is, turn the unknown-unknowns into known-unknowns. For instance, no one could have predicted that Microsoft cofounder Paul Allen would be diagnosed with Hodgkin's lymphoma, but any founding team can plan for the possibility that one of its members is suddenly forced to cut back or leave for medical or personal reasons. Teams who are willing to surface and discuss such scenarios will be able to transform some unknown-unknowns into known-unknowns and to work out contingent agreements to deal with them. Certainly the UpDown team, knowing the 50–50 lottery that drove the awarding of work visas, could have discussed the repercussions of each possibility and planned how the equity should change if only Georg, only Michael, or neither one received a visa.

No matter how thoroughly teams try to render unknown-unknowns into known-unknowns, there are still going to be surprises and upsets. At such times, the team must rely on the trust that has been developed among the members. Such trust, if it has had a chance to become strong before tension-filled problems arise, allows cofounders to act outside their immediate self-interest—above and beyond the call of duty—confident that, in the longer term, they will reap as they have sown.[23] Although it is easy for cofounders to assume that they will always trust each other, the trial by fire of founding a startup often burns a team instead of forging a stronger team.

For this reason, the members of a founding team need to take constant care of their mutual trust; at any moment, it might be the rope that keeps them from going over the cliff together. Even if a founder is trying to take steps to increase the success of the startup, his or her cofounders might see it as a violation of mutual trust. Michael's desire at UpDown to have his equity stake match his contributions was initially seen by his cofounders as greedy and selfish, rather than as an attempt to make the team more stable in the long run. However, his willingness to communicate openly with his cofounders and to adjust the equity stakes in the template to meet their needs enhanced the trust within the team. Thus, the tension-filled, high-stakes equity-split negotiation is itself a double-edged sword, an experience that can leave the team wiser, stronger, and more unified, or can undermine the trust within the team. In particular, some founders forget that the equity-split negotiation is one in a series of negotiations that will determine the founders' individual and collective success. A founder who pushes hard for every last percentage point of equity may leave the other founders feeling they'd better watch their backs, which will make it harder for the team to handle the inevitable unknown-unknowns when they arise. As Jim Triandiflou observed about such situations, "The juice isn't worth the squeeze."

The UpDown team's extensive discussions over equity actually solidified their mutual trust. Reopening the equity negotiations in February 2007 and arriving at an agreement that they all felt was fair gave them valuable insights into each other's motivations and goals, helping them clarify Michael's role, appreciate Phuc's contributions, and understand where the startup ranked on Georg's list of priorities. Thus, when Georg did not get his visa and left the country after graduation, the team was again able to renegotiate calmly. In 2007 and 2008, Georg returned two-thirds of his stock but kept one-third in consideration of the time and effort he had contributed to the startup. In contrast, at govWorks.com, the extensive negotiations with Chieh destroyed the trust between him and the rest of the team.

Protecting Yourself from Your Cofounders: Self-Imposed Vesting

Vesting is the most common type of dynamic equity agreement. Vesting terms require founders to earn their equity stakes, either over a specified time or when they accomplish specific milestones, rather than owning the equity from the start, as is the case with static equity splits. Founders who leave a startup before their equity has fully vested must relinquish the unvested portion to the startup or to their cofounders, thus either shifting it to the cofounders who will continue to build the value of the startup or allowing them to reallocate it to someone who will replace the drop-out founder. Vesting terms thus help serve as "golden handcuffs" that either give each founder financial incentives to continue contributing to the startup, rather than dropping out while keeping the full equity stake, or help protect the remaining founders when one founder leaves. Founder-imposed vesting also enables core founders to test whether their potential cofounders intend to stay with the startup for the long term and to set expectations about involvement and roles. If Robin Chase had proposed vesting to her cofounder, she might have learned from the reaction whether Antje planned to join the startup full-time.

Nevertheless, founding teams usually resist adopting vesting until forced to do so by their first outside investors. Founders often worry that proposing vesting terms will be seen as a lack of trust in their cofounders' dedication, or resent the idea that their own equity will have to vest, or even fear how they might be treated down the road before their equity has vested—without considering how vesting *protects* them.[24]

The two major types of vesting are time-based vesting and milestone-based vesting. With time-based vesting, each founder who is actively involved in the startup earns predetermined portions of his or her equity stake as each month, quarter, or year passes.* This type of vesting assumes that the passage of time approximates the addition of value to the startup, a valid assumption as long as work proceeds according to plan. But when the work proceeds more slowly than planned, as is often the case, founders can earn full equity stakes well before making the contributions that had been expected of them. In effect, time-based vesting that is too short releases the "golden handcuffs" and increases the risk of losing a founder while the startup is still being built. (For this reason, time-based vesting has been derided—perhaps unfairly—as "paying for a pulse.")

Milestone-based vesting is one solution to such a problem, but it can cause its own problems. Team members earn a specific amount of equity for each of a well-defined set of milestones that, if accomplished, would add concrete value to the startup. For business-oriented founders, the milestones may pertain to fund-raising, customer acquisition, revenues, or the establishment of partnership agreements. For technical founders, milestones may be tied to completing a prototype, conducting a successful beta test, or introducing the full initial version.

While this approach aligns each additional award of equity with the addition of value to the startup, it is effective only when the team can (a) define objectively when each milestone has been achieved and (b) clearly link the achievement of each milestone to the founder(s) responsible for achieving it. If the milestones are more subjective, milestone-based vesting can increase the tension and conflict as the founders disagree over which milestones have been achieved. If the achievement of a milestone is dependent on

---

*The most common time-based vesting schedules use an initial "cliff" of a year, at the end of which the founder earns the equity for that year, followed by monthly vesting thereafter. For four-year vesting, for example, at the end of the first year the founder would vest 25% of the equity, followed by three years of monthly vesting, with 1/36 of the remaining equity vested each month.

the efforts of several founders, only one of whom will receive an additional equity stake when it is achieved, the others will be motivated to focus only on those milestones that affect their own equity stakes, increasing the tension within the team and reducing its ability to achieve milestones.

In fast-changing companies, adopting rigid milestones can be hazardous and should be done carefully. Down the road, necessary changes in the startup's strategy may render obsolete a milestone on which part of a founder's equity depends, requiring another round of tension-filled negotiation over equity stakes and milestones or else leaving that particular founder feeling cheated or creating destructive rigidity as he or she continues to pursue an obsolete milestone. One founder-CEO related how one of his fund-raising milestones had defined three metrics that had to be met by his next round of financing: a certain minimum amount of capital raised, at a certain minimum valuation, before a certain date. Even though "I ended up getting multiple VC offers," some of the offers "did not meet the criteria [but] were arguably better for the company." This financing milestone, which had been designed to align the founder's incentives with those of the business, thus caused a significant misalignment instead. As with all high-powered incentives, vesting terms should be designed with such unintended consequences in mind. Boards and founders should "stress test" their tentative milestones against a variety of scenarios, assessing whether each milestone would work well in all the scenarios and adjusting milestones that, in some scenarios, might cause misalignment.

However, if used wisely, dynamic terms can provide a team with considerable flexibility in dealing with unique situations. For instance, at the corporate-concierge startup Circles, the two cofounders focused on the known-unknown of what might happen if either cofounder gave birth to a baby. Even though they thought that the new mother would probably want to continue working, they used vesting terms to account for the possibility that she might want to cut back on the days worked per week. The founders agreed that if that cofounder wanted to cut back to 80% or 60% time, her vesting would adjust at that rate. They also agreed that working less than

60% time would be equivalent to leaving the company or would require a more extensive discussion of what to do then. At Ockham Technologies, the founders designed a buy-back system whereby if Ken, the idea person, cut back to half time, his equity would be cut accordingly, and, if he had not joined by the end of the first year, his equity could be completely bought out. Conversely, as we saw earlier, the Lynx team agreed that the non-idea founder would vest while the founder who had had the idea would not, a flexible arrangement that fit that team's needs.

High Attraction, High Motivation

We can now better appreciate the power of dynamic agreements. We saw how splitting equity early can help attract cofounders but can undermine the founders' motivation and foster free riding, while late splits can bolster the founders' motivation but interfere with attracting cofounders. Dynamic agreements offer a way to avoid this trade-off. Defining the equity split (both its core terms and its contingent terms) early in the life of the startup allows the core founders to attract cofounders with concrete equity terms. Making the split dynamic—changeable in accordance with each founder's continuing contributions—helps keep cofounders motivated to build the startup's value.

Ockham's early equity split, for example, allowed Mike and Jim to be fully attracted and committed to the startup (by receiving equity early), while its equity-buyback clause encouraged them to continue to work diligently for success because they would have to relinquish their shares if they "ceased to perform." This contingency plan prevented a possible disintegration when Ken decided to drop out.

CASH COMPENSATION

For many founders, the main financial motivation to join a founding team is the equity stake rather than the cash compensation. Cash-poor startups generally cannot pay much salary or bonus, but confident, passionate founders usually believe that their equity stakes will eventually repay that sacrifice. For Ockham cofounder-CEO Jim Triandiflou, not receiving a salary was an entrepreneur's badge of honor: "April 19 was the first day of Ockham because that's the first day we did not have a paycheck. You're not getting paid, so you're now an entrepreneur."

On the one hand, my analyses show little association between cash and equity within most founding teams, suggesting that decisions about the mix of rewards are relatively ad hoc. On the other hand, as we will see, some founders have a clear picture of the role of cash compensation among the rewards they seek. For instance, within the UpDown team, Phuc Truong had a clearly stated trade-off he was willing to make between cash and equity, trading off less of one for more of the other.

Two striking patterns of founder compensation are the equality of pay within many founding teams and the below-market salaries often paid to founders (the "founder discount"), the latter of which can give us some insights into founders' attachment to their startups.

Salary Equality versus Inequality

While Jim Triandiflou gloried in his initial lack of salary, cash compensation remains important for some founders, particularly those accustomed to making a considerable amount. Phuc Truong, for instance, was making $200,000 a year on software-development consulting contracts and was adamant that UpDown compensate him for most of this lost income should he join full-time. He wanted a salary of $110,000, and his lower limit was $70,000, but for every $10,000 below $110,000, he wanted an additional 0.25% of equity. In contrast, Michael, who was a full-time student, cared very little about receiving a salary. Thus, the team ended up with cofounders making roughly equal contributions but earning very different salaries.

Given the differences among founders, we shouldn't be surprised to find the members of a founding team earning very different pay. And indeed, some suggestive quantitative analyses of my

2009 dataset revealed that, of the startups that had not yet raised any outside capital but still had at least two cofounders working in the startup, 63% paid the founders unequal salaries.* As would be expected, the founder-CEO was often the highest-paid cofounder. However, in almost one-third of these unequal-salary startups, a non-CEO cofounder actually earned more than the founder-CEO, a striking figure given that, in large companies, the CEO almost always makes significantly more than anyone else.[25]

While salary equality for founding teams is not the rule, it is common in young startups and may last for a long time; Lynx's three cofounders received the same salaries throughout the life of the startup. In my quantitative dataset, 37% of the pre-financing startups that still had at least two cofounders were paying their founders the same salary. This percentage dropped with each successive round of outside financing, with only 19% of the teams having salary equality after they had raised their third round of outside financing. Salary equality was more common in two-founder teams than in three-founder teams—40% and 33%, respectively. Although the percentages dropped by the third round of financing, the relationship between two-founder and three-founder teams remained: 20% of the two-founder teams and 13% of three-founder teams had salary equality.

The Founder Discount—Dedication or Exploitation?

The founders of Lynx Solutions were very discouraged with their cash compensation. At first, they had voluntarily accepted below-market—in fact, zero—salaries, believing that it would be better for the startup if they used all resources to get it off the ground. When they raised money from venture investors, they negotiated with their new board for salaries of $60,000 each. This was still far below market, but the founders believed they were "doing the

---

* Within these unequal-salary startups, the median gap between the highest-paid and lowest-paid cofounders was 30%. (This percentage did not vary much by financing rounds, always staying within a narrow range of 29%–32%.)

company a favor" by not asking for too much. However, when the founders later sought a raise to bring their salaries more in line with industry norms (well over $100,000), their board would grant them only $90,000. The three founders were on the verge of threatening to leave if the board did not agree to pay them fairly—after all, they themselves had responded to such threats from the startup's non-founding employees. As we will see, though, such threats were far less effective coming from founders.

The Lynx founders are not alone in being underpaid. In analyses of my quantitative dataset, I examined the compensation of 1,238 founding and nonfounding C-level executives in 528 private startups. Controlling for differences across the startups (such as company age, size, resources, and industry segment) and differences across the executives (such as equity holdings, educational and work backgrounds, and tenure in the organization), I found that founders received $25,000 less in salary than equivalent nonfounders did—clear evidence of a "founder discount."[*]

Two influential theories of corporate management—agency theory and stewardship theory—can shed light on the compensation differences between founders and nonfounders. According to agency theory, executives are "agents" acting in their own self-interest as opposed to the interests of the company; company owners therefore have to structure compensation (and monitor their agents' behavior) so as to tie an executive's self-interest as closely as possible to the organization's goals.[26] Nonfounding hires are classical "agents," self-interested individuals who take a job for the personal income and benefits. Founders need to align this self-interest with the interests of the company by structuring compensation to make it contingent on firm performance. In contrast, founders (especially founder-CEOs) tend to act more like the principals or "stewards" of stewardship theory—people who identify closely with their organizations and thus derive higher satisfaction from promoting organizational interests than from purely

---

[*] See Wasserman (2006b) for more details on the theories, samples, and results.

self-serving behavior.* In beginning a startup, founders incorporate their startups into their self-identities to the point where their own self-esteem becomes deeply tied to the startup's success or failure. While this situation sounds ideal in that it aligns the interests of the startup with those of its founders, it also has a dark side: It can severely limit a founder's bargaining power for compensation, resulting in the founder discount.

We thus have two explanations for the founder discount, one voluntary and one involuntary. Founders receive a great deal of psychic income and personal satisfaction from working on their ideas and may even embrace taking less compensation in order to help the startup. This was why the Lynx founders were underpaid—at first. But a labor of love can become a trap after the startup receives outside funding or forms a board of directors. Founders like those at Lynx, who feel underpaid but cannot bring themselves to leave their beloved startups in order to earn better pay, can be forced by their boards to continue to accept a salary discount.

In the end, Lynx's founders couldn't credibly threaten to leave on account of a raise. As founder James Milmo explained, "The board knew we were so attached to the company that we wouldn't walk away—we had too much vested in building the company to leave over short-term cash compensation. So they knew it was a bogus threat. . . . [Our artificially low salaries] ended up being an albatross around our necks" and a significant distraction.

However, a founder's power to negotiate a raise should increase over time. As a startup grows and its founders are forced to cede more and more ownership to investors and employees, we might expect them to become less profoundly attached—less like stewards and more like agents. Boards would then do well to adjust by closing the compensation gap between founders and nonfounding

---

* Stewardship theory tries to identify the psychological and situational circumstances in which an executive will be most likely to pursue organizational interests, even if they conflict with his or her self-interest (Davis et al., 1997). Agency problems are caused by the separation of ownership and control. However, young entrepreneurial firms are a classic instance of the union of ownership and control (Fama et al., 1983), making founders more likely to act as stewards or principals than as agents.

executives; that is, relying less on attachment/stewardship and more on compensation/agency. This is, in effect, what happened at Lynx. When the startup was several years old, the founders finally were able to negotiate a bigger slice of the rewards through an equity carve-out. My empirical results reinforce the notion that the founder discount shrinks as the startup grows. By the time startups grow to 100 employees, there is no significant difference between founder and nonfounder compensation. This evaporation of the founder discount is consistent with the disappearance of both its voluntary and involuntary causes.

CLOSING REMARKS

Splitting the equity is one of the most complicated and tension-filled of the founder's dilemmas. The natural inclination is to bypass the tension by taking the simplest route—an equal and static split. Founders should resist this urge, which is fraught with longer-term peril. Instead, they should seek the right time to split and use the right approach to doing so.

Splitting the equity too early is a recipe for continual renegotiation. If the business is still amorphous and the team composition is in flux, the founders should hold off negotiating the equity split. At the same time, an external event (such as an investment offer) or the need to provide a key cofounder with clarity about equity stakes (e.g., if he or she is being offered another opportunity) may force the team to split earlier than they want. In such a case, the dynamic element described below takes on even greater importance.

When things start to solidify, the founders should engage in a detailed attempt to match the initial split to each founder's expected long-term contributions. The template used by the UpDown team in Figure 6.6 offers a model. Although its details do not apply to every founding team (and some of its details were controversial even within the UpDown team itself), its overall structure and the process that that team followed can be generalized. Adapting this template to a particular startup provides the founding team with a structured approach to discussing complex emotional issues and

arriving at an initial split. As the founders begin to agree on particular terms, they should document those agreements in writing to
avoid later misunderstandings or miscommunication. Investor Jeff
Bussgang observes, "I find that the most common source of tension is the 'he said/she said' disagreements down the road, which
can be avoided by having well-documented, clear agreements or
contracts."

In the midst of negotiating such a tension-filled issue, each
founder should remember that working together is a long-term
proposition and that the equity-split negotiation can make or
break the team's relationship. Founders who treat the negotiation
as a "transaction" and try to maximize their own short-term deals
may poison the relationship and lose in the long term, securing a
larger slice of a smaller pie or increasing the chances that there will
be no pie at all.

It is possible that careful negotiation will arrive at the same
equal split that a quick handshake could have secured. Yet when
the time comes for the first round of financing, quick handshake
splits are associated with lower valuations than negotiated splits
(even negotiated equal splits). Why? One reason is that the equity-
split negotiation often acts as a trial by fire: If the founding team
survives the negotiation, it is often a stronger team able to tackle
tough issues. Better to find out sooner that the team has insurmountable difficulties making tough decisions together than to find
that out after each founder has sunk a lot of time and money into
a doomed startup.

The initial split should be accompanied by a dynamic element. To
take an extreme counterexample, if a team is sure that (a) its strategic focus, business model, customer base, and competitive situation
will not change and (b) each founder will remain fully committed
and contributing at a high level and that nothing will happen in his
or her personal life to affect that (which is obviously impossible to
know), then the team can decide on an equity split once and for all.
Otherwise, setting an early equity split in stone, without any way to
adjust it to expected or unexpected events, is one of the biggest mistakes a founding team can make. In a fast-changing startup, early

plans often change dramatically, making one cofounder's contribution more valuable than expected and another's less so. Even the most well-intentioned cofounder can cease contributing as he or she learns about the demands of a startup or as life intervenes. Such changes can leave the most important founders undercompensated while underperforming founders are overcompensated, leading to destructive tensions within the team.

Rather than succumbing to their natural optimism, founders should structure their equity split on the assumption that some aspects of the startup (such as its business model or strategy) and their founding team (such as the founders' roles or levels of commitment) *will* change. They should (a) define how foreseeable scenarios should affect the equity split and (b) "plan for the unforeseeable" by including buyout terms or similar means by which an underperforming cofounder's equity can be reclaimed by the other founders. Such terms encourage each founder to continue contributing and, failing that, let the remaining cofounders redeploy the underperforming cofounder's equity in order to replace him or her. Each founder is protected and so is the startup overall.

There is an inherent conflict in the fact that founders' contributions (relative or absolute) can never be precisely defined or measured while their equity stakes and cash compensation can be specified down to the decimal point. Nevertheless, cofounders have a very strong sense of what is fair or unfair. Indeed, my analyses with Matt Marx showed that cofounders who received less equity than they appeared to us to deserve (based on their backgrounds and early contributions to the startup) were significantly more likely to depart during the startup's early years.[*]

Founding teams who want to avoid the potentially disastrous consequences of an early and static equity split should do their best to devise a compensation plan (including the equity split) that (a) reflects each member's past and expected contributions as accurately as possible and (b) motivates each cofounder without seeming

[*] For more details, including how we estimated how much equity each cofounder "deserved," see Wasserman et al. (2008).

unfair to the others. Teams should also keep in mind that the deal is never completely done. Circumstances will change, and the equity split and compensation may need to change, too, in order to accomplish what these essential tools are meant to accomplish—an issue we will examine in Chapter 7.

CHAPTER SEVEN

THE THREE Rs SYSTEM: ALIGNMENT AND EQUILIBRIUM

IN EARLIER CHAPTERS, WE SAW HOW EVAN WILLIAMS'S INDIVIDUAL decisions about relationships, roles, and rewards affected Blogger. Now we can step back to see how those decisions acted in concert with each other to cause the Blogger founding team to disintegrate. For example, Evan's decisions to found with Meg, a prior girlfriend, and share the decision making with her gave Blogger an egalitarian structure that was seriously at odds with Evan's motivation—to maintain control of Blogger—as seen by his insistence on the CEO title and having more equity than Meg. Meg's status as a close friend coupled with the daily sharing of decisions led her to believe she shared control over Blogger; eventually Meg refused to accept Evan as the primary decision maker and left the startup. For Evan, deciding instead to found with a stranger or with a junior prior coworker (or to be a solo founder) and being careful not to share decision making would have aligned the roles and relationships with the unequal equity split and his own motivation, and would probably have avoided the painful and distracting team breakup. Misalignment can cause disaster.

BEYOND THE INDIVIDUAL DECISIONS: CONTEXT AND LINKAGES

On a test, each answer you give is right or wrong independently of the others. But for founding teams, multiple decisions must be

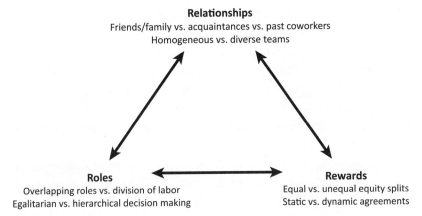

Figure 7.1. The Three Rs System

aligned in order to achieve successful outcomes for the startup. A decision made at one point can make a subsequent decision turn out badly, even if that subsequent decision might have turned out well in different circumstances. Decisions about relationships, roles, and rewards not only send startups down certain paths of development themselves, but also work against or in concert with one another in the struggle for growth, the acquisition of resources, and the retention of control of the startup. As suggested in Figure 7.1 and detailed below, our Three Rs are linked. Thus, a founding team's solutions to its relationship, role, and reward dilemmas must make sense not only individually but also collectively. As we will see throughout this chapter, the alternative to decisions that are aligned is a set of decisions that are at cross-purposes. At best, misalignment of the Three Rs will bring tension and dissension; at worst, it can blow up the founding team.

There is no perfect alignment that fits all situations and avoids all problems. The founding of Ockham Technologies, for example, began with a relationship decision: Jim chose to found with Mike, his former subordinate, and Mike chose to found with his former boss. They then chose roles and rewards that were aligned with their previous relationship: Jim became CEO with a 50% equity stake and Mike became vice president with a 30% equity stake.

This set of aligned decisions worked well. But it would surely not have worked so well at UpDown. Within that team of strangers and new classmates, crowning a CEO and adopting a very unequal equity split at the time of founding would have been out of alignment with their decision to found with people about whose capabilities and motivations they still knew so little. (Below, I describe theoretical reasoning and empirical evidence that support the riskiness of having these factors misaligned.) For this team, adopting an egalitarian approach to decision making, assigning overlapping roles to the two similar cofounders, and splitting the equity equally except for a small idea premium was a better-aligned system of decisions—yet one that would not have been aligned for Jim and Mike at Ockham.

Several times in Chapters 3 through 6, we saw the unhappy consequences of making quick and easy Three R decisions by default. The potential for disastrous consequences as a result of decisions like these is multiplied by the fact that there are linkages between the Three Rs. Understanding the causes of tension can be difficult for teams: Even one seemingly small decision, if misaligned with others, can tip the balance, and even one founder who is out of alignment with the others can cause an emotionally draining breakup. Because the effects of seemingly unrelated Three R decisions can be cumulative and hard to pinpoint, the concept of alignment offers an important tool for troubleshooting and resolving tension within a founding team. As we will see, the Three Rs framework gives such teams a structured approach for diagnosing the causes of tension— that is, for understanding the nature of the misalignments, resolving them, and creating a new equilibrium.

We have also seen that almost all the decisions a founding team makes are trade-offs. Even the "best" decisions about relationships, roles, and rewards bring risks as well as benefits. When these Three R decisions are aligned, those risks and benefits are brought into productive equilibrium. But, even when a team reaches a consistent equilibrium across the Three R system of decisions, it must be careful to reevaluate the system as the startup evolves and as unexpected events occur. As UpDown evolved, for example, the team's Three

Rs decisions—so well aligned at first—later became wholly inconsistent, bringing the team to the brink of a breakup, until it could achieve a new equilibrium. The need for dynamic alignment will be addressed later in this chapter.

We will start by examining the linkages between each pair of Rs—relationships-roles, relationships-rewards, and roles-rewards—to see how they can be aligned or misaligned, and then examine the need for a dynamic approach to the Three Rs system.

LINKING RELATIONSHIPS AND ROLES

In this section, we will look more closely at the linkages between relationships and roles. For example, how does the prior relationship influence the roles that founders play within their startups? Are there optimal ways to delegate roles and decision making depending on the type of prior relationship? We will treat each of our three types of prior relationships in turn, examining the role implications of founding with friends or close family, coworkers, and strangers.

Founding with Friends and Family

Prior relationships imply expectations of two kinds. We have descriptive expectations based on what we know from experience about another person's abilities, feelings, behavior, and so on. We also have prescriptive expectations that a friend or relative will not hurt our feelings, will not double-deal, will not throw away a friendship or family unity for the sake of a business advantage. But if these expectations are founded only on nonwork experience, they can be severely tested in the context of founding a startup, which can often be an extreme form of work experience. Such was certainly the case when Steve Wozniak found himself on the short end of a dishonest business deal made with the person he was expecting to behave as his best buddy.

Aside from the parent-child relationship, we do not expect our relatives and friends to have any more power over us than we grant them out of respect or affection. It would seem, then, that an egalitarian role structure would be better aligned with the decision to found with social relations than a hierarchical role structure would be. And indeed, I found in my dataset that the closer the prior social relationship, the more likely the team is to adopt an egalitarian approach to decision making. Teams of friends, for example, were 8% less likely to name a CEO than were teams of nonfriends. Used to being peers on a social basis, such cofounders tend to transfer the peer relationship to their professional relationship within the startup. The Stanford Project on Emerging Companies (SPEC) also found evidence of this strong linkage within high-tech startups. Of all startups in their study, 30% adopted the "commitment" model in which (a) employees are selected and monitored based on cultural fit and are attached to the organization like a family and (b) the founders emphasize universal buy-in for all major decisions. But of the startups in which family or friends of the founder were listed as key partners, fully five-sixths adopted the commitment model.[1] This effect of founding with family or close friends provides evidence that prior relationships can have a substantial influence on decision-making structures.

Founding with Coworkers

In contrast to teams with prior social relationships, teams of prior coworkers often find it more natural and better aligned to adopt a hierarchical structure, especially if one cofounder is more experienced than the other or if one has worked for the other. The roles and relationships reinforce each other rather than operate at cross-purposes, and there is less tension than there would have been otherwise. As noted in Chapter 4, this was the decision made by the founders of Ockham Technologies; their subsequent tension underscores the initial alignment of their original decision. At first, these prior coworkers—Mike had worked for Jim—adopted clearly hierarchical roles: Jim was founder-CEO and Mike was a vice president reporting to him. Tension arose when Jim included Mike in most of the decision making and on the board of directors. This de facto egalitarian decision-making structure gave Mike a role in his own mind that was at odds with his official role and, more to the point, with the role he had in Jim's mind. Thus, their relationship and their roles were no longer well aligned and had to be brought back into alignment. One possibility was to change the relationship: That is, they could agree to think of each other as peers rather than as former boss and subordinate—a hard shift to make. The other possibility was to change their roles. That is, Jim could take care to work with Mike as a vice president and not as a co-CEO. In fact, they took the latter route to realignment.

The cofounders of StrongMail—Frank Addante and his former subordinate Tim McQuillen—faced a similar dilemma. They, too, adopted a hierarchical role structure seemingly well aligned with their earlier work relationship: Frank became CEO and McQuillen was second-in-command. They, too, found this arrangement somewhat at odds with the more egalitarian day-to-day experience of founding a startup together. "The hardest part," Frank explained, "was transitioning from a role where he worked 'for' me to a role where we were building a business together. But [at Strong-Mail], I was still the CEO so technically he worked 'for' me. . . . [O]verall, it was a big positive because we had already developed mutual [professional] trust for each other."

In each case, the two cofounders discovered that early on, the demands of the startup made it more natural to adopt overlapping roles and collective decision making. This required an adjustment from their prior hierarchical relationships. However, as the startup grew and required a hierarchical structure, the cofounders' hierarchical roots enabled them to make that transition more smoothly.

Founding with Strangers

Relationships and roles must be aligned in terms of division of labor as well as of hierarchy. Choosing a cofounder with whom one has no prior relationship can affect the degree to which roles within the team are well defined and exclusive, though the effect can vary from one team to another. In part, this is because there is an inherent difficulty in aligning roles (or rewards) with what is actually the *lack* of a relationship.

One approach that at first seems to make sense is to adopt a clear division of labor in order to circumvent uncomfortable ambiguity. As Tim Westergren, founder of Pandora Radio, explained, "You need history if you want to do overlapping roles; if you don't have history, it's probably better to go for more defined roles. If you have overlapping roles [but no history together], you start to look at each other and wonder if you both need to be here." Such early clarity is understandably tempting to entrepreneurs as a way to reduce tension in the short term.

However, a quick division of labor carries the longer-term risk that, as the founders get to know each other and adapt to life within the startup, one or more of them will see a reason to reallocate roles. As Vivek Khuller of Smartix observed, "When the team doesn't know each other very well, where there are different domains, where you have little history of working together, it's best to delay it because things are still unknown and changing." Vivek's approach—adopting vaguely defined and overlapping roles until the cofounders know enough about each other to apportion the labor more precisely—can help avoid the risks of allocating roles blindly, but at the cost of early tension over roles. For instance, it took two earlier startups for members of FeedBurner's founding team, Dick Costolo and Steve Olechowski, to finally divide the roles among themselves. Even though they had worked together in the past, Dick did not realize that Steve would want to move away from pure software engineering and into business-oriented tasks—things that had traditionally been Dick's role—causing tension that was resolved as their startup grew enough to accommodate two business-oriented founders. Dick reflected, "There are lots of things you have to learn about each other. You can't anticipate how the executive team should split things up or what roles you should each play." But by the time they started FeedBurner, Dick explained, "we didn't need to discuss roles or equity. . . . We knew that Steve would be doing much less on architecture and programming. Now it was a given that he'd be the business-operations guy, dealing with legal, accounting, operations."

Reflecting on his team's experiences across their four startups together, Dick Costolo said, "Mapping out our roles early would certainly have helped." Amid the chaos of a startup, such role clarity is particularly attractive, and Dick naturally would prefer to have avoided the tension he experienced with Steve. However, with teams who are just getting to know each other, jumping too soon to define roles can be a big mistake, for if the roles are not allocated well and then have to be reassigned, tensions will be heightened rather than reduced, and the quality of work produced by the reassigned founder is likely to suffer. Thus, had Dick gotten his wish and split roles early with cofounders he barely knew, the team might not have made it through multiple startups together and not been together to build FeedBurner into the success it became.

LINKING RELATIONSHIPS AND REWARDS

Prior relationships have powerful determining effects, not only on role decisions, but also on the oft-contentious decision of how to split equity in a startup. A founding team's reward decisions must be aligned with the cofounders' prior relationships. As we have already seen in Chapter 6, when the differences within a team are below a certain threshold, the team tends to split the equity equally, but when they're above that threshold, the team tends to split the equity unequally. However, the team's prior relationships can have a strong impact on how high or low that threshold is. In particular, my analyses with Thomas Hellmann show that family relationships tend to raise the threshold. All other things being equal, if a founding team included at least one set of family members, it was more likely to split the equity equally. Researcher Martin Ruef's analyses of small-business equity splits also show that family relationships can skew equity stakes: When a core founder included a family member on the founding team, that family member received an equity stake that was 1.11 times the stake of a comparable non-family cofounder.[2] This can make for a serious misalignment if the family and non-family cofounders are not actually making roughly equal contributions to the startup. The cofounders of Dimon, a computer-game startup that Georg Ludviksson had cofounded before cofounding UpDown, had exactly this problem. Three of the six cofounders were siblings and the rest were close friends, so an equal equity split was far "easier" than a conflict-filled negotiation among friends and family members. But when investors required the three nonfamily cofounders to buy out the three family members who were no longer active in the startup, the buyout was "really painful" and left the three siblings feeling "unfairly treated."

We have already cautioned against the impulse to make quick equal splits in an attempt to avoid difficult negotiations. Yet in practice, we consistently see the association of family relationships with equal equity splits. To explain this tendency and determine its implications for the stability of the founding team, let's take a step back to examine equity theory.[3] Equity theory highlights the tight linkage between social factors (relationships) and economic factors (rewards). Prima facie, founding teams can be categorized as operating under a *social logic* or a *business logic*, depending on the type of prior relationship shared by the cofounders. For teams operating under a social logic, preserving personal relationships takes precedence over maximizing business success; for teams operating under a business logic, maximizing business success takes precedence over preserving personal relationships. Even a husband-and-wife founding team has to care about growth and profits, but such a team (if it is truly operating under a social logic, as one would expect) would choose a suboptimal business outcome if the optimal outcome could be achieved only at the cost of their marriage. When it comes to splitting equity, teams operating under a social logic will find the rule of *equal distribution*—distributing rewards equally, even if individuals have very different levels of contribution[4]—to be most aligned with the priority they give to their relationships. For instance, college roommates who operate under a social logic reward each other equally despite differences in individual performance.[5] In contrast, teams without prior social relationships and operating under a business logic (e.g., teams of former coworkers or teams of strangers) will find the rule of *equitable distribution*—distributing rewards in proportion to the value of each individual's

	Prior relationship	
	Social relationship (family, friends)	Prior coworkers
Rule of equal distribution	Stable team	Unstable team; inconsistent with business logic
Rule of equitable distribution	Unstable team; inconsistent with social logic	Most stable team

Basis for equity split appears at left spanning both rows.

Figure 7.2. The Linkage between Prior Relationships, Equity Splits, and Team Stability

contribution—to be most aligned with the priority they give to individual performance and business success.[6] Equity theory ultimately concludes that the best equity split for one type of team could be the worst equity split for another type of team, depending on the dominant logic operating in the specific circumstance.

Teams whose prior relationships and equity splits are aligned will, on average, be more stable and sturdy than those that are not. Indeed, Matt Marx and I, in our examination of founding-team turnover, found a compelling linkage among relationships, rewards, and team stability.[7] Figure 7.2 integrates the results of our quantitative analyses of founding-team stability with the field data from this part of the book and the theoretical lens of equity theory. Within the group of teams with prior social relationships (i.e., the ones presumably operating under more of a social logic), the most stable teams (i.e., the teams that are still fully intact after various amounts of time) tend to be the ones who split the equity equally. In contrast, within the group of teams with prior professional relationships (and presumably operating under a business logic), the most stable teams tend to be the ones who split equitably.

The results summarized in the figure drive home the dangers of making a key decision without considering its alignment with all of the other key decisions. Without knowing the cofounders' prior relationships, we can't state categorically that an equal split is better or worse for team stability than an unequal split. Knowing the type of relationship, however, does indeed lead to a particular approach to splitting that seems better aligned for team stability.

For founding teams of former coworkers, equitable (performance/contribution-based) equity allocations are well aligned with the cofounders' relationships in another way. Such allocations can act, over time, as a sort of natural selection: Poor performers may become dissatisfied with their comparatively lower rewards and leave,[8] increasing the team's proportion of high performers and therefore its long-term performance.[9] Such a weeding-out process would be painfully unaligned with the relationship choices of a team of relatives or friends.

Cofounders who have not only worked together previously but also founded startups together present a unique set of circumstances. Such "serial founding" teams (e.g., FeedBurner's team) possess far more knowledge about each other and a better feel for each other's commitment levels and motivations than any other grouping. They thus can make a well-aligned equity split much sooner, gaining the advantages of an early split without suffering many of the disadvantages otherwise associated with making such a decision too soon. However, even these teams should seriously consider adopting dynamic terms within the split, for the unexpected—illnesses, family crises, even visa problems—can happen to them, too.

Cofounders who have no previous acquaintance, either social or professional, need to align rewards with the relationship decision they have made; that is, with the lack of a prior relationship. The key here is for the cofounders to grasp how fully they do not know each other. Resumes, online bios, and even third-party recommendations can't tell you what makes a person tick and what contributions he or she will make, or fail to make, in the unpredictable growth of the startup, nor can they tell you a person's commitment level or whether he or she has what it takes to persevere through the scariest parts of the entrepreneurial roller-coaster ride. Such teams have much to gain by holding off their equity split until they have learned a lot more about each other, although they may pay a price for this benefit by sacrificing some of their ability to attract key cofounders (as did the Smartix team when it waited to split and thus lost the potential cofounder who had deep knowledge of and contacts in their industry). Once again, dynamic equity splits are an invaluable way for such teams of unfamiliar cofounders to deal with the trade-offs between attraction and motivation when facing the challenges of founding a startup.

LINKING ROLES AND REWARDS

While it is not surprising that hierarchy and division of labor affect equity splits, it is less commonly understood how their absence can also affect equity splits. Overlapping, nondistinct roles make it harder for cofounders to determine the value that each has contributed or will contribute to the startup and therefore make it more likely that the team will decide to split the equity equally. An unequal split would not be well aligned with such uncertainty about who really deserves what share.

On the flip side, clearly defined hierarchical roles tend to increase the likelihood of an unequal equity split. In particular, the person receiving the CEO title is often expected to contribute more value to the startup than anyone else. (A common exception is founding scientists or technologists in startups based on intellectual property they developed.) Evan Williams equated the CEO role with a bigger equity stake, as did Frank Addante; it wasn't until Frank was CEO in his later startups that he felt he could actively lobby for the largest piece of the pie. Both expected to make the largest contribution to the startup's success. At UpDown, Michael received a larger equity share than his original equal share and eventually became CEO as it became clear that he was making and would continue to make the largest contribution to the startup's success.

Indeed, my analyses with Thomas Hellmann show that, controlling for the other differences across founders, founder-CEOs receive a *CEO premium* (i.e., an additional amount of equity for being CEO) of 14 to 20 percentage points. The premium for founder-CTOs is lower—5 to 8 percentage points—but also highly significant from a statistical perspective. The idea premium discussed in Chapter 6 may also be, in part, a premium for adding greater value to the startup by initially articulating its vision, attracting other co-founders, and completing other critical early tasks often performed by the idea person. (Founders who serve on the official board of directors also play a different role than do otherwise similar founders. It is hard to assess whether such founders receive a *board premium*, because founders usually serve together on an informal board and often do not form an official board until after the equity split has been decided. However, serving on the board does provide executives with higher cash compensation than is received by equivalent nondirector executives;[10] eventual board membership could also affect founders' equity stakes.)

It isn't only teams that have to align their role and reward decisions; individual cofounders do, too. Cofounders who are motivated more by financial rewards than by control considerations should be willing to give up a better title or more central role in order to gain additional equity or cash compensation, while cofounders for whom becoming CEO is important might have to give up financial rewards to their cofounders in order to secure the title they want. My equity-split dataset suggests that some founding teams may be taking exactly this course: While in 39% of the startups, the founder-CEO held the largest equity stake (recall, there was an average CEO premium of 14–20 percentage points in this dataset), in 33% of the startups, the founder-CEO's equity stake was on par with his or her non-CEO cofounders, and, in 28% of the startups, a non-CEO member of the founding team received a higher equity stake than the founder-CEO did.* In some of these latter startups, the founders made conscious trade-offs between roles and rewards so that each cofounder would gain his or her own highest priority and be motivated to stick with the startup and give it his or her all. In others, the non-CEO contributed a scarce and critical nonmanagerial skill.

More broadly, as described briefly in each chapter of this part of the book but delved into more deeply in Part III, this need to make

---

* In half of the startups in which a non-CEO had the largest equity stake, he or she had received a VP-level title (which is unambiguously lower than a CEO title); in almost all of the others, the founder-CTO or founder-CSO received the largest equity stake.

trade-offs between (a) roles and decision-making control and (b) financial rewards recurs throughout each of the key dilemmas faced by founders, beginning with the first decisions they make regarding when to found and how to build their founding teams and continuing through the hiring, investor, and exit decisions that we will discuss in Part III. Chapter 11 highlights how these recurring decisions help determine whether the founder achieves a Rich outcome, a King outcome, neither, or, in rare cases, both.

The relationship between roles and rewards can also flow in the opposite direction; people who receive larger equity stakes may gain influence. One founder admitted that whenever people voiced an opinion or disagreed during a discussion, their relative equity stakes came to mind and affected how much weight he gave to their opinions.

The interaction of role decisions and equity decisions can have another important, long-term economic impact. Equity stakes are a scarce resource, and the allocation of equity is usually more efficient when the team has distinct roles than when the founders have overlapping roles and are therefore somewhat redundant. Instead of using scarce percentages of equity on overlapping founders, the startup could have used that equity to attract a cofounder with a missing type of human, social, or financial capital who would make the startup more valuable. In this way, the rewards structure would be better aligned with people's roles. Or, further down the line, those equity stakes could have been used to attract hires or investors to fill those holes and add value, as will be explored in Part III below. (This issue is exacerbated if the equity stakes are being held by fully vested drop-out founders, whose equity could have been reclaimed and redeployed if the team had adopted a dynamic equity agreement.) Thus, early inefficient uses of equity rewards within the founding team can leave the team handcuffed when it needs to fill necessary roles.

CLOSING REMARKS

When each pair of decisions is aligned, the team has achieved a "Three Rs equilibrium" in which tensions will tend to be low and the team can focus on building the value of the startup. But even then, there are at least three challenges that make the equilibrium particularly difficult to maintain.

Communication

Relationships, roles, and rewards are all sensitive issues that most teams try to avoid discussing. As the founder of a marketing-automation company observed to me about the tensions within his team, "The elephants in the room that no one wanted to bring up all fall into those categories." Some types of prior relationship, such as previous work experience together, facilitate raising role and rewards discussions within the team, but most types of relationship lead teams to avoid the tension of tackling those issues. If two cofounders find themselves stepping on each other's toes, for example, or one finds himself or herself working much harder on an exciting lead while the other is working on incremental product development, they may keep their frustrations to themselves so as not to disturb the team spirit. In a classic case of "not discussing elephants," it was the thought of losing his best friend that kept Steve Wozniak silent about his increasing unhappiness and frustrations at Apple. However, even reaching verbal agreements is often insufficient; founders should capture such agreements in writing to ensure clear communication and avoid later disagreements.

Change

Startups regularly face unexpected changes in personnel, competition, technology, economic conditions, regulation, and so on. Even if a team has achieved early alignment, it must be ready to adapt its arrangements or must have done the hard work early on to craft effective dynamic elements in its agreements, so that it can realign itself after the unexpected happens. As we will see in Part III, a particularly jarring change is when outside investors enter the picture, often changing the roles played by the founders, forcing realignment of their equity holdings and altering their relationships.

Inertia

Although early alignment can contribute to early success, it can also cause inertia and complacency that prevent effective adjustments to rapid shifts in the organizational environment.[11] So even when things seem to be proceeding smoothly, teams must proactively look ahead to the changes that will be caused by startup growth and evolution, plan for those changes (e.g., by setting expectations about when each founder might relinquish his or her C-level position), and regularly reassess the alignment of those arrangements.

Both change and inertia challenged the UpDown team, which seemed to have achieved an early equilibrium. The team's equity agreement in November 2006 was a quick, mostly even split, with 5% more to Michael for having the idea. The team shared decision-making power but assigned reasonably clear roles: Michael and Georg, who had similar backgrounds and skills, would focus on developing the business, while Phuc (the software engineer) would work on product development. All the founders planned to work full-time on the startup starting in the summer of 2007. Thus, the fairly equal equity split was in alignment with the expected contributions of the team members.

However, as the startup evolved over the next two months, Michael took the lead in business development, while Georg vacationed in Europe with his family and Phuc continued to work on his previous consulting commitments. Michael concluded that Georg's and Phuc's motivation and commitment—and therefore their contribution to the startup—were not equal to his. He recalled his frustration with the way the team responded to the first real possibility of gaining an outside investor: "I had planned to go on [a] student trip, but I cancelled that to work full-time on [UpDown]. At that point in time I also talked to Georg, but he said he was going to stay in Iceland until the end of the vacation. And Phuc was still involved in his prior consulting projects. So I was feeling very alone . . . while I was here working full-time. None of the [other] two were really working hard at that point in time. . . .

I [was] kind of scared [about] whether this [was] the right team to work with." The roughly equal roles and rewards that had previously been agreed upon were no longer in alignment, and the cofounders' relationship had progressed from being relative strangers to knowing each other much better.

Michael's crisis brought the team to the brink of dissolution and sparked a renegotiation of their roles and rewards in February 2007. The team recognized that their original assessment of each founder's past and future contributions had been incorrect, decided to award Michael more equity in consideration of his more involved role, and reached a new equilibrium. Yet that summer, an unexpected event threw the Three Rs out of alignment again: Georg failed to obtain a work visa in the visa lottery while Michael did receive one. Again, the cofounders had to realign their roles and rewards, with Michael receiving the CEO title and Georg receiving a greatly reduced share of the equity since he could no longer contribute an equal share of the work. This was their third equilibrium within a year, but they would have paid a far stiffer price had they refused to realign their relationships, roles, and rewards to their oft-changing circumstances.

Throughout this part of the book, we have examined how founders' natural inclinations can create pitfalls for their decision making and for their ability to build their startups. Passionate, confident founders often hear about the problems introduced by mixing social relationships with business roles, adopting egalitarian decision-making processes, and agreeing to quick-handshake equity splits, but want to believe that *they* are different, that *they* will be able to deal with it. One founder lamented to me, several months after his startup had failed, "Even after you showed us the data about the risks of founding with a friend and of splitting 50/50, we just figured, 'Those things happen to other people, they won't happen to us.'"

Cofounders who make these common decisions should know that they are playing with fire. Founder passion and confidence can blind them to the future implications of these early decisions. Heightened tension and instability within the founding team can make it hard for the startup to scale smoothly and can undermine the founder's ability to grow value while maintaining control. Founders are therefore imperiling their startups, and possibly their personal lives, if they do not force themselves to plan for the worst and to vigilantly watch for signs that their Three Rs equilibrium has fallen out of balance and needs to be reevaluated or renegotiated.

PART III
BEYOND THE
FOUNDING TEAM:
HIRES AND INVESTORS

INTRODUCTION

The dilemmas do not end once the founding team is in place. Founders continue to face momentous decisions about whether and how to involve other important parties in the startup. In particular, if the team has remaining holes, or as growth introduces a need for new human, social, and financial capital, the founders have to look to nonfounders who can provide these resources. The two most important of those parties are nonfounding hires—people who join the team as employees—and investors, who provide capital and might join the board of directors. Any startup that wants to grow beyond the founding team has to face the hiring dilemmas of whom to hire, what roles they should play, and how to structure their rewards.

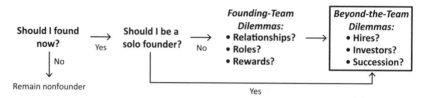

Figure III.1. Beyond-the-Team Dilemmas, in the Context of the Broader Set of Founding Dilemmas

Although fewer startups face the full range of investor dilemmas, most startups face important decisions about sources of financing and will benefit from understanding the full range of options and their repercussions. Often, the most important of those repercussions is founder-CEO succession, an outcome we examine in depth at the end of this part of the book. Figure III.1 places these new decisions about hires and investors in the context of the founding dilemmas examined throughout this book.

Founders must grapple with hiring and investor dilemmas over a long period, during which their startups can change dramatically regarding resources and the degree of formalization.[1] During the earliest *startup stage*, when the business idea is still being developed, the startup has little in the way of formal structure or processes and is usually severely resource-constrained. The founding team is often tight-knit, and the culture is informal and emphasizes creativity. Startups then go through a *transitional stage* that is most clearly characterized by two inflection points that affect the degree of formalization and the availability of resources: closing on the initial rounds of outside funding and completing the development of the first product. Both changes add resources (outside capital and customer revenues, respectively) but also call for new skills and processes within the organization. The division of labor deepens and decision making increasingly shifts away from the founders. As the startup enters the *mature stage*, it becomes relatively well funded and usually has a steady revenue stream from a standardized product or service line. Decision making is decentralized across functions and becomes more hierarchical; there is much less of a premium on flexibility. New executives, often with prior experience in larger companies or with specialized skills, often replace or become managers above the early employees (or even founders), who do not have the experience, expertise, and networks to lead and grow an entire division or department.

As the startup progresses through these stages,[*] founders' preconceived ideas about how they want their organization to look and operate sometimes conflict with the needs of the growing organization or the agendas of the new players, adding complexity to the founders' hiring and financing decisions. Attracting hires and investors forces the founders to make difficult trade-offs, because the more scarce and valuable an outside resource is, the more its owner can demand for it.[2] (In the case of personnel, the owner *is* the resource.) To attract the best hires, for example, founders have to give up not only enough cash compensation and equity ownership but also some level of control over operational decisions; skilled people usually don't like to be told what to do. To attract the best investors, founders have to give up significant amounts both of equity and of control over many board-level decisions. As we will see, this means that attracting the best resources can put severe constraints on the founders. It can even cost them control of the CEO position and of the board of directors.

OVERVIEW OF CHAPTERS

The first two chapters of this part of the book introduce the major players and dilemmas in these beyond-the-founding-team decisions. The third chapter delves into what is sometimes the ultimate consequence of involving outside investors, founder-CEO succession, which requires the hiring of the first nonfounding CEO. A brief overview of the chapters in this part follows:

---

[*] Although we outline this general sequence of stages, different functions within startups may go through them at different rates. The technical function, for example, may reach Stage 3 (mature) while the sales and marketing function is still in Stage 1 (startup).

Chapter 8: Hiring Dilemmas—Even after launching the startup, the team may still have holes or the startup's growth may require new people with particular skills. In each stage of growth, founders face important trade-offs regarding whom to attract as employees (i.e., whether or not to hire people with whom they already have relationships), what roles to give them, and what rewards to offer in order to attract and retain them.

Chapter 9: Investor Dilemmas—Investors can provide founders with human capital, social capital, and financial capital with which to build the startup. However, different types of investors provide very different amounts of value and introduce different risks for the founders. In this chapter, we compare the trade-offs of taking money from friends-and-family investors, angel investors, and venture capitalists.

Chapter 10: Failure, Success, and Founder-CEO Succession— The replacement of the founder-CEO with the first non-founding CEO is a critical inflection point for many startups. We will look at why and how this happens (there are numerous variations), who triggers the change and how that affects the succession process, and what are the best and worst practices for the transition process.

Unless otherwise noted, the data in this part of the book come from the full decade of surveys, 2000–2009, which includes more than 19,000 founding and nonfounding executives from more than 3,600 private startups.

CHAPTER EIGHT

HIRING DILEMMAS: THE RIGHT HIRES AT THE RIGHT TIME

EITHER AS AN ALTERNATIVE TO ATTRACTING COFOUNDERS (SEE Chapter 3) or as a way to augment a founding team that still has gaps, hires play an important role in the growth of many start-ups. Yet, even the most adept founders—those who have proven their leadership abilities by assembling a well-functioning founding team—can find subsequent hiring decisions difficult and dangerous. Founders naturally bring their own preferences to these decisions, but often fail to appreciate how growth and change will force them to rethink their preferences and realign their organizations. Decisions that seem ideal at first can prove disastrous, as employees at all levels struggle to scale with the maturing startup.

For a serial founder, decisions that worked well for one startup can be entirely wrong for another. When Evan Williams founded Blogger, his vision of universal access to self-expression on the Internet was more important to him than maximizing the startup's value. He structured the startup like a loyal tight-knit family; his first hires were dedicated friends and colleagues, mainly young self-taught programmers like himself. Later, to keep Blogger running when money was scarce, Evan relied on volunteers, who were willing to work for the "love" of the company and its vision, and contract employees recruited from Craigslist and blog posts. He hired young and cheap.

By the time of his next startup, Odeo, Evan had worked several months at Google (which had bought Blogger) and had established an entirely different vision for his new startup: a more professional organization that valued the advanced experience and expertise of its employees and that would achieve maximum value as quickly as possible in anticipation of a lucrative exit. To this end, he raised a large amount of VC funding and used it to employ executive recruiters to hire several talented programmers and experienced, high-level executives to head up marketing and engineering. Evan's hires at Blogger had required close supervision, but now Evan had to relinquish decision-making power to these senior hires.

How can we understand the decisions that Evan made and how they affected his startups?

The work of the Stanford Project on Emerging Companies (SPEC) in its study of employee-relations "blueprints" in high-technology startups provides a useful framework for understanding founders' hiring decisions.[1] The study sorted the responses of a large sample of founders along three dimensions: recruitment, rewards, and control. Respondents articulated three bases of recruitment, three bases of rewards, and four means of coordinating and controlling work.[*] Although there are 36 ($3 \times 3 \times 4$) potential permutations of these factors, five of those permutations—which the researchers call "blueprints"—accounted for 67% of the startups.[†] SPEC also found that

---

[*] The three *bases of recruitment* were short-term skill set, long-term potential, and values/attitudinal fit. The three *bases of rewards* were "love" or affiliation, "work" or a purposive drive to create something great with the company, and "money." The four *means of coordinating and controlling work* were "formal" oversight through job descriptions and HR procedures such as performance reviews and job descriptions, "direct" oversight through monitoring and influencing behavior, "informal" control through peer reinforcement and culture, and "professional" control through hiring from elite sources and assuming a degree of prior socialization in the employee.

[†] These five are (a) the "star" blueprint, with recruitment based on potential, rewards based on cutting-edge work, and control through elite socialization; (b) the "engineering" blueprint, with recruitment based on skills, rewards based on cutting-edge work, and control through peer enforcement; (c) the "commitment" blueprint, with recruitment based on fit, rewards based on love of the organization, and control through peer enforcement; (d) the "bureaucracy" blueprint, with recruitment based on immediate skill set, rewards based on work, and control through formal HR mechanisms; and (e) the "autocracy" blueprint, with

sticking with the chosen blueprint was a vital factor in a startup's success. Throughout the course of the study, only 10.9% of startups deviated from their original blueprint along all three dimensions, and they were 2.3 times as likely to fail as firms that kept to one blueprint.[2]

Viewing Evan Williams's experiences through this lens, we can see that at Blogger, where Evan was motivated to pursue a vision, he used a "commitment" blueprint—recruitment was for fit with the family-like culture, pay was low because employees were willing to work for love of the startup, and control was informal. On the other hand, when he was motivated to maximize Odeo's value, Evan used a "bureaucracy" blueprint—recruitment was for experience and functional skills, pay was commensurately high (requiring outside financing), and control was through a formal hierarchy.

As we have seen throughout, decisions in one domain can affect another domain. For instance, Evan's choices of hiring blueprints affected the rate at which his startups passed through the stages of the organizational life cycle. His preference for control over Blogger—his wish to keep it focused on his vision—caused him to hire a small number of inexpensive employees, but this also meant that Blogger would grow more slowly than it might otherwise have done. With Odeo, Evan was more motivated by the prospect of a quick and profitable exit and took a professional—and resource-intensive—approach to hiring that would accomplish that.

The dilemmas that founders face in choosing new hires, like those they face in choosing cofounders, fall into the Three Rs framework of relationships (whom to hire), roles (what positions to create or upgrade, when to do so, and what types of people to hire into them), and rewards (the compensation and equity used to attract and retain hires). Founders have to make different Three Rs decisions depending on their motivations and blueprints, and then adjust their decisions during the different stages of the startup life cycle.

---

recruitment based on immediate skill set, rewards based on financial remuneration, and control through direct oversight.

RELATIONSHIPS

Where do startups find their senior executives? Do those hires already have strong ties to the founder-CEO or to others in the startup?[*] As with many of the decisions examined in this chapter, the answers depend in part on the stage of the startup.

The Founder-CEO's Hires versus the Investors' Hires

Founder-CEOs of fast-growing startups often find that the quickest and easiest way to meet the new challenges that continually arise is to tap their own networks to find executives for their teams,[3] or to rely on other members of the organization to help find them. My data show that, across all C-level and VP-level hires, founder-CEOs are the source of 49% of all hires—by far the biggest share.[4] Tapping their own networks to find hires provides the benefits of comfort and access, but also business benefits: Founders who hire via their networks are able to build more coherent organizations and to attract employees who are more receptive to the organization's control systems, freeing up the founders to focus on non-HR issues.[5] When founder-CEO Genevieve Thiers began to hire people for her startup, an online babysitting site called Sittercity, she used her personal network because "hiring and managing people is a new thing for me. I definitely don't want to come out of the gate and have the wrong hire. So initially I decided to hire people I knew because it felt less risky."

All three original founders of Pandora Radio, an online-music startup, preferred to staff their new company with friends and personal contacts, believing such employees would take more responsibility, make more sacrifices, and be more proactive for the company. Founder Tim Westergren explained his thinking about hiring friends:

[*] "Strong" and "weak" ties refer to the degree to which people are connected and have a prior interpersonal relationship. The strength of the tie depends on the amount of time people have been connected, the emotional intensity and intimacy of the relationship, and the degree of reciprocity. For more information, see Granovetter (1973).

"I'm a huge believer in hiring people you know. Friends will be the ones who go to the mat for you, do it out of loyalty, and would be in the boat with us, as opposed to just being employees. We were able to engender that sense of ownership in a very strong way." Research seems to bear him out. When hiring nonfounding executives, high-potential startups that relied relatively heavily on the founders' personal networks received valuations that were 37% higher than those received by startups that barely tapped the founders' networks.[6] Playing such a central role in hiring executives can give the founder-CEO a closer initial relationship with his or her direct reports, though at the cost of having to spend more of his or her own time recruiting those people than if an HR function or third-party recruiter were handling the task.

CEOs tend to feel more comfortable with hires they already know, especially compared to the hires who come from the next most common source—the startup's investors and board members. During the earliest stages of growth, investors are the source of few hires, but by the second round of financing, the founder-CEO is finding fewer members of the team and investors account for 19% of executive hires. Hires found through investors often have no tie to the CEO but a strong tie to the investor. Such hires may, in fact, be more aligned with the investor than with the CEO for whom they are supposed to be working, introducing potential agency issues and loyalty challenges that the founder-CEO has to manage.

This is particularly true for CFOs. Investors are a source of 26% of all CFO hires, a far higher percentage than for any other non-CEO position. If a CEO's network does not include solid CFO candidates, the investors may be playing a valuable role by finding CFOs for their startups. Some founders, however, take a darker view of the preponderance of investor-chosen CFOs; one referred to them as "the investors' eyes and ears, their spies on the team." Another founder observed that, while the founder is still CEO, the CFO position is one of "the main levers for investors" who focus on "picking a CFO who can keep tabs on how their capital is being used and on the startup's performance." In contrast, investors apparently focus much less on building ties to other potential executive hires, such as

CTOs (for which investors serve as the source of only 13% of hires), COOs (16%), and the layer of VPs below them (14%).

Of executive hires, 15% are found through a non-CEO member of the executive team; these hires do not have a strong tie to the founder-CEO but do have a strong tie to one of the CEO's subordinates or to another member of the founding team. When James Milmo, co-founder and chairman of Lynx Solutions, first started building the Lynx team, he and the founder-CEO realized that they were too busy to handle all of the hiring, "so we set out to hire someone to do the hiring. I got in touch with a friend from [college] whose judgment in people I really trusted. He had never done HR stuff before, but I asked him to be our head of hiring. . . . That was our most important hiring decision because he could hire a lot more people than we could. Plus, he did a great job of extending our hiring philosophy."

The founder-CEO's centrality in hiring diminishes as the startup grows. Figure 8.1 shows that, before startups have raised any outside financing, their founder-CEOs are the sources of two-thirds of their C-level and VP-level executive hires. But as the startup matures, this percentage drops, possibly because the founder-CEO is running out of good candidates he or she already knows. As Genevieve Thiers of Sittercity observed, "I realized quickly that, to get the best people possible, I would have to go outside my network." Also, at this point, new players—investors and other outside directors—start bringing in hires with whom the founder-CEO does not have a relationship. By the time the second round has been raised, the founder-CEO accounts for fewer than half of all hires; this percentage continues to drop in subsequent rounds but remains higher than that of any other source through the fourth round of financing.

Casting a Wide Net versus Getting Cultural Fit

After the Lynx founders had tapped their personal networks, they began casting a wider net. For instance, they placed want ads in newspapers: "Our job postings stood out. They seemed like they were not written by HR people. [One of our early hires] was a Columbia B-school intern who we got to drop out of school and join

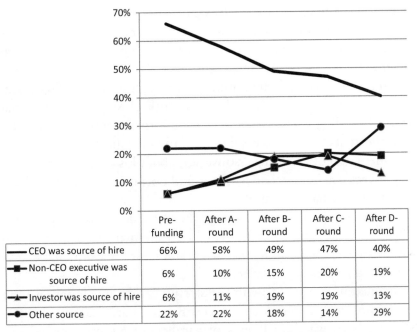

	Pre-funding	After A-round	After B-round	After C-round	After D-round
——— CEO was source of hire	66%	58%	49%	47%	40%
—■— Non-CEO executive was source of hire	6%	10%	15%	20%	19%
—▲— Investor was source of hire	6%	11%	19%	19%	13%
—●— Other source	22%	22%	18%	14%	29%

Figure 8.1. Sources of Executive Hires in Startups Led by Founder-CEOs

us full-time. He said the reason he applied to us was he saw our ad that said you could 'work in shorts.' It caught his eye." More broadly, hires can come from a variety of weaker ties, including executive-search firms, want ads, cold submission of resumes, and other sources beyond the networks of the founders and other participants in the startup. As shown in Figure 8.1, these weaker-tie sources of hires are important throughout all stages of startup evolution, accounting for between 14% and 29% of hires during each stage and averaging 20% across all stages. For job seekers of all types, weak ties can be a path to higher-status jobs.[7] For founder-CEOs, though, relying on such weak ties can make it hard to judge an individual hire's cultural fit with the rest of the organization and, overall, hard to keep turnover low.[8]

As the team grows beyond the founders, its dynamics change dramatically. The tight-knit founding team has to integrate executives and employees who may have very different motivations (they may, for example, see themselves as agents rather than stewards[*]) and skills (they may, for example, be much more specialized), but without whose contributions the startup cannot take the next step in growth. At the same time, new hires also have to be prepared for the challenges of integrating into a tight-knit founding team. As do other groups of people who work closely on challenging tasks, founding teams often develop informal routines, processes, and shortcuts that outsiders find hard to understand. Dick Costolo, founder-CEO of FeedBurner, observed about his cofounders, "Early employees can be shocked by the brutal openness and the less-than-courteous exchanges between people who've worked together for 11 years, and you have to manage the introduction of these people with clear messages such as, 'If we start annoying you with verbal shorthand, just remind us that we're not the only people here anymore and to please elaborate.'"

Evaluating a hire's fit with the startup can be much harder than evaluating his or her skills. At FeedBurner, Dick learned this lesson the hard way, but later saw parallels to his prior experience in improvisational comedy teams. Early in the startup, he recalls, "We had hired people who looked great on paper: the guy who had all the right credentials, great grades, knew all the programming languages. But during an interview, I often got the feeling, 'Not really one of us.' At [my prior startup] Spyonit, we would have hired him anyway, but seeing the problems it caused reminded me of the problems I had seen with the team of 'improv' all-stars, where the fit between personalities was so much more important than just finding people who [were very good comedians in their own rights]."

The Playing-with-Fire Gap: The Risks of Hiring Friends and Family

Given the comfort with people one already knows and the greater likelihood that they will fit in together, founder-CEOs find it very tempting to fill their teams with such hires. But this comfort comes at a cost, for such a team faces the same "playing-with-fire" risk that we

---

[*] See "The Founder Discount" in Chapter 6 for a brief description of agency theory versus stewardship theory.

saw founding teams facing in Chapter 4: Teams whose members have prior personal relationships may be less likely to discuss sensitive issues and may also face major damage to those relationships if things go sour in the startup. Recall that Evan Williams's team at Blogger included friends and former colleagues; when Blogger ran out of money, Evan not only lost employees, but also lost his social circle.

Tim Westergren enthusiastically hired friends at Pandora, but also experienced the downside: "You're mixing friendship with business. [At Pandora], we had to make a lot of thorny choices that negatively impacted our employees. The friendship had to come second because we had a higher responsibility to the collective. [But even though we made that choice,] we [still] suffered for that person. One of the quintessential questions for a manager is: If you are going to have layoffs, when do you tell people? When they are a friend you can see the absolute conflict, you want to give them fair warning—you want to give them all this time. But that's not the right answer for the company. So what do you do? It's a 'Sophie's Choice'—there is no winning answer for you as a person. You either do something that is against [your friend's] interest or against the interest of the broader company."

Hiring people who have strong ties to other cofounders can introduce similar problems in dealing with underperformance. One founder related, "I made the mistake of trusting my founder/friend to hire the right people for operations. He oversold his family members' abilities and I ended up in a company with people who are virtually impossible to fire and who get paid far more than their skill set is worth. They also don't want anyone rocking the boat for them." Another founder said, "After founding a software company with a friend who went and hired his family, my firsthand experience is that the dynamics of friendships—and worse, family—in a company can really create some miserable situations for people who are not part of the family power clique."

ROLES

Founders tend to start out with a flat, top-heavy organizational structure (described in Chapter 5), taking C-level titles for themselves and hiring few, if any, people below them to whom they can delegate tasks. However, as the startup matures, it gains more resources and becomes more formalized, enabling the founders to hire people below them to whom they can delegate tasks and thus make better use of their own time. They can gain efficiency, but must also face two major challenges described below: creating new C-level and VP-level positions that did not exist before and "upgrading" existing positions by replacing founders and early hires with hires more suited to the new demands of those positions.

When to Create New Positions?

Figure 8.2 shows that, as startups mature, executive teams go through two major changes. The first is a steady growth in the size of the team, from an average of about 3.5 executives to almost 6 by the time the startup raises its fifth round of financing. The second is the transition from top-heavy teams dominated by C-level executives (mainly founders, as described in Chapter 5) to teams in which VP-level executives finally outnumber the C-level executives after the fifth round of financing. But exactly which of those positions will be created and when?

At the C-level, the major new position is CFO. Only 4% of startups designate a founder as CFO (or head of finance) during their early stages. As startups mature and their financial challenges become more complex, they hire CFOs (or, less frequently, assign that position to someone already in the company); 70% of mature startups have a nonfounding CFO. Less common in young startups is the creation of the COO role (or, often interchangeably, the president role); before the first round of financing, 33% of startups have a COO/president (of which one-third are founders), but this percentage hasn't increased four rounds later. It may be that most young startups have little need for a COO/president beyond giving one of the founders a C-level title or backing up an operationally deficient CEO. Bill Holodnak, head of executive-search firm J. Robert Scott, says, "If a startup has a COO, it's a red flag: Either the COO doesn't belong or the CEO doesn't." Bill's statement paints all startups with

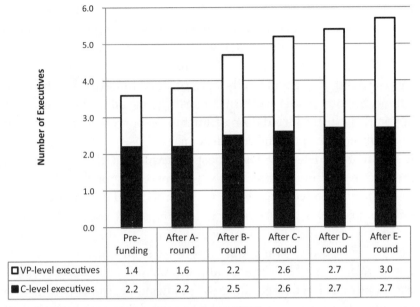

	Pre-funding	After A-round	After B-round	After C-round	After D-round	After E-round
☐ VP-level executives	1.4	1.6	2.2	2.6	2.7	3.0
■ C-level executives	2.2	2.2	2.5	2.6	2.7	2.7

Figure 8.2. Changes in Executive Teams as Startups Mature

a broad brush, but captures the need for startups to evaluate their teams carefully before adding such positions.

As suggested by Figure 8.2, many more new positions are created at the next level down, where the vice president title is typically used. The first VP-level position created is often the VP-sales; even before raising the first round, 37% of startups have a VP-sales (4% have a founder in that position, 33% have hired a nonfounder to fill it). The next most common early-stage VP position is VP-marketing (found in 22% of pre-financing startups), followed by VP-engineering (20% of startups), VP-business development (19%), and VP-human resources (19%). As startups mature, gain resources, and formalize, they steadily add these specialized roles. After the fourth round of financing, 57% of startups have a VP-sales, 44% have a VP-engineering, 37% have a VP-marketing, and 36% have a VP-business development. (Other startups may be using below-VP people to fill these roles. In addition, in three-quarters of the fastest-growing companies in the *Inc. 500*, a founder still served as the company's chief or only salesperson, even though the founder's title often did not explicitly acknowledge that role.)[9]

The one exception is the VP-human resources; even after the fourth round of financing, only 20% of startups have one. The team behind Spyonit and FeedBurner can help us understand why. At Spyonit, the team hired a VP of human resources early on, but in their subsequent startup, FeedBurner, they chose not to delegate that function. Founder-CEO Dick Costolo explained the evolution of the team's thinking on this issue: "[At Spyonit], none of us wanted to run hiring, so we brought in a person to run HR when we were only six people. A year later, we're looking at the code, asking why a certain component has so many bugs, and only then did we realize that we had hired several people who weren't cutting it! . . . The HR guy was telling us, 'This is a good person.'. . . A year in, we realized we should not have hired the guy. . . . Hiring decisions became the HR guy's decisions, not the team's." Dick said that at the team's next startup, FeedBurner, "We asked, 'What part of the General & Administrative [functions] do we want to offload first?' and this time we decided to offload finance instead of HR. . . . We wanted to do all the interviewing ourselves this time and it made it easier to have someone take responsibility for the finance stuff." Other startups combine the HR responsibilities with other tasks rather than having a person dedicated to HR, or use junior people to perform the administrative HR tasks.

As startups mature, they also begin hiring aggressively below the executive level. One metric we can use to examine this evolution is *structural leverage*—the number of nonexecutive employees per executive.[10] As shown in Figure 8.3, startups begin life with very low structural leverage, about 2.5 employees per executive, which steadily increases as the startup matures. By the time the startup raises its fifth round of financing, there is an average of 9.0 employees per executive, a situation with very different managerial challenges than the earlier low leverage. If an organization's tasks are such as can be delegated, and if the senior executives manage their employees effectively, increasing structural leverage can increase the

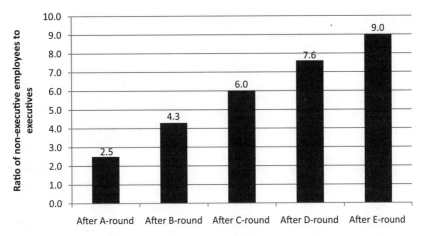

Figure 8.3. Changes in Structural Leverage as the Startup Grows

firm's performance as junior employees provide support for senior executives while learning best practices from them.[11]

The hiring process itself can force the organization to become more formalized.[12] Creating job postings is often the first time a startup has to concretely define job requirements and think about the differences between various positions or roles, making such postings the startup's first real job descriptions. Each new hire also puts added pressure on the organization to be more explicit about processes and decision criteria, especially when the new hires have prior experience with formalized organizations and yearn for the additional clarity that can come from formalization. Dick Costolo relates how, at FeedBurner, "We brought in a person on the West Coast to run partnerships when Steve and I were both spending time on partners, and this person ended up having some issues with, 'Who am I reporting to, you or Steve? I'm getting different answers from each.' As we start to grow, we can't have a loose oligarchy; we need people to be in charge of different things. . . . Pieces of the organization that we wanted to be very fluid, other people wanted to force them into having more structure." Alternatives to ordinary hierarchy, such as matrix structures or dual-report arrangements, can work in startups, but they introduce an even greater need for explicit discussion about roles and responsibilities.

When Should I Upgrade Existing Positions?

As startups grow, the demands on each position also tend to grow. For instance, the CTO whose job at first was to perform initial system design and development eventually becomes responsible for hiring and leading a technical team, which requires very different abilities. Likewise, the VP-sales, who began simply as the first salesperson, later finds himself or herself called upon to hire and lead a sales team and design a sales process and sales-compensation system, responsibilities that are very different from selling. Some founders and early employees are able to grow and develop as the demands of their positions accelerate and as they need to change from "player" to "coach." But in a fast-growing startup, the demands will grow more quickly than most people can learn and the startup must decide whether to leave a crucial task in the hands of a founder or loyal early employee who can't really handle it or to replace that person with someone who can handle it.

By any normal business standard, upgrading the quality of the person in the position makes more sense. Indeed, many startups do upgrade positions as they grow; in all C-level and VP-level positions, the percentage of founders is lower after the third round of financing than it was after the first round of financing.[*]

When some founder-CEOs sense that one of their employees is underperforming, they immediately act to remove the person. One said, "Knowing *for sure* that someone has to go is hard, but I have learned that if I start thinking someone needs to go, they need to go. It is always the right call to upgrade when you realize someone can't or isn't succeeding."

However, the decision to replace an underperformer is not always as obvious as it might seem. In a startup, the shock to a small, tight-knit team could be considerable. In many cases, even when the damage an underperformer is doing to the company's value is clear, the founder-CEO or other founders simply can't bring themselves to

---

[*] In my dataset, it was lower by 4 to 17 percentage points, depending on the specific position and controlling for changes in the number of all such positions.

throw one of their own overboard. Particularly when the division of labor is not very clear, the lack of individual accountability can be a trap. It can be too hard for the founder-CEO to justify an underperformer's dismissal to others on the team, or it can be too easy for the CEO to convince himself or herself that the underperformer isn't really doing that badly. Founders may not even be able to bring themselves to discuss the problem (and possibly find some other solution)—a perfect example of the playing-with-fire risk associated with teams whose members have prior personal relationships. But keeping the underperformer may also have real advantages, allowing the startup to retain valuable knowledge, connections, and relationships and showing other employees that loyalty is reciprocated. Upgrading can leave other team members disillusioned with the costs of growth; startups are often populated by people who value the mission and the camaraderie more than maximum profit. In addition, the more idiosyncratic the functional background of the first holder of a newly created position, the harder it is to find a replacement who will be able to stay in that position for a long time,[13] increasing the risk to the organization.

Such situations emphasize the dangers introduced when a founding team adopts early C-level titles. Title inflation may be good for attracting potential cofounders or early hires to the startup, but it can stand in the way of upgrading the team when that becomes necessary. According to Barry Nalls, founder-CEO of Masergy, "Early on, there's the CEO, and then you have to decide who else is hired at what titles. Do we hire him as a manager or as a VP reporting to the CEO? Early in the company's life, you don't have the ability to give them more salary, but titles are cheap to give out so you use that to make the package more attractive. They're currently a 'manager' in their company, so if they come in as a 'director,' they'll feel as if they've gotten a promotion. But, then they can't scale with the startup and that inflated title causes big problems." The person who enjoys having a senior title naturally resists being pushed a level or more downward by a new hire. This certainly caused problems for Nalls in his own high-growth company: "Our VP of sales started off managing two people the first year. Responsibilities quickly expanded the following year to managing people across the U.S. and, the year after that, to managing people in London and international sales. After three years, it was evident I needed to hire a 'true' VP of sales, so I hired a 'senior VP' above him. I realized that, in every place I could, I had to set expectations and explain to someone who was being hired as a direct report to me that, 'At some point in the future, I'll be hiring a boss for you. You'll have the ability to compete for the position, but someone else from outside the company could take the job.' Saying that doesn't quite work—anyone aggressive at all wants to believe they can work at a higher level. In fact, that aggressiveness is why we want them in the first place, but they usually don't scale." Clear communication and regular expectation setting are tough to accomplish, but a startup needs to have them. Even when it does, though, management challenges usually remain.

Whom to Hire When?

When deciding whom to hire into each of these new or upgraded positions, founders face at least two major trade-offs: hiring generalists versus specialists and hiring inexperienced versus experienced people. What's more, the trade-offs shift as the startup gains resources and becomes more formalized. Making the wrong decision at a particular stage of startup evolution can cause major problems, either immediately or down the road.

Generalists versus Specialists: Option Value versus Depth

Each time a startup hires a new employee, it faces a choice between hiring a specialist, who can usually be counted on to do a specific task well, or a flexible generalist or jack-of-all-trades, who cannot do any particular task as well as a specialist could but can move across multiple tasks more effectively than a specialist could.

Which choice is best depends very much on how formalized the function in question has become, which is dependent both on the startup's stage of development and on that specific function. When startups are founded, their founders often have a solid initial idea of what product or service they want to develop and sell. However, they face many uncertainties about their strategy for doing so, the business model they will use to make money, and even what the oft-changing idea will look like several months from now. They resist formalizing processes or creating specialized roles, allowing each person's tasks to change daily to match the fluidity of the startup's strategy, business model, and product-development efforts. At this early stage, flexibility is a priority.

Early-stage startups therefore tend to seek generalists who can pitch in wherever needed.[14] Even if a hire is assigned to a specific function, there is high "option value" in being able to move that person to another function as the work dictates. Founder-CEO Dick Costolo said that, of FeedBurner's first 20 employees, "In the end, five of our original twenty moved into radically different positions at some point." This flexibility is particularly important for functions that are still fluid or still face important uncertainties. For instance, if developing the product requires the team to resolve important technical or scientific uncertainties, then the technical or scientific functions will not be as stable and well defined as they are in startups for which the technology or science are well defined but there is much uncertainty about the market and its need.

During this fluid stage—and especially for functions that are still evolving—hiring specialists who excel at specific tasks but cannot, or would not want to, contribute to other tasks can be a big mistake. Hiring the world's greatest cellist could come back to haunt you if you're not sure yet whether you are an orchestra or a marching band and, if you turn out to be a marching band, the cellist or the band will be in for a tough time. Dick Costolo learned this lesson the hard way in his first startup, DKA, when the team hired an experienced and aggressive VP of sales, who immediately requested a demonstration version of the product to help the sales effort. The problem was that the product had not yet solidified enough for a true demo. Dick explained, "The user-interface people . . . put stuff in the demo that we couldn't implement later. So the customers saw things we could only do in a demo environment and it led to inevitable customer disappointment when they didn't get it in the product itself. It was a double negative; it also distracted our software people from getting actual product done for us to sell. It was a major time sink and opportunity cost." The team tried to slow the sales effort and redeploy that VP elsewhere, Dick recalled, but "we had hired a guy who was specifically a VP-sales and couldn't be anything else."

After that costly experience, Dick placed a premium on hiring flexible people in the early days of his subsequent startups: "We might be hiring for a specific role, but we . . . look for someone who could go do other things if the company heads in another direction in the next 5–6 months."

However, as major uncertainties are resolved and the startup begins locking down its technologies and strategies, flexibility becomes less valuable. The option value of being able to move employees from area to area is far lower and the value of having a specialist excel at a task is much higher. Over time, this accentuates what was earlier a less obvious cost of hiring generalists instead of specialists—the lower quality of the generalists' work. Drawing an analogy to athletes, Dick Costolo said, "With our early finance hire, it was like he had played wide receiver in college and we thought he could play defensive back in the pros so we drafted him. Then, we didn't use him as a defensive back and he ended up being only the third-best wide receiver. Oh well!"

As the organization grows, it usually tries to improve its efficiency by starting to formalize processes and structures. Dick recalled, "Our first CFO always wanted to have org charts for the board because they add a lot of structure to the board [presentation], but there was no org chart until the end of 2004. I was perfectly happy month to month moving people around when we didn't find people we wanted to hire." FeedBurner created its first formal organizational chart when it passed 20 employees and began to hire for specific and permanent positions. Mirroring a common pattern,[15] FeedBurner's technical functions were the first to become more specialized: "The business needs more of an emphasis on specialists now. In engineering, we need great Java architects who can jump into someone else's code and understand it and who specialize in writing great Java code. We've started to say, 'We need people who eat, drink, and sleep Java code.' I don't care anymore if they can do C++ code or if they can manage people. . . . Our job requirements have gotten very specific." During this transition, candidates' depth and expertise gain ascendance over breadth and flexibility, but not necessarily at the same rate for all functions. At FeedBurner, "The other functions are different; they're still like we were in the beginning. . . . With finance, operations, and business development, the culture is still about being able to juggle lots of things at once, being able to multitask."

It is often hard for founders to judge when to make this transition, to understand how it might differ by function, and to manage the disruption it might cause. James Milmo of Lynx Solutions reflected on how this transition affected Lynx: "What you don't realize until afterwards is that the early phase requires a different type of person. . . . At some point, a business begins to gel, [then you] want people who are less creative, less curious, and are fine with sticking with a job for a while. . . . [For us,] migrating to Phase Two quickly was tough." Likewise, the SPEC study of emerging companies found that transitioning from more fluid blueprints to a bureaucratic blueprint caused turnover to jump, heightening the challenge for the organization.[16]

Small-Company versus Big-Company Backgrounds:
"He Can't Actually Build the Crank"

A related trade-off is the one between hiring people with experience at a big company, where they often become more specialized and get used to working in formalized organizations, versus people who have worked for startups or small companies and might have developed the broader skills of a generalist. Many of the pros and cons of this decision mirror those of potential founders deciding whether or not to build a career in a big company before becoming founders, as described in detail in Chapter 2. On the one hand, people working in big companies have an opportunity to learn processes and systems in a company that has succeeded well enough to grow large. On the other hand, many of the habits people develop in large

companies can be counterproductive in a startup. As Frank Addante
explained about one of his hiring mistakes, "We hired [a VP of sales]
through a recruiter who was focused specifically on VPs of sales. He
had worked at Oracle and at IBM. He looked great on paper. We
brought him in and he talked a good game. Then he just sat there
for three months. He didn't do anything. He didn't hire anyone. He
didn't come up with a plan, he didn't create a strategy. He wasn't
comfortable creating something from nothing. It's like if you have a
crank, he can crank, but he can't actually build the crank. Building
something from nothing requires a different skill set."

Barry Nalls learned about the related divide between "doer" and
"manager" with an early hire at Masergy: "My first mis-hire was
someone who . . . had done sales and sales management at a mid-
sized-to-larger company, where he had a great team behind him.
When you hire senior people in larger companies, they're successful
because they can manage a team. They won't necessarily be effective on an individual level. I realized that in an early-stage company,
there's no such thing as a manager. Everyone is a contributor, including the CEO! People in mid-management and upper-management in
large companies, when they have to go back five or six years to find
a project they were proud of contributing to, that's a red flag."

Even if the hire is actively working on the startup's tasks, it may
be on the wrong tasks or in ways that are counterproductive. Early
in the life of Zipcar, founder Robin Chase felt she needed a more experienced executive on her team in order to raise capital. But hiring
a seasoned manager caused more problems than it solved. She said,
"Our mistake: hiring a big-company guy for a startup. He spent a
lot of money on lunches and parking, created huge lists and detailed
tasks and procedures that were 25% out of date by the time they hit
my desk and 50% out of date by the following day. He was used to
working at a much later-stage company where the goal was to put
procedures in place and follow them strictly."[17]

When Frank Addante started Zondigo, a wireless advertising
company, after his successful exit from L90, he wanted to assemble
a "dream team" of people experienced with marketing and technology. He hired people who had held senior executive positions

in established companies such as UPS, Visa, Coca-Cola, Columbia Pictures, and Intel. But his dream team failed to live up to expectations. As Frank explained, "They spent so much time thinking and pontificating and strategizing and analyzing, they could never make a decision together on how to move forward. They just kept debating. . . . The results were that nothing really happened."

Experienced versus Inexperienced Hires

The choice of generalist versus specialist is largely driven by the startup's emphasis on flexibility versus formalization. A related but distinct decision is how experienced each hire should be; this decision is often driven by how much experience the startup can afford. As shown in Figure 8.4, startups tend to hire relatively inexperienced employees before they have raised capital; that is, while they are still resource-poor. As they mature and gain additional resources, they tend to increase the seniority of their hires, in terms of both years of work experience and prior seniority in the given role.

The benefits of hiring experienced people include the following:

- **Skills, contacts, and credibility**—Experienced hires are more likely to bring human and social capital to the startup and to provide it with reputational advantages.
- **Hiring leverage**—By hiring experienced people, then delegating to them the task of hiring their own employees, founders can both leverage their own time and foster cohesion within each department in the startup. For example, one of the main reasons Frank Addante hired experienced people at Zondigo was because he "looked forward to relying on them to hire the people who would be working under them" and thus free Frank to pursue fund-raising.
- **Stability: Mr. Right versus Mr. Right Now**—Experienced hires lower the probability of having to upgrade the team in the long run; their relevant experience usually helps them scale more smoothly with the growing organization. If a startup can attract a Mr. Right, who will be able to excel in

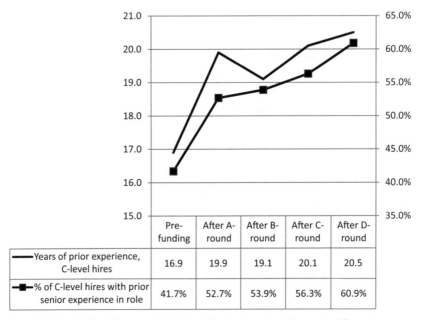

Figure 8.4. Seniority of Hires, by Maturity of Startup (number of rounds of financing raised)

	Pre-funding	After A-round	After B-round	After C-round	After D-round
Years of prior experience, C-level hires	16.9	19.9	19.1	20.1	20.5
% of C-level hires with prior senior experience in role	41.7%	52.7%	53.9%	56.3%	60.9%

the position through multiple stages of growth, rather than a Mr. Right Now, who can do the job now but will be out of his or her depth in the next stage of growth, that will save the startup a lot of trouble and disruption. Barry Nalls of Masergy was surprised by this aspect of startup growth: "High-growth companies change so much every quarter! That amount of change isn't normal and people can't be trained for it unless they've been in another [startup or small company]."

At the same time, there are also downsides to hiring experienced people. They include these:

- **Bigger paychecks**—At their current jobs, experienced candidates are probably earning more than junior candidates, making it more expensive to lure them to the startup and increasing the startup's "burn rate." Letting payroll get out of hand can cause not only dissatisfaction and turnover but also lawsuits. When Pandora Radio couldn't afford to pay its employees and had to defer salaries, it not only suffered a "pressure cooker" work environment, according to founder Tim Westergren, but also was sued for violating California employment laws.

- **Cultural control**—With bottom-up hiring, founders will be more in control of the culture they want to create. People lacking years of experience at established companies do not have such strong expectations of how a company should run and so are more open to the founder's blueprint.[18] James Milmo wanted his technology startup, Lynx, to be a home for creative "Renaissance" people; that is, people with high intelligence, creativity, and wide-ranging interests, but not necessarily with formal training in computer programming. James explained, "We hired a lot of Renaissance people who had backgrounds that were unrelated to what they would be doing for us. . . . Our culture was such that we got along with each other, spent a lot of time outside work together. We were a community. . . . People were more excited to be at Lynx because they loved who they worked with."

A startup hires inexperienced people hoping they will prove to be "rising stars" who can master new skills and grow into their roles. In contrast, experienced hires are expected to be "rock stars" who can contribute a lot of value right from the beginning. Genevieve Thiers, founder-CEO of Sittercity, explained how her ideas about hiring evolved throughout her startup: "[At first] I had brought in 'rising stars'—young people who would be able to grow with the company. But they were simply too emotional about the business swings of the company. It took too much of my time and energy to manage them. I felt as though I needed to find more senior 'rock stars' to help me take the company to the next level." She decided to focus more intensely on hiring a new executive team to replace those she had hoped would be rising stars and began searching for rock stars—people who were established and successful in their fields. Over the next year, Sittercity was able to attract 10 senior people by offering stock options and competitive salaries, by offering the chance to enter an up-and-coming industry at the ground level, and—being located in Chicago rather than in Silicon Valley or along Route 128—by not having to compete with a lot of other startups for local talent.

While Genevieve gave up on rising stars in favor of rock stars, other founders were able to "hit the hiring jackpot" by finding that rare commodity, the young, relatively inexperienced (and cheap) person who can learn and grow quickly to become a true asset to the startup. As Lew Cirne was ramping up Wily Technology, one of his first hires was Mark Sachleben, a recently minted Stanford MBA and a friend of Wily's outside board member. Lew was a little worried about bringing in an MBA at such an early stage, but felt that Mark's youth, potential, and working style might be a good fit with his young company and decided to make him CFO. "Mark was my gold-plated Stanford MBA," recalls Cirne, "though I wasn't able to pay him much gold. I really liked that he had incredible integrity and a self-effacing nature. . . . Rather than buying already-built desks, I remember my Stanford-MBA CFO hand-assembling the desks we had bought, rather than paying $50 for Office Depot to assemble them." As Wily grew, Mark proved to be a quick learner and a key member of the management team.

REWARDS

Cash-poor startups usually cannot afford to pay salaries and bonuses comparable to those paid by large companies. To compensate, startups have to use other financial (and non-financial) inducements, the most prominent of which is equity. Although the compensation packages of founders are often a mixture of incentives appropriate to both agents and principals, hires are usually classic agents who require different incentives. When designing compensation packages, startups can choose from contingent alternatives (i.e., performance-based bonuses) and noncontingent alternatives (salaries) and can tie financial rewards to individual performance (i.e., a bonus tied to the specific employee's performance[19]) or to the startup's collective performance (most prominently via equity stakes in the startup). The paragraphs below describe the drivers of each form of nonfounder compensation and then delve into some of the trade-offs between the different forms.

Cash Compensation

Nonfounder cash compensation can include both salary, paid regardless of individual and startup performance, and bonus, which is performance-dependent. Below, I describe the core salary and bonus patterns in the technology industry, then compare them with patterns in the life sciences industry.

The Ups and Downs of Salaries

Over the past decade, the technology and life sciences industries have experienced two full market cycles, from the heights of the economic boom in 1999–2000 to the depths of the bust in 2001–2003, then back to heights by 2007 and the subsequent recession in 2008–2009. As shown in Figure 8.5, the changes in nonfounder-CEO salaries in technology startups have largely followed the overall economic cycle, though lagging it slightly. C-level salaries declined during the downturns of 2001–2002 and 2009 and rose during the period in between.

Analyses of the salary data show that, across executives and startups, the major differences in salary are as follows:

- **Position**—As a group, C-level executives receive higher salaries than do VP-level executives, but there are significant exceptions. Across the full decade of compensation data for nonfounding executives, the two highest-paid positions were the CEO (average salary of $217,000) and the COO/president ($176,000). In the next tier, CTOs, CFOs, and the VPs of engineering, business development, sales, and

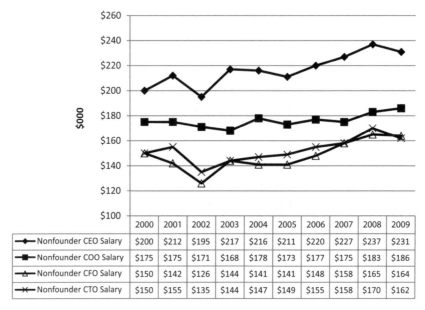

	2000	2001	2002	2003	2004	2005	2006	2007	2008	2009
◆ Nonfounder CEO Salary	$200	$212	$195	$217	$216	$211	$220	$227	$237	$231
■ Nonfounder COO Salary	$175	$175	$171	$168	$178	$173	$177	$175	$183	$186
▲ Nonfounder CFO Salary	$150	$142	$126	$144	$141	$141	$148	$158	$165	$164
✕ Nonfounder CTO Salary	$150	$155	$135	$144	$147	$149	$155	$158	$170	$162

Figure 8.5. C-level Nonfounder Salaries, 2000–2009

marketing all made between $147,000 and $155,000.* To the extent that salaries give us a window into which functions are most critical for mitigating the challenges or contingencies faced by an organization,[20] it is interesting to see the similarity of salaries across most of the executive team, a pattern that is found in both early-stage and later-stage startups.

- **Stage of startup**—The more mature the startup (the more rounds of financing raised) and the larger the startup (the greater the number of employees and the greater the revenues), the higher the cash compensation. For instance, splitting my 2009 startups into those that had raised two or

---

* A similar relationship holds for total cash compensation, which includes both salary and bonus. Over the decade, the average total cash compensation for a CEO was $296,000. For the COO/president, it was $228,000, and for the VP-sales, $230,000. At the next tier of nonfounder compensation, CTOs, CFOs, and the VPs of engineering, business development, and marketing all made between $180,000 and $189,000.

fewer rounds of financing and those that had raised three or more rounds, I found that the nonfounder C-level salaries were 12% to 17% higher in the later-stage startups. Splitting the startups into those with 40 or fewer employees and those with over 40, nonfounder C-level salaries were 17% to 19% higher in the larger startups. Splitting the startups into those with less than $5 million in revenues and those with $5 million or more in revenues, nonfounder C-level salaries were 10% to 12% higher in the higher-revenue startups.

- **Industry**—Executives in life sciences startups tend to make significantly more cash compensation than their counterparts in technology startups. For instance, in 2009, average nonfounder-CEO salary for life sciences startups was $285,000, compared to $231,000 in technology startups, a gap of $54,000. For the other nonfounder C-level executives, the gap was $31,000 to $36,000, or 19% to 22%, in favor of life sciences executives. Across the full decade, nonfounding life sciences CEOs received, on average, a salary 27% higher than that of their technology counterparts.[*]

Interestingly, geography does not seem to affect nonfounder salaries. In the technology "hubs" of California and New England, nonfounding C-level executives made only about 1% more than their

[*] There are some interesting divergences, but also parallels, between the compensation of CEOs in private versus public information technology and life sciences companies. Comparing cash compensation in private and public companies, the public-company CEOs make far more cash compensation than do their counterparts in private companies. According to the *Wall Street Journal*/Hay Group 2009 CEO Compensation Study, which analyzes compensation in public companies with more than $5 billion in revenues, CEOs of "technology" companies made $928,000 in salary and $1,084,000 in bonus and CEOs of "healthcare" companies made $1,200,000 in salary and $2,188,000 in bonus. These figures are much higher than the private-company compensation numbers shown in Figure 8.5 and described in the accompanying text. Slicing the pie another way and comparing cash compensation in information technology versus life sciences companies, the CEOs of public life sciences companies make significantly more than do the CEOs of public information technology companies, a relationship that also holds for private information technology versus life sciences companies.

counterparts in the rest of the country, a difference that is not statistically significant.

High versus Low Bonus-Sensitivity

For many executives, cash bonuses are an important component of cash compensation. Such bonuses are often tied to individual performance measures and to startup-level benchmarks, making them more sensitive than salary to actual performance. Across the full executive team, bonuses average 28% of total cash compensation. However, there are significant differences by position. Figure 8.6 shows bonus as a percentage of the executive's salary across the full decade of data for technology startups. Vice presidents of sales had by far the highest percentage of their cash compensation, 49%,[*] in the form of a bonus; for CEOs, the figure was 37%, and for all other executives, below 30%.

After two turns as a founder-CEO, Dick Costolo concluded that the "ideal compensation package" depended on the function: Salespeople were heavily motivated by performance-based compensation while software engineers primarily wanted to count on their monthly paycheck. As Dick explained, with salespeople, it's best to "make the compensation package based on how much more they'll make if they meet or beat quota and I, as CEO, have to be comfortable with their making four times as much as me, but with their having a low base and huge upside."

Bonuses also differ by industry. Cash compensation tends to be more at risk in technology startups; bonuses for nonfounding technology CEOs are 37% of their salaries, as opposed to 28% for nonfounding life sciences CEOs. Similar patterns obtained across the other positions. (As described below, the equity stakes of nonfounding life sciences executives were also lower than the equity stakes of their technology counterparts.)

---

[*] Having such a large bonus component boosts the average cash compensation for nonfounding vice presidents of sales into parity with nonfounding COOs, as detailed two footnotes above.

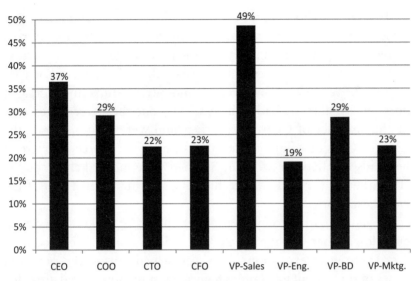

Figure 8.6. Bonus as Percentage of Salary for Nonfounding Executives in Technology Startups, across the Full Decade

Gender Gaps: Male versus Female Compensation

Studies of cash compensation in large companies consistently find a "gender gap"; that is, 20% to 25% lower compensation for women.[*] Even though large, bureaucratic organizations standardize their HR practices to minimize the effects of personal preferences and discrimination on employment and compensation decisions, this significant gap remains, partly due to the fact that men and women receive different job titles and are sorted into different occupational lines.[21] In pre-bureaucratic startups, lacking such rationalized HR practices, do we therefore see an even bigger gender gap, or are there counterbalancing effects? If there is a gender gap in startups, can it give us insight into the gender gap in large companies?

---

[*] For details, see Goldin (2008). Gender gap studies have been criticized for failing to control for differences in human capital and job function. In contrast, in my analyses, I was able to control for a wide variety of differences in executive backgrounds, positions, industries, geography, and other factors. See Note 22 of this chapter for more details.

My analyses show that, in startups, there is a much greater gap in the preponderance of women than in their compensation. Across the technology startups I analyzed, the percentage of women across the C-level and VP-level executives was only 10.7%; in life sciences, it was 17.6%.[22] Only 3.1% of technology startups and 7.9% of life sciences startups had female CEOs, but the percentages rose for the next tier of C-level executives and were even higher at the VP level. Outside of human resources (more than three-quarters of the heads of HR were women), women were most likely to be the VP-marketing (in 19.1% of technology startups and 41.9% of life sciences startups).

The gender gap in compensation was just over $10,000, or 5.6%, much lower than the typical 20% to 25% in large public companies. There were exceptions, however, which hint at the potential causes of the overall gap (and which suggest high-potential areas for research on the gender gap). The biggest distinction in gender gaps was geographic; the gap was $16,300 outside the entrepreneurial hubs of California and Massachusetts but too small to be statistically significant within them. Interestingly, as mentioned above, geography has no significant impact on startup compensation in general. Why, then, does it have such a strong impact on the gender gap? One reason may be gender-related differences in the balance of (labor) supply and (job) demand in those two job markets. There may also be a voluntary element: Women who choose not to work in the hubs may be trading off compensation for benefits such as a more balanced lifestyle; if such benefits are more important to women than to men, they could cause a gender gap.

Second, the startup's stage of development had a significant impact; there was a $12,300 gap in later-stage startups but no statistically significant gap in early-stage startups. This result has the most direct implications for our understanding of the gender gap in large companies, in particular for how it emerges and thus what the drivers are. Early in the life of a startup, there is no significant gap, suggesting that male and female executives are making similar trade-offs or that the startups operate as meritocracies. However, as startups grow, formalize their processes, or allow their employees to make more diverse trade-offs in compensation or lifestyle, a gap is introduced. Small at first, it widens as startups grow into the kinds of large, public companies that have been studied in the past. One (male) serial entrepreneur observed, "Early-stage companies are meritocracies, whereas mature companies are bureaucracies that reward factors other than performance and may be biased against women. . . . Most founder/CEOs get replaced by 'seasoned executives,' many of whom come from larger organizations. And those executives bring not only their 'own team' but they also bring their existing preferences and biases."[*]

The third big influence on the gender gap was the industry: Across all startups in the sample, there was a $13,300 gap in technology startups but no statistically significant gap in life sciences startups. One reason may be the aforementioned difference in the preponderance of female executives; they are much more common in life sciences than in technology.

If startups are indeed more meritocratic than large companies, making them relatively more attractive as places for women to work, we may see, in the future, an increase in the preponderance of women in startups, which may help reduce the gender compensation gap.[†] To the extent that the gap also represents men and women making conscious and different trade-offs, the gap may even be a good thing, for people of each gender may be getting what is most important to them. A female founder-CEO said, "I think women don't tend to leave because of salary whereas men do. A good work environment means a lot to us." However, to the extent that startup growth inherently nurtures the large, persistent, and involuntary gender gaps characteristic of large companies, it may be precisely

---

[*] This observation implies that, if founders are still around, particularly in the CEO position, we might see less of a gender gap. To test this possibility, I added a flag for whether a founder was still working as a senior executive and reran my gender-gap regressions. The presence of founders did counterbalance the gender gap a bit, reducing it by about one-third, but the effect was not statistically significant.

[†] The CareerLeader data described in Chapter 2—which suggest that women's motivations differ from men's, especially regarding the importance of financial motivations—lend some support to the suggestion that women like to strike different trade-offs than men do.

during the early stages of startup evolution that we should be trying to find out how this happens and how to stop it.

C-level versus VP-level Equity Stakes

During the early days of a startup, equity stakes tend to be individually tailored to each new hire. But as a startup matures, this ad-hoc approach can cause trouble. Dick Costolo ran into this problem as FeedBurner grew: "Our CFO had been a venture capitalist and pointed out that we needed to [clean up all our ad-hoc equity arrangements with our employees] so all new hires would be in the same boat.... [E]veryone's interests weren't aligned." Dick and the CFO were able to bring consistency to the equity packages for subsequent hires, but the inconsistency among early hires ended up causing alignment problems when FeedBurner later received an acquisition offer. Employees with one equity structure wanted to take the offer while others did not, causing divergence within the team at a crucial juncture.

Yet, even in the youngest of startups in my dataset, there are some consistencies. While the salaries of VP-level executives are often on par with those of some C-level executives (most notably, the CTO and CFO), equity stakes are much more strongly linked to organizational level. Nonfounding CEOs have significantly more equity than the rest of the C-level executives, who usually have more equity than VPs. Across the full decade of my dataset, nonfounding CEOs averaged equity stakes of 6.0%, COOs 2.9%, CTOs 1.7%, and CFOs 1.3%. The four main VP-level positions all averaged 1.0% to 1.3% of equity.

Figure 8.7 graphs the equity and cash compensation differences across these positions, using as a baseline the VP-marketing, the lowest-paid and lowest-stake executive in the core executive team. Most members of the team earn within 5% of the VP-marketing's cash compensation; even the CEO makes only 1.7 times as much. The equity-stake differentials, however, are far greater; the CEO's stake is more than 6 times that of the VP-marketing.

The stage of the startup also significantly affects equity stakes through dilution and uncertainty. First, each time a startup raises

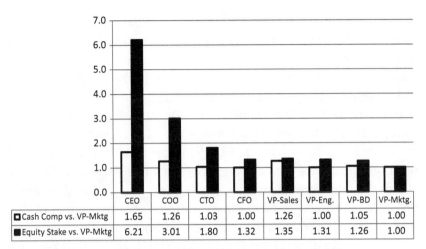

	CEO	COO	CTO	CFO	VP-Sales	VP-Eng.	VP-BD	VP-Mktg.
☐ Cash Comp vs. VP-Mktg	1.65	1.26	1.03	1.00	1.26	1.00	1.05	1.00
■ Equity Stake vs. VP-Mktg	6.21	3.01	1.80	1.32	1.35	1.31	1.26	1.00

Figure 8.7. Nonfounding Executives: Compensation and Equity Inequality

a round of financing, the equity stakes of existing equity holders decrease—they are "diluted"—because new shares are issued to the new investors. For instance, if a nonfounding CEO owns 10% of the startup and then the startup raises $5 million on a pre-money valuation of $10 million, the CEO's equity stake would be diluted to 6.7%. Second, during the early days of the startup, when uncertainty is high and hires are taking a big risk by joining, the startup has to offer larger equity stakes to attract them. But as the risk is lowered, startups can offer lower equity stakes,[*] reinforcing the negative relationship between startup maturity and the size of hires'

[*] To provide sufficient equity with which to hire key personnel, many startups create *option pools* containing shares of equity that will be assigned to upcoming new hires. These are usually created or "refreshed" during each new round of financing, but 46% of pre-financing startups also create such pools in order to facilitate hiring. This percentage rises to 80% of startups when the first round of financing is raised, and to more than 90% from the second round onward. In principle, these pools should be sized to match the amount of hiring the startup expects to do before the pool is refreshed again; that is, until the next round of financing. The data do indeed support this relationship: The size of the pool is largest during the early stages of startup evolution, when the firm needs the largest equity stakes to attract hires and when the greatest number of important positions have yet to be filled. In the youngest startups in my dataset, the option pools averaged 20% of fully diluted equity; this percentage declined with each subsequent round of financing. By the third and fourth rounds, the option pool has dropped to 11% and 10%, respectively, reflecting the lower number of key hires remaining to be made and/or the smaller equity stakes required to attract them.

equity stakes. In my 2009 technology-startup data, the nonfounding CEOs of early-stage startups that had raised two or fewer rounds of financing averaged 7.1% equity stakes; their counterparts in later-stage startups that had raised three or more rounds averaged 5.2%. In life sciences, the gap was even larger: 2.5% instead of 1.9%.

Industry also plays a small but significant role in equity stakes. Executives tend to have higher equity stakes in technology startups than in life sciences startups; in 2009, across all C-level and VP-level positions, technology executives each held an average of 0.5% more equity than did equivalent life sciences executives. All told, technology executives tend to have higher-powered incentives than do life sciences executives, with more of their compensation coming in at-risk forms of cash and equity: lower salaries, higher bonus percentages, and more equity.

Locking on the Golden Handcuffs

In Chapter 6, we examined the founding team's need to adopt dynamic equity arrangements, such as vesting schedules, in order to be able to adjust to future developments, such as a founder deciding to drop out or being forced by circumstances to curtail his or her commitment. The vesting terms used when assigning equity to hires give us a related window into equity arrangements within startups. Startups often use vesting schedules to handcuff a new executive; that is, to give him or her a strong financial motivation to stay with the startup for a certain number of years. (Vesting for nonfounder-CEOs is generally time-based, though about 10% of nonfounder-CEOs have performance-based vesting.) Ideally, each executive should be locked in for the horizon over which he or she is expected to add value to the startup. However, more than three-quarters of executive hires receive vesting terms of four years, as shown in Figure 8.8. The consistency of this arrangement across the various executive positions and throughout all parts of the market cycle, including boom times when startups are typically growing and reaching exits much more quickly and bust times when they may grow much more slowly, suggests that startups are following

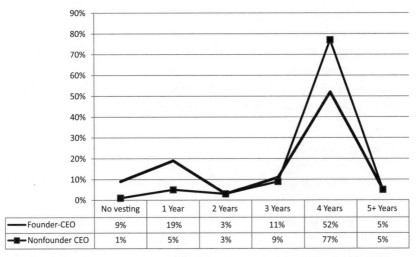

	No vesting	1 Year	2 Years	3 Years	4 Years	5+ Years
Founder-CEO	9%	19%	3%	11%	52%	5%
Nonfounder CEO	1%	5%	3%	9%	77%	5%

Figure 8.8. Years of Vesting for Founder-CEOs versus Nonfounder-CEOs, across All Stages of Financing

an institutionalized pattern rather than tailoring each vesting schedule to a specific executive and situation.*

It is also instructive to compare the vesting schedules for founders and nonfounders; boards give founders an average of six months less vesting than they give hires. As shown in Figure 8.8, founder-CEOs are much less likely to have four years of vesting and more likely to have no vesting or only one year of it than nonfounder-CEOs are, even after investors have entered the picture. When faced with an investor demand that they vest their stock, founders often push to get "credit for time served," which may account for some of the six-month difference. However, the shorter vesting for founders may also be due in part to an underappreciated benefit of founder

---

* Another vesting term—one that can unlock the handcuffs of vesting—accelerates the person's vesting if the startup is acquired or there is some other change in control. There are various forms of this *accelerated vesting on change in control* term (e.g., different triggers that are required before the accelerated vesting occurs), but a common pattern is that the more valuable the employee to the startup, the *less* of a chance that the handcuffs will be unlocked, otherwise the terms of the acquisition will probably be less attractive to the acquirer (under the expectation that the most valuable employees will be able to leave).

attachment to the startup. We saw in Chapter 6 that emotional attachment to the startup can handicap a founder's ability to negotiate an increase in pay, resulting in a founder discount. But the same
attachment may actually benefit the founder when it comes to vesting; investors may feel less need to impose "golden handcuffs" on a
founder they know would be most unwilling to leave.

Cash-versus-Equity Seesaw

Different mixes of cash compensation and equity can create different incentives, encourage different levels of risk taking, and direct
attention to corporate versus individual goals.[23] Startups, like larger
companies, often craft compensation packages that trade off cash
compensation for equity stakes; if a package is high in salary, it will
tend to be low in equity, or vice versa.[24] Such packages are designed
both to attract the right kinds of people to the startup and to provide them with particular incentives once they join. For instance,
as a way to learn about a potential executive's risk preference, Bill
Holodnak, head of the J. Robert Scott executive-search firm, shows
those executives a spectrum of compensation packages, ranging
from low salary/high equity to high salary/low equity, and asks the
recruit where he or she would like to fall on that spectrum.

Some startups choose to have all hires on one side of the seesaw or the other, while others allow each new hire to choose. Dick
Costolo said that, at FeedBurner, "Each hire would be either an
equity-heavy hire with below-market salary, or salary-heavy with
below-market equity. When we would make people offers, I would
ask, 'Do you want us to favor salary or equity?' For the ones who
favored salary, I told them, 'Well, no complaints when it comes time
to sell the company and your colleagues are going through the roof
and you mortgaged your future for more salary.'" Dick also learned
that different groups sometimes have different equity-versus-salary
priorities: "In Silicon Valley, the discussions are, 'Can you give me
more options if I take less salary?' [In Chicago], we always have the
opposite discussion with engineers."

In analyses of my nonfounder-CEO compensation data, I found
a strong and significant negative relationship between the CEO's

salary and his or her equity stake, even after controlling for a wide array of startup and executive characteristics (such as the startup's maturity and industry, and the executive's position and experience). Splitting the sample of CEOs into the higher-paid half (average salary of $253,000) and the lower-paid half (average salary of $181,000), I found that the higher-paid had average equity stakes of 6.46% while the lower-paid had average equity stakes of 8.49%. In exchange for greater salaries, such CEOs gave up a significant amount of equity, or vice versa. The same relationship held for the other executive positions.

Where employees come out on the cash-versus-equity seesaw can be affected by the founders' motivations as well as by the employees' own. Founders who want to retain more equity for themselves tend to offer a smaller equity stake to potential hires, preferring either to balance that with some other carrot (higher salaries if they have the resources, or intangible benefits) or to take the chance of losing the hire and having to hire a weaker candidate. Such a founder is often able to retain more equity but may build a team that is weaker or less motivated to build equity value. The founder thus increases his or her chances of ending up with a King outcome. On the flip side, founders who prefer to build a more valuable startup, even if their percentage of it is lower, will make the opposite decisions and increase their chances of ending up with a Rich outcome.

CLOSING REMARKS

Founders face the same dilemmas with hiring decisions that they face with cofounding decisions, but with the added complexity of aligning these decisions with the startup's stage of development, its level of formality (which may differ by function, complicating the challenge even further), and its available resources. Figure 8.9 summarizes the changes in hiring decisions that typically occur during each stage of startup evolution.

It is crucial for founder-CEOs not only to diagnose and correct the problems that arise from hiring the wrong person, but also to anticipate when a decision that was good at the time may need to be rethought because the startup has arrived at a new stage of

Startup's Stage of Development	Relationships	Roles	Rewards
Startup	• Personal networks of core founder are tapped to find loyal candidates who fit with the culture of the startup	• Generalists who cover multiple areas • "Flat" structure that has many C-level employees with few reports	• Low cash compensation • High equity compensation • Low gender gap • Less vesting
Transition	• Impersonal searches (e.g., newspaper ads, search firms) • The networks (and weaker ties) of investors and other participants in the startup are leveraged	• "Players" transition to "coaches," as functional VPs are delegated the responsibility to run and hire their own teams • Some early employees are usually unable to adapt to the changing needs of the company	• Moderate cash compensation • Lower equity compensation • Vesting equity stakes
Mature	• Investor networks are tapped • Executive search firms are hired	• The reporting structure is "pyramidal," with a few senior executives leveraged by many junior employees • "Professional" executives from large-company backgrounds	• High cash compensation • Employee stock options take the place of equity • The gender gap emerges

Figure 8.9. Evolution of Hiring Decisions as the Startup Matures

development. In the fast-paced world of startups, founders can't afford to become entrenched in a particular way of hiring but must expect their startup's hiring needs to change. For example, before hiring young employees during the early days of the startup, the founders should already be planning for the day when they will have to either replace those young hires or else hire more experienced people to supervise them; before building a team of generalists, the founders should already be considering how they will adjust when the startup requires the quality that can be provided only by specialists; before crafting a compensation package for the earliest hires, the founders should already be anticipating how different stages will require different packages. As we have seen throughout this chapter, the data indicate that each stage of a startup's evolution is marked by important changes in its hiring needs.

Another echo of the cofounder dilemmas can be found in the hiring dilemma of what to do when an underperforming or nonscaling employee is also a friend or family member. Founder-CEOs find it very tempting to fill their teams with such hires, given the natural comfort with people one already knows and the greater likelihood that they will all fit in together. But this comfort introduces longer-term risks, for such a team faces the same playing-with-fire risk that we saw founding teams facing in Chapter 4 and that we saw Tim Westergren facing earlier in this chapter. Founders who have prior personal relationships with their hires may be less likely to discuss sensitive issues and may also face major damage to those relationships if things go sour in the startup, both factors leading them to put off the issue until things are ready to blow up.

Just as it was critical for founding teams to create appropriate linkages among their own relationships, roles, and rewards, it is critical for the founders to create such linkages with their hires. For example, a bonus-heavy compensation structure tied to individual performance may be productive with a salesperson but counterproductive with a programmer who is part of a development team; that is, rewards properly linked (or aligned) with one type of role may be poorly linked (misaligned) with another type of role. Creative linkages can help solve sticky hiring problems, such as the ripple effects of dismissing a hire who has turned out to be a poor choice. Dick Costolo of FeedBurner said, "The worst problem with a bad hire is that they get into the organization, they become friends with people, and then it's, 'Why are you firing my friend?'" The result is that many founders become hesitant to hire—or make sure to "hire slow"—for fear of making a mistake. But linking rewards and roles can help solve this problem; for example, a highly con-tingent compensation structure for salespeople can turn off those who aren't confident in their skills while encouraging weak hires to leave. As Dick observed, "A salesperson will leave if he's not doing a good job and therefore not getting paid what he wants. If he doesn't work out, it solves itself quickly. It's 'hire fast, fire fast.'" Unfortu-nately, few first-time founders have such a nuanced understanding of how to balance hiring dilemmas; even for Dick, such understand-ing did not come until his fourth startup.

CHAPTER NINE

INVESTOR DILEMMAS:
ADDING VALUE, ADDING RISKS

Just as Evan Williams took widely differing approaches to his cofounding and hiring decisions at Blogger and Odeo, so he chose different kinds of investors for those two startups. In the early stages of Blogger, he and his cofounder, Meg Hourihan, financed the company with money they earned doing Web-development work for Hewlett-Packard. They hoped Blogger could avoid raising money and become "cash-flow positive" (when incoming cash is greater than outgoing cash) by increasing sales and software subscriptions, but Evan soon realized that they would need additional funding to complete the product development. With the dot-com boom heating up in 1999–2000, Evan could have approached venture capitalists, but he consciously decided not to do so because he wanted to avoid "losing a large percentage of our company." Instead, Blogger raised $500,000 on a pre-money valuation of $2 million from small investors, including Meg's parents, in return for 20% of the company. "We were consciously not taking a lot of money. . . . We were going to be frugal," explained Evan. "And the fact that we could still control 80% of the company was definitely appealing." When even that money ran out amid the bursting of the dot-com bubble, Evan resisted possible exits and instead financed the company by maxing out his own credit cards, eventually laying off all the employees and continuing to develop Blogger on his own.

After Evan sold Blogger to Google in 2002, he helped found the podcasting startup Odeo. This time, he seeded the startup himself by using some of the Google stock he had sold, but he quickly recognized the huge potential for the technology and the risk that competitors such as Apple would beat Odeo to market. Because Evan's small-but-successful exit at Blogger had made him a proven entrepreneur, he was able to raise $5 million from a top-tier VC firm which, in return, received 30% of the company and a 1.5x liquidation preference.[*] The two founders would have two seats on the five-person board of directors. Although Evan had a $1 million offer from angel investors, the VCs offered him $5 million, and he decided to take the bigger check.

Professional investors have played important early roles in financing and building some of the most successful startups, including such industry pioneers as Google, eBay, and Genentech. However, investors who are considering investing in a startup face many risks. The founder knows far more about his or her capabilities and motivations than the investors do and usually has a better understanding of the market potential. Investors can take actions, such as performing due diligence on the founder and the market, that will reduce their risks. But they must also structure the investment to reduce risk and to align the startup's interests with their own, so that "simply by following his or her self-interest," each party "advances the other's interests as well."[1] Sometimes, the terms that are used in those investment structures (e.g., the founder vesting, liquidation preferences, and board representation detailed below) are necessary to make the investment possible, but, as we will see, also cause increased tensions between the founder and the investors. Such was the case with some of the terms to which Evan agreed when he accepted the VC offer.

---

[*] A *liquidation preference* is a term agreed to in the initial financing deal between venture capitalists and entrepreneurs that governs the division of profits in the event of the venture's acquisition or liquidation. We delve into liquidation preferences later in this chapter.

ENTER THE INVESTOR

To survive and grow, startups need human capital, social capital, and financial capital. Core founders who lack any of these three often try to attract cofounders or hire employees who can provide what is missing. Sometimes that works. But for many founders, the startup's financial capital needs (e.g., for product development or for rapid growth) exceed the capital they can provide, and lead the founders to seek outside funding. When they do so, a brand-new player enters the startup—the investor—which can cause dramatic and sometimes unexpected internal changes.

No other topic discussed in this book has received as much attention from academics as investor and financing issues have. While the academic research has not focused on intrateam financing issues, such as the equity splits covered in Chapter 6, "Reward Dilemmas," it has much to teach us about entrepreneurial financing that involves outside investors. It is beyond the scope of this chapter to review all of that research and to delve into the nitty-gritty of each financing term. Instead, I will build on the research in order to focus on the investor issues that result in founders' dilemmas: the early financing decisions that have long-term implications for growth and control. We will pay particular attention to building and managing a board of directors, often the conduit through which investors make their impact on the startup.

We will first examine a key early decision—whether to self-fund or to take money from outside investors. We then delve into the implications of taking money from three of the most common outside options: friends and family, angel investors, and venture capitalists. We will focus on four factors that differentiate these options: the investors' sources of capital, which shape their motivations and incentives; the founders' abilities to access the investors; the investors' potential to add value to the venture; and the costs and risks faced by founders who take capital from each particular type of investor. Throughout this chapter, we will focus on the decisions faced by founders and teams including Evan Williams and the founders of Ockham Technologies, a sales-automation software startup.

SELF-FUNDING

As with the decision to found solo or to build a founding team and with the decision whether or not to complement the founding team with hires, founders have a "go it alone" option when it comes to investors. When Jim Triandiflou and Mike Meisenheimer started Ockham Technologies, they quickly attracted the attention of Monarch Capital Partners, which offered them $2 million. But they decided not to take the money and instead seeded the startup with $150,000 of their own money. "We just felt that we should go sell something [first]," Jim explained. "We knew we'd make the company more valuable by doing that and first getting some validation of our idea." Serial entrepreneur Frank Addante, after one startup failed and he had to give back VC funding, decided to self-fund his next company, avoiding investors until he had a solid business plan and proof of concept.

In 77% of founding teams in my dataset, at least one founder contributed seed capital early in the life of the startup. Even in those teams, though, the capital usually runs out pretty quickly. In the startups that had not yet raised an outside round of financing, the median monthly "burn rate" (the amount of cash being used) was $75,000 and the median startup was a little more than four months away from running out of cash. A startup with a small cash cushion is more vulnerable to liquidity problems and more likely to disband.[2] As Professor Bill Sahlman points out, in startups, money buys time: time to experiment, to collect and evaluate data about what worked and what did not, and to adjust the strategy and operations based on what was learned.

Barry Nalls's first startup, for example, was a completely self-funded two-person consulting business. Barry recalled how hard those years were: "There were two absolutely painful parts—I never got a day off and this was all my money. . . . When there's no payroll, it means you have no money [to pay yourself] either, so you're as broke as you can get. It was very tough financially and emotionally." When Barry ran out of money even for groceries, he said, "I started calling [customers], telling them I needed to collect from them. I started working my customer network really hard." Eventually the pace of the business and lack of financing drove Barry back to the job he had left at GTE.

The startup's industry, the macroeconomic context in which it operates, its degree of capital-intensity, and its business model all have powerful impacts on its financing strategy.[3] However, even when all of those factors point to trying to raise money from investors, some founders choose to avoid external sources of financing. Such founders are usually motivated to retain control of their startups, to be able to make all the decisions themselves, and not to have to spend time managing investors rather than growing the business. Either from prior experience or from the stories they have heard from mentors and from more experienced founders, they have learned the disadvantages of outside funding (which will be described below) and decided to avoid them. Brian Scudamore launched his startup with the clear idea of *never* involving investors: "Even if someone would have offered, I wouldn't have taken outside money," he said. "It's something I got from my dad—that you don't go out and take money from someone. You should start small and grow it on your own."[*]

It is possible to get away with this if the business can bring in customer revenues very early; for example, by consulting or by getting customer prepayments. For businesses with tangible assets, such as capital equipment or accounts receivable, which can serve as collateral, debt financing is an option.[4] But high-potential startups in the technology and life sciences industries rarely have such assets, so debt financing is rarely an option for them. Among the startups in my dataset, only 2% raised debt financing, with this percentage remaining relatively consistent across all stages of company evolution.

WHEN INVESTORS BECOME DESIRABLE

Startups for which alternate sources of capital are not available, or whose growth ambitions require more capital, will need outside

---

[*] Likewise, a distinct group of technology founder-CEOs, such as Joel Spolsky of Fog Creek Software, proclaim their aversion to taking money from VCs and similar investors (e.g., Spolsky, 2003).

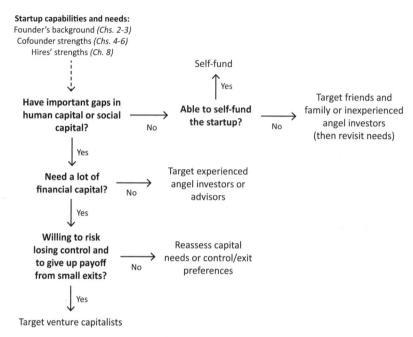

Figure 9.1. Central "Investor Dilemmas" Questions for Startups That Can Attract Outside Financing

investors.[5] Figure 9.1 shows the core questions that should be asked by founders and how the answers should lead founders to target different types of investors. As shown, founders have to assess whether they are still missing the human capital, social capital, and financial capital needed to grow the startup and to compete successfully; whether the different types of investors can play a role in filling those gaps; and whether the risks of involving those investors are worth the potential benefits of doing so.

Outside investors can provide founders with two broad benefits: (a) the capitals needed to get to the next stage of development and (b) improved governance, which includes bringing additional discipline to the startup,[6] helping hone its strategy, and providing outside perspectives about the startup's prospects and its people's abilities. When founders consider potential sources of capital, they have a wide variety of options, each with its own pros and cons. The spectrum of investors is usually described as ranging from "dumb money" or "money-only" investors who only contribute financial capital, to "smart money" or "money-plus" investors who contribute all three types of capital. In between, there are many options; the "angel investor" category alone includes a wide spectrum of investors, ranging from inexperienced investors informally investing in the company to "super-angels" or to formal and experienced multi-angel groups that approximate early-stage VCs in their attention to due diligence and their relevant prior experience. We lack space here to cover all of the options, but below we examine the pros and cons of three prototypical investors: friends and family, angel investors, and venture capitalists. For each type of investor, Figure 9.2 summarizes the key differences, which are detailed in this chapter.

These three types of investor tend to enter startups sequentially—first friends and family, then angel investors, and finally venture capitalists.[7] However, the sequence should be seen as a sharply narrowing funnel, because many more startups can raise money from friends and family than from angels, and, in turn, many more can raise from angels than from VCs.[*]

It should be noted, though, that many founders, even when they have started raising money from outside parties, continue to invest some of their own capital, often to maintain ownership stakes or to show confidence in the startup's prospects. As shown in Figure 9.3, even in their A-round of financing (the first round where they tap outside investors), 32% of founding teams continue to invest their own capital in the round, followed by 16% of founding teams who invest in the B-round and 13% in the C-round.[8] However, once a startup's founders can no longer finance it themselves, they often look to the next easiest source of financing: their friends and families.

---

[*] At the same time, attracting one type of early investor may preclude the attraction of a different type later. For instance, taking money from—and/or giving board seats to—some family members or angel investors may turn off a VC or lead to tough negotiations over the VC's desire for those relatives or angels to leave the board, something they might be loath to do.

Investor	Investor's Main Source of Capital	Founder's Ease of Accessing the Investor	Value Typically Added to Startup	Risks to Founder
Friends and family	• Personal wealth (small)	• Easiest. Personal networks of core founders are tapped.	• Little to none. Family members often do not have business skills.	• May send an unprofessional signal • Lax standards may enable founders to pursue marginal ideas • Playing with fire
Angel investors	• Personal wealth (medium to large)	• Intermediate. Third-party networking and impersonal searches such as angel forums can be used.	• May have broad business experience • Role on the founder's board • Social capital • More financial capital than friends and family	• Less "constructive discipline" and oversight/assistance than VCs • Can be difficult to manage • May introduce complications that later turn off potential investors

| Investor | Investor's Main Source of Capital | Founder's Ease of Accessing the Investor | Value Typically Added to Startup | Risks to Founder |
				Wealth / Control
Venture capitalists	• Limited partners (very large)	• Hardest. Angel investors and professional contacts are often used.	• More—and more predictable—financial capital than angel investors • Social capital (to find hires, future investors, and professional CEOs) • Reputational effects • Guidance through taking an active role on the board and regular communication	**Wealth** • VCs demand equity, which dilutes founder stakes • Liquidation preferences affect exits • Forced vesting of founder equity stakes • Forced equity reallocations among the teams **Control** • Board seats • Protective provisions and supermajority voting rights with preferred stock • Differing risk levels than founders can cause conflict • Staging of funds • Drag-along rights can affect exit

Figure 9.2. Pros and Cons of Investor Options

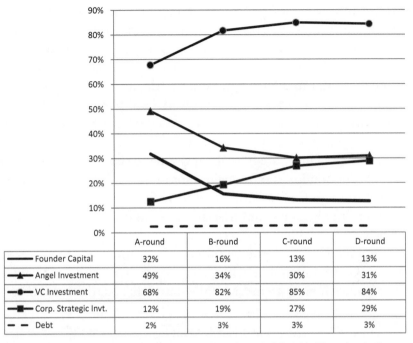

	A-round	B-round	C-round	D-round
—— Founder Capital	32%	16%	13%	13%
—▲— Angel Investment	49%	34%	30%	31%
—●— VC Investment	68%	82%	85%	84%
—■— Corp. Strategic Invt.	12%	19%	27%	29%
– – Debt	2%	3%	3%	3%

Figure 9.3. Types of Investors Participating in Each Round of Outside Financing in the CompStudy Dataset

ACCESSIBLE BUT RISKY: MONEY FROM FRIENDS AND FAMILY

Founders often have a small set of friends and relatives with whom they have frequent contact, long-term trusting relationships, and an emotional connection.[9] Such prior relationships tend to make friends-and-family investors easier to access than angel investors, who also invest their own capital but tend to be more "professional" about it than friends and family. Investments from friends and family are often what make a startup possible in the first place. Meg Hourihan's parents invested in Blogger; Pandora used money from the father of a college friend of one of the cofounders; Scott Cook of Intuit, described below, took loans from his father.

While early investments from friends and family can be crucial, they also have certain limitations compared with more professional investments. Because friends and family are investing their own money, they usually invest much less than professional investors do. Because friends and family typically lack expertise or credibility in the most important business issues, they usually have little human or social capital to contribute. Because friends and family are usually inexperienced investors and not very hard to convince, their investments don't boost the startup's credibility in the eyes of outside parties such as potential customers or other potential investors.

Friends and family are typically investing to support someone they love, like, or admire—not to make a lot of money. Lew Cirne, whom we will study in Chapter 10, raised $100,000 in seed money for his startup from his family and friends. "They didn't understand any of it," he explained, "but they were willing to bet on me." While such faith grants the founders a certain freedom from the demands and scrutiny that would come with professional investors, it also introduces a much more extreme risk if the startup fails, as discussed below.

Motivation to Take Friends-and-Family Money: Comfort, Desperation, or Ignorance?

The advantages and disadvantages of friends and family as investors are similar to their advantages and disadvantages as cofounders (discussed in Chapter 4). Such people are easy to reach, and there is an initial feeling of comfort and trust. Many founders jump at the chance to take this "easy money"; as one said, "Always take the money. You have to start somewhere." To the extent that founders tend to be very confident in their startup's prospects, they may even be more inclined to take money from friends and family, happily imagining those close to them sharing in the startup's future success. One founder-CEO, acknowledging that complete certainty is almost never attained, said, "If you *know* that you won't lose their money, you should take it." In fact, whether a founder is willing to risk taking money from friends or family may be a good indicator of whether or not that founder has laid a solid groundwork for success. One founder-CEO said that "if you think there is a real possibility that you might lose their investment, maybe you haven't addressed all the risks" and should take the hint to think again and try harder to reduce them.

However, many other founders see friends and family as, at best, a last resort. Brian Scudamore was uncomfortable with the idea of taking money from relatives, even though at one point his startup was about to fold for lack of cash. He explained, "My dad could have given me the money. However, I didn't want him to worry that things weren't going well . . . I wanted to show dad that I could do it myself, even if that meant stretching things a bit too far. Also, taking money from him would cause problems if things went sour."

Brian's last point worries many other founders and investors. Just as cofounding with friends and family creates the Playing-with-Fire Gap discussed in Chapter 4, taking money from friends and family can put important—even crucial—relationships at risk and, if thing go badly, leave them in ruins. Founders who are confident in their startups' prospects and who are passionate about their ideas often discount the possibility that the startup could fail, but founders and investors who have already been burned by playing with fire take a very different view. One experienced advisor of startups observed, "If you go into business with money from friends and family, then you will either lose the business or lose your family, and have a very good chance of losing both." A serial entrepreneur explained, "Out of principle, I do not include family in business/financial transactions or pursuits. The fact is, money stands to be the very thing that can dissolve the strongest of relationships. Added to the prospect of 'family drama' (of which everyone seems to have plenty), it's not worth it."

One way around this can be to treat an investment from a friend or relative as a gift rather than an investment; that is, with no particular expectation of being paid back. As one founder put it, "To avoid any problems, just ask them to close their eyes and donate money to you." Speaking from the other side, one investor said about investing in a startup founded by a friend or relative, "I sometimes do it, but I regard it as a gift, not an investment."

In addition to introducing playing-with-fire problems, taking money from friends and family may send a negative signal about the startup's prospects, especially if the startup is beyond the early launching stage. One serial entrepreneur observed that founders who fail to raise capital from professional investors and then have to raise from friends and family should think twice about the startup: "If you can't convince someone more objective than your friends and family to invest in you, there's probably a flaw with your business, which will result in them losing their money and you feeling terrible. Even if you have a dozen rich uncles, I would suggest you find someone outside that circle who believes in you and your idea." An experienced investor said, "It's a shame to lose friends or family because they invested their savings in the business and lost it all. It becomes a tragedy when the business concept was flawed from the beginning. . . . Why do people take such a risk when there's plenty of other money out there? Because [friends-and-family] money is too easy to obtain, which encourages people to start marginal businesses. Beyond that, friends and family do little diligence, have no real objective judgment, and can't advise/prevent you against doing something completely stupid."[10]

Another experienced VC suggests that some founders may simply not know what their funding options really are: "The reason people usually go to [family and friends] is that they don't have other choices—or more likely, they don't know they have other choices."

Pulling together these considerations, one serial entrepreneur offered this rule of thumb: "If your family comes from a business background and are well-informed about finances *and* they know to keep business and friendship strictly apart, you should utilize them. However, there are clearly too many ifs, ands, or buts in this scenario, so founders would be well advised to search for financing in other places." Just as cofounding with friends and family should be accompanied by carefully constructed firewalls and explicit discussions about worst-case scenarios, so too should any financing from friends and family, or else founders should resist the temptation to take such money.

"Burning the Boats": Productive Motivation or "Entrepreneurial Suicide"?

Taking money from friends and family may not only make a startup possible, but also profoundly affect how—and even why—the founders try to grow or exit their businesses. For instance, taking such money may enable founders to persist through the scary drops of the entrepreneurial roller coaster, not simply because they have money with which to do so but because they don't dare give up. Scott Cook, the founder-CEO of personal-finance software company Intuit, tried to avoid raising capital from friends and family.[11] But 25 failed pitches to professional investors later,[12] he gave in and borrowed from his parents' retirement savings and from his cofounder's friends. Altogether, he "spent about $350,000 on Intuit, a sum pieced together from life savings, home-equity credit, credit cards, and loans from his father."[13] During one particularly difficult period, he said, "What kept me going was just fear that I didn't know how I'd ever pay back the money."

Similarly, Tim Westergren, founder of Pandora Radio, persisted with his startup long after others might have called it quits, in large part because he could not face the idea of losing the money invested by his cofounders' friends or reneging on the $1 million in salary deferrals the company owed its employees, most of them personal friends of the founders. As Tim explained, "I've brought everyone into it and can't turn back. My persistence might look like a virtue, but I have to put myself through this because of all the people I've involved who I have ties to." Indeed, objective observers might question whether such persistence is virtue or vice, skewing founders' incentives and possibly leading them to throw away years of their lives, or to throw good money after bad.

Some founders refer to taking money from friends and family as "burning the boats," referring to the legend of the Spanish conquistador Hernando Cortez, who, after arriving in South America with 700 men seeking to conquer the continent for Spain, ordered them to burn their boats so they could not even think of retreat. One founder said, "Once the money is in, a whole new dynamic is involved. With the relationship at risk, the entrepreneur (the good ones anyway) will move heaven and earth to not lose the investment. And moving heaven and earth is often what it takes."

An experienced startup advisor takes a more negative view, comparing "burning the boats" to "entrepreneurial suicide." He explains,

"If one sets oneself up in situations where you must 'succeed or die,' then your fundamental motivation must be called into question. . . . Instead of taking prudent risks to maximize your chance for succeeding, you live constantly on the edge in a world of 'possible success.' If this is the case, then the business is your 'addiction' that you're asking your friends and family to support. Further, founders and entrepreneurs should have a 'safe haven' if they are to have any hope to survive the rigors of the startup company lifestyle. Where do you go for physical/psychic nourishment and comfort when the world is crashing in on you? Family serves this purpose often and best. 'Burning your boats' undermines this support structure and thus is setting oneself up for failure."

For other founders, taking money from friends and family may make them more risk-averse than they might otherwise have been, which can result in a lower exit value. An experienced investor explained, "When an entrepreneur has all of their own personal wealth or their family's wealth tied up in a deal, they are more likely to be risk-averse and more likely to sell out at a smaller number." Founders who prefer a higher-probability small exit to a lower-probability large exit would see this as a good thing.

Although the effect of taking money from friends and family will differ depending on the founders involved and the specifics of the situation, friends-and-family investors introduce a more emotional element to the business as it moves forward, regardless of whether that heighted emotion is beneficial or detrimental to the founder and the startup.

HIGH VARIANCE: ANGEL INVESTORS

"Angel investors" refers to a wide range of individual investors who invest their own money and usually don't already know the founder. They invest at an earlier stage of startup development than do venture capitalists, often with the goal of attracting VCs to invest in a subsequent round of financing. One analyst of angel investments writes, "The angel market is essentially the farm system for the next wave of high growth investments."[14]

Angels differ from friends and family in almost all of the dimensions described above:

- **Motivations**—Angels are much more financially driven than are friends and family. They typically prioritize getting a good financial return from their investments, but many also have nonfinancial motivations, such as mentoring the next generation of founders, passing on their own hard-earned lessons, and applying their deep industry knowledge to help build the next generation of companies.
- **Access**—As shown in Figure 9.4, 13% of angels were investors in a founder's previous startup. However, for the typical first-time founder, angels are much harder to reach than are friends-and-family investors and there is far less initial trust and comfort. Most founders have to rely on weaker ties to access angels, either being introduced by someone they know or applying to make presentations to "angel forums" such as TechCoast Angels, a Southern California network with over 300 angels, or CommonAngels, a Boston network of about 70 angels.[15] In my data, 58% of startups were referred to their eventual angel investors by someone with a common tie (i.e., by a friend or family member of a founder or of an early executive in the startup), 7% of the startups approached the angel by submitting a business plan or making a cold call, and 4% were referred to an angel by a service provider such as an accountant or lawyer.
- **Human capital**—Occasionally, a friend or family member has experience or contacts that are directly relevant to the startup. For instance, if the person worked in the same industry or had worked in another startup, he or she might be able to provide advice and guidance or be able to introduce the founders to potential customers or partners. However, such value addition is more likely to be gained from professional angels, who usually have more business experience.[16] Early on, some play an active counseling role and may even sit on the board of directors until VCs begin investing. But

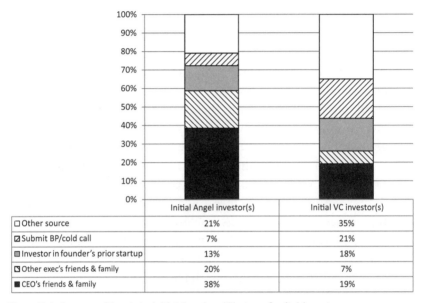

Figure 9.4. Sources of Leads to Initial Angel and Venture-Capital Investors

	Initial Angel investor(s)	Initial VC investor(s)
☐ Other source	21%	35%
☒ Submit BP/cold call	7%	21%
▣ Investor in founder's prior startup	13%	18%
◨ Other exec's friends & family	20%	7%
■ CEO's friends & family	38%	19%

their participation on the board usually does not last beyond the entry of VCs, and thus is less sustained than their participation in providing capital; by the second round of financing, few angels still sit on startup boards.

- **Social capital and credibility**—Depending on the backgrounds and reputations of its angels, a startup may gain a lot of credibility from them.[*] Angels can also play a direct role in bringing VCs into a startup. In 10% of the startups in my dataset, angels introduced the startup to a VC who eventually invested in it. The angel may also have customer contacts, industry expertise, or relevant skills that can add a lot of value to the startup.

---

[*] The connections and credibility added by top-tier angel investors can exceed those of many VCs. For instance, since 2007, angel investor Ron Conway, one of the first to invest in Google, PayPal, and many other successful startups, has been among the top 10 investors according to the *Forbes* "Midas" rankings, higher-ranked than the vast majority of VCs.

- **Financial capital: Amount invested**—Unless the founder chose his or her parents (or social circle) very carefully, friends and family are usually limited in the amount of money they can invest in the startup. Angels can fill the gap between friends-and-family investors and institutionalized investors such as venture capitalists. Between 2001 and 2009, the average size of an angel round was approximately $450,000, which falls right in between the amounts invested by friends-and-family investors and by venture capitalists.[17] Although most individual angels invest modest amounts, some organized angel groups invest much more; TechCoast Angels targets investments of up to $1 million, and CommonAngels targets deals that total $500,000 to $5 million.[18]
- **Financial capital: Continued investment**—Although angels mainly get involved in the earliest round of outside financing, many also try to invest in later rounds in order to maintain a minimal level of ownership in the startup. (This is also in contrast to friends-and-family investors, who often do not continue investing substantial amounts in later rounds.) As shown in Figure 9.3, angels participated consistently in 30% to 34% of the second through fourth rounds.
- **Personal risks**—Although, as we will see, taking money from angels can increase some types of risk dramatically, the playing-with-fire risk is much lower with them. There is usually no prior social relationship that will be damaged by failure, and professional angels are usually investing only a small percentage of their net worth in any one startup.

Among professional investors, venture capitalists usually get the lion's share of attention, but angel investors actually account for many more investments per year. Analyzing data from the University of New Hampshire Center for Venture Research's annual surveys of angel investors, I found that angels accounted for an average of 49,000 investments a year between 2001 and 2009, an order of magnitude greater than the annual number of VC investments during the same time period.* But VC investments, as described below, tend to be much bigger; despite the much greater number of angel investments, total angel capital invested per year averaged $22 billion, less than the venture capital invested annually over the decade.[19]

One advantage of angel investors is the diversity of industries in which they invest. Venture capitalists tend to target technology and life sciences startups; for instance, "Internet-specific" investments accounted for more than 20% of capital invested by VCs in half of the years between 2000 and 2009 and for over 30% in 2000 and 2008.[20] Startups in other industries have a better chance of being targeted by angel investors. Excluding the temporary spike in software investments during the dot-com boom, no single sector accounted for more than 20% of the capital invested by angel investors in any year between 2001 and 2009.[21]

The downsides of many angels include a general lack of understanding and experience with respect to both the business and their role as investors. In addition, because angels each invest smaller amounts, founders end up with a larger group of investors to manage. As Dick Costolo of FeedBurner explained, "We didn't know any VCs but we knew people who had sold companies and were interested in investing. We got a dozen accredited investors who took all common stock, no preferred stock at all. So far, so good. However, there were a few investors in the syndicate we didn't know well and they became problematic. They were making high-risk investments in a new company, but didn't feel like they could afford to lose their entire investment. It was a recipe for disaster. I had 13 people who, now that they had $20,000 invested, wanted to call me and ask about an article in the *Wall Street Journal*, taking 45 minutes of the CEO's time when he should be running the business!"

Dick also explained that angel investors do not demand the level of "constructive discipline" and accountability that more professional investors would require of a startup: "We didn't form a

* It should be noted that, due to problems with the transparency of the angel market, the angel data most probably understate the actual number of angel investments (Aldrich, 2010).

board because it was an angel round. We did things randomly for six months, paying ourselves randomly. We ended up having to go back and put our books in order when we did a [VC] deal later and it was a painful process. A board would have forced us to do things right and would have pointed out that the way we were hiring people could have used more rigor."

At Ockham, Jim Triandiflou's experience negotiating with angel investors illustrates some of their advantages and drawbacks. When Jim was ready to raise funding for Ockham, he first approached a group of angel investors led by Bobby Crews, a real estate developer from Texas whom he had met through a business associate. "Their term sheet was extremely interesting," Jim recounted. "They would give us $10 million: $3 million now and another $7 million as we needed it. They would take 50% of the company on Day One and then would keep their hands out of the business." Jim also liked the fact that, if he took the Texas money, Ockham's board would be small, and the founders would have two of the three seats. The major drawback, explained Jim, was the angels' lack of industry experience: "They didn't understand anything about the business. Bobby's a real estate guy! He would talk about it at cocktail parties and it'd be kind of cool, the little Atlanta software company he's funding." The lure of "no strings attached" angel money was quite powerful for Jim, as it is for many founders.

STRIKEOUT OR HOME RUN: VENTURE CAPITALISTS

Venture capitalists are professional investors who focus full-time on investing in high-potential startups. They receive business plans from the founders of young startups,[*] evaluate the plans, meet with the founders, perform due diligence to investigate the startup's team and potential, negotiate investment terms with the startups in which they want to invest, then help build the startup (often as

---

[*] As shown in Figure 9.4, 21% of the startups in my dataset initially approached their VCs by submitting a business plan. In 18% of initial VC rounds, the founder had already worked with the VC in a prior venture.

board members) in the hopes of exiting from their investment at an appropriate time.

VCs raise capital from limited partners (LPs), most of which are large institutions—foundations, university endowments, public pensions, and the like—that invest in a wide portfolio of assets and allocate a relatively small percentage of their capital to venture capital. The VCs have a fiduciary duty to those LPs and are evaluated on the financial returns from their investments. VCs are paid a management fee (usually 2%–2.5% of their assets), which they use for salaries and operating expenses, and a share of the financial gains ("carry") that averages 20% of the aggregate profits from their investments. VC firms are usually founded by a small group of general partners (GPs) who have to raise the funds they will invest, organize the operations of the firm, and sometimes hire junior people (analysts, associates, principals, and others) to whom they can delegate tasks in order to make better use of their own time.

More than any other type of investor examined here, VCs are motivated to prioritize financial gains and take any actions they believe will increase their returns. VCs raise funds that last a decade (often with an option for short extensions); they usually invest the majority of the fund during the early years, then have a few years to build and exit from each startup before the fund ends. VCs who want to continue investing must therefore raise a new fund every few years, requiring them to justify their performance and the solidity of their strategy to LPs. To maximize financial returns while reducing the risk of their investments, VCs seek to invest in a portfolio of startups, often numbering in the dozens for each fund. For each investment, VCs are seeking to return a large multiple of the amount of money they have invested, so they look for startups with the potential to be extremely big. The most common exits for VC investments are acquisitions by larger companies (as when Google bought FeedBurner), initial public offerings (as when Google itself went public), or, much less attractive, the bankruptcy of the startup. In a recent study of more than 22,000 venture-backed companies from 1987 to 2008, 26% of the startups had merged or been acquired, 9% had gone public, 15% had been liquidated or had gone bankrupt, 19% were expected not to return any money to share-holders, and 31% remained private.[22]

In the following two sections, we will see that founders can gain a lot, both financially and nonfinancially, by taking VC money. But there can also be serious losses of ownership and control.

Benefits of Venture Capital

Venture capitalists can provide founders with more financial capital, social capital, and human capital than the typical friend-or-family investor or angel investor can. Although there are always some who question whether those benefits outweigh the costs of taking VC money, many entrepreneurs persist in seeking VC investment. In fact, the more reputable, experienced, and well connected the VC firm, the more unfavorable the terms an entrepreneur will accept in order to secure an investment from it: A study of entrepreneurs who had received offers from multiple VC firms showed that, on average, entrepreneurs were willing to give up more than $4 million in valuation to get a better VC firm on board.[23] However, it is important to note that the entrepreneurs in this and similar studies are those who chose to seek VC investment to begin with; some of those founders who did not seek VC investment are likely to disagree that a VC investment is worth that price, as we will see below. (Capturing the spirit of this latter perspective, one founder insisted, "The goal of every board meeting is to end it.")

Financial Capital

VCs are attracted to high-risk/high-reward investments, which excludes most startups and which makes VC portfolios more volatile than portfolios of lower-risk/lower-reward investments would be. Within each portfolio, VCs tend to have a few "home runs" they hope will make up for the majority that either fail or produce only small returns.[24] One study estimated that, if the financial market's overall volatility is defined as 1.0, VC returns have a much higher comparative volatility (called a "beta") of 1.7.[25]

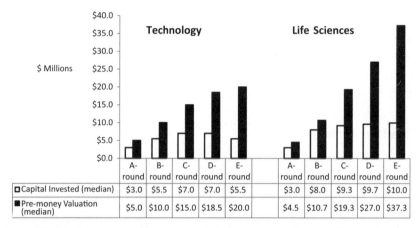

Figure 9.5. Capital Invested and Pre-Money Valuation for Each Round of Financing

As shown in Figure 9.5, even the smallest round that includes VCs (the A-round, which averages $3 million) is far bigger than rounds raised from friends-and-family investors and angel investors, which rarely surpass $1 million. Subsequent rounds get even bigger, especially in life sciences, where startups are often more capital-intensive, requiring nearly $10 million per round after the initial round.

VC investments are generally not only larger than friend-and-family and angel investments, but also longer-term. VCs invest with the intention of continuing to invest through multiple rounds of financing and usually budget their capital carefully to make sure they can continue to invest if the startup is making good progress (as described below), in contrast to friend-and-family investors who rarely continue into later rounds and to angels whose continuation is uncertain. Each round of financing, VCs decide whether to continue investing in each startup or to shift their capital toward more promising startups.

At the same time, the availability of professional capital is also heavily dependent on market conditions. During the dot-com bust, total VC capital invested plunged by 52% between 2000 and 2001 and by another 41% in 2002.[26] VC investments then jumped 57% during the turnaround in 2005–2006, only to drop again by 37%

during the early part of the recession in 2008–2009. Even if VCs invest with a long-term perspective, their sensitivity to the business-cycle roller-coaster ride is quite pronounced, limiting the confidence that startups can place in venture capital as a consistent source of funding.

Social Capital: Connections and Credibility

Founders of startups often rely on their investors and board members to make up for their own potentially fatal lack of connections, particularly connections to those who might serve as further sources of capital.[27] In a survey of VCs regarding the startup-related activities in which they were most involved, they ranked obtaining alternate sources of equity financing and interfacing with other investors second and third, respectively.[28] (Their top-ranked activity is discussed below.) In a follow-up survey asking startup CEOs to rank the contributions made by their VC investors, introductions to other potential investors was ranked second.[29] In my own dataset, VCs were more effective than other investors at making connections to future investors. For instance, initial VC investors connected 31% of startups to subsequent VC investors, while angel investors did so for only 10% of the startups. Similarly, VC investors connected 14% of startups to their initial corporate investors;[30] angels did so for only 5% of the startups.

High-status investors can also give a young venture some of the legitimacy it lacks. Startups with more prominent investors receive higher public-market valuations; the boost from prominent investors is especially significant for younger, less-proven startups for whom a boost in credibility is most important.[31] Frank Addante experienced the "halo effect" of top-tier venture firms when he began talks with Sequoia, a famous Silicon Valley VC firm. Although Sequoia's term sheet for Frank's startup, StrongMail, was not as attractive as some of the other offers he had in hand, Frank chose to do business with Sequoia because of their legendary reputation for helping build valuable startups. After meeting with Sequoia's partners at their office, he recalled, "I realized I was sitting in the same chair Steve Jobs had sat in, the same chair Larry Ellison and a lot of other big names had sat in." Having Sequoia on board helped convince potential hires and customers of StrongMail's prospects. As we saw in Figure 8.1, by the B-round of financing, investors are the second biggest source of executive hires, accounting for 19% of hires and helping make up for the founder-CEO's declining (though still strong) centrality in hiring.

Human Capital: Guidance and Mentoring, Both Informally
and through the Board of Directors

Do VCs provide guidance to their startups? In a survey of VCs to gauge the startup-related activities in which they were most involved, the highest-ranked item was "serving as a sounding board to the [executive team]."[32] Through their own websites, interviews, blog posts, and other forums, VCs tout their ability to add value. For their part, founders who have taken money from VCs do report that their investors had an impact, often positive, on how they ran the business. In the aforementioned survey asking CEOs to rate their VCs' contributions, the top-rated activity was serving as a sounding board to the executive team.[33] In another study, startups that received VC financing were 47.7% more likely than those with other kinds of investors to report that their investors were influential in shaping human resource management policies and initiating other professionalized practices.[34] In yet another study, VC firms with a high level of industry experience were able to get their term sheets accepted by entrepreneurs despite offering valuations that were, on average, 10% lower than those of competing offers.[35] This seems to indicate that founders expect to benefit more from the more experienced VC firms. Founders should recognize, though, that even if the VC firm has a great reputation, that is no guarantee that all of the firm's individual partners will be effective and committed. As a general partner from a top firm observed, "Not all money from Sequoia is the same color—it's different if you get [senior partners] Mike Moritz or Doug Leone instead of one of their newbies."

How is this valuable guidance being delivered? A lot happens informally or during one-on-one meetings between investors and founders. The issues covered in those discussions can vary greatly from startup to startup and from investor to investor, but are most likely to include strategic, personnel, operational, and financing issues. For instance, a VC will often serve as a "strategic counselor" who helps the founder-CEO hone in on the central strategic uncertainties facing the startup and who challenges the founder's core assumptions, "generally, pushing the CEO to step back from the day-to-day tactical operational activities and focus on the true value-creating decisions that need to be made."[36] The frequency of these informal meetings tends to change as the startup matures. As one VC explained, "The stage of the business has the biggest effect on mentoring frequency. In the first two years, as the team is being built, the strategy is getting set, etc., [the interactions are] many times per week. Some email traffic, some instant messages, some calls, some in person one-on-ones." After that, as the team and strategy solidify, such interactions become less frequent and more ad-hoc.

Another vehicle by which VCs provide guidance is formal meetings of the startup's board of directors. In fact, the very existence of a formal board is often a direct outcome of VC involvement. As described in Chapter 5, "Role Dilemmas," startup boards usually begin as informal decision-making bodies made up of the founders and sometimes one or two trusted advisors. By the time the first round of VC financing closes, there is a formal board of directors that includes at least one VC investor. (When multiple VC firms participate in the round, either multiple VCs join the board or the VC who "led" the round does.)

Thus, VCs not only demand a board, they generally demand to be on it, and the VC presence tends to increase over time. Furthermore, it tends to increase at the expense of founder representation. This is, of course, a significant control issue, as discussed below, but for our current purposes, it also has implications for guidance and mentoring, for the following reasons:

- **Longevity.** In contrast to angels, who usually leave the board of directors once VCs begin investing, VCs tend to remain on startup boards much longer. This longevity can help them provide better guidance than if board members were regularly being replaced, and CEO-board relationships are often more productive when the CEO has a chance to develop relationships with the board members.

- **Size.** The larger the board, the more industry knowledge and business expertise the CEO might be able to tap. In my dataset, after the first round of financing, 80% of boards had 3 to 6 members, with an average of 3.9. After the second round of financing, that average was 4.8 members. After that, the growth slowed; the average was 5.2 members after both the third and fourth rounds. By the fifth round of financing, 89% of boards had between 5 and 8 members, averaging 5.7.* (Despite their potential advantages, though, larger boards also introduce their own challenges, described below.)

- **Experience.** Board members with significantly more experience can gain added authority—the more so the smaller the board. The VC members of a startup board are likely to have more pattern recognition than the founder members and, in particular, are more likely to have experience as board members. In my dataset, 48% of outside directors had prior experience as directors. Most of those were venture capitalists who had sat on the boards of other startups in which they had invested, had seen common problems encountered by management teams, and had negotiated multiple financing rounds and company exits, in contrast to the founders themselves, who accumulate few such experiences.

- **Frequency of meeting.** Startup boards also meet more frequently than the quarterly schedule maintained by most large-company boards, although the frequency itself changes over time. This reflects the fact that startups are evolving with a speed and intensity not found in large corporations.

---

* Boards also often include "observers"—people who can come to board meetings but usually do not actively participate in them and do not vote on decisions. As a condition of their investments, VCs and other investors may negotiate the right to have an observer on the board, but those observers do not have a say in board decisions.

It also reflects the fact that startups are often being run by an executive team with less experience than would be found in a large company. Such a team may need a different quantity and quality of guidance from its board, guidance that becomes available once the board includes VC members. In my dataset, boards averaged 7.9 meetings a year, far more often than large-company boards. There was a wide variation in meeting frequency, but a consistent pattern was that boards met more frequently when the startup was younger, then less frequently as the startup matured. An experienced VC talked about how he insists on monthly board meetings while the startup is young, but that "[o]nce the business is well 'metric-ed,' is firing on all cylinders, and has a complete team, 60 days between meetings works." In other words, as ventures become more formalized and have metrics with which performance can be tracked, and as the executive team is completed, there is less need for the VCs to use board meetings to monitor the startup's performance and less need for them to provide guidance and recruiting assistance, so meetings can be held less frequently.

All of these factors suggest that startup boards serve as powerful conduits for the influence of VCs, an influence that seems, on the whole, to be viewed from both sides as helpful to the startups. My research with Warren Boeker suggests another dimension of this influence; namely, that the CEO's background is strongly linked to the degree to which VCs are actively involved in the startup.[*] To examine this, Boeker and I used my dataset of 450 technology startups to examine the proposition that three aspects of the CEO's background—functional background, years of work experience, and whether or not he or she was a founder—affect three aspects of the board—size, frequency of meetings, and composition (particularly the percentage of directors with prior board experience).[37]

---

[*] Future research could shed light on the VC side of this, examining whether the different backgrounds of VCs result in different levels of engagement with their startups, different types of value addition, and other factors.

We found that different kinds of CEOs do indeed have very different boards.[*] These differences could affect how much value the board will provide and how challenging the board is to manage.

First, CEOs with a midrange amount of prior work experience have the largest boards and meet most frequently with them. Both results suggest that those CEOs have the most opportunity to receive guidance from their boards. While this is good news for those CEOs with a moderate amount of experience, it does not bode well for inexperienced CEOs, who are most in need of guidance.[38] At Odeo, Evan Williams struggled to develop a product roadmap and looked to his board for guidance about how to do so, but grew frustrated with how little useful advice he got from them.

Second, regarding functional backgrounds, CEOs with experience in an external or output function, such as sales,[39] have smaller boards that meet less frequently and have less-experienced directors; CEOs with experience in an internal or throughput function, such as technology, have boards that meet with them much more frequently. For instance, Wily Technology's founder-CEO, Lew Cirne, who had a deep technical background, would be more likely to meet frequently with his board than would Jim Triandiflou of Ockham Technologies, who had a deep background in sales. Apparently, for technical founders, getting the guidance you need from your board can also come at the cost of having a larger board to manage and having to spend more time meeting with it.

Third, even after controlling for differences in the CEOs' levels of experience and functional backgrounds, there was a very strong relationship between a CEO's founder/nonfounder status and the board's experience: Founder-CEOs had much more experienced boards than did nonfounder-CEOs. There may be several reasons for this. To the extent that founders are overconfident and passionate, and thus can benefit from having a board that can serve as a reality check on their tendencies, their more-experienced boards are more capable of playing that counterbalancing role. As Bagley and Dauchy suggest,

---

[*] The results described here regarding formal board meetings were statistically significant even after including a proxy for the frequency of the informal board-founder interactions.

"The most effective boards give independent, informed advice to management and challenge the CEO, rather than acting as a rubber stamp."[40] Ideally, says one VC, "Boards should be encouraging the type of learning to allow a company to 'pivot' by making important changes in its strategy." To the extent that some founders have trouble focusing on a single idea rather than pursuing new projects, boards can also serve as a check on that tendency. Evan Williams, for example, was famous for jumping from project to project and failing to focus on the core deliverable at hand. Evan himself recalled that, in his first startup, a family-funded Internet publishing company, "I realized I had started 32 different projects during the previous year and not finished any of them. I was constantly thinking up new ideas and found it better to abandon the current thing so I could work on the new idea. I was very shortsighted." Evan eventually closed the company, losing all of his father's investment. A strong board might have kept Evan on track and avoided this fate.

All told, these results suggest that boards are often built with the CEO's weaknesses and strengths in mind. Except for the least-experienced CEOs—who seem to get less guidance than they might need, possibly because they are less attractive mentees—the CEOs who have the most need for guidance (those with a moderate amount of experience) seem likelier to get it. There is a wide-open opportunity for research that can show what is actually happening and why. For example, are founders seeking board guidance, or are VCs on boards making sure CEOs get it?

I should mention a further factor that can limit the intensity of VC influence through the board. The geographic proximity of a startup's VCs plays an important role in board composition and significantly affects the degree to which VCs can engage in close monitoring and CEO counseling, which are most effective in person. Controlling for a wide range of differences among VC investments, Professor Josh Lerner found that the closer a startup is to its VC's office, the more likely the VC will be to take a seat on the startup's board. The probability that a VC investor located within five miles of the startup will serve on the startup's board is 47%; for a VC located over 500 miles away, the probability shrinks to 22%.[41]

Costs of Venture Capital: Giving Up Ownership

There are two major rights affected by ownership in a startup: economic rights and control rights. By selling equity stakes to investors, founders give up some of both.

Changes in Overall Ownership

In each round of financing, the founders/insiders sell more of their startup's equity to investors, decreasing their own ownership percentages. When the startup returns money to its owners—often through an exit when it is acquired or goes public but sometimes also from a share of the ongoing profits—the owners receive that money in proportion to their ownership, unless there are other investment terms that affect the payments, such as the liquidation preferences described below (and many other terms that we lack space to cover here).

Figure 9.6, based on my dataset, shows how the percentage owned by each major type of shareholder changed after each round of financing. The most striking pattern is that after the C-round of financing, VCs finally owned more than half the equity—53% on average. (After the B-round, VCs averaged 46% ownership.) The increases in VC ownership were accompanied by steady decreases in the percentage owned by founders and employees, whose collective stakes plummeted from 41% after the A-round to less than half that after the D-round.

These changes do differ by industry. Life sciences startups tend to be more capital-intensive, requiring the founders to give up more equity in order to get the capital they need. After each round of financing, life sciences founders/insiders owned three to six percentage points less equity than did their technology counterparts. In addition, within each industry, the more attractive the startup and the fewer its weaknesses, the higher the ownership stake typically retained by the founders and inside executives.[42]

Founders/insiders are particularly likely to lose ownership in a *down round*, commonly defined as a round in which the venture's share price is less than it was in the previous round,[43] which means that the founders and insiders now have to give up more ownership

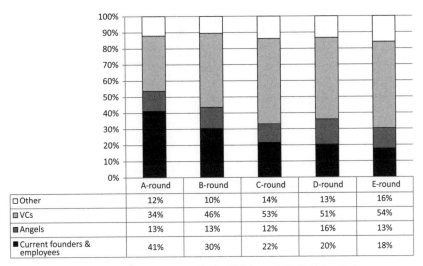

	A-round	B-round	C-round	D-round	E-round
□ Other	12%	10%	14%	13%	16%
▤ VCs	34%	46%	53%	51%	54%
▩ Angels	13%	13%	12%	16%	13%
■ Current founders & employees	41%	30%	22%	20%	18%

Figure 9.6. Capitalization Tables: Average Equity Holdings of Each Major Party

to raise a given amount of capital. Across all rounds in my dataset, 7% were down rounds. Sometimes, a down round occurs when the startup misses milestones and underperforms. One startup, having earlier raised an initial round of $1 million, wanted to raise a second round of $1 million. Because it had become evident that the startup was not going to achieve its milestones for bringing its system into operation, the investors demanded a higher percentage of ownership—and a lower share price—in return for their investment. As the company continued to experience "missteps and missed deadlines," the startup's investors invested another $2.7 million, bringing their ownership stake to 75% of the company's equity as the startup's price per share sank.

Figure 9.7 shows that down rounds are also closely tied to the business cycle: During the high points in the cycle, such as the late 1990s and the mid-2000s, the percentage of down rounds decreases; during bust times, such as the early 2000s and the late 2000s, the percentage increases markedly.[*] Thus, a startup's exposure to the

---

[*] Further analysis of down rounds shows that 4% of B-rounds were down rounds (i.e., at a lower valuation than the A-round) and 7% of C-rounds had a lower valuation than the B-rounds, followed by 9% for the D-rounds and E-rounds.

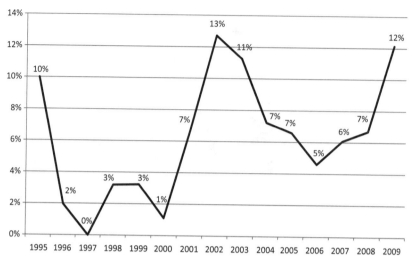

Figure 9.7. Percentage of Financing Rounds That Were Down Rounds, by Year the Round Was Raised

negative effects of a down round can be due both to its own ability to execute and to factors outside of its control.

Liquidation Preferences: Giving Up "Small" Exits

The percentage of equity owned by each party tells only part of the ownership story. Other terms in the investment agreement affect how much each party would receive in various exit scenarios. Perhaps the most important of these terms affects each party's payouts, particularly when there is a small exit. That term is called the *liquidation preference*, which dictates that if the startup liquidates or is acquired, then the VCs get back the amount they invested, or a multiple of that amount, before other shareholders (most centrally here, the founders) receive any proceeds.[44] During the first round of financing, 78% of the startups in my dataset agreed to give their investors a "1×" liquidation preference; that is, if the startup would sell for the amount of capital invested by those investors (or less), those investors would receive all of those proceeds and the founders and other early shareholders who own common stock would receive nothing.* (Once the liquidation preference has been paid out, the common stock holders usually begin receiving some proceeds.)[45]

Far more drastic are the liquidation terms to which the other 22% of startups agreed: 9% agreed to liquidation preferences of 1.1x–2x, 5% agreed to 2.1x–3x, and 8% agreed to greater than 3x. In this most extreme latter category, the startup would have to exit for at least three times the amount invested in order for the founders and common-stock holders to see a penny of return. As startups raised further rounds, the percentage of startups agreeing to preferences greater than 1x increased, from 22% during the first round to 33% during the fourth round of financing.

Investors require such terms so they can reduce their risks and align the founder's incentives with their own. Without such terms, the investors might be unwilling or unable to invest at all, would have to reduce the amount of capital, or would have to use other—more costly—terms. Why, though, do founders agree to such terms? Sometimes, it is simply because they sorely need the capital and lack the negotiating power to resist. However, another important factor is entrepreneurial optimism. Filled with passion for their idea, confident in their abilities, and dreaming of building a large and valuable company, founders often shrug off the possibility that their startup may sell for only a small "nice" price. They figure, "There's little chance we'll sell for less than $X, so if the VCs want a liquidation preference for that amount, I'll give it to them and I'll take the more likely upside of a big sale or IPO." At Lynx Solutions, the founders agreed to standard 1x liquidation preferences that meant that the startup would have to sell for more than $29.5 million (the amount invested by the VCs) for the founders to earn a dollar from the sale.

---

* A related term, which can also affect the founders' eventual payouts, is whether the investors' preference includes *participation*. After the initial preference is paid out to investors, participation governs how the remaining proceeds are paid out. There can be full participation (investors share pro rata in the remaining proceeds as if they had converted their preferred shares into common stock), no participation (investors have to choose whether to keep their liquidation preference or to convert their preferred stock to common stock), or capped participation (a midrange option). For more details on this term and for the potential misalignments that each option can cause, see Wilmerding (2004) and Bussgang (2010).

Amid a market downturn, Lynx did not receive any offers greater than $25 million, which introduced major misalignment between the founders (who did not want to sell and go entirely unrewarded for their years of hard work) and the investors (who preferred a moderate exit to what they saw as a good chance that the startup would fail).[*]

Some founders, having gotten burned signing such terms, begin to feel that their investors took advantage of their early passion by having them sign large liquidation preferences. They regret that, with all their eggs in one basket, they did not push back against the much more diversified venture capitalists rather than bear the risk themselves. But a wiser course would be for founders to take the small-exit scenario seriously from the beginning, however confident they are of something better. In fact, the more confident they are, the more helpful it would be to get some impartial advice on the rational probability of a small exit and consider whether they really are willing to give up any possible gains from such an exit.

But aside from optimism and overconfidence, founders may have more rational reasons to sign such terms. Evan Williams, for example, agreed to a 1.5x liquidation preference for Odeo's investors, largely because he felt that time was running out for the startup to bring its product to market ahead of well-funded competitors. Other founders think carefully about the probabilities and seek outside advice to counterbalance their confidence and passion, then still decide that the increase in potential return is worth the new risks.

Whatever the motivation, giving investors a liquidation preference increases the pressure on founders to "swing for the fences" and to adopt higher-risk/higher-return strategies, since they now have nothing to gain from a "small" exit to which they might otherwise have agreed. Founders who are incented to swing for the fences are more aligned with investors who likewise want to hit a home

---

[*] The impasse was resolved only when the investors finally agreed to create a small "equity carve-out" that would give the founders and some key personnel small shares in the sale.

run, but founders (for whom this might be their only swing at the ball) do so at the cost of increasing their risk, often dramatically.*

Investors Forcing Ownership Shifts within the Founding Team

Investors may also have a powerful impact on ownership within the founding team itself. The most common impact is when VCs insist that the equity held by founders and nonfounding executives must vest—that is, be earned back—over a preset number of years or after the achievement of predetermined milestones, in order to provide "golden handcuffs" to keep them working for the startup. (See Chapter 6 for details on founder vesting and Chapter 8 for nonfounding executive vesting.) For instance, at an early Web startup, the venture capitalist insisted, as a condition of the A-round and as a way to incent the founders to keep working at the startup, that the two founders' full equity stakes had to vest, effectively returning their economic ownership to zero and forcing them to re-earn their old stakes. Taken aback but needing the capital, the founders fought the change—in vain.

A less common, but still very important, way in which investors can affect founders' stakes is when the investors insist on reallocating those stakes to more closely match the individual founders' contributions. Investors want the most important members of the team to own the largest equity stakes in order to both retain and motivate those members. Investors will therefore assess whether the "right" founders have the largest stakes and, if they detect too great an imbalance, will often insist that the founders reallocate their equity as a condition of the financing round. One founder said, "I was the cofounder of a startup and as part of the Series A, the investors actually required my stake to be increased. They felt the original founder's equity was lopsided and wanted to ensure incentives were properly distributed across the team." A VC explained why he might insist on an equity adjustment before investing: "We spend

---

* Among VC-backed startups, 75% of founders received no financial return from their years of hard work building the startup (Hall et al., 2010).

time during our diligence process understanding how [the founders' equity splits] came to be. By the time we look at a company for investment, there has usually been enough development so that issues resulting from 'quick handshakes' or disproportionate equity splits have made themselves visible. From my experience, both equity-split scenarios can lead to suboptimal behavior."

Attracting investors is usually associated with an increased chance of organizational survival and a reduced liability of newness.[*] However, my research with Matt Marx suggests that founding-team turnover actually increases dramatically when the startup raises its first round of financing; success at attracting investors is associated with having founding teams become less, rather than more, stable. This might be because investors may force renegotiation of equity stakes and roles within the founding team, which is almost guaranteed to raise the tensions within the team.[46] This important hidden cost of attracting investors should be considered before hunting for capital.

Costs of Venture Capital: Losing Control of Decision Making

Although the board can provide guidance to the executive team and monitor the team's progress, its most fundamental role is often decision making. For instance, boards not only review the startup's strategy and performance but also help decide if the strategy should change. They not only evaluate the CEO's performance but also decide how the CEO should be compensated and whether or not he or she should be replaced (see Chapter 10). Boards may also make decisions about financing (e.g., whether or not to raise new rounds or to change financing approaches) and about when and how to exit. Having a say in all of these decisions is a key way in which investors protect their investments. However, all of these decisions create the potential for divergence between the wishes of the founders and the wishes of the investors, making the board a key arena in which founders and investors wrestle for control.

---

[*] For more on the liability of newness and Stinchcombe's (1965) arguments about the factors that underlie it, see the beginning of Chapter 1.

Board Control

As described in Chapter 5, a startup's board tends to start out dominated by the founders. With each round of financing, however, the
lead investor is likely to want a board seat. Sometimes a new seat is
added, but more often, to avoid having the board grow unwieldy,
the lead investor replaces a founder or an early angel investor on
the board. In my dataset, after the A-round of financing, founders
were already a minority within the average board, holding 34%
of the seats, while outside directors already held 59%. After the
B-round, founders were down to 21% of the seats, with 72% held
by outside directors, the clear majority of whom were investors.[47]
The board's changing composition often becomes a critical issue
that affects how much control the founders will continue to have
over certain decisions.

Boards usually start out including the founder-CEO along with
one or more other founders. A founder-CEO who wants to stay on
the board can push for his or her seat to be defined as a "founder
seat," in which he or she will still sit even if replaced by a nonfounding CEO, rather than as a "CEO seat" that will be taken by the new
CEO, possibly leaving the founder without any seat on the board.
When FeedBurner was raising its A-round, the founding team negotiated that its newly formed three-person board would include,
in addition to the lead VC, two founders rather than one founder
and the CEO. Founder-CEO Dick Costolo, knowing that he could
be replaced as CEO by a nonfounder, pushed for this provision so
that he and the team would have more sustained representation on
the board.

In some cases, the VCs' presence on the board may lead to much-
needed professionalization and discipline within the executive
team.[48] The VCs may also help shape the startup's strategy in productive directions. In other cases, though, it may constrain the founders
from adjusting their strategy or making other changes. For instance,
Evan Williams believed that Apple would beat Odeo to market with
a superior podcasting technology, so he wanted to abandon the
podcasting strategy and quickly develop a new status-update tool.

Evan's VC-controlled board, however, was starting to worry about its investment and about Odeo's lack of progress. "It's the board's job to question what I am doing, but I don't want to be required to explain myself [so much]," Evan said. "Having a board is killing our ability to try new things."

Although many board decisions are decided by majority rule, investors may negotiate "supermajority" or veto rights that give them extra power when deciding specific issues, such as whether to sell the startup. In the same way that liquidation preferences give investors more ownership rights than they would have based strictly on the percentage of equity they own (as we saw above), supermajority or veto terms can give them greater control rights than would be indicated by their percentage of ownership. At one startup, even though the founders retained board control, the VCs negotiated veto rights over certain decisions. One of those was approval of the annual budget. Years later, during the dot-com crash, the VCs wanted to exit and tried to force the startup to accept an acquisition by vetoing all proposed budgets. One founder said, "Their vetoes made it impossible for us to give our employees pay increases or bonuses and it really was holding us back," forcing the company to find new investors to buy out the VC firm.

During the downturn of 2008–2009, some founders complained that their boards had become risk-averse and opposed to any actions that would require additional resources, preventing the founders from taking advantage of the downturn by acquiring competitors who had fallen on hard times and from making other aggressive competitive moves. At the other extreme, because VCs try to pick out startups with the potential to be very large, they often push those startups to adopt grander—and sometimes riskier—strategies. One of the VCs on the board at Lynx Solutions, for example, pushed the company to make a radical shift away from its consumer-based product and focus instead on an enterprise-based system in order to capitalize on the "hot" market for enterprise technology, even though its founders believed this would be a major mistake.

Boards often aspire to make unanimous decisions that have everyone's support. However, for many decisions, this is unrealistic and may not even be desirable (if it leads to lowest-common-denominator decisions), resulting in board votes that are much more split. Sometimes, every seat counts:

- **Split board, plus one independent director**—Many boards have equal numbers of insiders and outsiders, with one additional seat held by an independent director (i.e., a director who is not a major investor, current executive, or founder). A three-person board would have one founder, one investor, and the independent director; a five-person board would have two founders, two investors, and the independent director. On boards with more than three members, founders are usually aligned with each other, as are investors, making the independent director the "swing vote" whenever a decision is to be made by majority rule. Of course, this heightens the stakes in the negotiation over who gets to choose that independent director. After FeedBurner's B-round of funding, the company established a five-person board: two founder seats, two VC seats, and an independent board member to be nominated by founder Dick Costolo. Dick nominated Matt Blumberg, the founder-CEO of another high-tech startup. "I love having another CEO on the board," explained Dick. "Matt's the only person involved in the company who knows exactly what I'm dealing with, is my peer, and generally feels the same way I do about the next steps in the life of the company." When VCs choose the independent director, such alignment between that director and the founders is much less likely.
- **Evenly split boards and board gridlock**—Many startup boards are evenly split with no independent tiebreaker, despite the obvious risk of board gridlock. In fact, after the A-round of investment, a full 46% of boards have an even number of members (24% have four members and 11% have six). This percentage stays relatively constant through the first four rounds of financing, ranging from 43% to 49%. Boards with only four members—two insiders (founders or

early executive hires) and two outsiders (often investors)—
are most common during the first two rounds of financing
(before outside investors gain control of more than half the
board) and are most prone to gridlock.*

Managing the Board: The Middle of the "Hourglass"

The CEO plays a central role at every board meeting. However,
a board meeting is not just an event, it is a process. The founder-
CEO has to prepare for the board meeting, conduct the meeting,
and perform follow-up tasks after the meeting. All of this comes on
top of his or her duties managing the executive team. FeedBurner's
Dick Costolo described this two-sided challenge: "As founder-CEO,
you're alone at the center of an hourglass-shaped reporting structure in which all the employees report up to you and then you report up to all the investors/shareholders." New founder-CEOs are
often surprised by the amount of time it takes to perform their "up-
ward" board-management tasks. Masergy's Barry Nalls recounted
the enormous amount of time he spent preparing for board meetings: "The preparation of my first board package took a full week.
We had monthly board meetings, and after one of them, I realized
I had spent 25% of my month getting ready for it. The amount of
work to prepare for a board meeting was stunning!"

Although founders can learn how to perform these tasks more efficiently, the challenge of managing the board continues to grow as the
board grows. As Jim Triandiflou of Ockham Technologies said about
the perils of having a large board of directors, "You spend all your
time managing your board members."[49] Serial entrepreneur Furqan
Nazeeri commented about boards in young startups, "I have found
that a five-person board for early-stage (A-round) companies is too

---

*To avoid such decision-making gridlock, the millennia-old Talmud goes out of its way
to ensure that no court ever has an even number of judges. At the beginning of its main vol-
ume on jurisprudence (TB Sanhedrin, p. 2a), the Talmud outlines nearly three dozen widely
varying types of court cases, from small monetary claims to capital cases, which are judged
by courts ranging in size from 3 to 71 judges. The Talmud mandates that every single one of
those courts have an odd number of judges.

large. The CEO will spend as much time managing the board as he or she will managing the team, which is probably the same size. It's also very difficult to remove a board member, particularly a VC, as the company grows. It's not uncommon for B-round and later-stage VC-backed companies that start with five-member boards to grow to six- or even seven-member boards, which is just too cumbersome."

Lynx Solutions experienced this very problem. It was raising a new round of financing and its board had grown to four investors and three founders. The founders resisted growing the board to accommodate new investors and instead scaled it back to five members. Founder James Malmo said, "If we hadn't cut back, we would have been a tiny company with a board fit for GM. . . . We already had a minority from the management group anyway, and that wouldn't change. . . . [Cutting back to five] would give us room to grow. It felt minor league to have just VCs and management on the board; a serious VC-backed company brings in prominent outsiders who can add value. That was part of the rationale: Leave room to bring on someone from the outside world."[50]

The Effects of Board Formalization

When the full board is making decisions together, members who are founders or inside executives can have an important impact. However, just as startups become more formalized as they grow, boards also become more formalized as they grow. In particular, they usually adopt a committee structure, in which subsets of directors serve on specialized committees making decisions about specific issues. For instance, a compensation committee may be responsible for setting (or recommending changes to) executive compensation and an audit committee may be responsible for monitoring the quality of the startup's performance, accounting, and tax data. These committees are often made up of outside directors with the appropriate experience or expertise, and some committees (e.g., the compensation committee, which recommends executive compensation) cannot include founders who are still executives, potentially reducing the impact of founders and inside executives on those decisions.

Within my dataset, after the first round of financing, 30% of boards had established formal compensation committees and 21% had established formal audit committees. These percentages rose steadily and, by the fifth round of financing, 42% of boards had compensation committees and 34% had audit committees.

Staging as a Control Mechanism

Gaining control of the board is the most direct way for VCs to gain control over decision making. A less direct but still powerful way is by "staging" their investments; that is, committing small portions of capital sequentially, rather than committing up-front the full amount of capital that will be needed by the startup. VCs know that they will have the most leverage over a startup when it needs their money to grow or just to continue operating.

Before the initial round of financing, a VC firm's due diligence might reveal risks that it wants addressed before it agrees to invest; the VC may therefore require such changes as a condition of its initial investment. Each subsequent round of financing also provides the VC with a key lever of control over the startup. Before each new round, the VC reassesses the startup's prospects and decides whether to reinvest in the next round, to make new demands before reinvesting, or to abandon the investment. If the VC decides to reinvest, it will try to provide enough capital for the startup to achieve its next major milestone. This "staging" of capital allows the VC to learn more about the startup's prospects and to reduce its own risks (and potential agency problems) by not having to commit all of the necessary capital up-front.[51]

A key decision for both startups and investors is how long to wait between rounds of financing. The technology ventures in my dataset averaged 15 months between rounds; the life sciences ventures averaged 17 months.* On the investor's side, Professor Paul

---

*The time between rounds was very consistent across levels of startup maturity: In technology startups, the intervals were 15 months between A-round and B-round, 16 months between B-round and C-round, 16 months between C-round and D-round, and 14 months between

Gompers has shown that VCs are willing to allow more time between rounds when the startup has a higher percentage of tangible assets; because such startups pose lower agency costs and fewer information problems, VCs can invest for longer periods. On the other hand, they allow less time between rounds when the startup is more R&D intensive and dependent on intangible assets; such startups pose higher agency costs and more information problems. On the startup's side, Professor Bill Sahlman suggests that how long entrepreneurs wait between rounds of financing is partly determined by the balance they strike between fear and greed; that is, the fear of running out of cash and having to shut down versus the desire to keep a higher percentage of the equity by waiting to make more progress and increase the startup's valuation. Interestingly, founders suggest that the decision is also partly based on their respect for the "disciplining effect" of not having a wealth of resources and their fear of the bad habits that can develop when a startup has raised too much capital.

DIVERGENT PATHS: WEALTH VERSUS CONTROL WITH INVESTORS

Founders face a wide spectrum of investor choices that can pose stark trade-offs. Perhaps even more so than for the previous dilemmas examined in this book, each investor choice can enable or imperil very different things for the founders. For instance, resisting investments from professional investors can enable the founders to keep control of the board and of key decisions, but imperil their ability to fill holes in the startup's human capital, social capital, and financial capital, thus making it harder to quickly bring a better product or service to market. In contrast, taking money from outside investors can enable the founders to tap into the resources needed to grow value, but at the expense of imperiling control.

For instance, when Ockham Technologies was faced with a choice between taking money from informal angel investors whose

---

D-round and E-round. Within life sciences startups, the intervals were 17 months, 17 months, 15 months, and 16 months, respectively.

only real contribution would be capital and taking money from a top regional venture capitalist, founder Jim Triandiflou had to carefully weigh the potential benefits and pitfalls of each path. On the one hand, the Texas angel investors required less total equity while investing more money ($10 million), promised to stay out of the day-to-day management of the company, and would accept a small board on which they had only one representative. The drawback to the angels was their complete lack of industry and startup knowledge. If Ockham's founders took the angel money, they would be completely on their own.

On the other hand, Noro-Moseley, one of the most reputable VC firms in its region, offered only $2 million, wanted a liquidation preference, gave Ockham a lower valuation, and required a board of directors with five seats, of which only two seats would be held by the founders. (One seat would be held by an independent director.) Jim wanted to avoid losing control of the board. But Noro was a proven player, had partners with direct experience in Ockham's industry, and would give Ockham the credibility that a young startup needed to attract the best employees and to sell its software to customers such as IBM.

Jim, a first-time founder, explained how he and his cofounders made their choice: "We weren't overly confident that $10 million from the Texas guys would be enough. If things happened that we didn't expect, the Texas guys might run for the hills, but for Noro, this was their business. The terms of the Noro deal were the least attractive, but we wanted to get the smartest, best people we could, and we didn't let our equity 'delusions' stand in the way of that." In the horse race between fear and greed, Jim's fear of running out of cash, given the uncertainties faced by a first-time entrepreneur, won out over his "greed" for a higher percentage of equity.

As we will see in Chapter 11, different founders *should* be making very different investor choices, informed by their own core motivations. With each type of investor, founders should also make very different choices about the specific investment terms to which they agree. For instance, we focused above on how board composition will affect control of the startup, but founders who are particularly concerned with keeping control of their startups should also fight back most strenuously against *protective provisions* that give investors extra voting rights and *drag-along rights* that determine who can authorize the sale of the startup to another company. Prioritizing these control-related terms will increase the founder's chances of remaining king of the startup. Founders who are less concerned with control rights than with maximizing their financial value should be willing to accept the provisions listed above and instead fight to maximize their ownership stake overall and in various exit scenarios, thus increasing their chances of achieving a Rich outcome. In addition to the liquidation preferences described above, they should fight to minimize secondary terms, such as the investors' *anti-dilution protection* (which protects the investors' ownership stake in a subsequent down round of financing) and the *dividends* that investors can accrue. At Ockham, for example, Noro-Moseley wanted an "accruing dividend" that would lock in an 18% annual return before the company could make payouts to other shareholders.[52]

CLOSING REMARKS

Vigilance about investor decisions is particularly important, given (a) the potential disconnects between taking outside capital and maintaining control of the startup and (b) the natural inclinations that can get founders into trouble when making investor decisions. Prior to "signing on the dotted line," founders should understand the repercussions of taking outside money, guard against their own optimism, and arm themselves with negotiating leverage whenever possible.

One of the major repercussions of taking outside money arises when investors move to gain control over key decisions in order to protect their investments, imperiling the founder's control over the startup. For founders who are wealth-motivated, gaining confidence that a VC will be able to add value to the startup often makes it easier to relinquish some control to the VC. But for other founders, their control motivation may not be compatible with outside investment and they should be very hesitant to raise capital or, if it is absolutely necessary, should try to craft terms that will give them the maximum amount of control for as long as possible.[53] Investors are usually more attracted to startups with wealth-motivated founders, with whom they will be better aligned than with control-motivated founders, so founders who truly want— and understand the repercussions of—outside funding should check that they are sending the appropriate "wealth-motivated" signals to potential investors.[*]

A founder's natural optimism can also introduce long-term problems when taking early investor money. Founders who agree to standard investment terms—for instance, to give their investors a liquidation preference—because they are confident that their startups will grow big, are giving up claim to a moderate gain. Yet it is much more likely that a startup will grow to moderate size than to huge size. The Lynx Solutions team, for example, agreed to a liquidation preference for their A-round that led to problems three rounds later when they were weighing acquisition offers that were below their cumulative liquidation preferences and thus would not give the founders any financial return from their years of hard work. Instead of assuming that such a term will never apply because the startup is sure to become big, optimistic founders should take the small-exit scenario seriously from the beginning and should consider whether they really are willing to give up any possible gains from such an exit.[†]

---

[*] Term sheets and investment deals should be formulated differently for wealth-motivated founders (who, for example, are likely to be more open to being replaced by a better CEO) and for control-motivated founders (who, for example, may be averse to accepting the necessary outside capital unless their control of the startup can be solidified). Adeo Ressi's influential founder-oriented website, TheFunded.com, has created a set of "founder friendly" model term sheets to complement model term sheets created by the National Venture Capital Association. Such models make it possible for founders and investors to create a coherent spectrum of choices that recognizes how founders differ regarding control-versus-wealth trade-offs and how those different incentives can be aligned with those of investors.

[†] Investors could help founders avoid some of the ill-fated decisions that result when founders default to natural human tendencies rather than consciously deciding what to do. For instance, as examined in Chapter 4, founders commonly found with friends or family—a

Dealing with investors can be daunting, particularly for new entrepreneurs, but there are several strategies that founders can use to gain leverage. Jim Triandiflou deliberately waited until his startup had a solid product, cash flow, and customer contracts before approaching VCs, judging correctly that this strategy would result in higher valuations. He also avoided working with a single VC firm, in order to avoid the control over decision making that a single VC with two board seats would have. Instead, he split the first round between two VC firms, each of which took one seat on the board. "Two guys from the same firm can monopolize decisions, and not giving any one person or group control is critical," Jim explained. "My having board control is less important than my making sure someone else doesn't have it."

For FeedBurner's Dick Costolo, gaining leverage in a VC negotiation meant having appealing alternatives. In one round, he had gained leverage by getting competing term sheets from different VCs. In another round, he put off approaching VCs until he had received acquisition offers from Yahoo and Google: "Having the potential acquirers involved changed the dynamic with potential investors. It kept acquirers from wasting our time with stupid offers and prevented a lot of back and forth with the VCs on harsh terms." Dick also made sure that he negotiated with VCs well in advance of running out of cash: "If we take it down to the wire, the VC will sit on it for a few weeks until they know we don't have money, have to sign their term sheet, and have to take their terms."

As we have seen, core founders are often missing skills, connections, and financial resources needed to build the most valuable startup possible. They can make up for this by attracting complementary cofounders or by hiring talented nonfounders. A third possibility is to add investors to the team, but founders must first think

---

very natural tendency—but fail to erect firewalls to make sure that the team does not blow up (and take the founder's most treasured relationships with it). Likewise, as examined in Chapter 6, natural human inclinations lead founders to avoid structuring dynamic equity agreements, despite the probability that static agreements will harm the team and the startup. Investors could offer creative incentives to avoid such missteps; for example, by making the implementation of specific firewalls or dynamic agreements a condition of investment.

carefully about the often-hidden implications for themselves, for the startup, and for the board of directors. For a founder-CEO, losing control of the board is only the first step on the way to losing control of the major decisions in the startup and may culminate in one of the most critical inflection points in the life of a startup, the replacement of the founder-CEO by a nonfounding CEO. That inflection point is the subject of our next chapter.

CHAPTER TEN

FAILURE, SUCCESS, AND FOUNDER-CEO SUCCESSION

THUS FAR, WE HAVE EXAMINED FOUNDERS MAKING THEIR VERY FIRST decisions, from becoming founders early or late in their careers, to going solo versus building a founding team, to making choices about hiring and about attracting investors. Through the experiences of Evan Williams and a host of other entrepreneurs, we have become acquainted with the many ways founders can make mistakes. In this chapter, we turn to one of the most important outcomes affected by early decisions, which also happens to be one of the most critical points in the life of a startup and of its founder—the point at which the founder-CEO is replaced as CEO. As we will see, although some founders, such as Evan Williams, are able to orchestrate their own successions, for many others, it comes as a shock.

In contrast to some of the founders we have seen, Lew Cirne avoided many early pitfalls. From the very beginning of his career, Lew made choices that would enable him to start and grow a successful startup. After earning a degree in computer science at Dartmouth, he furthered his technical education by taking a job at Apple Computer. While performing his core tasks there, he also conceived an idea for a diagnostic tool for Java-based enterprise systems and began to make plans to launch his own high-tech startup. He decided to gain more experience in both technology and management while also getting an insider's view of a startup by working for two years at Hummingbird, a young IT company. "I wanted to learn how to be a founder or an early employee of a new company," said Lew. "I wanted to gain breadth, compared to my more focused role at Apple.... Part of my motivation to start [a company] was to grow professionally by achieving as a businessperson, not as a technologist." While at Hummingbird, Lew picked the brain of a former entrepreneur who helped him hone his idea and gave him insights on hiring and fund-raising.

Lew decided to fly solo, founding Wily Technology on his own and raising $100,000 from angel investors. From the beginning, he was passionately attached to his startup and made personal sacrifices designed to benefit Wily. Lew worked alone and feverishly for a full year to develop his Java-based technology. He sent a white paper about his idea to IBM, which resulted in Wily's first sale. Lew then hired a "generalist" who could take on the nontechnical tasks while Lew himself continued to work on the product. When his early board members (the angel investors) dragged their feet on giving the new employee equity, Lew carved out some of his own equity. "I transferred [some of my shares] to [my employee]," he explained, "rather than dilute the rest of the shareholders." The principle Lew was following was, "Don't worry about your own dilution, worry about Wily."

As Lew continued to refine the product and the business plan and bought his first suit so he could make sales calls, he realized he needed to raise more money for full-scale product development. Based on the strength of his technology and his vision for the product, he raised $2 million from outside investors. He then hired one of his former Apple colleagues to take on the chief scientist role. This was "a pretty challenging thing for a technical founder to do," Lew said, but the new version of the product benefited from the new leadership. Lew hired more key people, paying them more than he himself made as CEO.

Lew continued to build Wily with help and guidance from his VC investors and the startup continued to meet or exceed all its early milestones. Lew was particularly excited as the company began shipping its new version of the product and started negotiations on

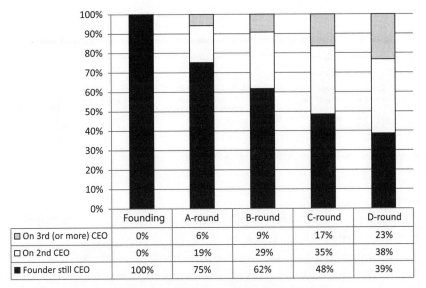

	Founding	A-round	B-round	C-round	D-round
▨ On 3rd (or more) CEO	0%	6%	9%	17%	23%
☐ On 2nd CEO	0%	19%	29%	35%	38%
■ Founder still CEO	100%	75%	62%	48%	39%

Figure 10.1. Percentage of Startups Still Being Led by the Founder-CEO

a new round of financing. His excitement quickly turned to shock when his backers insisted that he step down as CEO as a condition of the new round. "Things became really tough after that," Lew recalled. "All I could think was, where have I messed up? What have I been doing so wrong?" In the end, Lew's potential replacement as CEO, Richard Williams, refused to take the job unless Lew also gave up his position as chairman of the board. At this point, Lew faced a major dilemma: Refuse to hire the professional who could build Wily's value, or hire the pro and be completely sidelined in the startup he had nurtured as if it were his only child.

How could this happen to such a successful entrepreneur? The move to replace Lew came as Wily was raising its third round of financing; we can see in Figure 10.1 that, by that time, more than half of startups have replaced their founder-CEOs. In fact, 17% of them have already replaced CEOs more than once. But why? How often is it by choice and how often is it forced on the founder-CEO? What happens to the replaced founder? These and related questions are central to one of the most critical inflection points in the evolution

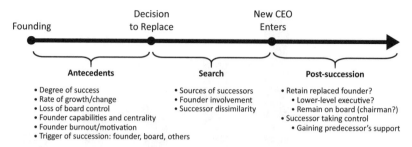

Figure 10.2. The Founder-CEO Succession Process

of a startup: the "succession" from a founder-CEO to a "professional" (nonfounding) CEO.

Throughout this book, we have focused on startups in which a founder is still CEO. However, a startup's first-ever CEO transition is a particularly challenging and jarring juncture. To help us delve into founder-CEO succession, we will both examine large-scale data about the antecedents, dynamics, and aftermath of such events and delve into the stories of several founder-CEOs and the professional CEOs who replaced them. We will analyze why successful founder-CEOs like Lew get fired as CEO, observe in detail the process of replacing them, and explore whether they should remain active in the startup. Figure 10.2 is a graphical depiction of the most important stages of the founder-CEO succession process and some of the factors affecting each stage.

Although we have already seen many decisions in which control-motivated founders diverge from wealth-motivated founders, the divergence is most stark during the founder-CEO succession process, affecting who triggers the succession, how the search for a new CEO is conducted, and what—if any—role the replaced founder-CEO will play in the startup.

TRIGGERS FOR CHANGE

Founder-CEO succession can be initiated by the founder-CEO, the board of directors (which is officially responsible for selecting and monitoring the CEO), or some other party, such as investors who do not serve on the board. In my dataset, founder-initiated changes were relatively uncommon, accounting for only 27% of succession events.[1] The lion's share of CEO changes—73%—were initiated by the board or by another party.[*] Board-triggered successions are usually the most tense. The founder-CEO often resists the change, heightening the risk to the startup. After examining the smoothest type of succession—voluntary succession triggered by the founder—we will look at two types of board-initiated succession: first, when the board fires a poorly performing founder-CEO and, second, when the board replaces a high-performing founder-CEO. The latter confronts us with what is known as the paradox of entrepreneurial success.

Voluntary Succession

Voluntary succession is when the founder-CEO decides to step aside for a new CEO, who almost always comes from outside the startup. This is usually the least stressful transition, but given the tight attachment between founders and their startups, and the typically high level of confidence founders have in their skills, it is a rare founder who willingly gives up leadership of his or her startup. As Lew Cirne said, "Prior to Richard [the professional CEO] coming along, I felt it was my company—'Lew's company.'" For such a founder, voluntarily handing over the reins of the startup is as inconceivable as voluntarily putting up for adoption the child he or she has raised since birth.

Founders who willingly volunteer to be replaced may be those who are most self-aware and have become convinced that the demands

---

[*] In all, 62% were triggered by the board. Other triggers of succession—such as investors who were not on the board, a recent executive hire, or even a non-CEO cofounder—accounted for the remaining 11%. Note that this does not include unsuccessful attempts to fire the founder-CEO. Field research suggests that such attempts are not uncommon, but has not yet established systematically how frequently they occur or how founder-CEOs survive them.

of the CEO job are beyond their abilities.* Alternatively, they may be those who feel burned out from riding the entrepreneurial roller coaster, putting in seven-day weeks month after month. In either case, the founder begins to realize that the value of the startup is going to suffer. By the time Mike Brody, founder-CEO of Transcentive, told his replacement, Les Trachtman, that he was in favor of stepping down, he had been CEO for over fourteen years and was, as Les explained, "a little older, a little more tired," and motivated to hand Transcentive over to a professional CEO who could lead it more effectively.

Founders primarily motivated by building wealth are often quicker to step aside as CEO when they see the startup's value—and therefore the value of their equity—suffering. In contrast, control-motivated founders will be more likely to fight for their CEO positions and thus end up having the board initiate the change. As we will see below, waiting for the board to trigger the change can have important consequences for the founder's role after succession. Founders who maintain some control over the succession event often end up in better positions. For example, Mike Brody at Transcentive was able to retain his position as chairman of the board, largely because he took an active role in his own succession.

Fired for Failure

A board may trigger CEO succession if the startup has been performing poorly under the founder-CEO's leadership and the board believes a new CEO could do better.[2] (Such a situation is typical in large companies, where firing the CEO almost always comes after underperformance or a failure to meet expectations.) VC Tim Connors says that, in startups, boards "look for a CEO to raise money, hire a team, and set and hit a financial plan," and that failure in those areas will cause them to replace the CEO.

---

*Sometimes that self-awareness is enhanced by participation in regular meetings of a CEO forum or by working with an outside "CEO coach" who becomes a trusted, unbiased advisor. Participation in a forum can also mitigate the loneliness of being a CEO, which Dick Costolo described as being "alone at the center of an hourglass."

In startups, however, failure is harder to judge than in big companies, especially when the startup has not yet completed product development. There are no sales or revenue figures, customer acquisition has not begun, and other market-driven metrics are not available. However, startups do have a variety of milestones—such as completing development of each major module of the system or hiring an experienced VP of marketing—that they are actively tracking and sharing with the board. When those milestones are missed, or missed one after the other, the board may conclude that the leadership team, particularly the CEO, is dropping the ball, whether by choosing the wrong milestones, inaccurately forecasting when they will be achieved, or choosing the wrong processes or people to achieve them. One founder-CEO, for instance, came up with an industry-changing idea, launched his startup, developed a prototype, and raised $2 million in two rounds of financing. Nevertheless, he was fired by his investors after more than a year of consistently missing product-launch targets and was replaced with a successor who got the company back on target.

The Paradox of Entrepreneurial Success

Lew Cirne was neither a volunteer nor a failure. He was enjoying his role as CEO, he felt confident he was up to the job, and Wily was unquestionably doing well. By almost any metric, Lew was a smashing success as CEO. He had built a 50-person company and led it through a very successful product-development process. As a result, Wily's revenues were rising quickly and the company was headed toward profitability. To get the "rocket fuel" to invest in product development and hire his team, he had raised two large rounds of financing from venture capitalists—and top-tier ones at that. Attracting rocket fuel was not only an essential ingredient of Wily's success, but also an important certification of that success; VC investments serve as both a stamp of approval for the startup's progress and a boost to its credibility.[3] One investor, Greylock Venture Partners, went so far as to state on its website its "belief in the entrepreneur as 'Star' and Greylock as 'Invited Guest,'" and Lew certainly had every right to feel like a star entrepreneur. Like many founders, he referred to his startup as his "baby." He was brimming with pride in its growth and enjoyed being at the center of its operations.

Why, then, was the father of this baby being fired by his "invited guest"?

The seeds of such founder-CEO succession events are planted much earlier. Quantitative analyses of my data along with my field research highlight two types of success—product development and fund-raising—that spark crucial but underappreciated internal changes that, in turn, put successful founders such as Lew at risk of being fired.[4]

Succeeding at Product Development

The major operating challenge in the initial phase of a startup is to develop a product or service that can be sold to customers. This requires the accomplishment of many complex steps: defining specifications, developing an architecture, surmounting technical or scientific hurdles in development, coordinating team efforts to develop different yet intersecting pieces of the product or service, gaining any necessary regulatory approvals, and the like. At this stage, there is a premium on technical or scientific skills and on leadership at the project-team level. For Wily, Lew Cirne's expertise was particularly important in the fast-developing world of Java applications. When the original client-side product didn't get the traction Lew had anticipated, he was able to quickly regroup and redesign the product in time to catch the growing server-side wave. Founders with relevant technical or scientific backgrounds, such as Lew, are often the best leaders for the product-development phase of the startup, for they are best suited to address the technical contingencies and challenges of that stage.

However, once the product or service has been developed and is ready to be sold, the startup becomes much more complex and the CEO faces dramatically different challenges. The startup is no longer primarily a technical team developing a product. It must add new functions such sales, marketing, and customer support. A technical founder-CEO such as Lew, who had to buy his first suit in order to make a sales call, now has to interview and hire salespeople, understand how their motivations differ from those of technical whizzes, and know how to structure their incentives and compensation. Few founders who were adept at the early technical challenges are equally—or even sufficiently—adept at these very different challenges. Managing a technical team is quite different from managing multiple functions that must interact and with most of which the CEO has little direct experience. At this point, the startup's finances and metrics also become much more complex, requiring a level of financial sophistication possessed by few founder-CEOs.[*]

The leap from leading product development to leading a multifunction startup challenges not only the founder's skills, but—perhaps even more profoundly—his or her values. During the early days, when founder-CEOs are still relying heavily on their own networks for hiring (see Chapter 8), they tend to bring in people they already know well and build a tight-knit culture. "Whom we hired was important," Lew insisted, "because we were trying to build a culture that felt like a family." Founder-CEOs therefore tend to exhibit fierce loyalty to their early employees. Those early employees often prove unable to meet the challenges of the startup's next stage of growth, yet the founder-CEO, prizing loyalty and not wanting to imperil the carefully constructed family culture, often keeps them in key positions long after they have reached the limits of their capabilities. The startup has reached the point at which those early employees must be managed much more objectively than the founder-CEO can do. After professional CEO Les Trachtman

---

[*] Some startups later face a second dramatic shift in their customers and their market focus when they try to "cross the chasm" (Moore, 2002). Companies developing products that are innovative or based on new architectures (or both) have to transition from an early market dominated by a few early adopters to a larger mainstream market. The chasm such companies must cross includes a huge difference in the skills and operations required to serve these different markets, a huge difference in customer preferences, and other key issues that involve multiple functional areas. Although the challenges of crossing the chasm are classically seen as a marketing problem, they also require new capabilities at the top of the startup and thus often require a new CEO. Far from being just a marketing issue, the challenges of crossing the chasm should be seen more broadly as a leadership and operational-management issue.

succeeded founder-CEO Mike Brody at Transcentive, he reflected on how hard it would have been for Mike to make the personnel changes that the startup required at that stage of growth, particularly to replace his own brother, who had long ago ceased to be an effective CFO. "[Mike was in] a tough situation," Les recalled. "A couple of people he knew were in the wrong positions, but because he valued his personal relationships with those people, he didn't want to make the moves he knew were necessary. I think I was brought into the firm because the board realized that Mike couldn't jettison the staff that needed to be let go. He had developed such strong ties with his employees. . . . I [also] think Mike knew that his brother was not the right person for the CFO job," but couldn't bring himself to change CFOs.

The founder-CEO may also be attached to his or her original idea for the startup, while the startup itself has reached the point at which the original idea may have to be adjusted. At Megaserver, an earlier startup at which Les Trachtman had worked, the technologist-founders had spent years developing their idea for a "virtual supercomputer" and kept finding ways to give it more functionality and add "bells and whistles." Finally, the startup's chairman decided that it was time to move past the stage of developing "cool technology" and to get to work developing a usable system that customers could understand and would want to buy, a change in emphasis that the founders would have trouble accepting. To help effect such a change, the chairman hired Les, a sales-oriented technology executive, to be Megaserver's first nonfounding CEO. As Les explained, "We needed to highlight a specific functionality of the technology so that we would not confuse consumers. The [founders], on the other hand, felt that by taking this route, consumers would never know that the technology had a lot of other great functionality."

The next stage of the startup's development often requires the development of new processes, the formalization of the organizational structure, and other changes foreign—or even antithetical—to the typical founder-CEO. One influential model of startup evolution emphasizes that each stage of startup development has a very different "dominant problem" that the startup must solve, but that the solution often causes the startup's next crisis.[5] For instance, solving the early "creativity" challenge in a startup leads to a crisis of leadership, which is solved in the next stage by an increase in direction, which in turn causes a crisis of autonomy. The skills and personal characteristics needed to solve one stage's dominant problem often become obstacles to solving the next stage's dominant problem. The radical differences between stages require radical shifts in the capabilities of the executive team.[*]

To add to the injustice, the more quickly a founder-CEO leads the startup through these early stages, the more quickly he or she will need to develop new skills or capabilities and the sooner he or she may find the challenges winning the race. Thus, the founder-CEO's very success at leading a fast-growing startup through product development is likely to accelerate his or her own obsolescence and replacement. Quantitative data show that it is precisely at the point where the startup has completed product development that the founder-CEO's chances of being replaced rise significantly.

Succeeding at Fund-Raising

For many startups, a key challenge is attracting outside capital. Such capital not only helps the startup bring its product or service to market, but—if it comes from professional investors—also increases the startup's credibility with potential customers and other external parties.[†] Yet meeting the fund-raising challenge can set off an even bigger change within the startup. With each round of financing, the startup sells equity to outside investors and adjusts the composition of its board accordingly. As described in Chapter 9, the founders, once they begin raising capital from outside investors, quickly

---

[*] In a different realm, how often has the right person to lead a revolution proved to be the wrong person to subsequently lead a government? For instance, long ago, in ancient biblical history, King David was a warrior king who led the Israelites during the conquest of their country and their capital city, Jerusalem, but was deemed unfit to establish the Great Temple and other administrative features of a stable kingdom. Instead, his successor, Solomon, was far more suited to carrying out those tasks, and did so successfully during his 40-year reign.

[†] See Chapter 9 for more details.

lose control of board-level decision making. Thus, the startup's success at raising outside capital has not only accelerated its growth rate, but has also caused a fundamental shift in the power structure within the board—which hires and fires the CEO. The new board, made up of investors and independent directors who are motivated by the creation of shareholder value, may have a very different view than the CEO does of who is the best person to tackle the startup's next set of challenges. Investors may well believe that a new CEO is needed for the startup to reach its potential value during the next stage of growth, and they now control the body that can make that decision. Thus, with successful fund-raising comes loss of control of the board and, with it, the risk that the founder-CEO will lose his or her own position as CEO.

For Lew Cirne, the VCs' demand for a new CEO coincided with the raising of Wily's third round of financing. Lew's seed round had been with family and friends—angel investors who did little more than act as an advisory board. After the first round of VC financing, Wily's board consisted of Lew (chairman), an angel investor who had been Lew's mentor and fully supported him, and the VC who had led the first round. After the second round of financing, Wily's board gained another VC, the lead investor in the new round. It was this newly constituted board that soon insisted that Lew step down as CEO. Henry McCance, chairman of Greylock Venture Partners, explained how changes in the challenges facing Wily sparked the investors' desire for a new CEO: "When we get into the go-to-market phase, when sales-and-marketing becomes a bigger issue, in most cases the entrepreneur doesn't have that in his background, as was the case with Lew. So we put it out there that there will come a time when we need a CEO with different skill sets."

In general, the more critical a resource is to a startup, the more the startup must give up to attract it.[6] If that resource is capital, the startup's founders typically must sacrifice control of the board and the founder-CEO must sacrifice control of his or her destiny. Quantitative analyses confirm that the chances of founder-CEO succession rise with each new round of financing, the more so the more capital is raised in that round.

Implications for Succession

As the founders and employees of startups celebrate each milestone, feeling that much nearer to the success they envision, they seldom realize that they may also be that much nearer to the day when the "fearless leader" who hired them and has brought them this far will be replaced.

Some founder-CEOs are aware of this possibility—perhaps having already been replaced in a previous startup, or having heard stories from their mentors who were—which can introduce perverse incentives. As one commented, "If the company tanks, I'm gone. But if it's a big hit, I'm also gone. If I want to remain CEO, should I only aim for middling success?" Confirming this founder's intuition, young companies are indeed more likely to experience the departure of the founder-CEO when their revenue and employment growth are very low or very high; middling growth rates lead to the lowest rate of founder-CEO departure.[7] Control-oriented founders in particular may prefer to sacrifice fast growth in order to grow at a rate closer to their own ability to learn and to adjust to the shifting challenges they know they will face. At Sittercity, for example, COO Dan Ratner acknowledged that founder-CEO Genevieve Thiers was able to remain CEO for several years because of the slow growth Sittercity experienced after being founded during the dot-com bust and before it faced real competition. "You don't normally have a four-year run-up to the starting line like [Genevieve] has had," explained Dan. "She . . . had the time to learn how to get through roadblocks. . . . No matter how smart you are, you need a certain amount of time, not just time to absorb but to make mistakes."

Understandably, even wealth-motivated founder-CEOs often disagree with VCs over the right time to change CEOs, with VCs preferring an earlier change than do the founder-CEOs. VCs have voiced the opinion that, when it comes to changing CEOs, "if in doubt, better to pull the trigger too soon than too late," while founder-CEOs almost always prefer to receive the benefit of the doubt as long as possible. As a result, CEO changes often occur later than investors prefer, but earlier than founder-CEOs prefer. In my data-set, for example, VC-triggered successions occurred an average of 6 to 12 months earlier in the life of the startup (3 to 3.5 years into the startup's life) than did founder-triggered successions (approximately 4 years after founding).

The final challenge introduced by the founder-CEO's success is that this very success makes it harder for the founder to believe that a different CEO is needed. After all, the founder's worthiness to lead the startup, while it may have been a gamble at the beginning, has now been proven. (In contrast, a founder who is failing, drowning in problems he or she doesn't know how to solve and wishing for assistance, is usually much more receptive to the earthshaking message from the board of "You're not the right person to lead us into the next stage.") Indeed, a very experienced VC told me, "One of the toughest jobs I have is firing CEOs who have *succeeded* in rapidly growing their companies."

SEARCHING FOR A SUCCESSOR

About one-third of replaced founder-CEOs leave the executive team within a month after the decision has been made to replace them. The percentage varies according to which party triggered the change: When the board initiates the change, the founder leaves the executive team 37% of the time; when the founder-CEO initiates the change, he or she leaves the team 24% of the time. In either case, the founder-CEO abruptly goes from being his baby's very attached parent to having no custody at all. But for everyone else, and for the two-thirds of replaced founder-CEOs who remain as non-CEO executives, the next step is the search for a new CEO.

Sources of Successors

In large companies, a high percentage of new CEOs come from inside the organization. For instance, in a broad study of 1,035 large-company succession events, 81% involved inside successors.[8] Promoting an inside executive is seen as healthy for the organization and gives the board confidence that the new CEO will fit with the organization and its culture. One notable exception is when the organization has been performing badly and requires dramatic changes; in such cases, an outside hire is much more common.[9]

In startups, however, the new CEO almost always comes from outside the existing executive team. In my dataset, only a handful of startups chose a successor from within the executive team. The new CEO is usually being brought in to make major changes, whether in the organizational culture (e.g., moving from Lew Cirne's "family culture" to a professionalized one), in the strategy (e.g., altering the founder's original business idea), or in the team (e.g., replacing cofounders or early hires who aren't performing well). In short, the new CEO is being hired to do what the founder-CEO either *could not* do (for lack of skills or knowledge or because of deeply ingrained mental models or schemata) or *would not* do (given his or her nonwealth motivations or his or her attachment to longtime participants or to the original strategy or idea). The startup's small executive team seldom offers the board enough good candidates. In addition, as noted by venture capitalist Jeff Bussgang, "Great general-management and operational executives don't typically take startup roles running a single function," requiring the startup to look outside for such executives.

Wily's search for a new CEO touched on a wide variety of both internal and external sources. Lew Cirne's initial inclination was to promote Vic Nyman, the VP of sales and marketing. "Vic was an absolutely key person in the growth of Wily. He was a great team player who would take on whatever job we needed him to do," said Lew. "At the same time, he was clearly aspiring to be a president or CEO. He served the company and the team very well, but all the while accomplishing his own objective of gaining breadth in his own career." However, David Strohm, the VC from Greylock who served on the Wily board, immediately rejected the idea because he was "not comfortable with the internal candidate." David added, "The leadership team at Wily largely consisted of people who had grown into jobs within Wily, some without extensive prior experience at leading teams or managing functions. . . . [Also, Vic's] sales and marketing functions were where most of the growth-induced conflict was occurring."

Wily therefore began a search for outside candidates. The startup spent three months engaged with a small boutique search firm, but the few candidates it sent were, according to Lew, "disastrous," "a bad fit with our culture," and "people who were out of work and should continue to be." Wily then searched through its own network of contacts, but "the first candidates we approached didn't want to take our call. It was hard to get a high-quality person's attention to even hear our elevator pitch," lamented Lew. Several more months went by and Wily engaged another search firm. Within a few weeks, the new firm had found "solid candidates" for the board and Lew to consider. But after looking at 120 resumes and interviewing 20 candidates, the new investor in the upcoming C-round instead recommended one of its own "favorite CEOs," Richard Williams, who had a "reputation as a superstar." Thirteen months after the search process started, the board and Lew agreed that Richard would be the right choice for CEO.

Wily ended up finding a new, outside candidate, but in some cases, startups have prior familiarity with their potential new CEOs. Some hire new CEOs who have served on the startup's board or served the startup as a consultant. Transcentive's Les Trachtman, for example, had forged a strong working relationship with founder-CEO Mike Brody, first as a consultant and then as VP of operations, before succeeding Mike when Transcentive's board felt the need for a professional CEO. Similarly, Lynx found its professional CEO, Clark Evans, when he came to conduct an all-day strategy session. He was well received by the employees and, as a veteran of a large consumer-products company, had the business-process skills that Lynx's founders lacked. As founder James Milmo recalled, "People breathed a sigh of relief that we founders were smart enough to bring in someone like that."

Founder Involvement

While the interval between deciding to replace the founder-CEO and hiring a new CEO can be as little as a month, this is uncommon.

In my dataset of founder-CEO successions, 6% of the startups hired a new CEO in the same month that the decision was made to replace the founder-CEO. Much more often, the search is drawn out. In fewer than one-third of the startups was the CEO hired within a year of the initial decision; Wily's 13-month search was fairly normal. This is especially true if the founder-CEO who is being replaced is playing a central part in the search process. For the outgoing founder-CEO, hiring a replacement is sometimes akin to approving a husband for his or her only daughter; no one is good enough.

Legally and formally, it is the board's responsibility to choose the new CEO. But boards often make the founder a central part of the search process, in an attempt both to get input about candidates from the person who best knows the startup and to help gain the support of the replaced CEO. However, when the founder's motivations (e.g., to maintain the culture and ensure that loyal early employees are not laid off) conflict with those of the investors (generally, to find a CEO who will maximize the financial return from the startup), involving the founder in the search process can introduce new risks and delays. "I didn't want us to rush," Lew asserted. "When you have high pressure to find the right CEO, you're going to rush into taking the person who 'looks good' on paper but doesn't fit too well with your organization and its culture. An important and challenging thing is to provide pushback to investors on the fit piece, because they'll be pushing hard on the people whose resumes look really good. But the investors aren't the ones who have to spend every day with them—we are!" Boards must carefully consider what they might gain from a certain level of involvement on the outgoing founder-CEO's part versus what that level of involvement might cost. Who will conduct the first screening interview of prospective candidates, the founder-CEO or the board? Will the board solicit input from the founder-CEO but retain full control over the final decision? Will the founder-CEO have veto power?

Lew's intimate involvement with the search process and his intangible criteria for finding the right person caused him to reject several candidates favored by the investors, particularly at the beginning of the process. Lew explained, "I believe it's . . . the intangibles that will make or break this turning point for the company. I was very happy with the people I had hired and the culture we were building and wanted someone who wouldn't feel that he needed to put his mark on the company, to assert control and feel like he had to make changes in the team." Lew also didn't want someone overconfident who "hadn't made any mistakes yet . . . so no humility." He vetoed one person who he felt "used motivation by fear," and he avoided people who were "younger, very ambitious with the constant need to prove [themselves]."

When the board involves the founder in the search process, CEO candidates have to meet the criteria of two very different parties. The candidates have to be aligned with the board members, in particular the investors, who are wealth-motivated and are changing CEOs in order to increase the value of the startup. The candidates must also be acceptable to the founder-CEO, who may well be control-motivated and seeking every way to retain control of key decisions. Even if the founder-CEO is wealth-motivated, he or she may have other and conflicting motivations, such as emotional attachment to the startup or worries that his or her contributions will be forgotten and his or her legacy weakened.

At Wily, the family culture led to even broader involvement in the hiring process by people who did not serve on the board. At the beginning of the search process, Lew took an open approach to hiring. He invited most of the company's senior managers to sit in on interviews and to read resumes to ensure that the team would feel comfortable with the hiring process and that the new CEO would fit Wily's culture. But this approach scared off the highest-quality candidates. As David Strohm, Wily's VC, explained, "When you include everyone in it, the process quickly becomes a plebiscite, which can be quite off-putting to serious candidates. It can also result in a 'least common denominator' outcome, with the candidate who is least threatening or most agreeable to everyone on the team surviving."

Successor Dissimilarity

During the search process, homophilic tendencies—the tendencies for "birds of a feather to flock together"—can lead founder-CEOs to feel drawn to candidates who share their backgrounds and skills.* At the same time, for many founders, the more different the candidate is, the more acceptable, if those differences address important contingencies the founder couldn't address. Thus, a founder-CEO who lacks sales experience but whose startup is ready to sell its product will more clearly see the value of a candidate with a strong sales background. A founder with 10 years of work experience will more clearly see that a candidate with 30 years of experience may be a better choice than a candidate with the same 10 years. For Lew, the fact that Richard had a different skill set made the change more palatable for him. "What got me comfortable with being on board with [the succession] was recognizing that [Richard] couldn't have done the job I had done to get the company to where it was. I felt better about myself, that I had done something uniquely valuable for the company. I had gotten the company from A to B, but now we have to go from B to Z."

It is also easier for the former CEO to accept a position as a subordinate if the new boss is unambiguously more experienced, or at least more experienced in a crucial way. Even so, the more different the successor-CEO's functional background is from the founder-CEO's, the more likely the founder-CEO's exit from the startup,[10] heightening the need for boards and successors to focus on facilitating a smooth post-succession transition.

If the founder-CEO was fired because of the startup's success, that success can make the startup more attractive to new CEO candidates. Henry McCance of Greylock explained how Wily's success affected the CEO search: "As Wily hit more milestones, the team realized they could shoot for a more capable and experienced CEO." At the same time, if the replaced founder's prior success makes him or her unhappy with the change, this can cause problems for the new CEO, leading many successors to prefer losing the "irreplaceable founder" rather than retaining a disgruntled founder in an important role.

---

* See Chapter 4 for more details about homophily and its powerful impacts on team composition.

AFTER THE SUCCESSION

Even after the startup has found its new CEO, much hard work and many land mines remain for the replaced founder-CEO, the incoming professional CEO, and the board of directors. Decisions made at this point can still make or break the transition and spoil the startup's prospects.

"A Tidal Change"

Even when founder-CEOs have been convinced to support—or at least not actively oppose—their own succession, they are ill prepared for the jarring change it introduces. As professional CEO Les Trachtman observed, "The founder-CEO says, 'Okay, I'm ready for this,' but they don't have a clue what it means. They think it's a *title* change, not the *tidal* change it really is." This can be true even when the founder-CEO was the one who initiated the succession. Mike Brody at Transcentive, despite being fully on board and supportive of Les taking over as CEO, still experienced a rocky transition. "Mike really didn't know what this change meant," explained Les. To complicate matters, Mike found it hard to let go of day-to-day decision making, and his role on the board signaled to employees that he was still in charge. "He was still the person that people went to when they had problems. It was still, 'Mike, may I?'—which disempowered me a bit," reflected Les.

Before joining the startup, a CEO candidate needs to assess whether the startup and the founder are ready for such a drastic change. At the startup level, is the startup at the inflection point where a new CEO's skills are needed and he or she can have an immediate and positive impact? For instance, is the startup heading into a potential "market chasm" that the new CEO's skills will help it cross, as was the case for Les Trachtman at Transcentive, or is the startup still facing early technical challenges? (The latter was the case when Les failed at Megaserver, the first startup into which he was hired as professional CEO.) Will there be fierce opposition to an outsider taking over, or do the key employees understand the need for change and see a new CEO as the solution to the startup's problems? Does the board fully support the incoming CEO, or are there sensitivities and constraints that the new CEO needs to consider when making strategic, cultural, and personnel decisions? At the individual level, is the outgoing founder-CEO control-motivated and thus likely to vehemently resist the change, or is he or she wealth-motivated and more likely to see the value to be added by a new CEO? Is the founder still intensely driven, or is he or she burned out? If the outgoing founder-CEO does not fully support the succession, will his or her loyalists also resist it? Or do they, despite their loyalty to the founder-CEO, see the need for change better than he or she does?

In any company, it is an uphill battle for a new outside CEO to learn how the organization operates, develop relationships with the key players (many of whom might be unhappy with the change), and take hold of the reins. Startups typically add two more complexities to this challenge. First, the new CEO is being hired specifically to make dramatic changes in a fast-paced environment, which both denies him or her the luxury of taking a long time to get to know the organization and its people and also makes resistance more likely. Second, the replaced founder-CEO, in many cases already disillusioned with the change, is usually kept on in a prominent position.

The Replaced Founder's New Position

In large companies, the replaced CEO almost never remains on the executive team and generally leaves the board of directors as well. This is invaluable for helping the new CEO take charge and for signaling that "there is a new sheriff in town." In most startups, though, the replaced founder-CEO remains on the executive team and on the board. In my dataset, even when the board initiated the succession, 63% of the replaced founders remained in the startup as executives; when the founder-CEO initiated the change, 76% remained in the startup as executives.

The trigger of change had an even more dramatic impact on whether the founder remained on the board and on which sub-CEO position he or she assumed. At the board level, if the founder-CEO initiated the change, he or she remained on the board 96% of the time; if the board initiated the change, that number dropped to 60%. Either way, in a majority of startups, the new CEO had to deal with having the replaced founder on the board of directors.

Some boards try to smooth the founder-CEO's transition by letting him or her become or remain chairman of the board of directors. Clearly, this can cause problems for the incoming CEO who wants to send a clear message about who is in charge and wants to sideline any potential sources of resistance to the upcoming changes. At Wily, Richard Williams would replace Lew Cirne as CEO only if Lew also stepped down as chairman of the board. Lew recalled Richard's words: "Lewis, I think the world of you, but you're not the right person to be chairman. I want David [Strohm, the VC] to become chairman instead. I'll only take the CEO job if he is the chairman." From Richard's point of view, this would send a clear signal that he, not Lew, was now in charge of Wily. But for Lew, this was close to the last straw. "With my president and CEO titles going away, being chairman takes on more importance with my knowing that I still have a role that goes beyond technology leadership."

At the executive level, Figure 10.3 shows that if the founder initiates the change and wants to remain in the startup, he or she is almost guaranteed to receive a C-level position, but if the board initiates the change, the chance of receiving a C-level position plummets. Founder-CEOs with technical backgrounds are most likely to move into the CTO or VP-engineering positions; founder-CEOs with business backgrounds are most likely to move into the VP-business development position, followed by the VP-marketing position.

Even though the predominant pattern is for the percentage of founders in executive positions to decrease as the startup ages (due to founder attrition and the hiring of nonfounders), there is a distinct temporary uptick in the percentage of founders in sub-CEO positions as former CEOs are moved downward into those positions. For instance, before any outside financing is raised, only 12% of VPs of business development are founders, but that jumps to

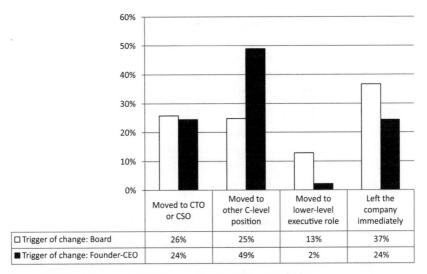

Figure 10.3. Post-Succession Positions of Replaced Founder-CEOs

	Moved to CTO or CSO	Moved to other C-level position	Moved to lower-level executive role	Left the company immediately
☐ Trigger of change: Board	26%	25%	13%	37%
■ Trigger of change: Founder-CEO	24%	49%	2%	24%

38% after the first round as replaced founder-CEOs are moved into that position. Before raising financing, 43% of CTOs are founders, but that jumps to 57% after the first round as replaced founder-CEOs are moved into that position; the percentage increases again slightly after the second round.

For Lew Cirne, who was replaced when Wily had a relatively complete organizational structure, such a redeployment to a lower-level position could have been even more disruptive had it required him to displace one of the loyal executives he himself had hired. "It was a real challenge," Lew said. "We had a VP of engineering, a chief scientist, a VP of product management. I had given them responsibility and I didn't want to now take that back. Everyone was very cognizant of, 'Where does Lew fit?'" Wily had not hired a CTO, however, so Lew was given that title. Yet even this decision was not as harmless as it might seem. When Lew saw the new org chart, he realized that his role as chief technology officer would be symbolic at best; with no direct reports, he would be "chief" of no one. This could certainly have been taken as an insult and have further provoked Lew to resist the new CEO.

Keeping the Founder: High Risk, High Return?

By keeping Lew around, Richard Williams gained the benefit of his insights, institutional knowledge, and customer relationships, as well as greater buy-in from the employees Lew had hired. Had Lew left before Richard came on board, the startup would have suffered a setback in employee morale and technical direction. As a VC observed, "You can replace a CEO, but you can't replace a founder."

On the other hand, keeping the founder around can be risky, especially if the founder is control-motivated, unhappy with the change, or both. The transitions at Segway, maker of the two-wheel electric vehicle, highlight the perils of keeping the founder around when changes are needed but the founder does not want to give up control. Early on, founder Dean Kamen decided that his new company needed a strong and experienced leader—someone who could lead the product-development engineers, leverage knowledge of the automotive industry, and bring the product to market quickly. He wanted someone who could realize the product's enormous, game-changing potential and who "knew what was required to make a global business."[11] Through one of his board members, Dean found Tim Adams, then a senior VP at Chrysler and "responsible in large part for the company's fabled turnaround."[12] Dean convinced Tim to join Segway with assurances that Dean wouldn't micromanage the company. However, soon after Tim came on board, Dean began to find fault: "You talk to [Tim] and he says a few bright things, but he says the same few things every time. He's a simple guy in a lot of ways. . . . He's not nearly as bright as most of the engineers I have, even though I pay him two or three times as much as any of them."[13] Dean placed restrictions on the terms that Tim could offer prospective employees and suppliers, dragged his feet on permission to build a factory, and prohibited test-marketing in order to preserve secrecy. Dean was the only one who could grant clearance to see the prototypes. Eventually, Dean replaced Tim and proceeded to hire and fire CEOs nearly annually, severely impacting the growth of Segway over the next decade.

The challenges faced by a startup's first nonfounding CEO are steep enough that a VC once told me, "When I search for a CEO to replace the founder, I usually have to find two CEOs because the first one often fails." Similarly, another investor compared the first nonfounding CEO to "a new organ being transplanted into a body that will try to reject it." In Figure 10.1, we can see that by the time of their D-rounds of financing, 23% of the startups have had a least two nonfounding CEOs.

The risk that a professional CEO might fail (or simply decide to leave) further complicates the question of whether to keep the former founder-CEO on board. The founder can serve as an insurance policy: In case the body does reject its new organ, the board can hand over the reins to an experienced hand rather than suffering a void at the top.

Smoothing the Transition: The Board's Role

As we have discussed, it is natural for a founder-CEO, especially a successful one, to resist his or her own succession. Such resistance can be extremely disruptive—even dangerous—for the startup. For this reason, many professional investors, as part of their due diligence before they initially invest, try to gauge whether the founder-CEO will resist an investor-driven succession when the time comes. In what one VC referred to as a "rich-versus-king test," they assess whether the founder-CEO is motivated by control of the startup or by financial gains. If the former, many VCs will shy away from making the investment, expecting the founder-CEO to resist succession should it become (in their eyes) necessary, a resistance that could bring down the startup or at least substantially reduce its value. (At the very least, the succession is likely to be very tense and disruptive.) If the latter, the VCs can be more confident that the founder-CEO's interests will be aligned with their own (financial) interests and that he or she will be more likely to agree with them on the need for a new CEO who can better advance their mutual interests (although even the most financially motivated founders often hesitate when the time comes to step down).

Investors who have the tough pre-investment conversation with the founder—laying out their succession expectations before emotions and tension are heightened—can often lay the groundwork for a smoother transition when the time comes. Leaving such a tension-filled discussion for the last minute tends to increase founder resistance and organizational disruption. In addition, investors—once they have invested—should make sure that the board conducts regular, candid, written reviews of the founder-CEO's performance to help provide a flow of developmental feedback, building trust and reducing the risk of unpleasant surprises.

When the time comes to make a change, if the investors have already and correctly diagnosed the founder as wealth-motivated, they should highlight for him or her precisely what the new CEO will be able to do to build the startup's value that the founder cannot do; for example, the professional CEO has a deep sales background that will be immediately useful and which the founder lacks, the professional CEO has already successfully managed a complex startup whereas the founder has not managed anything bigger than a project team, or the professional CEO will be able to upgrade the executive team while the founder is held back by longstanding personal relationships with team members. Les Trachtman, for example, was able to remove longstanding employees and founders and cut free from the family culture at Transcentive, which founder-CEO Mike Brody had been unwilling to do. Les was also able to enhance many of Transcentive's business processes—including a complete reorganization of the sales-and-marketing function, which resulted in sales growth of 40% per year—an accomplishment that was well beyond Mike's skills.

As we discussed above, founders who can't see much difference between their own capabilities and those of their potential replacements will find it harder to support their own succession, but wealth-motivated founders who see distinct, material differences will be more likely to do so. Lew Cirne's successor at Wily, Richard Williams, had 30 years of high-level experience working at companies such as IBM and Novell. He had been VP in a variety of positions, including VP of sales, and had led two turnarounds and several successful exits. Lew could therefore admit that Williams could be a "vitally important leader of the company. We had different things we could bring to the table and we respected and worked with that." In fact, Lew felt that helping recruit someone of Richard's caliber was one of the most valuable things he had done for Wily. "What made me comfortable about getting on board with [the change]," Lew explained, was the knowledge that, as one investor said, "[a] person like Dick Williams would not have the know-how or the interest in being a CEO of a startup, doing what Lew did."

As we have seen, many founders don't appreciate the dramatic changes that occur between the different stages of a startup's growth. The board may be able to make the founder-CEO more supportive of succession by helping him or her understand what those changes will be. Once Lew got over his initial shock of being replaced, his mentors were able to help him see how different the startup was becoming: "What helped me get through the shock was the realization that the world's best speedboat captain isn't able to pilot an oil tanker. It's not who's the best flat-out leader, but who's best suited to the tasks at that stage of development."

Even if the founder is not primarily wealth-motivated, boards can point to other ways in which the transition is consistent with the founder's motivations. If the founder loves to plot technical direction or lead scientific tasks, but has found the business aspects of the CEO position less enjoyable, boards can highlight the advantage of bringing in someone else to take those tasks off the founder's hands so he or she can concentrate on more satisfying work. If the founder aspires to build a long-term, multi-startup career as a serial entrepreneur, the board can highlight how a smooth transition can support rather than hinder that aspiration. Recall that Lew Cirne had aspired "to grow professionally by achieving as a businessperson, not as a technologist" even before founding Wily. As CEO of Wily, Lew was building his business skills gradually through trial and error. However, the board could have emphasized that by accepting a position under a very experienced CEO, Lew would be able to "learn from the best" and gain a more solid grounding in the business skills he lacked. Shifting Lew's perspective from his immediate losses to his potential longer-term gains could have been a crucial step toward getting his support. The argument that Richard could increase the value of Lew's equity share, which he could then invest in his next startup, would also help Lew see how a smooth transition could boost his longer-term career.

Rather than forcing an abrupt and permanent transition, some boards use an interim approach to smooth the transition. Lynx Solutions hired Clark Evans as a "bridge CEO" who would be at the company for only 18 months. As founder James Milmo explained, Clark wanted to help the founders "bring stability to a small fast-growing company, then leave to take on the next one." Clark introduced formal processes and structures and helped change the strategic direction. Clark's status as an interim CEO made him less threatening to the founders and helped alleviate their tensions concerning loss of control, while giving the startup the new skills it would need for its next stage of development. Another interim approach is a two-stage transition, such as Les Trachtman's at Transcentive, wherein a potential CEO is hired as a non-CEO executive who might eventually take over as CEO once the founder, the potential successor, the board, and the rest of the startup become more comfortable with such a transition.

Gaining the Predecessor's Support: The New CEO's Actions

The new CEO can also play a critical role in gaining the support of his or her predecessor. When taking over from Mike Brody at Transcentive, Les Trachtman gained Mike's support by paying close attention to the Three Rs that affect the tensions within a startup team:

- **Relationships.** Les spent considerable time getting to know the founder, the company, and the employees. His engagement with Transcentive began when he was a consultant, then deepened when Mike asked him to become CEO. But before taking on that role, Les insisted on taking the role of VP of operations. This helped him evaluate the situation before deciding whether to accept the CEO position and gave him a solid foundation for taking charge once he did accept it. By the time Les had taken over as CEO, he and Mike had a productive working relationship, Mike respected Les's abilities, and they had developed trust in each other's motivations. (This was quite a contrast with Les's first startup as a professional CEO, Megaserver, when he dove in and began taking action with no prior working relationship with the chairwoman or the former founder-CEO.) Experienced facilitators can also help founders and successors develop such trust.

- **Roles.** After taking over as CEO, Les seized opportunities to educate Mike about his new non-CEO role, gently moving him away from the day-to-day functions. "Mike came to me a few weeks after I became CEO," Les recalled. "He said to me, 'I'm concerned about how much we're spending on milk for employees.' I told him, 'Mike, I see my job as freeing you up to focus on things that really count. This isn't one of them. From now on, if it's not a $100,000 problem, don't spend your time on it.'" These incidents helped Mike begin grappling with the "tidal" change in small ways, which over time created a very different relationship between the founder and the startup with which he had been so deeply involved. The most effective approach is a blend of keeping the founder *out* of tasks he or she should no longer be involved with and involving him or her *in* targeted decisions. Sometimes, the founder can take over and be accountable for a specific function for which he or she is particularly suited. At Wily, for instance, Richard Williams kept Lew engaged with hiring, which helped Lew feel more valued as part of the startup while providing Richard with insights about how each candidate would fit into Wily's culture. At other times, the founder might be better suited to a "special projects" role that falls outside of the startup's functional boundaries.

- **Rewards.** Perhaps one of the most important actions that Les took was to help Mike gain significant wealth at the same time that he had to give up control. Les negotiated a partial sale of the business to two strategic partners, but used most of the proceeds to cash out the founders and early employees who had recently been fired as part of the transition. Les explained how this "partial founder buyout" affected both him and his predecessor: "The partial buyout acted as a pressure-release valve for Mike. He heaved a big sigh of relief . . . and didn't care as much about what happened after that. Abruptly, he said he was moving to Virginia and was no longer going to participate in day-to-day. For me, it was a different kind of release. I had effectively gotten rid of Mike's brother and the three quasi-founders, but now that they had something tangible to take away from it, that made me feel great!" In other startups, the board may provide financial incentives for a smooth transition by giving the founder a "CEO transition" bonus or by awarding the founder additional equity that vests.

The particulars will be different in every case, but by paying close attention to each of the Three Rs, professional CEOs can help their boards smooth the founder-CEO succession, decrease the risk of a failed transition, and increase the chances that the replaced founder will remain productively engaged with the startup he or she founded.

CLOSING REMARKS

Both boards and founders should see founder-CEO succession not as an event but as a process. As an event, it is likely to be traumatic, but as a process, it has more opportunity to be productive and rewarding as well. From the board's perspective, the process begins even before investors participate in their first round of financing, when they have to assess whether the founder-CEO's motivation will hinder or facilitate a smooth transition, should the need for one arise. At that point, the investors should openly discuss the possibility of succession and the conditions that might trigger it.* The process continues with the board's ongoing coaching of the founder-CEO as he or she encounters new challenges and with new hires who can bolster the founder-CEO where he or she has weaknesses. As the process continues, it may come to the point where the board can no longer put Band-Aids on the founder-CEO's deficiencies and decides to replace him or her. Bob Davoli, a venture capitalist at Sigma Partners, describes this progression: (a) Let the CEO run the company; (b) when a problem occurs, the board should identify it and try to work with the CEO to solve it; (c) if that doesn't work, "fire him."[14] Other VCs describe this approach as "coach, then replace."

The process should also include frank dialogue about the start-up's upcoming challenges and whether the board has confidence that the founder-CEO will be able to tackle them. At Wily, board member and investor David Strohm made it clear from the outset that Lew would eventually be replaced. "Our initial . . . investment and my involvement in Wily had been predicated on an understanding that we would need to bring in an experienced CEO." Even so, confident, passionate founder-CEOs often fail to receive that message, especially when they are succeeding. Lew Cirne, for his part, was later blindsided by David's explicit request that he step down, describing his reaction as "shock." Clearly, he either had not heard or had not grasped David's earlier assertion that he would have to give up leading Wily relatively soon. Henry McCance, the chairman of Greylock, observed, "An entrepreneur who is anxious to receive capital, may say, 'Okay, sure, I will do whatever it takes.' But he may be thinking, 'I'll show them that I can do it all!'" Even when directors think they have sent the message about succession, they must realize that, most likely, the message was not understood clearly, not taken as seriously as it was meant, or tuned out altogether.

---

* If investors do not raise the issue, founders should *not* assume that this means they will never be replaced. Even though it is natural for a founder either to be optimistic about the probability of remaining CEO throughout the life of the startup or to want to avoid a tense discussion about succession possibilities, founders who are concerned about being replaced (and who might think twice about taking capital from investors who might want to replace them) should fight those inclinations and raise the issue before accepting the capital.

Founders, by acknowledging succession as a process that starts early in the startup's life, can at least gain more control over how and when they lose control of their startups. As we will see in Chapter 11, even before founding their startups, founders should reflect deeply on their core motivations and then make founding decisions that are consistent with those motivations. If those early decisions include taking capital from outside investors, the founder must understand that he or she may already have taken a key step toward his or her own succession.

Founders should also realize that they can gain some control over when they lose control of the startup by "getting ahead of the board" and initiating the succession themselves.* Founder-initiated succession and board-initiated succession can have very different outcomes. As described above, when the founder triggers the change, he or she is less likely to leave the startup immediately, more likely to play a central role in the search for and choice of a successor, more likely to remain in a senior executive role, and more likely to remain on the board of directors. Triggering one's own demise as CEO is wrenching but, for some founders, is worth the price if it can ensure their remaining a prince of the realm after relinquishing the throne.

---

* In contrast, VC Jeff Bussgang observes, "If your board is 'ahead' of you on CEO succession, it's a problem."

PART IV
CONCLUSION

CHAPTER ELEVEN

WEALTH-VERSUS-CONTROL DILEMMAS

THE PATH FROM FOUNDING TO SUCCESS IS A LONG AND WINDING one, with dilemma after dilemma forcing founders to make decision after decision, all with important—and sometimes surprising—short-term and long-term consequences. Throughout this book, we have examined a wide variety of players—ranging from core founders to cofounders, hires, investors, and successors—and a wide variety of dilemmas. Those who have made the decision to found a high-potential startup must decide whether to go it alone or to assemble a founding team. Those who choose to assemble a team need to make decisions about the relationships, roles, and rewards of their cofounders. Both solo founders and founding teams are likely to have to make decisions about the relationships, roles, and rewards of their hires. For many founders, there will be further decisions about the various kinds of investors.

We have also seen a wide variety of outcomes that result from those early decisions. Sometimes, they were what the founders had hoped from the start to achieve. However, we have also seen many ways in which things don't work out as the founders want, from Kaleil and Tom having to pay off their former govWorks.com cofounder, Chieh, to Lynx cofounders James Milmo and Javier Pascal facing the prospect of having to sell their startup for only enough money to pay back their investors—not themselves—to Lew Cirne being forced out of his CEO position at what appeared to be the height of his success.

We have looked at each of these outcomes in light of the decision points that led up to them. We are now in a position to understand them collectively in yet another light—a "wealth versus control" dilemma that coexists with all the other dilemmas (once one has decided to found at all). But first, let's step back and once more look at the basics.

What is entrepreneurship? A widely used definition is "a process by which individuals pursue opportunities without regard to the resources they currently control."[1] That sounds straightforward, even romantic, but it has a dark side: When a founder of a high-potential startup chooses to pursue an opportunity regardless of whether or not he or she has the necessary resources, a critical piece is usually missing—often several critical pieces. One study estimated that founders are 60 times more likely to be resource constrained than to have all of the resources they need.[2] Yet, pursuing an opportunity *fully* requires having a full complement of the relevant human, social, and financial resources.[3] The more resources a startup can control and the more quickly it can gain control of them, the better its competitive position.[4] Lacking resources is a big reason why new ventures have such a high failure rate.[5] Lack of resources lies behind all the dilemmas we have described so far. If a founder started out with all the human, social, and financial resources he or she needed, there would be no need for cofounders, hires, or investors, nor any need for him or her to be replaced as CEO.

Attracting outside resources, especially those in short supply,[6] requires founders to give up valuable assets.[7] Outside resource providers often want two major things in return for their contributions to building the value of a startup: economic ownership and decision-making control. Regarding ownership, resource providers are often motivated to contribute their resources by the chance to gain a share of the economic winnings should the startup succeed. Cofounders and hires who know their own value want to have a hand in important decisions in return for the skills and contacts they contribute; investors also demand a degree of control over the organization's decision making in return for their guidance and capital.[8] Control of a startup can be contested in two ways: whether the entrepreneur remains CEO or is replaced,[9] and whether outsiders or insiders control the board of directors.[10] Founders who refuse to give up ownership and control in either or both of these ways will be less likely to attract the resources they need and thus not be able to fully pursue the opportunities they envision. It appears, then, that each of our founding dilemmas is also a dilemma of what resources to acquire at what cost in ownership and control. This is the dilemma behind all the other dilemmas. As we will see, it can be the harshest of the dilemmas in this book.

A CENTRAL DILEMMA: WEALTH VERSUS CONTROL

It is harsh because it pits the two most common entrepreneurial motivations—wealth and control—against each other.[*] Most founders embark on their entrepreneurial journeys with passion and confidence, expecting to build a valuable startup and then run it throughout its life. They want to be the next Bill Gates of Microsoft or the next Anita Roddick of The Body Shop, prominent founders who managed to achieve both value creation and control. However, few founders are able to maximize both goals because, at every stage of startup evolution, the actions that maximize one inherently hinder the other, and most founders are forced to choose between one or the other of these goals. In short, there is an inherent tension between achieving one and the other. (While other entrepreneurial motivations can be important, they lack this inherent tension.)

To show this pattern more clearly, Figure 11.1 summarizes some of the key dilemmas already covered in Parts II and III of this book, but now reveals them to be a sequence of necessary trade-offs between maintaining control and creating a valuable startup or, as we noted above, a recurring dilemma of what resources to acquire at what cost in ownership and control. As discussed below, the

---

[*]See Chapters 1 and 2 for empirical evidence of the preponderance of these two motivations.

Potential Participants in the Startup	Decision Area	Decisions Oriented toward Maintaining Control	Decisions Oriented toward Maximizing Wealth
Cofounders	Solo vs. team	Remain solo founder (or attract weak cofounders)	Build founding team; attract best cofounders
	Relationships	First look to immediate circle for "comfortable" cofounders	Tap strong and weak ties to find the best (and complementary) cofounders
	Roles	Keep strong control of decision making; build hierarchy	Give decision-making control to cofounders with expertise in specific areas
	Rewards	Maintain most or all equity ownership	Share equity to attract and/or motivate cofounders
Hires	Relationships	Hire within close personal network (friends, family, and others) as required	Aggressively tap broader network (unfamiliar candidates) to find the best hires
	Roles	Keep control of key decisions	Delegate decision making to appropriate expert
	Rewards	Hire less expensive junior employees	Hire experienced employees and incent them with cash and equity
Investors	Self-fund vs. take outside capital	Self-fund; "bootstrap"	Take outside capital
	Sources of capital	Friends and family or money-only angels; tap alternative sources (e.g., customer prepayments or debt) if possible	Target experienced angels or venture capitalists

	Terms	Resist investor-friendly terms (e.g., refuse any supermajority rights)	Be open to terms necessary to attract best investors (e.g., supermajority rights)
	Board of directors	Avoid building official board; when built, control composition and makeup	Be open to losing control of board if necessary to get best investors and directors
Successors	Trigger of succession	Avoid succession issue until forced	Be open to initiating succession when next stage of startup is outside one's own expertise
	Openness to succession	Resist giving up the CEO position	Be open to giving up CEO position to better CEO
	Desired role after succession	Prefer to leave than to remain "prince"	Want to remain executive in position that matches skills and preferences
Other factors	Preferred rate of startup growth	Gradual to moderate	Fast to explosive
	Capital intensity	Low capital intensity	High capital intensity
	Core founder's "capitals"	Well equipped to launch and build startup without much help	Important gaps that should be filled by involving others
Most likely outcome		Maintain control; build less value	Build financial value; imperil control

Figure 11.1. Wealth-versus-Control Dilemmas

decisions listed in each column are the decisions that each type of founder *should* make, given a goal of either maximizing personal control or maximizing the eventual payoff. In real life, the choices are seldom as consistently aligned as they should be.

The decisions in the first column consistently prioritize maintaining control over building financial value. Even when a potential cofounder, hire, investor, or successor would add important human capital, social capital, or financial capital to a startup and enable it to build more value, a founder who consistently makes control decisions will forgo that extra value in order to maintain control of the startup. Founders who consistently make control decisions (a) remain solo founders or choose only cofounders who will allow the founder to retain control, (b) hire inexperienced people and keep control of decision making, (c) self-fund or raise capital only from investors who won't interfere with the founder's control of the startup, and (d) choose to remain CEO throughout all stages of startup evolution. Such founders take full responsibility for development and implementation of their visions and aim to rely largely on their own human, social, and financial capital. The data (see below) confirm that such founders are more likely to maintain control for a longer period of time but end up with less-valuable equity stakes.

Conversely, decisions in the second column consistently prioritize building value over maintaining control. This second type of founder (a) strives to attract cofounders whose expertise fills important holes, (b) hires experienced people who take control of their domains, (c) raises money from investors who add enough value to the startup to justify the control they demand over decisions, and (d) watches for the point when someone else will be able to do a better job leading the startup during its next stages of development. If a potential cofounder, hire, investor, or successor would add an important piece to the startup (skills and human capital, contacts and social capital, or financial capital), the founder who is making wealth choices is willing to do what it takes to attract that person, even if doing so imperils the founder's own control.

Many founders, especially first-timers who haven't yet experienced the outcomes of their decisions or do not have an experienced mentor to guide them, often do not realize that their early decisions are leading them in one or the other of these directions. Unfortunately, Figure 11.1 is only a normative description of the systematic decisions that different founders *should* make—but often do not. As we have seen throughout this book, systematic consideration of early decisions can yield much better outcomes than an accumulation of reactive decisions; founders need to "decide rather than default."

Divergent Outcomes: Rich versus King

At each fork in the road, the decision that maximizes value tends to threaten the founder's control, and vice versa. There is an inherent conflict between maintaining control and building value in high-potential startups because the latter requires value-added players who demand some control.

Founders who consistently make control decisions are more likely to reach what I call the "King" outcome, in which the founder retains the throne but does not rule as big and rich a kingdom as might otherwise have been possible. Founders who consistently make wealth decisions are more likely to reach what I call the "Rich" outcome, in which the founder generally loses the throne but sees his or her venture pursue its business opportunity to the fullest. Figure 11.2 summarizes these two outcomes, the outcome of achieving both control and value creation ("Rich and King," also known as "the entrepreneurial ideal") and the outcome of achieving neither control nor value creation ("Failure").

My quantitative analyses suggest that few founders—especially first-time founders—can maintain control *and* create maximal value.* As we saw in Chapter 10 on founder-CEO succession, few founders—even the extremely successful ones—are still CEO when their startups become very big or go public. Bill Gates and Anita Roddick are so well known precisely because they are the

---

* Likewise, in power-elite theory, the "corporate rich"—powerful and wealthy top executives—are also a very small, elite subset.

| | | Financial Gain | |
		Far Below Potential Value	Achieving Potential Value
Retention of decision-making control	*Minor player*	Failure	Rich
	Major player	King	Rich & King

Figure 11.2. Rich versus King Outcomes
Adapted and reprinted by permission of *Harvard Business Review*. From "The Founder's Dilemma," by Noam Wasserman, February 2008. Copyright © 2008 by the Harvard Business Publishing Corporation; all rights reserved.

exceptions. Yet, many founders have so much confidence in their startup's prospects and in their own abilities and feel such intense passion for their idea that they systematically underestimate their need for further resources or overestimate their ability to remain in control of the startup even as they take on a wide range of outside resources. These natural entrepreneurial inclinations can lead founders away from becoming Rich or King as they make decisions that leave them with either too few resources or too little control of the startup.*

My analyses also suggest that founders who keep control personally give up a significant amount financially. Such founders tend to build a less valuable startup while keeping a larger share of equity in it, but it turns out that the value-seeking founder's "smaller slice of a larger pie" is generally greater than the control-seeking founder's "larger slice of a smaller pie." Controlling for a wide variety of differences across the 460 startups I analyzed,[11] founders who had kept control of both the CEO position and the board of directors held equity stakes that were only 52% as valuable as those held by

---

* Throughout this book, we have looked at how overconfidence can skew founding decisions. Overconfidence can also mislead founders about the probability of achieving the entrepreneurial ideal, leading them to attend to only those exceptional founders who grew valuable startups while maintaining control throughout, or else to assume that their own chances are higher than the typical founder's. The choices they make because of this misperception may increase the chances of their failing, rather than enabling them to achieve their top priority, whether it be maintaining control or maximizing wealth.

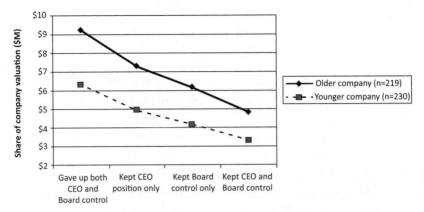

Figure 11.3. Value of Founder's Equity Stake, Depending on Degree of Control Maintained
Reprinted from "Rich vs. King: The Entrepreneur's Dilemma," by Noam Wasserman, *Best Paper Proceedings of the Academy of Management*, 2006.

founders who had given up both the CEO position and control of the board, as shown in Figure 11.3. (The founders' equity stakes had an intermediate value if they had given up control of either the CEO position or the board but not both.) This result held in both younger startups and older ones, suggesting that founders face a trade-off between wealth and control, *and* that this trade-off persists throughout the stages of startup evolution.

To assess whether founders tend to make consistent decisions, I compared solo founders (whom we would expect to be more inclined toward control) to the core founders who attracted cofounders.[*] This dataset included 1,658 technology startups that completed surveys between 2005 and 2009, and it controlled for a wide variety of founder and startup characteristics, such as capital intensity,

---

[*] From a revealed-preferences perspective, in which we examine people's actions to learn about their preferences, solo founding is one of the clearest indicators of a founder's control orientation. However, it does not enable us to separate solo founders who intended to (and did) found alone from those who tried to find cofounders but failed. (Given the "noise" introduced by this, the analyses described here should be conservative, underreporting the statistical significance of the independent variables.) As described below, future research should examine further indicators of control motivations, possibly including self-reported measures of motivation or survey questions similar to the CareerLeader survey questions detailed in Chapter 2.

industry segment, and startup maturity. The statistically significant results indicated some consistency that extended across our founding dilemmas, as summarized below:

- **Hires**—Solo founders hired younger employees than multi-founder startups did, suggesting that solo founders favored more inexpensive hires.
- **Investors**—Solo founders (a) were almost twice as likely to use debt, which does not dilute the founder's ownership, as a source of financing; (b) raised their first institutional round of financing later in the lives of their startups (possibly because investors were more hesitant to invest or possibly because the founders wanted to wait longer); and (c) raised less capital in their first institutional round of financing (which again may be due either to investor preference or to founder preference).
- **Chairman role**—Solo founders were more likely to retain both chairman and CEO titles (i.e., remain a "double King") after their first round of financing.

Solo-founded startups received lower pre-money valuations than did multifounder startups, confirming the price that control-motivated founders pay for making control-motivated decisions. However, the results above also suggest that, while solo founders raised less capital, they may have done so on more friendly terms, a trade-off that control-motivated founders are usually willing to make.

Using the Wealth-versus-Control Lens to Revisit Evan Williams's Decisions

Throughout this book, we examined the very different choices that Evan Williams made as he was founding and building Blogger and Odeo. With the tension between control decisions and wealth decisions in mind, let's take one more look at Evan's choices. At Blogger, he consistently made control decisions rather than wealth ones. He founded with a former girlfriend, Meg Hourihan, who did not have experience in startups or in the industry. He hired young and inexperienced friends to build the product at inexpensive salaries, later replacing them with an even more extreme choice—volunteers. He was adamant about keeping a controlling interest in the company, refusing to split the equity equally with Meg and avoiding selling equity to professional investors. When he disagreed with Meg, he overruled her or simply ignored her concerns in favor of pursing his own vision for the company. He avoided talking to VC investors, even in the midst of the dot-com funding frenzy, preferring to accept funding from friends, family, and angel investors, and even taking donations during a public "Server Drive." His board was advisory in nature, offering little guidance. When Meg challenged Evan for the CEO position, he refused to give it up, leading her to leave the company. He also refused an acquisition offer that threatened his control of the startup, even though that refusal meant losing his entire staff. In fact, after making this last decision, Evan felt relief: "The next day, mixed with the sadness and the loss was an incredible amount of liberation."

With Odeo, Evan consistently made wealth decisions that threatened his control of the startup. He founded with Noah Glass, a business acquaintance who had experience in the podcasting segment, and gave Noah both the CEO position and the lion's share of equity. When Evan realized the great potential of Odeo's podcasting technology, he steered the startup into a series of decisions designed to help Odeo grow quickly. He negotiated with a venerable VC firm to raise $5 million, which he used to hire high-level experienced executives, technologists, and sales managers who would drive decisions within their functions. After that, Evan's board, which was dominated by representatives from his investors, became highly involved in the decision making at Odeo.

Within each startup, Evan's choices were quite consistent. At Blogger, he made the control decisions shown in the left column of Figure 11.1 and ended up with full control, but it was full control of a startup that sold for much less than its potential warranted, considering that Blogger was, at the time, the tool of choice for a rapidly expanding user base. With Odeo, Evan made the wealth decisions shown in the right column of Figure 11.1, choices that increased the chances of growing a valuable startup at the cost of much of his own equity and decision-making control.

The further evolution of Odeo is also quite instructive, for it shows us how Evan tried to balance his control inclinations with the desire to pursue big opportunities. As Apple's iTunes gained traction in the marketplace, Evan and his team realized that Odeo's prospects were much diminished and turned to brainstorming other ideas. Jack Dorsey, an engineer at Odeo, proposed a status-updating tool that would allow users to send short text messages instantly to a group of "followers." The team decided to develop a prototype, and two weeks later a product called Twitter was born. While Evan and his fellow engineers saw the wisdom in switching to developing Twitter, it was much harder to convince the VCs on the board. By the time he had gotten to this point, Evan had realized that he needed full control of Odeo if he were going to be able to explore and develop Twitter's full potential, but that his earlier decisions had caused him to sacrifice that control. To reclaim the creative freedom he craved, Evan made the nearly unprecedented decision to put up $3 million of his own money to buy out his investors and retake control of his company. A year later, Evan sold Odeo's podcasting assets to Sonic Mountain for over $1 million, then spun out Twitter with the idea founder, Jack Dorsey, as CEO.

In 2008, as Twitter's growth began accelerating by adding millions of users per month, Evan again felt the need to retake control. With the board's approval, he moved Jack from CEO to chairman and took over as CEO. Evan was later quoted as saying, "It's hard and confusing . . . I think there's few cases in history where the CEO steps down and is also the founder and reports to someone and that works."[12] For his part, Jack said that being removed from his position at Twitter "was like being punched in the stomach."[13] Along the way, Evan was careful to raise capital only at times and on terms that were compatible with his desire to retain control. But Evan struggled; in his words, he and his team were "just hanging on by our fingernails to a rocket ship."[14] He couldn't hire or put processes in place quickly enough to keep the system running. Twitter also lacked a monetization strategy. To fill these holes, in September 2009 he hired Dick Costolo, the former founder-CEO of FeedBurner whom we've also gotten to know in these pages, to be his chief operating officer. Following the playbook described in Chapter 10, after "trying before buying" for a year, Evan named Dick his successor as CEO in September 2010 and moved himself into a product-strategy role before transitioning out of Twitter a few months later. Dick Costolo's fifth startup would thus be one in which he took over from the founder-CEO, applying all of the lessons he had learned from his first four startups to lead someone else's startup through its next stage of development.

Other Alternatives: Second-tier Resources

There are two ways in which Evan's decisions were more extreme than those of many founders: Each choice was at an extreme of control versus wealth, and, within each startup, his choices were extremely consistent.

Figure 11.1 presents a series of binary choices: avoiding bringing on a specific high-quality resource—which may add the most value but may also pose the biggest threat to the founder's control—versus bringing on that resource. In real life, however, there are in-between or "second-tier resources"[15] that may add more value (but not the maximum) but with less threat (though not without any) to the founder's control. Rather than solo founding or attracting the best cofounders, founders can choose to attract "adequate" cofounders. Rather than hiring either inexperienced or very experienced executives, founders can hire midrange executives. Rather than self-funding or taking money from a top VC firm, founders can take money from second-tier investors. Rather than taking no VC money or the most they can get, founders can raise smaller rounds of financing and face less risk of being replaced as CEO.[16]

For instance, Frank Addante used second-tier resources for his startup StrongMail when he recruited a "B team" of inexperienced people through Craigslist. By using a B team rather than expensive top-college grads or experienced executives, Frank was able to lower his burn rate and bootstrap the company while he worked to gain proof of concept. The downside was that Frank spent valuable time having to direct his team and was frustrated by their lack of

motivation and self-direction. However, the B team fulfilled its function of buying Frank the time that he needed to build the company,
develop the product, and attract VC attention. He eventually raised
outside capital and replaced his B team with top-tier hires.

Other Alternatives: Hybrid Paths

We have seen that Evan's decisions were remarkably consistent
within Blogger and during the early stages of Odeo. Each individual
decision a founder makes can contribute incrementally to building
the startup's value or to maintaining control of decision making.
We would expect consistent control-oriented decisions to markedly
increase the founder's chances of maintaining control (though of a
smaller startup) and consistent wealth-oriented decisions to markedly increase the founder's chances of growing more value (while
losing control of decision making). Some founders, however, pursue
a hybrid path—a mix of control and wealth decisions—which they
hope will increase the chances of achieving both Rich and King.*
For instance, they could maintain full control by remaining solo
founders and by hiring only employees who will not challenge that
control. If they are using this period of total control to develop an
initial product and achieve key early milestones, they might have
more control over the terms they get from outside investors. They
can then shift strategies toward making wealth-oriented decisions
and try to "hit the accelerator" by attracting the best investors they
can find and leveraging their investors' capital and guidance to scale
the startup and the team. Hinting at such a strategy, the chairman
of the Buffalo Angel Network was recently quoted as saying, "The
hardest decision a founder, inventor, or entrepreneur needs to make
is 'when do I give up some control to grow the company.'"[17]

At the beginning of her startup, Sittercity, Genevieve Thiers made
control-oriented choices.[18] She chose to be a solo founder; used
friends and family connections as advisors, employees, and angel

---

* Of course, it may be a rare founder who is able to smoothly move back and forth between such opposing actions!

investors; and kept all the decision-making control and all the equity to herself. When Sittercity had been in business for eight years, however, she felt the time was right to seek venture capital to continue Sittercity's growth and maintain its first-mover advantage. Genevieve explained why she waited so long: "A lot of founders take funding too early and lose ownership in the company. The company starts to be run by the investors. . . . [For me,] being able to retain control was very important. We finally did decide to take venture capital money in 2008 because . . . I always felt that—at a certain time—having funding would be appropriate for the company. We were probably the latest-stage Series A our investors had ever seen. We were so successful, so big, and had this established team. Our investors could put their money in and just sit back." For startups such as Sittercity, with the luxuries of time and low capital-intensity, such a strategy can work. For other startups, however, such a strategy would increase the likelihood of slow or lower-quality product development (because fewer resources are being used to develop it) and of competitive disadvantage, harming the value that can be built and thus the chance of achieving the entrepreneurial ideal.

In deciding on a wealth, control, or hybrid strategy, founders should carefully assess which of the resources most critical to the startup's success are lacking, then carefully allocate equity, financial resources, and attention to attracting those resources. Such founders can try to make up for weaknesses in one area by bolstering their resources in another area. For instance, a solo founder who consciously avoids adding a cofounder (thus retaining all of the equity) may instead focus on using equity slices to attract the best post-founding hires. Solo founder Lew Cirne, for example, carved out some of his own equity to sweeten the pot for his first employees after his angel investors refused to allow their shares to be diluted.

Such hybrid strategies may indeed reduce the probability that founders will end up as exclusively Rich or exclusively King, but they may also increase the probability of ending up Failures. Just as entrepreneurial firms that pursue multiple strategies can get "stuck in the middle,"[19] so too should entrepreneurs who make inconsistent choices be more likely to end up with muddled strategies[20] and face greater risk of failure. For a brief and simple quantitative exploration of the pros and cons of hybrid strategies, see Appendix 11-1 at the end of this chapter. The model there suggests that founders who are unsure about their core motivations, and thus which outcome and accompanying set of choices are best for them, can hedge their bets by using hybrid strategies—but at high risk. This will markedly reduce the chances of achieving one outcome, slightly increase the chances of achieving the other, and significantly increase the chances of failing.

Another potential risk of hybrid or hedging strategies is that founders who shift strategy in the middle of building a startup may cause major tensions within the startup or harm their ability to attract the best resources. For instance, if they initially attract the best cofounders and hires (wealth), then refuse to raise money from outside investors (control), they may bring on major dissention and high turnover among critical employees and lack the resources to continue paying the ones who remain. When Dean Kamen—whose medical-product research-and-development company, DEKA, invented the Segway personal transporter—first realized Segway's potential, he began talks with scores of investors and hired an experienced executive team to manage the project, offering stock options to attract the best managers and engineers. Dean's subsequent insistence on control rebuffed potential funders and eventually caused Segway's experienced CEO, Tim Adams, who had been promised control of key decisions, to leave the company.[21]

"BETTER" AND "WORSE" OUTCOMES

If different decisions lead to such different outcomes, is one outcome better or worse than the other? Evan Williams made control-oriented choices at Blogger and then wealth-oriented choices at Odeo—was he right in one case and wrong in the other?

The Core Founder's View: Self-Knowledge and Decision Making

As we saw in Chapter 2, there is a wide range of entrepreneurial motivations. Many of these motivations—altruism, variety, and intellectual challenge, for example—are unlikely to provide founders with clear guidance as to which decisions to make. But maintaining power and control over the key decisions within the startup and gaining financially from building a valuable startup are the two most common motivations, and they do provide clear guidance.

For the founder, is one set of choices better than the other? In certain circumstances, it may be. Given a capital-intensive idea in a ticking-clock environment, for example, control-oriented choices will indeed be more problematic than wealth-oriented choices. But otherwise, wealth-oriented choices are neither better nor worse than control-oriented choices—as long as they are consistent with the founder's core motivation. What's "worse" is a set of choices that are inconsistent with each other, which means that some of them must be inconsistent with the founder's core motivation. Worst of all would be a consistent set of choices all of which were in opposition to the founder's core motivation.

A wealth-motivated founder who consistently makes control decisions may get to some kind of outcome, but it probably won't be the one he or she had hoped for; likewise for a control-motivated founder who consistently makes wealth decisions. Early in the founding of Wily Technology, Lew Cirne stated a goal of growing as a businessperson by being CEO. To this end, he consistently made control choices: founding, working alone for a year to develop the initial product, raising money from friends and family, and hiring junior people who might be able to grow. But then, to spark Wily's growth, he took multiple rounds of financing from top VCs, lost control of his board, lost his Kingship, and was sidelined within his own startup. Lew ended up having a nice payday when Wily exited, and a founder whose core motivation is to get rich would have been delighted with Lew's outcome. Lew himself, though, regretted having given up control and vowed to keep control in his next startup. "Next time," he exclaimed publicly, "I'm running it to a billion dollars, and I don't care what any VC says about that!"

Only by understanding the founder's motivations can we—or the founder himself or herself—judge whether the outcome was better or worse. (As discussed below, we also have to consider business characteristics or environmental circumstances that might force a founder to go against his or her own core motivations.)

What about Evan Williams? Did he truly have two different motivations as he pursued his two different startups? In Blogger, he risked everything to maintain control. In Odeo, he seems to have become a different person, willingly trading control for maximization of the startup's value. In fact, though, after Evan raised $5 million from VCs, he chafed under the scrutiny of his board of directors. "Anything I do," he complained, "I have to explain and justify it to the board.... It kills the creative part that can lead to something good.... I don't want to be required to explain myself. Having a board is killing our ability to try new things." He concluded, "I could believe in the company . . . only if I had complete control over it." It would seem then that he had talked himself into being wealth-oriented when, inside, he was still control-oriented.

Choosing between the options outlined in Figure 11.1 can be particularly hard for (a) founders who lack clear priorities and (b) founders who do not yet know themselves well enough and have not experienced the challenges faced by startup CEOs. (Founders who both have unclear priorities and lack self-knowledge and experience will be in for a really rough ride.) In the first case, the founders may be equally motivated by wealth and control. On the other hand, they may not be that strongly motivated by either and thus find it particularly difficult to make coherent decisions. In the second case, first-time founder-CEOs are often handicapped by at least four kinds of ignorance. First, having never been in a fast-growing startup, they do not understand how the stages of growth will differ. Second, they do not realize how those very different stages will cause dramatic changes in the challenges faced by the CEO and the executive team. Third, they do not yet know whether or not they have the skills and capabilities to address those challenges. Fourth, they have not had to reflect on whether they will be willing to trade off control versus value creation and are therefore less prepared to make decisions that are consistent with their core motivations.

As a first-time founder, Lew Cirne had little understanding of these four issues. He didn't realize that, by building Wily quickly, he would more quickly come to the point at which his experience and expertise could no longer fulfill Wily's needs. Lew only gradually came to understand that his career as a technical manager had not prepared him for the challenges of leading a maturing company. Having never dealt with venture capitalists, he didn't understand that he was risking his control of the company by accepting funding from them. Perhaps most importantly, Lew did not anticipate the intensely negative reaction he would have to losing control of Wily. Even though his investors had intimated that he would eventually need to be replaced, Lew clearly hadn't foreseen or planned for such an event. It was only after much discussion between Lew and his investors, and after more than a year of looking for a successor, that Lew realized, "It's not who's the best flat-out leader, but who's best suited to the tasks at that stage of development."

Some founders are self-aware even at the beginning of their first startup. The founder of Steria, an IT systems and services company, made decisions that resembled Evan Williams's control-oriented decisions at Blogger, but was much clearer from the outset that his primary motivation was "to remain independent and master of his own destiny," and he consistently aligned his decisions with that motivation.[22] Instead of taking capital from outside investors, he relied on founder capital and bank loans; he refused to grant stock to attract better hires to Steria; and he insisted on remaining CEO. As a result, Steria experienced slower growth than it would have had the founder taken outside capital, attracted better employees, and been more open to giving some control to experienced executives. Each of these latter choices held the promise of greater financial gain, but at the expense of the founder's maintaining control, and Steria's founder avoided them with open eyes.[*]

The Views of Other Participants: The Need to Assess the Founder

Core founders can find it enough of a challenge to make key decisions that are consistent with their own motivations. However, as soon as they involve other participants, such as cofounders, hires, and investors, the potential for misalignment grows dramatically. Thus, before

---

[*] Likewise, in *Life of Caesar*, Plutarch quotes Julius Caesar's clarity about his early need to accept a smaller kingdom in order to have control of it: "For my part, I had rather be the first man among these [lesser] fellows, than the second man in Rome."

joining the startup, those potential participants also need to assess whether the founder's motivations—and the corresponding decisions he or she will make in response to the inevitable sequence of founding dilemmas—may conflict with their own motivations.

Potential cofounders, in particular, need to share similar—or precisely complementary—motivations. At each fork in the road, cofounders will have to make a single coherent decision about how to proceed. For instance, they will have to decide together if they should raise outside money or continue to self-fund. If the cofounders are all wealth-motivated, they are more likely to agree on attracting the resources that can grow the value of the startup. A mixture of a control-motivated founder-CEO and wealth-motivated cofounders can be harmonious if the control-motivated founder-CEO is indeed the right person to be the CEO and will be able to build the startup's value most effectively (thus fulfilling his or her own desire for control and the other cofounders' desire for financial gains), but contentious if the wealth-motivated cofounders lack confidence in the founder-CEO's ability to build the value of the startup. However, other mixes of cofounder motivation may be far more dangerous. In particular, if the cofounders are both control-motivated, they may end up like Evan and Meg at Blogger, with intense startup-endangering fighting over who is CEO and who controls the most important decisions.

Cofounders may have very different ideas about what the startup should do regarding almost every dilemma examined here. Such divergences can introduce intense tensions into the team, threatening its stability and the startup's growth and survival. Potential cofounders who discuss these dilemmas before deciding whether or not to cofound together, walking carefully through each row of Figure 11.1 and discussing what decisions they would each want to make at each fork in the road, will be able to anticipate—and perhaps even avoid—such tensions. They may also realize that they simply shouldn't be cofounders to begin with.

For potential hires, diagnosing the founder-CEO's motivations can also be critical.[*] Wealth-motivated hires should try to work

---

[*] See Chapter 10 for a discussion of the need for potential successor-CEOs to diagnose the founder.

with wealth-motivated founders. If the founder-CEO is control-motivated, we would expect the hires to be attracted for other reasons: the founder's compelling vision, the chance to "change the world," the excitement of working in a startup, or other nonfinancial considerations. Such was the case at Segway, where talented engineers competed to work for Dean Kamen, even for below-market compensation. They were attracted to the culture of creativity, the flat organizational structure, and the pursuit of the next big idea with a visionary like Dean. "I owe Dean for giving me the greatest experience of my life," said one DEKA engineer.[23]

However, when the founder-CEO starts making control-oriented decisions, such as refusing to raise needed capital or to delegate decisions to experienced executives, the wealth-motivated hire is likely to chafe under the founder's leadership and to feel that the founder is sacrificing the hire's benefit (value creation) for the founder's own benefit (personal control). Had some of Segway's top hires probed their founder-CEO more deeply, they might have avoided being caught in a situation where Dean demanded control of all important decisions, even in areas where he lacked business expertise that others possessed.

Likewise, as described in Chapter 10, potential investors have to diagnose whether the founder of a startup in which they might invest will be aligned with their own wealth motivations. Down the road, if the founder's interests diverge from those of the investors—for example, if the investors believe a different CEO could do a better job building the value of the startup—will the founder be more on board with the change because it would be financially beneficial for everyone, or will the founder fight to retain control, even if it brings down the value of the startup—or possibly brings down the startup itself?*

---

* From the founder's perspective, we have argued that wealth and control motivations are equally valid as long as the founder's decisions are consistent with those motivations and with the overall context in which the startup is operating. However, as a society, should we care what motivates our entrepreneurs as long as they continue to be motivated to found startups? Very possibly. There is a tension between societal goals and some of the personal goals on which we have focused. A wealth-motivated founder makes decisions that maximize value creation, which may be aligned with societal interests. A control-motivated

CAN FOUNDERS CHANGE?

Evan Williams found it very hard to change his core motivation. Although he seemed to have changed from a control-motivated founder at Blogger to a wealth-motivated founder at Odeo, he came to regret his loss of control there and began to reverse his course, making choices designed to win back control of his startup. Once he realized that the problem with Odeo was his inability to make his own decisions, due to the powerful influence of his investors, he made the nearly unprecedented decision to use his own money to buy out his VCs—that is, to buy back the control he had mistakenly surrendered. Not that surrendering control is inherently a mistake, but it was a mistake for Evan because it violated his core motivation as a founder.

As described in Chapter 2, the CareerLeader data on entrepreneurial motivations suggest that those motivations may be very stable throughout a founder's life. However, people differ in the relative strengths of their wealth and control motivations. For some founders, such as Evan and Brian Scudamore, one is near or at the top of the list and the other much lower down; for others, the two motivations have nearly equal force. The former type would find it much harder than the latter to reverse the ordering of their motivations.

At the same time, the ups and downs of startup life can indeed shape the founder's motivations. On the down side of the entrepreneurial roller coaster, even the most control-oriented founder—burned out from months or even years of struggle—may be more willing to give up the reins and settle for wealth rather than control. James Milmo of Lynx Solutions said that he and his partner, who for months had fought each other for control of Lynx, were finally attracted to a buyout offer because "we were tired and we needed

---

founder, however, sacrifices value creation in favor of maximizing the chances of getting what he or she most prizes. A founder who has an idea with world-changing potential could build a startup that employs hundreds or thousands of people and delivers tremendous value to customers, but if that founder is control-motivated, he or she might make decisions that impede that value creation.

a break." Although the full buyout offer on the table was much less lucrative than other acquisition offers, James said that being able to walk away from Lynx was "very appealing." On the up side of the ride, a founder who fulfills one objective may change his or her emphasis to achieving the other. For instance, a control-oriented founder-CEO who has become rich may decide that further financial gain is no longer worth the hard work of being CEO and be willing to step aside. At Transcentive, founder-CEO Mike Brody experienced both of these effects. Mike was able to step away from the company he had controlled for more than 14 years when Les, the new CEO, negotiated a partial founder buyout that allowed Mike to retire as a rich man. Also, after so many years at the helm of his company, guiding it from a startup to a more mature company, Mike was ready for a change and, according to Les, "tired."

As founders gain knowledge and confidence in their skills, they may also seek to gain more control of decisions. For instance, when Tim Westergren first founded Savage Beast (later renamed Pandora), he had no prior business experience, having worked as a nanny, musician, and composer. He believed that his partner Jon, who had prior startup experience, was far more qualified to lead. Over the years, however, Tim's knowledge, skills, and confidence grew. He took on more of Jon's responsibilities and became the "evangelizer" who was the public face of Savage Beast's innovative service. Much to his own surprise, Tim found himself willing and ready to take over as CEO when Jon decided to leave.

The nature of a new opportunity may also cause the founder to shift his or her priorities. Evan Williams realized that podcasting would be a huge market and that other, more advanced companies, such as Apple and Yahoo, were sure to enter it with their own technology. Odeo had the early-mover advantage, having made a splash at a popular industry conference, and Evan felt a need to press his advantage by being first to market—a decision more typical of a wealth-motivated founder than a control-motivated founder. In addition, the relative ease with which Evan was able to raise VC funding for this hot technology placed him firmly on the path of fast, aggressive growth.

As the first-time founder sees the challenges that come with the later stages of startup evolution, he or she may also conclude that "I'm a startup person" who loves to get a startup off the ground and then move on to the next startup, rather than hanging in for what can seem like the long slog of the later stages of consolidation and formalization.

Founders who go on to found more startups can give us a window into how the learning process during a founder's first startup may cause a change in motivations that then shapes future efforts. As we have seen, first-time founders are often ignorant of their own capabilities, the outcomes of their early decisions, and the dramatic changes in each stage of startup growth. As they learn from their initial experiences, they go from being ad-hoc and naïve to systematic and informed. While building Wily Technology, Lew Cirne came to understand, for example, that startups required very different skills than more mature companies and that a successful startup CEO would not necessarily be the best person to lead the company as it grows. In Lew's words, he realized that he was more of a "speedboat captain" than "captain of an oil tanker."

While Evan's case shows a founder who traveled 360 degrees from King to Rich and back again, Frank Addante experienced a gradual 180-degree shift in priorities over his five startups. As a young and inexperienced entrepreneur, Frank was happy to cede control of and equity in his first two startups to his more veteran partners. In his third startup, Frank began to actively prepare to become a CEO. Finally, in his fourth and fifth startups, he gained control, setting out from the beginning to be "The Guy" who was "going to lead the army and go after that market and conquer it" instead of being a lesser member of the team.

OTHER CHOICES THAT AFFECT RICH-VERSUS-KING OUTCOMES

Figure 11.1 focuses on the founder's choices regarding other key participants in the startup. But wealth-versus-control outcomes are also affected by other choices, some of which are made even before founding. These choices include:

Preferred Rate of Startup Growth

Founders who want to keep control should prefer slower growth; at the least, the startup should be growing no more quickly than the founder's ability to learn the new skills required for each new stage of growth. Founders who lack confidence may also prefer slower growth; for some founders, "self-doubt about their management capabilities led them to avoid rapid expansion."[24] (In turn, the founder's growth goals should affect the type of financing used by the founder.)[25] In contrast, founders who want to maximize startup value should be open to faster growth if that's where the best opportunity lies. In some industries and in some stages of the business cycle—for example, in industries without drastic competitive pressures and during down parts of the business cycle—founders often have more control over the startup's growth rate. In industries with intense competitive pressure or during boom times, on the other hand, the founder's only choice may be "grow fast or die."

Evan Williams was under incredible pressure to develop Odeo's podcasting tool quickly, particularly after Apple engineers showed him the prototype of their new rival product, called "iTunes." Evan explained why he decided to raise VC capital so early in the startup's life, having shunned it altogether in his prior startup: "There was definitely pressure to . . . grow fast. . . . Apple came on, and then Yahoo launched a product within the same year, and every major media company announced something in podcasting and many of them were calling us, wanting to do deals. There was a feeling that this was all moving very, very quickly, and we needed to be ahead of it."

Capital Intensity

Similarly, founders who want to keep control should strive to begin startups that have low capital-intensity or that require few or no resources beyond those the founder already controls. Founders who want to maximize startup value, on the other hand, should be open to pursuing ideas that require high capital-intensity and to attracting the necessary resources.

Boundaries of the Firm

Capital intensity can be affected by which activities the founders decide to include within the boundaries of the firm. For instance, a startup could decide either to carry out all core tasks internally or else to outsource some of them.[26] At Ockham, Jim Triandiflou relied on outsourced software programmers to develop his sales-force-optimization product, saving him the trouble of adding a technical cofounder and deferring the need to raise capital. Dean Kamen, however, refused to allow outsiders to become involved in Segway's production, even though this decision forced him to raise considerable capital and hire several auto industry and production experts to build a complex production competency in-house. Franchising is another way to expand the traditional boundaries of the firm. Franchising can afford founders tangible benefits, such as enabling rapid growth in far-flung markets and sharing the risks and costs of expansion with highly motivated owner-operators.[27] Franchising allowed Brian Scudamore to build a highly valuable rubbish-removal empire without raising one penny of outside capital or sharing equity with a single cofounder.

INCREASING THE CHANCES OF ACHIEVING THE "ENTREPRENEURIAL IDEAL"

Future research could benefit from a focus on what distinguishes those few first-time founders who achieve the Holy Grail of Rich-and-King status. We could very well find that the major distinction is luck; for example, a rare window of opportunity such as IBM introducing its PC but needing an operating system for it and tapping startup Microsoft. However, outside of hoping luck will break their way or waiting for a once-in-a-lifetime idea to strike, what can founders do to increase the chances they will achieve both Rich and King?

Increasing Pre-founding Resource Endowments

Founders who begin their startups with more resources—that is, who made pre-founding career choices that enabled them to develop more of the human, social, and financial capitals needed to pursue the opportunity—will have a higher probability of achieving the entrepreneurial ideal. One such founder is Barry Nalls, whom we've gotten to know throughout this book and who will help us see how such founders prepare themselves to launch startups:

Human Capital

Founders who have accumulated the skills and knowledge needed to start and build their startups should be able to go without outside resources—and avoid the costs they impose—for a longer period of time. When they do eventually try to access those resources, they should be able to do so on more attractive terms, maintaining more control and giving up less ownership. Specifically, potential founders should work long enough to accumulate the managerial and functional skills required to be a founder-CEO throughout the stages of startup evolution, including the deep sales skills that become more critical as a startup matures. Potential founders should also try to work beforehand in the industry in which they are most likely to found.

After working for a decade at GTE, Barry Nalls attempted to start a small generalist consultancy, taking on whatever local projects he could find. It ended up being a very rocky experience, and he shut it down after a couple of years, returning to GTE. A decade later, when he decided to step back into the entrepreneurial waters, he was more prepared. First, he chose to found in an industry—telecom—that he knew extremely well. Second, he had gained additional managerial experiences that he believed would be attractive to investors: "I knew the technology. I had been an intrapreneur and had built a division from $30 million to $1 billion, so I had a real track record for [investors] to smell and validate." After GTE, Barry worked at two small startups, again gaining valuable experience by learning the pace and working environment at small entrepreneurial firms.

Social Capital

Social capital plays a central role in attracting other resource providers. At GTE, Barry Nalls had gained contacts with many telecom industry players who were potential customers, employees, and investors—contacts he leveraged to obtain financial and human capital. More broadly, founders can leverage their social capital to enhance both the startup's potential for financial gain and their own control of decision making.[28] Entrepreneurs with more social capital earn higher returns from the opportunities they pursue[29] and increase the likelihood that their startups will go public.[30] On the control side, greater social capital should increase an entrepreneur's control over his or her startup.[31] Prior ties reduce information asymmetries and investor risk,[32] thus reducing the degree of control investors will feel they need in order to protect their investments. Resource providers with prior ties to an entrepreneur are usually willing to incur greater risk and to be less likely to take actions detrimental to the entrepreneur.[33] Board allegiance, which often derives from prior ties, can forestall a CEO's dismissal,[34] at least in part because people with prior ties enjoy a deeper level of trust.[35]

Financial Capital

Potential founders should be avid savers, adopting a low "personal burn rate" even when they are receiving comfortable corporate salaries so they can accumulate as much seed and post-seed capital as possible. Such founders should enjoy greater bargaining power when they negotiate with resource providers.[36] An entrepreneur's initial investment of financial capital can help eliminate liquidity constraints[37] and might affect the startup's ultimate level of success.[38] Barry Nalls had negotiated a six-month severance from his last company, giving himself that long to start a new firm. "I gave myself six months to put together the complete plan, and raise money from investors," he recalled. "If I couldn't do it in that six-month window, I'd go get a job. We wouldn't have starved, wouldn't be on the street." Moreover, the positive signal sent by entrepreneurs who invest their own resources should improve access to outside resources.[39] Combined with a solid resource base, such positive signals should help attract better cofounders and hires.

Anticipating Trouble

We have seen how founders' early decisions can drastically hinder their efforts to build value and to retain control of the startup. For instance, "playing with fire" by founding with friends or family can cause major damage to the startup, the founding team, and the founder's social relationships outside the startup. Splitting equity in a static fashion can cause drop-out founders to make off with equity desperately needed to replace them or can enable them to hold up much-needed rounds of financing. Taking capital from a VC firm that tends to change CEOs at the first hint that the founder-CEO might not be able to handle every aspect his or her job can lead to early founder-CEO succession fireworks.

Founders who understand the long-term risks introduced by these common early decisions can anticipate those problems and take action to avoid them. In particular, founders who play with fire by cofounding with those close to them (hoping to gain the benefits of doing so) can proactively erect strong firewalls to protect themselves and the startup should those personal relationships blow up. Founders splitting equity can include terms for buying out cofounders if irreconcilable differences arise within the team or can structure dynamic equity splits that adjust to future changes. Before taking capital from potential investors, founders can perform their own due diligence on those investors to learn from past founders whether, for example, the investor tries to "coach the founder-CEO to success" when the startup hits a rough patch or tends to pull the trigger and replace the founder as CEO.* Founders who take steps in advance to recover from such problems are more likely to create more value, retain more ownership, and/or maintain control, thus increasing the chances of maximizing wealth while maintaining control.

---

* In recent years, websites such as Adeo Ressi's TheFunded.com have made it much easier for founders to perform such due diligence on their potential investors, further increasing their abilities to proactively prevent such problems.

Getting Closer Each Time: Serial Entrepreneurs

We have focused on first-time founders. Serial entrepreneurs—
founders of multiple startups in succession—often did not achieve
Rich-and-King status in their early startups, but eventually accumulated knowledge and resources to help them get closer to achieving the entrepreneurial ideal in subsequent startups. For instance,
my data show that serial entrepreneurs receive larger equity stakes
within their founding teams (increasing how wealthy they can become from the startup) and remain CEO for longer (increasing their
reigns of control) than first-time founders do. As we saw in Chapter
9, "Investor Dilemmas," 18% of founders take capital from investors who had invested in the founder's prior startup. By leveraging such preexisting ties, serial entrepreneurs should also be able to
negotiate investment terms that leave them more in control and/or
owning a larger percentage. Other recent research also suggests that
serial entrepreneurs have a higher probability of startup success.[40]

Although power and wealth are often at odds in a founder's first
startup, his or her increased wealth after a successful startup may
result in "delayed power" in a subsequent startup. Lew Cirne, for
instance, after handing the reins of Wily Technology to Richard Williams, was sidelined within his own startup but a couple years later
ended up a rich man when Computer Associates bought Wily for
hundreds of millions of dollars. In his second startup, New Relic,
Lew consciously kept tighter control over the early decisions by solo
founding, self-funding until he had enough leverage to get the benefits of VC money without the risk of losing control, and carefully
choosing each person whom he involved as a hire or board member.

FeedBurner's "serial founding team" was able to go from near
failure in its first startup to achieving better results in each subsequent startup until it achieved the entrepreneurial ideal in its fourth
startup. Along the way, the team learned lessons at every level at
which our founding dilemmas occur. Team members ironed out
early role problems and learned how best to split the equity. With
hires, they learned not to hire specialists too soon, how to strike
the right balance between flexibility and depth, and how different

functions develop at different rates and have to be compensated differently. They learned how to gain bargaining leverage with investors, which terms were most important to negotiate, and how to build, manage, and maintain control over a board. As a result, these founders retained control throughout the evolution of FeedBurner while leading the startup to a lucrative exit.

IMPLICATIONS FOR "UNSOLVED PUZZLES"

In Chapter 1, we previewed several unsolved puzzles concerning founders. We are now in a position to shed light on each of them.

Is the Missing "Private Equity Premium" Really a "Puzzle"?

Microeconomists have wondered why entrepreneurs, despite the higher risks they take and their presumed financial motivations, do not tend to make more money than they could in paid employment—probably even less on a risk-adjusted basis. The wealth-versus-control trade-off provides a straightforward and empirically supported explanation for this lack of an entrepreneurship premium: Although some founders are motivated to maximize their financial gains, many other founders are motivated by control, passion for the idea, and other motivations and therefore make decisions that sacrifice financial gain in order to maintain control or to maximize other nonfinancial benefits. Research on entrepreneurs should become less puzzling when researchers take into account the different kinds of success different entrepreneurs are motivated to seek.

Founder Power?

In academic sociological research, an executive's status as a founder has been used as a proxy for his or her greater power within the startup.[41] However, my research shows that founder status can indicate exactly the opposite. Founders' attachment to their startups causes them to suffer financially and to lose control of their startups (as described in Chapters 6 and 10, respectively). This is one example of how the entrepreneurial arena can help us shed light on power-elite theory, which assumes that the corporate power and economic wealth of top executives reinforce each other, with corporate positions serving as the source of wealth while "money provides power."[42] In contrast, the research described throughout this book highlights recurring conflicts between wealth and power, examining the circumstances in which they are in tension.

We have also seen how early sources of a founder's power can later become liabilities.* Founders' early successes often depend upon their optimism, persistence, and passion. However, if they are not careful, these very traits can skew their decisions and lead them to make mistakes at every stage of startup evolution. For instance, optimism may mislead potential founders into making the leap before they are ready (see Chapter 2), underestimating their need for cofounders (see Chapter 3), discounting the dangers of founding with friends and relatives (see Chapter 4), misjudging their ability to be effective CEOs through multiple stages of startup evolution (see Chapters 5 and 10), fighting for larger equity stakes than they objectively deserve (see Chapter 6), failing to fill holes with appropriate hires or even to recognize those holes (see Chapter 8), or agreeing to investment terms (e.g., liquidation preferences) that they think will never apply to them (see Chapter 9). Any of these and other missteps can weaken the founder's power, harm the value of his or her startup, and even imperil his or her ability to remain involved or for the startup to survive.

Stewards Rather Than Agents?

The predominant lens in microeconomics studies is agency theory, which posits that problems are caused by misalignment between

---

* Morgan McCall's research on *executive derailment*—when successful managers who were expected to continue being successful fail instead—highlights four common dynamics that have parallels to some of the dynamics described here. McCall's four are that the managers' prior strengths become weaknesses in a new situation, their existing flaws do not become salient until they are in a new situation, their success leads to arrogance, and they experience bad luck. For more details, see McCall (1998).

the individual "agent" and the organization (or its owners).[43] The theory proposes that organizations can reduce agency problems by means such as incentive alignment and monitoring. Stewardship theory, on the other hand, posits that, in certain contexts, executives' interests will be aligned with company interests and be more intrinsically motivated than predicted by agency theory.[44] The findings in this book suggest that, in many cases, stewardship theory can better represent the relationship between founders and their startups and more accurately predict founder behavior than agency theory can. Even so, my research exposes a dark side of stewardship theory, for the close attachment between founder-stewards and their startups causes problems for founders regarding both wealth (resulting in a greater founder compensation discount) and control (causing founder-CEO succession to be even more disruptive to the founder and the startup). Founders' stewardship inclinations can negate their power and even become destructive.

BOUNDARY CONDITIONS AND OPPORTUNITIES FOR FUTURE RESEARCH

The data and case studies at the core of this book come from for-profit American startups in the two largest industries for high-potential startups—technology and life sciences. The dilemmas examined throughout the book apply specifically to the founders of such startups. It is still unknown whether and to what extent they are specific to the United States. We have also focused on subsets of the possible motivations, types of founders, and founding dilemmas. These limitations and boundary conditions must be kept in mind regarding the results and patterns described in this book, but also suggest avenues for future research.

Testing Boundary Conditions

The two major boundary conditions are the types of organizations examined here and the country from which the data were collected.

Specific to High-Potential Startups?

Both the field cases and the quantitative data presented in this book come from high-potential startups.* In such startups, founding dilemmas are often stark, for the founders are usually very resource-constrained, rarely have all of the skills and connections needed for the startup to reach its full potential, and tend to face significant risk of losing decision-making control. Some studies of small businesses have begun to suggest that, even in low-potential startups, founders may sacrifice financial gains for nonfinancial benefits.[45] However, these researchers have not directly examined if and to what extent small-business entrepreneurs give up control of their organizations and, if they do give up control, whether they gain financially from doing so. Answering these questions would help establish whether the dilemmas faced by those small-business founders differ from the dilemmas examined here.

Nonprofit organizations and family businesses also offer good opportunities to examine the tension between wealth and control. Nonprofits face the core entrepreneurial challenge of pursuing opportunity while having to gain control of necessary resources,[46] suggesting that the founders of nonprofits may face dilemmas similar to those examined in this book. As nonprofits grow, they also face distinct changes in the skills needed to lead the organization, posing major challenges for the founders' abilities to continue leading them. However, nonprofits and their founders may face even more extreme challenges because the founders may become even more central to their organizations than other founders do, more attached to them, and more identified with their missions, making it even harder to transition to a new generation of leadership. Also, many nonprofit founders are motivated by "impact" and the chance to improve things for the community or the world. Maximizing that

---

* As defined in Chapter 1, *high-potential startups* are startups, often technology- or science-based, that have the potential to become large and valuable, even though their founders may subsequently make decisions that limit their growth. See Chapter 1 for a brief discussion of the differences between high-potential startups and small businesses.

impact calls for attracting the necessary resources, but that, in turn, may imperil the founder's control of decision making.[47] Do non-profit founders face a trade-off between impact and control that parallels the wealth-versus-control trade-off we have been examining, or does that pair of motivations result in different trade-offs and different dilemmas for nonprofit founders?

In the family business realm, does the motivation to maintain control of the business so that descendants can continue to run it introduce trade-offs that parallel the trade-offs examined here, or does it introduce different dilemmas? If multiple members of the family have a say in the business, but differ in their motivations, how do they resolve those differences? Not only would a wealth-versus-control lens help us deepen our understanding of nonprofits and family businesses, but that deeper understanding should in turn enrich our understanding of the core dilemmas encountered in high-potential startups.

Specific to the United States?

Almost all of the cases and data in this book come from the United States. We do not know yet whether the dilemmas examined here are specific to the American culture, legal regime, and regulatory structure or whether they apply more universally. Culture certainly affects the propensity for founders to found alone, to do so with family members, to split roles in an egalitarian fashion, to split equity equally, to hire inexperienced people, and to avoid (or not have access to) professional investors. Whether the differences mean that the actual dilemmas differ, or just that the different choices within each dilemma occur with a different frequency, remains to be established.

At the same time, data collected by the Global Entrepreneurship Monitor (GEM) project, a multi-institution effort to understand entrepreneurship around the globe, suggests that most countries have similar mixes of Rich versus King founders. GEM surveys entrepreneurs about their core motivations, categorizing them as being motivated by "independence" (i.e., control) or by the desire to "increase income" (i.e., wealth).[48] Across the 42 countries in GEM's report, including 23 high-income countries and 19 middle- and low-income countries, almost every country had a relatively even split between the two types of motivation. In every country, at least 35% of entrepreneurs were control-motivated and, in all but two, at least 30% were wealth-motivated.[49] The split in the United States—about 57% control motivated and 43% wealth motivated—was similar enough to the splits in other countries to suggest that the U.S.-based results in this book might extend to many of those other countries. But we still need solid evidence that this is true.

Opportunities for Future Research

Throughout *The Founder's Dilemmas*, I have presented the results of a wide variety of analyses of my quantitative dataset. These results provide an initial look at how the patterns described here affect such outcomes as the propensity to found alone, founding-team stability, startup valuation, and the ability to remain CEO of the startup. Future multivariate research could (a) test other important outcomes and (b) test other propositions about how these outcomes are affected by the variables and contingencies described in this book. Other opportunities for high-potential research include broadening the picture to include other entrepreneurial motivations, the experiences of serial entrepreneurs, other participants in the building of startups, other dilemmas faced by founders, and the relative risks and returns of founder exits. Because any honest model of a complex human phenomenon has to acknowledge the many unknowns, these opportunities for future research are integrated into the cohesive model of founder decisions presented in Appendix 11-2.

Beyond Wealth and Control: The Effects of Other Motivations

Although wealth and control motivations are the most common for entrepreneurs, they can coexist with others. For instance, a founder who is equally motivated by wealth and control motivations, and thus lacks clarity about what to decide regarding a specific dilemma, may use a secondary motivator, such as intellectual challenge, as a tiebreaker, which might lead to different decisions than those made by a founder who uses yet another motivation—say, altruism—to break the same tie. Also, the framework in this book applies to the majority of founders, who are indeed wealth- or control-motivated, but not to founders with less common motivations.[*] It thus cannot provide solid guidance to those founders about what decisions to make when facing the dilemmas described in this book. Developing such guidance requires both the theoretical groundwork to understand the linkages between their motivations and the decisions they should make, and the empirical testing to validate those relationships.

Beyond First-Time Founders: Serial Entrepreneurship

My consistent focus has been on first-time founders, occasionally contrasting them with serial entrepreneurs such as Dick Costolo, Evan Williams, Lew Cirne, and Frank Addante. Academia has begun taking a more concentrated approach to studying serial entrepreneurs,[50] and, for each of the dilemmas examined here, there is a fertile opportunity to research the systematic differences between first-timers and serial entrepreneurs. In what ways does the decision making of serial entrepreneurs evolve? How do their motivations evolve, and is that affected by how successful they were in their initial startups? Do any of these changes create underappreciated pitfalls for the serial entrepreneur?

Beyond Founders, Hires, and Investors: Other Potential Participants

This book has focused on the most central participants whom founders might involve in their startups: cofounders, hires, and investors. However, other participants might also play important roles as alternative resource providers. For instance, rather than gaining full control over some resources, founders may create corporate

---

[*] As shown by the CareerLeader data in Chapter 2, wealth and control motivations dominate the list of entrepreneurial motivations, but altruism, variety, and intellectual challenge are also top-four motivations for some age cohorts.

partnerships with companies that have complementary resources or companies to which they can outsource important tasks. These founders will thus face "whether to partner" dilemmas.

Such partnerships may involve different wealth-versus-control trade-offs than those involved in attracting cofounders, hires, and investors. For instance, crafting a corporate partnership may cause a founder to give up control of some decision-making power (because the startup will no longer be doing everything in-house) and of some financial gains (which will now have to be shared with the partner), but might increase the founder's chances of retaining a moderate amount of control (because he or she didn't have to take as much capital from outside investors) and of securing at least some financial gains from his or her hard work (by staying focused on the core of the business, remaining nimble, getting to market and scaling the business more quickly, or keeping costs down). In this sense, corporate partnerships may be a way to achieve "75% Rich, 75% King."[51] Such participant issues can become "boundary of the firm" decisions that can also have important implications for how much control the founder can keep over decision making and how valuable a startup he or she can build.

Where to Found, Exits, and Other Important Dilemmas

A dilemma that is not addressed in this book is one of the earliest decisions a founder faces: where to found the startup.[52] Locating in hubs can help founders attract the best cofounders and hires (who might already be living there and not want to move elsewhere) and the best investors (who like to invest in clusters of nearby startups).[53] However, if such a hub is not the best place for the founder or his or her family, he or she may decide to locate where the resources are not as available and thus limit the potential value the startup can achieve. (This is one way in which the personal, career, and market factors from Chapter 2 can affect eventual outcomes.) Barry Nalls returned to North Texas from California because of the resources available there for his autistic son, even though California might have been a better place to find the resources he would need for his startup. Genevieve Thiers moved Sittercity from Boston, where she had contacts and employees, to Chicago, both to pursue her avocation in opera at a master's program at Northwestern and because her fiancé was born there and wanted to move back home. The FeedBurner team was adamant about staying in Chicago for their families' stability, even to the point of negotiating specific buyout terms that would ensure they would not have to move.

A final dilemma that deserves attention is whether to sell the startup to an acquirer or to go public. Appendix 11-3 presents an initial field-based exploration of these exit decisions, but much more research is required to establish the patterns and best practices. How do wealth-versus-control trade-offs affect such "exit dilemmas"? How are the founders' decisions affected by their tendencies toward overconfidence, optimism, and attachment? How do nonfounders, including professional CEOs and investors, affect the exit decision, and how often do their interests diverge from those of the founders? What are the most effective mechanisms for resolving such divergences (e.g., founder carve-outs or earn-outs)?[54]

Other Outcomes: Realized Exits and Risk Differences

Quantitative examination of founders' exit dilemmas would have a further benefit. Because the data in this book come from operating startups, we can compute only the current value of the founders' equity stakes—their "paper gains"—but not their "realized" values—the wealth eventually received from the startup. A dataset that included startups that had exited and returned actual money to their shareholders (a much smaller dataset than the one used here) would help us to assess how closely startups' interim paper gains approximate their eventual realized gains.

In addition, although we have deemed some choices riskier than others (e.g., founding with friends or family members and doing quick-handshake equity splits) and have some information about outcomes such as the breakup of a founding team, we don't have the final outcomes that would give us the last word, so to speak, on which decisions are safer than others. For instance, how often is a control-oriented founder able to sell a startup, of which he or she owns 100%, for $5 million, and how often is a wealth-oriented founder able to sell a startup, of which he or she owns 5%, for $100 million? How much longer do control-motivated founders take to exit compared to wealth-motivated founders? Is one exit a longer shot than the other? If so, how should differences in risk profile affect the founder's early decisions?[*]

CLOSING REMARKS

There is a great deal of mystique around founders, some of it well deserved but some of it also dangerously unexamined. Many founders and would-be founders see themselves—and are seen by others—as having a calling. This is true and very inspiring, but founders—and those who join their startups—need a clearer picture than that. Different motivations call for very different decisions. Many founders have learned the hard way how their own choices undermined their motivations. As the Roman playwright and philosopher Seneca wisely observed, "If one does not know to which port one is sailing, no wind is favorable."

But knowing one's motivation is only one piece of the puzzle. Founders often embark on their entrepreneurial journeys feeling like Lewis and Clark as they set out across the continent, having a rough idea of where they want to go, but seeing no clear road ahead nor fully anticipating the dangers they might encounter. Once on their way, they often fail to realize when they are at a crucial fork in the road they are on, about to make a decision that will have important consequences for the journey. Perhaps they see a path to the right but not the path to the left. Nor do they see that, just around the bend, the path to the right heads straight over a cliff. Neither instinct nor luck can consistently guide their way, mile after mile, as reliably as a clear understanding beforehand of the many forks in

---

[*] In Hall et al.'s (2010) study of VC-backed startups, 75% of the startups returned $0 to the founders. How does that compare to the return to King founders, and how do the risks of losing the CEO position differ for each type of founder?

the road, the options at each fork, and the implications of each of those options.

I have called these forks "founding dilemmas," which sounds more like a warning than an invitation. But they are not unsolvable. Scientific study and the wisdom of the experienced can each help. I have gathered as much as I can of both into this book. As an academic, I am interested in both success and failure, but to those who use this book, I wish only success on the path ahead.

APPENDIX 11-1—A THOUGHT EXPERIMENT: WOULD A HYBRID PATH BE BETTER?

Let's engage in a brief thought experiment regarding founder decision making. In this simple world, a founder has decisions to make about each of three people to involve in the startup—one decision about cofounders, one about hires, and one about investors—and has two choices within each decision—a control-oriented choice, which maintains control at the risk of not attracting the person, and a wealth-oriented choice, which attracts the person but heightens the risk of losing control. Let's assume that each control-oriented choice will result in an 80% chance of maintaining control and a 20% chance of building the full value possible, and that each wealth-oriented choice will result in a 20% chance of maintaining control and an 80% chance of building the full value possible.

If the founder consistently makes the control-oriented choices, it will lead to the following probabilities of each result:

- Maintain control: 80% × 80% × 80% = 51% probability
- Build fullest value: 20% × 20% × 20% = 1% probability

In contrast, if the founder consistently makes the wealth-oriented choices, it will lead to the following probabilities of each result:

- Maintain control: 20% × 20% × 20% = 1% probability
- Build fullest value: 80% × 80% × 80% = 51% probability

Founders who make consistent choices across all three levels will thus be approximately 51 times more likely to achieve one result than the other. According to this model, these founders will also have a slightly better than 50/50 shot at reaching one of the desired outcomes, rather than failing to reach either outcome, but also a less than 1% chance of achieving both outcomes.

If the founder is less consistent about his or her decisions, the probabilities change markedly. If a founder chooses control for two of the decisions and wealth for the third (though not necessarily in that order), it will lead to the following probabilities of each result:

- Maintain control: 80% × 80% × 20% = 13% probability
- Build fullest value: 20% × 20% × 80% = 3% probability

The chance of maintaining control has dropped by a factor of four, while the chance of building the full value of the startup has risen to only 3%. The chance of complete failure—not achieving either outcome—has risen dramatically, to better than an 80% chance. Likewise, for one control-oriented choice and two wealth-oriented choices, there will be a 3% chance of maintaining control and a 13% chance of building the startup's full value.

A hybrid strategy may indeed provide one benefit: Founders who aren't sure which outcome they prefer can "hedge" their bets by mixing some wealth-oriented choices with some control-oriented ones. By making consistent choices, founders have only a 1% chance of achieving the less likely outcome, but by making mixed choices, they can increase that probability to 3%. However, the cost of this hedging is dramatic, causing the probability of achieving the more likely outcome to drop dramatically and increasing dramatically the chance of achieving neither of the desirable outcomes. For founders who aren't sure which outcome is more valuable to them, such a hedge might make sense; however, if those founders could figure out their core motivation before making those decisions, they could dramatically increase their probability of achieving the more attractive outcome.

Future research could examine empirically how often founders use consistent versus hybrid strategies and begin establishing whether hybrid strategies are the best or the worst of both worlds.

APPENDIX 11-2—A MODEL OF FOUNDER DECISIONS

Throughout this book, I have described a wide variety of decisions faced by founders and the factors that might affect the outcomes they achieve. These factors range from the founder's motivations and behaviors to strategic and environmental influences. Where relevant, I have presented my initial research results and provided suggestions for future research. Figure 11.4 integrates all of these factors into a cohesive model of founder decisions.

The figure begins with the founder's motivations, which include the wealth and control motivations on which we have focused as well as altruism, variety, intellectual challenge, and others. Those motivations, shaped by strategic factors, affect founders' pre-founding career decisions; their founding-team, hiring, and investor decisions; and their decisions about where to found, whether and how to form corporate partnerships, and whether and how to exit from the startup. The interplay of these decisions with the founders' own capabilities and consistency and with their teams' interpersonal dynamics affects the outcomes for the individual founders, their teams, and their startups. Meanwhile, founder motivations, decisions, and outcomes are all affected by the environmental factors described throughout the book. To top it off, this whole tangle of interactions is dynamic. Founders learn from the results of their decisions, adjust their goals, and develop further skills and contacts that, in turn, affect their motivations and subsequent decisions.

There's a lot going on—that's one of the most important messages of this book. A less obvious message of this book is that we have a lot to learn. Throughout the book, I have presented the results of my initial research and of research conducted by others, but I have frequently pointed out where the necessary research has yet to be done. As indicated by the asterisks throughout Figure 11.4, productive opportunities for future research abound. I invite founders to help remove those asterisks by sharing their own insights about the many factors we have seen at play and which they will have experienced firsthand. I invite researchers to help remove asterisks with their future investigations into those factors.

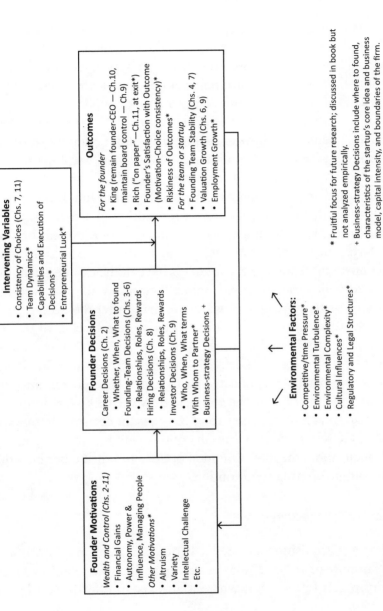

Intervening Variables
- Consistency of Choices (Chs. 7, 11)
- Team Dynamics*
- Capabilities and Execution of Decisions*
- Entrepreneurial Luck*

Founder Motivations
Wealth and Control (Chs. 2–11)
- Financial Gains
- Autonomy, Power & Influence, Managing People

Other Motivations
- Altruism
- Variety
- Intellectual Challenge
- Etc.

Founder Decisions
- Career Decisions (Ch. 2)
  - Whether, When, What to found
- Founding-Team Decisions (Chs. 3–6)
  - Relationships, Roles, Rewards
- Hiring Decisions (Ch. 8)
  - Relationships, Roles, Rewards
- Investor Decisions (Ch. 9)
  - Who, When, What terms
  - With Whom to Partner*
- Business-strategy Decisions [+]

Outcomes
For the founder
- King (remain founder-CEO — Ch.10, maintain board control — Ch.9)
- Rich ("on paper" — Ch.11, at exit*)
- Founder's Satisfaction with Outcome (Motivation–Choice consistency)*
- Riskiness of Outcomes*

For the team or startup
- Founding Team Stability (Chs. 4, 7)
- Valuation Growth (Chs. 6, 9)
- Employment Growth*

Environmental Factors:
- Competitive/time Pressure*
- Environmental Turbulence*
- Environmental Complexity*
- Cultural Influences*
- Regulatory and Legal Structures*

* Fruitful focus for future research; discussed in book but not analyzed empirically.

[+] Business-strategy Decisions include where to found, characteristics of the startup's core idea and business model, capital intensity, and boundaries of the firm.

Figure 11.4. A Model of Founder Decisions

When launching their startups, many founders dream of the Promised Land of going public, seeing the sale of equity to public shareholders as the ultimate exit. However, as we saw in Chapter 9, even startups that manage to attract venture capital are almost three times as likely to be acquired as they are to go public.[*]

Our focus has been on the dilemmas faced by founders when deciding whether and how to involve new players in their startups. A founding team's decision about whether, when, and how to exit can be deeply affected—and constrained—by those earlier decisions about bringing in cofounders, hires, investors, and professional CEOs. Indeed, some of the long-term wealth and control implications of those early founding decisions may become evident only as the startup nears the finish line. For instance, early decisions may affect how strong a voice the founders have in the exit decision, the extent to which they disagree among themselves about it, and the contribution they are able or willing to make after the exit.

Yet academic research has paid much more attention to the investors and acquirers than to the founders, and we lack a detailed picture of the factors that affect founders' decisions to exit. To address this gap, I have conducted early-stage field research into the major factors that should be considered by the lucky few founders who face—and have a strong voice in—the exit decision. In this appendix, I describe the initial results of this field research, beginning with acquisition, the more common option, and then describing the initial public offering (IPO) option.

Should We Sell Our Startup?

Not only is acquisition a more likely outcome than an IPO, but it is also far more of an "exit" for the startup and for the founders. Once a startup gets to the point where it attracts an offer from a larger

---

[*] In Hall et al.'s (2010) study of venture-backed companies from 1987 to 2008, of the startups that had exited (half of their sample), approximately 52% had merged or been acquired, 18% had gone public, and 30% had been liquidated or had gone bankrupt.

Reasons *Not* to Sell ⟵————————⟶	Reasons to Sell
• Will lose control of decision making	*Eroding prospects for startup:*
• Will lose chance to build further value, then sell at a better price	• Adverse market changes or dangerously low cash
• May not be able to preserve startup's culture	• Founder burnout or rising tensions between founders
• May not gain financially if investment terms (e.g., liquidation preferences) mean founders won't share in exit payments	• May soon lose control of exit decision and terms
	Attractive post-acquisition possibilities:
	• Achieve wealth goals
	• Use as stepping stone to become serial entrepreneur
	• Gain resources to build startup
	• Work for attractive parent company

Figure 11.5. Reasons Not to Sell versus Reasons to Sell

player, it faces a dilemma that could have dramatic implications for the company and for the founders. When deciding whether or not to accept an acquisition offer, founders have to weigh the following factors (summarized in Figure 11.5).

Reasons Not to Sell

The founders' core motivations have played a fundamental role in the decisions we have examined throughout this book and they do so in the exit decision as well. Control-motivated founders may not want to sell because it means losing a lot of decision-making control. Some fear that being swallowed by a large company will spoil the culture they have spent years building. Acquiring companies also usually want to control strategic decisions and to decide who should remain with the startup as it is integrated into the acquirer's core business. Early in the life of Blogger, Evan Williams received an acquisition offer of $1 million. For Evan, selling Blogger would have been the way out of several sticky problems; he was dangerously short on cash, and he would soon need to lay off his entire staff. His cofounder and employees pushed strongly for the sale. But Evan couldn't give up on his baby and decided not to sell. Even when Google made an offer months later, Evan initially rejected it: "After four years of pouring my heart into Blogger, I saw a lot of risk in giving up control."[55]

Yet even wealth-motivated founders, offered a payday after years of hard work, may not want to sell. Some believe they can still build significant value by remaining independent. For example, when the acquisition market for Internet companies started to improve in the mid-2000s, FeedBurner started to attract acquisition offers, but cofounder-CEO Dick Costolo wasn't ready to cash out: "I wanted to stay in because I felt there was a lot more stock value to be built," he explained. In 2008, when Facebook made a lucrative offer for Twitter, Evan Williams successfully pushed his investors to refuse the offer because of "what we could accomplish by when [and] why there's still so much we have left to do."[56]

While Dick's decision not to sell was founded on years of working in technology startups, other founders' decisions are driven by their optimism and passion. They may have unduly rosy pictures of the startup's potential, causing them to underestimate their upcoming growth challenges, to misread the competitive landscape, or to anticipate a better offer that never materializes.

Just as early decisions can affect a founder-CEO's options in the event of his or her own exit from the role (the founder-CEO succession discussed in Chapter 10), they can also affect the founding team's exit options. For instance, founders who signed term sheets with liquidation preferences that prevent them from getting any proceeds from the sale until the investors get back the capital they invested will usually resist mightily any offers below that amount, finding numerous ways to hold up the acquisition. At Lynx Solutions, cofounders James and Javier had liquidation terms that would have required that their investors be paid back their investments of almost $30 million before the founders' and employees' equity stakes could be honored. Lynx's two potential offers, both for a lot less than $30 million, would have left the founders without any reward after years of hard work, many of those years without pay. "The reason we became entrepreneurs in the first place and had survived all of our ordeals was that we never lost sight of the upside," explained James, "and if we did have some kind of exit, we didn't want to end up with nothing in the end, didn't want to become victims of a $30 million overhang."

Reasons to Sell

Major reasons to sell include both eroding prospects for the startup and attractive post-acquisition possibilities, but may also include more intangible factors, such as founder burnout and incompatibility.

Eroding Prospects for the Startup

The founders may be worried about the startup's future, particularly if cash is running low, as was the case at DKA, Dick Costolo's first startup, when the firm's strategic investor decided not to fund a B-round and other potential investors also shied away. Eventually, a sale was the only viable option, short of closing the company, and the founder-CEO was able to find an acquirer at the last minute. "Our CEO pulled a rabbit out of his hat," explained cofounder Dick Costolo. "Selling became our only avenue because of how we had financed the company before."

Founders may also worry that changes in the industry will threaten the startup's core business. Les Trachtman, CEO of Transcentive, a stock-option software company, explained how various forces changed the stock-option industry. "The market in 2001 was saturated, legislation had passed that was cracking down on stock options, and the market was demanding a global presence. Our customers were moving from stock-option plans to overall compensation plans, which meant that we would need to fill in holes in our offerings. To do that, we either needed to invest heavily in our software or find companies we could buy to fill those holes." When the board rejected his idea to acquire a company, Les found a company interested in acquiring Transcentive.

Within the startup team, years of pressure may be eroding the relationship among the founders or within the broader executive team. As these relationships suffer, the startup often does, too. Under such circumstances, an acquisition offer can feel like a lifeline, a chance for the team to solve its internal problems—by having one or more players leave or be reassigned—while also benefiting financially. At Lynx Solutions, which had recently become profitable after several years of losses, the burned-out and bickering cofounders decided that selling the company would be the best resolution of their irreconcilable differences.

Some founders choose to exit while they still have the power to drive the acquisition negotiations. Waiting until after another round of financing may mean that their equity share or their control of the board has dipped below the point where they could negotiate the acquisition terms most important to them. For Dick Costolo, the inflection point came when he was contemplating the choice between an offer from Google to buy FeedBurner or a C-round term sheet from VCs. Dick chose the buyout over the financing, in part because, after the C-round, the investors would own over 50% of the company and have a three-seat voting bloc on the board. For Dick it was sell now, when he had full control, or wait and perhaps be forced by his investors to accept a deal that would not be as beneficial to the founding team. Founders who think ahead about the point at which they are likely to become secondary players in the exit decision should be in a better position to control that decision.*

Attractive Post-acquisition Possibilities

Rather than running away from an eroding startup, some founders are running toward an attractive post-acquisition situation. For wealth-motivated founders, an attractive offer is the goal they set out to reach years before—walking away from the startup with a lot of money. Even control-motivated founders may be happy to take such an offer if they see it as a stepping stone to their next stage of life. They could use their payday to shift gears in life or to become serial entrepreneurs, building a new startup over which their increased financial capital will give them more control. For instance, after handing over the reins of Wily Technology to Richard Williams (see Chapter 10), Lew Cirne remained with Wily as founder-CTO. When Wily was sold to Computer Associates in 2006 for $375 million, Lew stayed a year, then left to found New Relic, another performance-management software company. Lew explained that he viewed New Relic as a "do-over" in which he could correct the mistakes he had made with Wily. Most importantly, he built New Relic as a software-as-a-service (SaaS) or subscription-software business, which gave him lower up-front costs, much higher recurring

---

* As Shakespeare stated (in *As You Like It*, 2:7), "All the world's a stage, / And all the men and women merely players; / They have their Exits and their Entrances."

revenue, and a business model that fit his skills. Lew was thus able to self-fund the company during its early stages and to maintain decision-making control longer.

The post-acquisition possibilities may also be more attractive if the acquisition enables the startup to gain valuable resources it would not otherwise have had. Both Evan at Blogger and Dick at FeedBurner felt that being acquired by Google would provide the financial capital to fulfill their visions and would put the best and brightest engineers and business minds to work on their projects.

For founders who have put in years of long intense hours, a steady job at a larger company may look attractive. For some, it offers a better balance between work and personal life without having to abandon the startup to which they are still attached. If the acquirer respects, rewards, and fosters the founders' strengths, they may also be glad to work for that company. For instance, two of FeedBurner's engineering-focused founders were excited about being acquired by Google and working for an innovative and fast-growing company.

How Should We Structure the Sale?

Acquisitions can be structured in a wide variety of ways, each of which may cause repercussions for the founders. Two of the major options are to structure it as a cash-only deal, in which the acquirer pays shareholders for their equity stakes, or as an earn-out, in which a significant share of the potential payoff for the startup's key executives (including founders) comes in the form of performance-dependent payments *after* the acquisition. For an acquirer planning to replace the startup's management with its own people, a cash-only deal often makes sense. However, if the acquirer wants to retain some of the startup's people or if it senses that using an earn-out structure will help it filter out any startup whose own executives lack confidence in its prospects, an earn-out structure is more attractive. It lets founders who are still confident in their startup's prospects benefit from the acquisition right away (from the non-earn-out part of the offer) while preserving future upside (through the earn-out). Acquirers who can tie a significant portion of the acquisition price to future performance are often willing to pay a higher price for the startup.

At Lynx Solutions, the founders faced competing offers from two wireless companies, Mobilink and Spotlight.* Mobilink wanted to close within 30 days and to buy out and replace the cofounders immediately, but offered only $20 million in cash. Spotlight offered $25 million in cash and stock plus a $10 million earn-out upon Lynx meeting challenging milestones over the subsequent two years. The founders would remain working for those two years, focused on achieving those milestones.

Earn-outs appeal to confident founders and sometimes reward them handsomely, but can also come back to bite them. At one startup, the earn-out was tied to the founders hitting $150 million in revenues, the amount they had projected before the acquisition. But they achieved only $59 million and would have done better to take a much lower offer with more of the money up-front.

Founders who remain with the startup to build more value face a more fundamental risk: They will lose a certain amount of control over the very decisions that affect how much value they can build. When Evan sold Blogger to Google, he agreed to work there for two years, but he soon became disillusioned. Google hired most of Blogger's team as contractors rather than employees, and it didn't come through with all the resources Evan had expected. When Google went public less than two years after the acquisition, Evan cashed out some of his stock and left the company shortly thereafter. Similarly, when Dick Costolo sold his third startup, Spyonit, to 724 Solutions, he found he hadn't anticipated the potential downsides of his three-year earn-out clause. As Dick explained, "Unfortunately, we did the deal in September 2000 and, right after that, the stock deteriorated. Also, after the sale, we weren't in control of our company any more. We were no longer responsible only to ourselves. There was now a big company in Canada that we had to report to. They had very different priorities. It was a drastic change."

*These names are pseudonyms.

Acquisition by a larger company may force the startup team that has spent years pursuing its vision unhindered to sacrifice that vision if the new mother company has interests that conflict with it. After Google bought FeedBurner, Dick Costolo and his cofounders expected their execution risks to drop, only to find them replaced by new risks. "We learned that selling the company doesn't de-risk all of the execution risk. If you think, 'I'm going to sell because the money's good and they have all these resources and I'll make my baby into this beautiful thing,' sometimes [a sale] actually increases risk because of the parent company's competing interests."

For the Lynx founders, accepting an earn-out would conflict with their major reason for exiting in the first place: They were burned out after years of riding the entrepreneurial roller coaster, and they wanted out. They therefore accepted the offer from Mobilink—millions of dollars lower than Spotlight's offer—because Mobilink wanted to complete the sale immediately and replace the founders. "For us personally, their approach was attractive," James explained. "We wanted to move quickly and we really didn't want to stick around for two more years to run things. We were tired and needed a break."

Should We Go Public?

Even for the few founders who are able to remain in a startup until an IPO, this Promised Land is often less attractive than expected, bringing many changes that make life harder.

The most tangible positive change for the company may be that it is now able to access a new source of capital—public shareholders. At L90, founder Frank Addante believed that an infusion of capital from the public markets and the chance to have a publicly traded stock currency would enable L90 to acquire smaller competitors and thereby expand its services. An IPO would also add credibility and engender the trust of larger accounts, enabling L90 to bring in new customers. Candace Kendle, founder-CEO of life sciences startup Kendle International, Inc., made a similar observation: "The number-one best thing is having the public currency with which to complete acquisitions. Otherwise we wouldn't have gone that [IPO] route. It's about having money and getting more money."

For founder-CEOs, however, going public can have adverse effects. Academics have theorized that having broadly dispersed shareholders after going public might increase the founder-CEO's control of the startup,[57] but newly public CEOs often lament the scrutiny and tougher regulations, not to mention the substantial cost of mandatory financial disclosure.[58] Frank Addante reflected, "When you're private and you take investor money, you have a finite set of investors to manage. You get to decide who you work with. You look at them eye to eye and get to know whether they believe in your vision, so they share your expectations. When you're public, you don't know who is buying stock. You have people who don't understand your full vision and are looking at it for a variety of factors. Some are short-term, some are long-term, some are buying into the metrics and the fundamentals and some are simply buying based on vision." Kendle International's stock suffered from many such ups and downs. Candace Kendle observed, "If you miss your numbers . . . even on a quarterly basis, there is a huge price that you pay."

For Kendle's other cofounder, Chris Bergen, going public had more personal implications. "There is a benefit to the public exposure," he explained. "We enjoy a position in the business community . . . which we wouldn't otherwise enjoy and that's good. There's a downside to that: Our finances are more public than they once were. To the extent that people know how much money you make and how much stock you own, that's not something that we're comfortable with because we're not very public people, we're very private people." Within Kendle, going public had implications further down the organization chart, too. Chris said that, at first, "Employees were absolutely ecstatic. . . . [But later], when [the options] are underwater, they think maybe it's not such a great deal. Everyone's happy when things are going well; the trick is to make them happy when things aren't going well."

The IPO is much more of an exit for VCs than it is for founders.[59] Not only do VCs get returns from their investment, but one study showed that 62% of VCs leave the board once a portfolio company goes public.[60] (As a result, many founder-CEOs of newly public startups are answering to new boards of directors.) For the founders, as for the startup itself, an IPO is sometimes less an exit event than the next in a series of financing events. The founders' previously illiquid stock is now liquid, yet it is only after a multi-month post-IPO "lockup" period that founders are able to sell some of their stock and enjoy financial gains from their hard work. Even after that, they are subject to constraints on how much they can sell; large sales might send a negative signal about the company's prospects, harming its stock price. For some founders, there may also be self-imposed constraints on selling their stock. Frank Addante, for example, had trouble getting himself to sell his stock in L90: "There's a conflict in your mind between selling the stock and holding onto it. It makes you feel that you're selling because you believe that you can't create more value in it. It's an emotional struggle internally. . . . Anytime I thought about selling some stock, I was never able to pull the trigger."

Divergence within the Team

Exit dilemmas can be hard enough to resolve when the founding team is aligned in its motivations; they become even harder to resolve if the founders' motivations diverge. For instance, some founders may be more risk-averse than others, preferring to take the safe option (such as a "sure" acquisition offer) rather than taking a chance on a risky future (such as building more value before selling). Dick Costolo explained how risk tolerances diverged and split the Feed-Burner team into two camps: "With the different risk profiles within the founding team, some are ready to do the deal, while others say, 'Let's tell them to go to hell. We need 25% more.' You might think you're all going to be on the same page, but when the real number comes in, people [will be tempted to take what's on the table.] . . . Eric and I are always more willing to take more risk, leave it all out there, keep going. Steve and Matt are more like, 'Let's not look back on this with regret. Let's take something off the table.'"

Likewise, if one founder is wealth-motivated and the other control-motivated, the former may want to grab an offer while the latter founder resists. Indeed, whether or not to exit was the only major disagreement between the cofounders of a financial-services outsourcing company. One wanted to take a buyout offer from a large public competitor, but the other resisted. The latter cofounder later said, "I did everything I could to stop the sale, but eventually realized that the rock was falling anyway and that it would be better to be on top of it than under it. It is hard to say that taking $250 million cash is a bad decision, but [the startup] was my baby and I loved it."[61]

Early decisions about equity splits may also set up the team to disagree about the best timing for an exit. Dick Costolo explained how members of DKA's founding team had different views on their startup's sale: "It was not a home run, so there was a lot of grumbling. [And] because we had differing amounts of equity, we had differing levels of desire to exit and that caused a real divergence within the team." Key nonfounding employees can also hold up the acquisition if they are not aligned with the rest of the team. Dick described his dilemma when an employee's compensation package threatened to derail FeedBurner's sale to Google: "One early employee had a funky option deal that won't work out with the way the deal is done, so he doesn't want it. But Google was saying, 'That person's a key employee,' so that person can hold the deal hostage."

ACKNOWLEDGMENTS

WRITING A BOOK IS A TEAM SPORT. EVEN IF THE PLAYER IS THE ONE with his picture on the baseball card, he would not have achieved the statistics on the back without a squad of coaches, scouts, and support staff. Similarly, without my coaches here at Harvard Business School and at other schools, the scouts who decided to place early bets on me (including Seth Ditchik, who was willing to bet on a rookie author), and the people who provided support for every phase of this book-writing process, this book would never have made it up to bat.

It was Nitin Nohria who sparked my interest in an academic career and, for more than a decade, has provided mentorship and support on all levels. Paul Gompers, Josh Lerner, Bill Sahlman, George Baker, Jerry Green, and Peter Marsden were invaluable early research mentors who encouraged me to focus on rigorous inquiry into the black box of founding teams. Lynda Applegate and Teresa Amabile not only have mentored me ever since I was a rookie in the recently created Entrepreneurial Management unit, but also became deeply engaged with the early drafts of this book, helping shape its final state in a myriad of ways. During the same stretch, Tom Eisenmann provided terrific career guidance, companionship through many lunches, and targeted feedback on how to improve this book. Toby Stuart, Geoff Jones, Nancy Koehn, and Kash Rangan were very early and influential supporters of the idea of writing a book to tie together a decade of research. Ben Esty, David Garvin, Andre Perold, Bharat Anand, Ranjay Gulati, Mihir Desai, and Jan Rivkin provided sagacious input during my early days on the faculty of Harvard Business School, while I was developing the course on which *The Founder's Dilemmas* is based and at other key junctures of my career. Further afield, but still foundational, are my debts to Howard Aldrich, Donald Hambrick, Kathy Eisenhardt, and Howard Stevenson, four of the giants on whose shoulders my research stands.

The seeds for the book's data were planted early and have had several key nurturers. Brian Hall facilitated my initial dialogue with Bill Holodnak and Aaron Lapat about a potential collaboration. Bill and Aaron in turn trusted a young doctoral student to write the CompStudy survey instrument and analyze its results. Mike DiPierro and Evan Brown have kept everything moving smoothly year after year, even when they found themselves having to keep more balls in the air than we expected. Furqan Nazeeri, an invaluable collaborator on multiple projects, was a terrific sounding board for my early research.

A wide variety of collaborators helped me craft the cases and papers described in this book. Thank you to Deepak Malhotra, Henry McCance, Eric Olson, LP Maurice, Antony Uy, Rachel Gordon, Rachel Galper, and Rosy Fynn for coauthoring the case studies that form the backbone of my MBA course and of the book; to Jeff Bussgang, not only for coauthoring a case but also for the plethora of subsequent projects and collaborations that case has sparked, and also for making a wonderfully insightful pass through an early draft of this book; and to all of my case protagonists for their openness and honesty in helping me learn about the toughest dilemmas they had faced and for their help in crafting case materials that helped share their knowledge with the next generation of high-impact founders. Thank you to all of my Entrepreneurial Manager and Founders' Dilemmas students (and Kauffman Scholars) for continually showing me new sides of our material (two of which resulted in research projects that would not have existed otherwise) and for giving me firsthand appreciation for R' Chanina's ancient Talmudic saying, "I have learned much wisdom from my teachers, more from my colleagues, and the most from my students."

On the research side, Matt Marx, Thomas Hellman, and Warren Boeker have been delightful collaborators, often at all hours of the night, on three of the papers profiled in this book. Matt Marx also believed in the Founders' Dilemmas course enough to stake his early MIT teaching career on becoming my "first franchisee." Wendy Torrance likewise believed in the importance of the material, making it a central part of her Kauffman Global Scholars program. Thank you to Matt and to Ginger Graham for helping make teaching a delight as our weekly three-professor teaching group brainstormed about the material we would be covering and the best ways to educate our future founders about the dilemmas awaiting them.

In addition to being wonderful colleagues throughout the years, Ramana Nanda, Mukti Khaire, Bill Kerr, Monica Higgins, Rakesh Khurana, Boris Groysberg, and David Scharfstein provided key input at various points in the research and book-writing process. Likewise, Bill Schnoor, Janet Kraus, Tim Butler, Evan Richardson, Tim Connors, Amar Bhide, Tony Mayo, and Ari Ginsberg provided well-timed, high-impact input on specific parts of the book.

Thank you to Lisa Brem and Kyle Anderson for the depth and breadth of their contributions to this book, sharpening the final product in so many ways while making the writing process lots of fun, and to John Elder for his input into every piece of every chapter. Day in and day out, Theresa Gaignard and Matthew O'Connell provided supremely competent and enjoyable administrative support.

Finally, *acharonim chavivim*, thank you to my *eishet chayil*, Chana, for being an incomparable wife and mother; to Talya, Tamar, Yair, Liat, Naava, Avital, and Yishai for amazing and amusing me every day with their accomplishments, enthusiasm, and delightful personalities; to my wonderful parents and in-laws for laying the foundation on which three generations have been built; and to Hakadosh Baruch Hu for making it all possible.

APPENDIX A
QUANTITATIVE DATA

THIS BOOK'S QUANTITATIVE DATA COME FROM A UNIQUE DATASET of thousands of startups, founders, and executives collected over the last decade, from 2000 to 2009. This appendix describes the survey process that was used to collect the data, the demographics of the respondents, and the contents of the survey instrument.

SURVEY PROCESS

When I started doing systematic research on founders and high-potential startups in 1999, one of the major challenges I faced was the lack of publicly available data. In contrast to public companies, which have to publicly file detailed disclosures about compensation, company operations, executives, and other important aspects of the company, privately held companies can keep all of those details to themselves. There is no private-company version of the SEC's Edgar database. The few databases that have tried to compile such data are extremely limited in their scope and plagued by missing-data problems. In particular, startups are extremely secretive about executive compensation,[1] capitalization tables, financing valuations, founder-CEO succession events, and founders' equity splits. There are no good sources even for some less-sensitive data points, such as the founders' prior relationships and pre-founding backgrounds. Most research on high-potential startups has therefore either used field-oriented approaches or focused on companies that had recently gone public (at which point the founders rarely still number among the top executives). For instance, a seminal 1994 study of "young company" compensation that used data on newly public companies was not able to examine founder compensation.[2] Researchers who have tried to examine founders in large companies discovered that founders made up less than 10% of the executives in their datasets, precluding definitive founder-related conclusions.[3]

To solve this problem, I started collecting my own data using a survey of private high-potential startups. In 1999, I partnered with three national professional-services firms—Ernst & Young (an accounting firm), J. Robert Scott (an executive-search firm), and Hale and Dorr (a law firm)—to conduct our first survey of technology startups. I designed the survey instrument, pilot-tested it with 10 companies, and revised it based on their feedback and my analyses of their responses; the three partner firms developed a website to administer the survey, which we named "CompStudy" (a name we extended to the survey and to the reporting site, www.compstudy .com); and I analyzed the data and compiled detailed breakdowns of the results. For the first decade of the survey, we focused on the United States, given its important role in entrepreneurship and our intimate knowledge of the country, but we are now expanding the survey to four other countries in which entrepreneurship is either strong or growing—the United Kingdom, Israel, China, and India.

Given the breadth and sensitivity of the survey questions, we decided to target the CEOs and CFOs of the startups, with the expectation that a single senior executive would complete the entire survey for each company.[*] To provide incentives to those executives, we interviewed CEOs and board members of startups and learned that they lacked solid data on executive compensation. (They were facing the same lack of data that we faced as researchers!) As a result, they did not know how much salary, bonus, and equity to offer potential hires and were losing many battles for that talent; they faced problems retaining their own staff because they could not accurately gauge what the market was paying for executives; they feared that they were overpaying some executives even though the typical startup is cash-poor and can't afford to overpay; or they found that they had given away too much equity to their hires and were left with little themselves.

As a "carrot" to drive participation, our research team promised participants that we would compile the survey's compensation data

---

[*] Survey respondents consistently report spending an average of one hour completing the survey.

into a detailed "Compensation Report" that would slice the data for all C-level and VP-level positions by founder/nonfounder status, company maturity, industry segment, geographic region, and other dimensions. We would provide the report only to participants who completed the survey—at no charge to them. To help ensure valid and complete submissions, we built data-validation capabilities into the online survey.

Over the past decade, the annual Compensation Report (commonly referred to as the Ernst & Young Compensation Report or the Harvard Business School Compensation Report) has become highly visible within the industry, serving as a standard benchmark for startups making hiring and retention decisions and deciding how much to budget for compensation and equity stakes. The data have also served as the backbone of a series of academic papers.[4]

The initial invitation list to participate in the survey was derived from multiple listings of technology startups across the country, including the membership lists of regional and statewide technology councils, the VentureOne database of companies that have raised venture capital, the client lists of the professional-services firms with which I was partnering, and recommendations by private-company investors. As will be described below, respondent locations closely matched the distribution of high-potential startups across the country rather than being concentrated in just one or two regions. Regular tests of geographic location and of startup maturity and size have shown no statistically significant differences between respondents and nonrespondents; details are provided below and in the references.[5]

Analyses of the first three years of responses indicated that a 20% response rate was achieved over those years,[6] a relatively high response rate considering the sensitivity of the questions and the level of the executives targeted.[7] Those calculations were possible due to our having a clearly defined list of startups to which we were mailing survey invitations. Since 2004, though, the invitation approach has been augmented in two ways: We developed relationships with professional investors who forwarded survey invitations to all of the companies with which they were involved, and we contacted respected bloggers who posted the invitations for their readers and subscribers. These changes have made it harder to calculate precise response rates, since we cannot know how many legitimate candidates for the survey received the forwarded emails or saw the blog posts. (These changes have also increased our need to validate each response.) However, the growth in the survey's visibility, reputation, and usefulness would suggest that response rates were probably maintained from the rate achieved when the survey was in its initial years.

Any database of currently operating companies is susceptible to survivorship bias. For instance, the databases of public companies that are commonly used in academic research include only companies that survived long enough—and succeeded well enough—to go public, but there are systematic differences between those companies and the broader population of all companies. Although the CompStudy dataset is much less susceptible to such biases because it catches startups soon after founding, some CompStudy analyses may be susceptible to survivorship bias. Whenever possible, I have used methods and analyses to assess the level of potential bias or to correct for it, or else I report differences by stage of startup evolution. For example, as described in Chapter 11, I performed two separate analyses—one using the younger half of startups and another using the older half—to analyze the trade-off between the value of founders' equity stakes and the degree of control the founders kept, and then compared and reported the results.

Over the years, the percentage of repeat respondents has increased from almost none to about 20%.[*] In analyses that would be sensitive to autocorrelation problems, or where only one observation was desired per startup (e.g., when doing analyses of founding teams, wherein repeat respondents would have multiple identical entries for each founding team),[†] multiple methods were used to

---

[*] A low rate of repeat survey participation is not surprising, given the high rate of failure among startups, demands on the time of their CEOs and CFOs, the exclusion of startups that had gone public or been acquired, and other factors.

[†] The increase in repeat respondents has also enabled us to test the reliability and accuracy of survey submissions by comparing the answers from repeat respondents.

avoid such problems, including dropping repeat respondents, recalculating robustness models to see if the results changed, and including fixed effects in the models.

DEMOGRAPHICS OF RESPONDENTS

The 2000 and 2001 surveys targeted technology startups. Those two years, we received complete responses from 211 and 178 startups, respectively. In 2002, to enable cross-industry comparisons and enable us to cover both of the major industries for high-potential startups, we broadened the survey to include life sciences startups and received complete responses from 168 of them. In subsequent years, the number of responses grew steadily, though more quickly in the technology industry than in life sciences. From 211 startups in its first year, the technology survey grew to include 489 startups in 2009; the life sciences survey grew from 168 startups in 2002 to 214 in 2009.

The full decade of data include a little more than 3,600 startups (32% from life sciences, 68% from technology), 9,900 founders, and more than 19,000 executives. The distributions of startups regarding location, financing stage, number of employees, and age of startup was as follows:

- **Geography**—The geographic distribution of respondents closely matches accepted profiles of the startup population, with the two biggest entrepreneurial hubs making up the two largest segments of CompStudy respondents. For the decade, 32% of CompStudy startups were in California, 22% in New England, 19% in the Mid-Atlantic, 15% in the western United States (excluding California), and 11% in the southern United States. These percentages were almost identical for the technology and life sciences industries, with no region differing by more than 2 percentage points.
- **Financing**—The respondents to the first technology survey were almost all VC-backed, matching the distribution of startups in VentureOne and other standard databases that

include only startups that have received institutional financing. Over the years, the percentage of startups that had not raised any outside financing grew from 2% to 11% (12% in technology, 9% in life sciences). Across the decade, 7% had not raised any financing, 18% had raised one round, 28% two rounds, 23% three rounds, 12% four rounds, and 12% five or more rounds. This suggests that the sample is biased toward founders who are willing to take outside financing; wealth-motivated founders seem to be overrepresented. To the extent that control-motivated founders are underrepresented, the quantitative results should understate the strength of any wealth-versus-control differences; those differences should be even more stark with a dataset that has more control-oriented founders.

- **Number of employees**—On average across the decade, the startups had 28 full-time-equivalent employees (FTEs). In the technology industry, 34% of the startups had 1 to 20 FTEs, 28% had 21 to 40 FTEs, 20% had 41 to 75 FTEs, and 19% had more than 75 FTEs. Life sciences startups were smaller, with a little more than 50% of the startups having 1 to 20 FTEs and lower percentages than technology startups in each of the other buckets.

- **Age of startup**—The average age of the startups in the full dataset was 6.8 years, with a standard deviation of 4.4 years. The 25th percentile was 3.7 years, the median was 6.1 years, and the 75th percentile was 9.0 years. Of the startups, 84% were founded between 1996 and 2006.

SURVEY CONTENTS

The core survey questions cover company founding, dates on which key product-development milestones were achieved, financing history, backgrounds of the members of the executive and founding teams, executive compensation, and the composition of the board of directors. Note that these questions take a "revealed preferences" approach to understanding founders; rather than asking founders about their preferences and inclinations, we focus on their actual decisions and actions as a more revealing window into their preferences and inclinations. The same core questions have been used (with only minor refinements) since the first year of the survey, but some sections have been expanded since then. In particular, in 2006, the founding-team section was expanded to include detailed questions about founders' equity splits and their prior relationships. Those questions play a central role in Part II of this book. In 2008, the section on founder-CEO succession was expanded to include more questions about the trigger of succession, the replaced founder-CEO's post-succession role, and other questions that are used in Chapter 10.

The specific questions from each major section of the survey are as follows:

- For **each company:**

  ○ Date company founded
  ○ Industry segment, location
  ○ Date on which development of the initial product or service was completed (or is expected to be completed)
  ○ Company revenue, whether it is profitable, headcount
  ○ Average monthly burn rate, cash on hand
  ○ Capitalization table: percentage of equity owned (fully diluted) and percentage of equity owned (current) for:

    ■ Current employees, former employees
    ■ Angel investors, VCs, corporations/strategic investors
    ■ Option pool for future hires
    ■ Other equity

  ○ Number of CEOs
  ○ Current CEO's functional background

- For **each founder:**

  ○ Prior experience

    ■ Whether founder had previously founded another company

- Years of work experience before founding this company
- Whether founder had prior experience managing people

○ Founder(s) whose idea it was to begin this venture
○ Initial position in the company
○ Whether founder was working full-time for the startup from the day it was founded
○ Amount of founding capital contributed by this founder
○ Percentage of company's equity received at time of initial equity split
○ Whether founder is currently employed with the company

- If not currently employed with the company, number of months this founder worked as a full-time employee in this company

- For **each founding team:**

○ At the time of founding, how many months had any of the founders already worked on this project with the intention of founding a company?
○ Prior relationship within the founding team: Before founding this company . . .

- How many of the founders had previously worked together?
- How many of the founders had founded another company together?
- How many of the founders were friends but *not* coworkers?
- How many of the founders were related to each other?

○ Equity split process

- Date the founders initially split the equity
- How much time the founders spent negotiating the initial equity split
- When the founders split the equity, whether they did so informally (i.e., not in writing) or formally (in writing)

- If a founder had left the company soon after the equity was split, would the founder have had to give up a significant amount of his or her equity?
- When the first institutional round of financing closed, what percentage of the founders' equity was fully vested?

- For **each round of financing:**

  - Date round closed
  - Pre-money valuation
  - Gross equity proceeds
  - Participants in the round: founders, angels, VCs, corporate/strategic investors, debt providers, public equity markets
  - Number of VCs participating in the round
  - Liquidation preferences: none, 1×, 1.1×–2×, 2.1×–3×, more than 3×

- Sources of **equity investment leads:** How company found initial angel investor, subsequent angel investor(s), initial VC, subsequent VC(s), initial corporate investor, subsequent corporate investor(s)

  - Friend, family, or past coworker of the CEO; friend, family, or past coworker of other team member; investor in past company of a founder; through submission of business plan or cold call; referred by existing angel investor; referred by existing VC or member of board of directors; referred by investment bank or other outside professional (e.g., lawyer, accountant, commercial bank); other source

- For **each executive** (C-level or VP-level):

  - Prior experience

    - Number of years of full-time career work experience before joining company
    - Academic degree(s)

- Before joining this startup, was this person ever before the senior-most executive within his or her function?

○ Date joined the startup
○ Source of hire: Prior connection to CEO (e.g., past co-worker, friend, family member), title of another member of the executive team with whom this person had a prior connection, referred by existing investor or member of board of directors, other source
○ Whether founder or nonfounder
○ Gender
○ Compensation

  - For previous and current years: annual base salary
  - For previous and current years: cash bonus (planned and received)
  - Percentage of current-year bonus that is guaranteed

○ Equity holdings:

  - Percentage of company's total outstanding equity currently held (fully diluted)
  - Percentage of company's total outstanding equity granted at time of hire (fully diluted)
  - Equity vehicles used at time of hire: incentive stock options (ISO), nonqualified stock options, restricted stock, common stock
  - Vesting: Number of years over which full vesting occurs, whether vesting is performance based, whether executive would have accelerated vesting upon change of control
  - Frequency of equity grants after time of hire

○ Whether executive was eligible to receive a severance payment if fired and, if so, number of months of severance

- For **each board member**:

  ○ Date joined board of directors

○ Background

- If current employee, title in company
- If former employee, last title in company
- Whether angel investor, VC, executive in same industry, executive from outside the industry, academic, other

○ Compensation

- Equity stake: percentage of fully diluted shares granted to join board, currently held percentage of total outstanding shares (fully diluted, including both stock and options)
- Annual equity retainer: percentage of total outstanding shares (fully diluted)
- Annual cash retainer
- Committees: serves on audit committee, executive committee, compensation committee, or other committee

- **For each company that had replaced the founder-CEO:**

  ○ First nonfounding CEO's background

  - Years of prior experience
  - Functional background:
  - Whether had prior work experience in the industry, as a C-level executive, in a private company, in a public company

  ○ If first nonfounding CEO has been replaced, for how many months he or she remained CEO of the company
  ○ Date when decision was made to replace the founder-CEO
  ○ Main trigger of the change in CEO: board, founder-CEO, board and founder-CEO equally, non-CEO employee, other
  ○ After being replaced, did the former founder-CEO remain at the company in an executive position?

  - If yes, which position: CTO, other C-level position, lower-level executive role

- ○ After being replaced, did the former founder-CEO remain on the board of directors?

  - ▪ If yes: became chairman, remained chairman, moved from chairman to non-chairman director, remained non-chairman director

- ○ Annualized percentage sales growth

  - ▪ In the 6 months before the founder-CEO was replaced
  - ▪ In the 12 months after the founder-CEO was replaced

APPENDIX B
SUMMARY OF STARTUPS AND PEOPLE

THE TWO TABLES BELOW PRESENT ALPHABETICAL LISTINGS OF THE startups described in *The Founder's Dilemmas* and of the people (mentioned in the book) who founded or worked in them. The startups table also includes references to the full case studies that have been published about those startups.

Table B.1
Table of Startups

Startup Name	Year Founded	Protagonist (Initial Title in Startup)	Other Founding Team Members (Initial Titles)	Prior Relationship with Cofounder(s)/Partner(s)	Mentioned in Chapters (brief mentions in parentheses)	Original Idea for Startup
38 Studios[1]	2006	Curt Schilling (Founder-President-Chairman)	N/A (solo founder)	N/A	2, (11)	Develop a best-of-breed online role-playing game with a rich story component.
Apple Computer[2]	1976	Steve Wozniak (Cofounder)	Steve Jobs (Cofounder) Ron Wayne (Cofounder)	Close friend Stranger	4, (5), (6), (7)	Develop and sell a personal computer based on Wozniak's design.
Blogger[3]	1999	Evan Williams (Founder-CEO)	Meg Hourihan (Vice President)	Ex-girlfriend	1, 4, 5, 6, 7, 8, 9, 11	Online self-publishing (blogging) tool.
Circles	1997	Janet Kraus (Cofounder-CEO)	Kathy Sherbrooke (Cofounder, President/COO)	Fellow MBA student	(1), (4), (6)	Provide "everyday services" to individuals, such as dog walking, errands, etc.

ConneXus[4]	1996	Humphrey Chen (Cofounder)	George Searle (Cofounder)	Fellow MBA student	2	Develop a network of computers that will automatically catalogue music playing on the radio and allow consumers to access song information, listen to the song, and purchase it via a touchtone phone or Internet website.
Digital Knowledge Assets (DKA)[5]	1995	Dick Costolo (Co-VP of Technology)	Eric Lunt (Co-VP of Technology) Two other founders (CEO, COO)	Coworker (subordinate) Strangers	(8)	Collaboration and publishing software company.
FeedBurner[6]	2003	Dick Costolo (Founder-CEO)	Eric Lunt (CTO) Matt Shobe (Product Design) Steve Olechowski (COO)	Cofounders	1, (3), 5, 7, 8, 9, 11	Intermediary between online publishers, advertisers, and distributors.

(continued)

Table B.1
(Continued)

Startup Name	Year Founded	Protagonist (Initial Title in Startup)	Other Founding Team Members (Initial Titles)	Prior Relationship with Cofounder(s)/ Partner(s)	Mentioned in Chapters (brief mentions in parentheses)	Original Idea for Startup
Kendle International[7]	1981	Candace Kendle (Founder-CEO)	Christopher Bergen (President and COO)	Colleague, fiancée	Appendix 11-2	To build a clinical research organization (CRO) to perform clinical drug trials for pharmaceutical companies.
L90[8]	1997	Frank Addante (Founder-CTO)	John Bohan (Founder-CEO)	Business contact	(6), (8)	Merge ad server with ad broker to take advantage of synergies.
Lynx Solutions[9,a]	1998	[a] James Milmo (Founder-President-Chairman)	[a] Doug Curtis (CEO)	Acquaintance	2, 5, 6, 8, 9, 10, 11	Advertising-supported screensavers for handheld wireless devices.
			[a] Javier Pascal (CTO)	Friend		
Masergy[10]	2000	Barry Nalls (Founder-CEO)	N/A (solo founder)	N/A	1, 2, 3, 8, (9), 11	Telecom service provider for enterprise and B2B customers.
Megaserver[11,a]	~1996	Les Trachtman (professional CEO)	Mother (Chair of board)	Family members	10	Enable multiple computing platforms to form a supercomputer.

		Father (Inventor/technologist) Son (COO, former founder-CEO)			
Nike[12]	1964	Phil Knight (Founder-President)	Coach	(6)	Create and market an innovative running shoe.
		Bill Bowerman (Vice President)			
Ockham Technologies[13]	1999	Jim Triandiflou (Founder-CEO)	Coworker (subordinate)	2, (3), 4, 5, 6, 7, 9, (11)	Sales-force-optimization software.
		Mike Meisenheimer (VP Product Management)			
		Ken Burows (COO)	Coworker		
Odeo[14]	2004	Evan Williams (Cofounder-investor-advisor)	Acquaintance	1, (2), 4, 5, 6, 8, 9, 11	Podcasting technology.
		Noah Glass (CEO)			
Pandora[15] (originally Savage Beast)	2000	Tim Westergren (Founder-Chief Music Officer)	Acquaintance	1, 2, (3), 4, 5, (6), (7), 8, 9, 11	A music decision engine that plays/suggests songs based on attributes of songs/artists the user chooses.
		Jon Kraft (CEO)			
		Will Glaser (CTO)	Stranger		

(continued)

Table B.1
(*Continued*)

Startup Name	Year Founded	Protagonist (Initial Title in Startup)	Other Founding Team Members (Initial Titles)	Prior Relationship with Cofounder(s)/ Partner(s)	Mentioned in Chapters (brief mentions in parentheses)	Original Idea for Startup
Proteus Biomedical[16]	2001	Andrew Thompson (Founder-CEO)	George Savage (CMO)	Fellow MBA student	2	To develop technology that could insert miniature computers and sensors into drugs and medical devices.
			Mark Zdeblick (CTO)	Acquaintance		
ReaXions[17]	1997	Frank Addante (Cofounder)	"Cary" (Cofounder)	Friend/ colleague	6	Advertising software that tracks and schedules a company's online advertising.
Rubbish Boys[18] (renamed 1-800-GOT-JUNK)	1989	Brian Scudamore (Founder)	"John" (Cofounder)	Friend	(2), (3), 9, 11	Trash-removal service.
Segway[19]	1999	Dean Kamen (Founder)	N/A (solo founder)	N/A	10, 11	Create a low-cost, low-emission personal transportation device.
Sittercity[20]	2001	Genevieve Thiers (Founder-CEO)	N/A (solo founder)	N/A	1, 2, 4, 8, 10, 11	An online matchmaking service for parents and babysitters.

Company	Year	Founder/Role	Other people	Relationship	Numbers	Description
Smartix[21]	1999	Vivek Khuller (Founder-CEO)	Kirill Dmitriev Saurabh Mittal — Unnamed technical cofounder	Fellow MBA students — Coworker (subordinate)	1, 2, (3), 4, 5, 6, 7	Create an electronic ticketing technology for sports and entertainment venues.
Spyonit[22]	~1998	Dick Costolo (Founder-CEO)	Eric Lunt (CTO) Matt Shobe (Product Design) Steve Olechowski (Business Development/ Programmer)	Cofounder Coworkers (subordinates)	(3), 8	Alert systems for Internet consumers.
StrongMail[23]	2002	Frank Addante (Founder-CEO)	Tim McQuillen (Cofounder)	Coworker (subordinate)/ friend	2, 7, 9, 11	Create an email messaging infrastructure software package and sell to enterprise clients.
Transcentive[24]	1981	Les Trachtman (VP Operations, later professional CEO)	Mike Brody (Founder-CEO)	Mike's family members	10, (11)	Corporate stock-option software.

(continued)

Table B.1
(Continued)

Startup Name	Year Founded	Protagonist (Initial Title in Startup)	Other Founding Team Members (Initial Titles)	Prior Relationship with Cofounder(s)/ Partner(s)	Mentioned in Chapters (brief mentions in parentheses)	Original Idea for Startup
			Mike's brother (Founder-CFO)			
UpDown[25]	2007	Michael Reich (Founder-CEO)	Georg Ludviksson (Co-CEO) Phuc Truong (CTO)	Fellow MBA students; stranger	3, (4), 6, 7	Create an online social-networking site for investors.
Wily Technology[26]	1998	Lew Cirne (Founder-CEO)	N/A (solo founder)	N/A	(3), 8, (9), 10, 11	Self-diagnostic software for computer operating systems.
Zipcar[27]	2000	Robin Chase (Founder-CEO)	Antje Danielson (VP-Environmental affairs and strategy)	Friend	(2), 6, (8)	Create a car-sharing business based on a German company and market it in the United States.
Zondigo[28]	2000	Frank Addante (Founder-CEO)	Two unnamed cofounders	Business contacts	5, 6, 8, 11	Create technology for "on-the-go" advertising direct to wireless devices.

a Disguised name.

1 Noam Wasserman, Jeffrey J. Bussgang, and Rachel Gordon, "Curt Schilling's Next Pitch," HBS No. 810-053 (Boston: Harvard Business School Publishing, 2010).

2 Noam Wasserman, "Apple's Core," HBS No. 809-063 (Boston: Harvard Business School Publishing, 2009).

3 Noam Wasserman and LP Maurice, "Evan Williams: From Blogger to Odeo (A) and (B)," HBS Nos. 809-088 and 809-093 (Boston: Harvard Business School Publishing, 2008).

4 Monica Higgins and Noam Wasserman, "Humphrey and Cecilia," HBS No. 810-702 (Boston: Harvard Business School Publishing, 2010); Monica Higgins, Adam Richman, and John Galvin, "Video Case: Humphrey Chen (Preview Note)," HBS No. 498-036 (Boston: Harvard Business School Publishing, 1997).

5 Noam Wasserman and Eric Olson, "Lather, Rinse, Repeat: FeedBurner's Serial Founding Team," HBS No. 809-089 (Boston: Harvard Business School Publishing, 2009).

6 Noam Wasserman and Eric Olson, "Lather, Rinse, Repeat: FeedBurner's Serial Founding Team," HBS No. 809-089 (Boston: Harvard Business School Publishing, 2009).

7 Dwight B. Crane, Paul W. Marshall, and Indra A. Reinbergs, "Kendle International Inc," HBS No. 200-033 (Boston: Harvard Business School Publishing, 2000).

8 Noam Wasserman and Antony Uy, "Frank Addante, Serial Entrepreneur," HBS No. 809-046 (Boston: Harvard Business School Publishing, 2008).

9 Noam Wasserman, "The Tale of the Lynx (A), (B), and (C)," HBS Nos. 807-151, 807-152, 807-153, (A and B): 807-112 (Boston: Harvard Business School Publishing, 2009).

10 Noam Wasserman and Rachel Galper, "Big to Small: The Two Lives of Barry Nalls," HBS No. 808-167 (Boston: Harvard Business School Publishing, 2008).

11 Noam Wasserman and Rosy Fynn, "Les Is More, Times Four," HBS No. 807-173 (Boston: Harvard Business School Publishing, 2008).

12 Noam Wasserman and Kyle Anderson, "Knight the King; The Founding of Nike," HBS No. 810-077 (Boston: Harvard Business School Publishing, 2010).

13 Noam Wasserman, "Ockham Technologies: Living on the Razor's Edge," HBS No. 804-129 (Boston: Harvard Business School Publishing, 2004).

14 Noam Wasserman and LP Maurice, "Evan Williams: From Blogger to Odeo (A) and (B)," HBS Nos. 809-088 and 809-093 (Boston: Harvard Business School Publishing, 2008).

15 Noam Wasserman and LP Maurice, "Savage Beast (A) & (B)," HBS Nos. 809-069, 809-096 and (A1) 801-051 (Boston: Harvard Business School Publishing, 2008).

16 Richard Hamermesh, Lauren Barley, and Ginger Graham. "Proteus Biomedical: Making Pigs Fly," HBS No. 809-051 (Boston: Harvard Business School Publishing, 2008).

(continued)

Table B.1
(Continued)

[17] Noam Wasserman and Antony Uy, "Frank Addante, Serial Entrepreneur," HBS No. 809-046 (Boston: Harvard Business School Publishing, 2008).

[18] Noam Wasserman and Rachel Galper, "Rubbish Boys," HBS No. 808-101 (Boston: Harvard Business School Publishing, 2008).

[19] Richard Hamermesh and David Kiron, "Managing Segway's Early Development," HBS No. 804-065 (Boston: Harvard Business School Publishing, 2003).

[20] Noam Wasserman and Rachel Gordon, "Playing with Fire at Sittercity (A) & (B)," HBS Nos. 809-009 and 809-010 (Boston: Harvard Business School Publishing, 2009).

[21] Noam Wasserman, "Smartix: Swinging for the Fences," HBS No. 808-116 (Boston: Harvard Business School Publishing, 2009).

[22] Noam Wasserman and Eric Olson, "Lather, Rinse, Repeat: FeedBurner's Serial Founding Team," HBS No. 809-089 (Boston: Harvard Business School Publishing, 2009).

[23] Noam Wasserman and Antony Uy, "Frank Addante, Serial Entrepreneur," HBS No. 809-046 (Boston: Harvard Business School Publishing, 2008).

[24] Noam Wasserman and Rosy Fynn, "Les Is More, Times Four," HBS Case No. 807-173 (Boston: Harvard Business School Publishing, 2008).

[25] Noam Wasserman and Deepak Malhotra, "Negotiating Equity Splits at UpDown," HBS No. 809-020 (Boston: Harvard Business School Publishing, 2008).

[26] Noam Wasserman and Henry McCance, "Founder-CEO Succession at Wily Technology," HBS No. 805-150 (Boston: Harvard Business School Publishing, 2007).

[27] Myra Hart, Michael J. Roberts, and Julia D. Stevens, "Zipcar: Refining the Business Model," HBS No. 803-096 (Boston: Harvard Business School Publishing, 2003).

[28] Noam Wasserman and Antony Uy, "Frank Addante, Serial Entrepreneur," HBS No. 809-046 (Boston: Harvard Business School Publishing, 2008).

Table B.2
Table of People

Protagonist	Startup Name	Title and Role in Startup	Highest Degree Received	Work Experience	Other Relevant Experience
Addante, Frank	ReaXions	Cofounder Product and business development, hired employees Negotiated merger to form L90	High school	Self-taught programmer; T1 line installer	Four years of college before leaving
	L90	Founder-CTO Technical development			
	Zondigo	Founder-CEO Business and product development Secured funding, hired team			
	StrongMail	Founder-CEO Business and product development Secured funding, hired executive team			
Bergen, Christopher	Kendle International	Founder, President and COO	MBA	Associate VP, Children's Hospital of Philadelphia	
Bohan, John[1]	L90	Founder-CEO Secured funding, directed public offering	Economics degree	Opened West Coast office of early website company; TV ad sales	

(continued)

Table B.2
(*Continued*)

Protagonist	Startup Name	Title and Role in Startup	Highest Degree Received	Work Experience	Other Relevant Experience
Bowerman, Bill	Nike	Vice President and director Product development	Four-year college degree	College and Olympic track-and-field coach	Developed running shoes
Brody, Mike[2]	Transcentive	Founder-CEO		CEO of digital photo lab Cofounder of Stockholder Systems	
Burows, Ken	Ockham Technologies	COO Business development Dropped out as founder	MBA in finance and strategic management	Systems integration consultant Director-Financial Information Systems Business development	
"Cary"	ReaXions	Cofounder Investor		IT consultant	
Chase, Robin	Zipcar	Founder-CEO Refined concept, market research, developed business plan & budgets, designed website Hired contract engineers for online reservation system	MBA in applied economics and finance	Healthcare consulting Private school director of finance and operations Managing editor of public health journal	

Name	Company	Role and contributions	Education	Experience
Chen, Humphrey	ConneXus	Cofounder Business and product development, secured funding	MBA	Five years IT experience in several companies, including online music store startup
Cirne, Lew	Wily Technology	Founder-CEO Product and business development, hired employees, early sales to customers, secured funding	B.A. computer science	Senior software engineer at Apple Computer Java project lead at Hummingbird Communications
Costolo, Dick	DKA	Co-VP Technology Product development	B.S. computer science	IT consultant/manager Developed British TV show
	Spyonit	Founder-CEO Business and product development Secured funding		Standup comedian
	FeedBurner	Founder-CEO Business and product development Secured funding		
Curtis, Doug[a]	Lynx Solutions[a]	Founder-CEO Business development, hired team, secured funding		Veteran entrepreneur
Danielson, Antje	Zipcar	Founder-VP environmental affairs and strategy, built relationships with car companies, specified in-car technology, environmental issues	Ph.D. geochemistry	Supervisor of undergraduate energy-policy research at Harvard University Car sales

(*continued*)

Table B.2
(*Continued*)

Protagonist	Startup Name	Title and Role in Startup	Highest Degree Received	Work Experience	Other Relevant Experience
Evans, Clark[a]	Lynx Solutions[a]	Interim President/CEO Business development, secured funding, scaled company		SVP of consumer products company	
Glaser, Will	Pandora	CTO Technical development	Degrees in math, computer science, and physics	Cofounded technology startup IT consultant	Amateur musician
Glass, Noah	Odeo	Founder-CEO Product development		Worked on an audio application for Blogger	
Hourihan, Meg	Blogger (originally Pyra Labs)	Founder-Vice President Business and product development, managed employees, and provided some seed funding	English degree	Technology consultant	
Kamen, Dean	Segway	Founder Business and product development Securing funding, hiring team	High school	Inventor of several highly successful medical products Founder-CEO DEKA	

Kendle, Candace	Kendle International	Founder-CEO	Pharm.D., D.Sc.	Senior faculty positions at several leading schools and colleges of pharmacy and medicine	
Khuller, Vivek	Smartix	Founder-CEO Business and product development Pitched idea to investors and venues	M.S., MBA	5 years at Bell Atlantic as a programmer and IT manager	
Knight, Phil	Nike	Founder-President and director Business development Secured funding Negotiated contracts with suppliers Hired sales and management team	MBA	Accountant	Track-and-field athlete in high school and college
Kraft, Jon	Pandora	CEO Business development		Founder-CEO of enterprise database startup	
Kraus, Janet	Circles	Cofounder-CEO	MBA	Technology consulting; director of social marketing for The Body Shop	

(*continued*)

Table B.2
(*Continued*)

Protagonist	Startup Name	Title and Role in Startup	Highest Degree Received	Work Experience	Other Relevant Experience
Ludviksson, Georg	UpDown	Co-CEO Business development support Sales and marketing strategy development	MBA	Computer programming Sales Cofounded computer game startup	
Lunt, Eric[3]	DKA Spyonit FeedBurner	Co-VP technology-product development CTO-product development CTO-product development	B.S.E. mechanical engineering	Software programmer at Andersen Consulting	
McQuillen, Tim[4]	StrongMail	Cofounder Chief Information Officer Director	B.A. psychology	Partner, business development at IT staffing companies Head of IT, sales, data centers	
Meisen-heimer, Mike[5]	Ockham Technologies	VP Product Management Product development, sales, and marketing Helped secure funding, hired team	MSM	Sales and marketing consultant	

Milmo, James[a]	Lynx Solutions[a]	Founder-President-Chairman Business development, secured funding Hired team, sales and marketing	Government major	Campaign worker Apprentice to a toy inventor Prior failed startup	Member of entrepreneurship club
Mittal, Saurabh	Smartix	Cofounder Business and product development	MBA	Investment banking internship	
Nalls, Barry	Masergy	Founder-CEO Business and product development, secured funding, hired employees, sales and marketing	MBA	GTE for 25 years, from technician to SVP	
Olechowski, Steve	Spyonit	Programmer Business development		Software programmer at Andersen Consulting	
	FeedBurner	COO			
Pascal, Javier[a]	Lynx Solutions[a]	Founder-CTO Product development, hired team	Engineering degree	Engineer	
Reich, Michael	UpDown	Founder-CEO Business development Secure funding, recruit team/sales force	MBA	Small champagne distributor startup; consultant; manager in startup	
Savage, George	Proteus Biomedical	Cofounder, Chief Medical Officer (CMO)	B.S. biomedical engineering, M.D., MBA	Cofounded other biotech firms (with Andrew Thompson)	

(continued)

Table B.2
(*Continued*)

Protagonist	Startup Name	Title and Role in Startup	Highest Degree Received	Work Experience	Other Relevant Experience
Sherbrooke, Kathy	Circles	Cofounder, President/COO	MBA		
Shobe, Matt	Spyonit FeedBurner	Product design Product design	Graduate degree	User-interface designer at Andersen Consulting	
Strohm, David[6]	Wily Technology	Partner: Greylock Partners Member of Board of Directors, advisor, investor	MBA	At Greylock since 1980	
Thiers, Genevieve	Sittercity	Founder-CEO Business and product development Hired team, sales and marketing Secured funding	B.A. English Graduate degree in music (opera)	Technical writer Babysitter	Opera singer
Thompson, Andrew	Proteus Biomedical	Cofounder-CEO	M.A. engineering and education; MBA	Cofounded other biotech firms (with George Savage)	

Name	Company	Activities	Education	Experience	
Trachtman, Les	Transcentive	VP Operations, later CEO Restructured sales/marketing/customer service; made several staffing changes to scale company Engineered and negotiated sale of company	MBA/JD	Director of corporate development VP Business development President/CEO of several technology startups	
	Megaserver[a]	CEO Secured funding; marketing, sales, and business plan development; created financial and internal controls			
Truong, Phuc	UpDown	Co-CEO Product development	A.B. economics	Technology startup Contract IT consulting	
Westergren, Tim	Pandora	Founder-Chief Music Officer Music database development	B.A. political science	Composer Rock band leader Nanny	Jazz pianist
Williams, Evan	Blogger (originally Pyra Labs)	Founder-CEO Product and business development, secured funding, hired employees	High school	Self-taught Web developer; marketing coordinator; developed websites for HP and Intel	Two years college
	Odeo	Cofounder, advisor, investor Eventually CEO, secured funding, hired employees, business development			Prior failed startup

(continued)

Table B.2
(*Continued*)

Protagonist	Startup Name	Title and Role in Startup	Highest Degree Received	Work Experience	Other Relevant Experience
Williams, Richard[7]	Wily Technology	President/CEO Hired to replace founder-CEO Lew Cirne	B.S. mathematics	22 years at IBM in various leadership roles Digital Research – President/CEO Novell-EVP Sales Illustra Information Technologies – President/CEO Quokka Sports-founding director	
Zdeblick, Mark	Proteus Biomedical	Cofounder, CTO	B.S. civil engineering, B.A. architecture, M.S. aeronautics and astronautics, Ph.D. electrical engineering	Background in micro-electrical mechanical systems (MEMS) technology; held several patents in atomic and biomedical products and processes	

a Disguised name.

1 John Bohan, "Biography," http://www.johnbohan.com/bio.html (accessed October 2010).

2 Exágo, Inc., "About Us," http://www.exagoinc.com/exago_aboutus.php (accessed October 2010).

3 BrightTag, "Management Team," http://www.thebrighttag.com/who_is_brighttag.php (accessed October 2010).

4 Businessweek.com, "StrongMail Systems, Inc., Executive Profile," http://investing.businessweek.com/research/stocks/private/person.asp?personId =932869&privcapId=8594882&previousCapId=8594882&previousTitle=StrongMail%20Systems,%20Inc (accessed October 2010).

5 NewSigma, "Management Team," http://www.newsigma.com/Management-Team.html (accessed October 2010).

6 Greylock Partners, "David Strohm," http://www.greylock.com/team/team/14/ (accessed October 2010).

7 Businessweek.com, "IBM Executive Profile," http://investing.businessweek.com/research/stocks/people/person.asp?personId=234687&ticker=IBM :US&previousCapId=19153&previousTitle=Benchmark%20Capital (accessed October 2010).

NOTES

CHAPTER ONE

1. (Gorman and Sahlman, 1989) The authors surveyed 49 well-established venture capitalists (VCs) about 96 of their portfolio companies that either had failed or were in danger of failing and asked the VCs to choose up to 3 out of a choice of 11 factors that were the major contributors to these companies' difficulties. For 91 of the 96 companies (i.e., 95%), the VCs cited problems within the management team as a top-three contributing factor, ranking it the most important contributing factor for 61 of those companies (i.e., 65%).

2. (Kaplan et al., 2004) The authors of this study analyzed 67 internal investment memoranda from 11 VC firms and categorized the various analyses of internal, external, and implementation strengths and weaknesses. The internal weaknesses that led the list for 61% of the startups included such items as "CEO is a rather difficult person," "Incomplete management team," and "Must strengthen management team and ensure involvement of VC as chairman. Will have to hire CEO."

3. (Bhide, 2000:1) He continues, "Cliché and anecdote—or laments about the ineffable nature of entrepreneurship—dominate the discourse about new and fledgling businesses."

4. These early decisions are particularly formative for the organization; in the early days of a startup, founders have much more control than they do after inertial forces set in (Hannan et al., 1989) and after the effects of that early imprinting begin constraining the organization (Boeker, 1988, 1989).

5. (Stevenson et al., 1990:23) This definition will play a central role in our analyses of the core trade-offs faced by founders.

6. (Aldrich et al., 2006)

7. (Baker et al., 2003; Baker et al., 2005)

8. When almost 3,000 small business owners were asked about the odds of success for their own businesses, they ranked their own chances as being an average of 8.1 out of 10. When asked about the odds of success for businesses *similar* to their own, they ranked them as being 5.9 out of 10. For more details, see Cooper et al. (1988).

9. Busenitz et al. (1997) surveyed 176 founders of firms in the plastics, electronics, and instruments industries and 95 managers from large public

companies. They asked six fact-based questions about death rates from diseases and questions that gauged the confidence the respondent had in his or her answers. The founders were overconfident in their choices in five out of six categories, whereas managers were overconfident in only three out of six categories. The researchers' overconfidence variable predicted sorting into entrepreneurship 70% of the time.

10. Hayward et al. (2006) argue that as overconfidence increases, founders attract smaller initial resource endowments because they overestimate customer demand, neglect the reference group of competitors, underestimate requirements for legitimacy, and overestimate their ability to develop social ties and secure needed resources.

11. In a sample of 201 founder-CEOs taken from the Dun & Bradstreet database, each respondent was given a six-item Life Orientation Test that measures a general sense of optimism about life. This variable was associated with a 20% decrease in revenue growth and a 25% decrease in employment growth. The authors suggest that optimism can cause startups to fail because entrepreneurs hold unrealistic expectation, discount public information, and mentally reconstruct past experiences to avoid contradictions. The negative relationship between optimism and performance increased in the presence of environmental dynamism (Hmieleski et al., 2009).

12. (Baron, 1998)

13. (Emerson, 1962; Pfeffer et al., 1978)

14. (Stevenson et al., 1990)

15. (Amit et al., 2000; Carland et al., 1984; Sapienza et al., 2003)

16. (Wadhwa et al., 2009:13)

17. (Hurst et al., 2010b, table 7)

18. (Scitovszky, 1943:57)

19. (Kirzner, 1973; Schumpeter, 1942)

20. (Amit et al., 2000:120)

21. (Moskowitz et al., 2002)

22. (Hall et al., 2010)

23. (Hamilton, 2000)

24. (Hamilton, 2000:622–623) Although this study has recently been criticized for relying on data sources that understate entrepreneurs' earnings by a significant percentage (Hurst et al., 2010a), even after adjusting for that underreporting, the result still holds that entrepreneurs earn less than would be expected, though the difference is smaller. Amid multiple guesses as to why this might be true, Hamilton speculates that the reason might be "that many entrepreneurs receive substantial non-pecuniary benefits, such as 'being their own boss.'" This possibility is one we will examine closely.

25. Two of these authors (Moskowitz et al., 2002) even asked about this "puzzle" in the title of their study.

26. (Zaleznik et al., 1975)

27. (Boeker et al., 2002; Wasserman, 2003)

28. (Wasserman, 2006b)

29. (Mills, 1956:162)

30. Renaissance Capital's data on IPOs from 2000 to 2009 show that technology startups accounted for almost 30% of all IPOs, and life sciences and healthcare for 18%. The financial industry accounted for almost 12%, and no other industry was above 8.3%.

31. According to my analyses of annual reports from the Center for Venture Research at the University of New Hampshire, which compiles perhaps the most reliable data on angel investments, technology investments (including software, hardware, telecommunications, and IT services) accounted for 45% of angel investment across the decade and life sciences investments (biotechnology, life sciences, and health) accounted for an additional 29% (Sohl, 2001–2009).

32. According to Thomson's Venture Expert Database, accessed September 16, 2010, technology investments (including Internet, computer software and services, communications and media, semiconductors and other electronics, and computer hardware) accounted for 56% of VC investments from 2000 to 2009 and life sciences investments (medical/health and biotechnology) accounted for 15%.

33. (Aldrich et al., 2006; Hurst et al., 2010b)

CHAPTER TWO

1. (Higgins, 2005a)

2. (Higgins et al., 2010)

3. This particular analysis included 2,732 first-time founders. Similarly, in a recent study of 86,000 science and engineering graduates, age was not a significant predictor of the transition to self-employment. Researchers drew their data from the National Science Foundation's Scientists and Engineers Statistical Data System (SESTAT) and focused on data from 1995 to 2001. Every individual in the sample had at least a bachelor's degree in a science or engineering field (Elfenbein et al., 2009).

4. This is consistent with other research, such as a study of 1,547 small-business entrepreneurs in the United States that found that the average age of the entrepreneurs was 36.7 years old, with a standard of deviation of 9.4 years. The sample was drawn from the National Federation of Independent Businesses (Gimeno et al., 1997).

5. Taking a multi-decade view of a subset of founders, the age distribution of founders appears to have become younger over the past few decades. A survey of MIT graduates found that between the 1950s and

1990s, founding ages dropped 12.5 years, leading the authors of that study to conclude that entrepreneurship was transitioning from a "mid-life career change" to an earlier-in-career option (Hsu et al., 2007).

6. In a sample of 229 founder-CEOs of architectural woodworking firms, passion influenced motivation by affecting the founder's confidence in his or her skills, the founder's goals for sales and employment growth, and how that growth orientation affected the firm's vision statement (Baum et al., 2004).

7. For example, Busenitz et al. (1997) compared the risk-taking preferences of 176 founders of firms in the plastics, electronics, and instruments industries to those of 95 managers from large public companies. Risk-taking preferences were measured using the Jackson Personality Inventory and did not significantly predict entrepreneurship. A meta-analysis (Stewart et al., 2001) of prior studies of risk differences between entrepreneurs and managers seems to suggest support for the proposition that entrepreneurs are more risk-tolerant than managers, especially among growth-oriented entrepreneurs. However, the study's methodology has been criticized for treating as independent multiple studies that used the same underlying dataset of growth-oriented entrepreneurs, and the authors have been criticized for not being "conservative" enough in interpreting their results. (See Miner et al. [2004] for details.) More broadly, decades ago, academics made a concerted effort to nail down the core characteristics of the "entrepreneurial personality," but in vain. "In the end," as one expert summed it up, "it turned out that there is no such thing as a well-defined 'entrepreneurial personality.'"

8. (Higgins, 2005a; Higgins et al., 2010)

9. In a 2007 study of 20,000 individuals from 27 European countries and the United States, Stam et al. (2008) found that respondents with self-employed parents were more likely to be entrepreneurs and their startups were less likely to fail. The authors attribute this to indirect learning from observing the entrepreneurial actions of role models.

10. The survey uses dozens of scenarios to assess how important each motivation is to the person.

11. The database had complete work-reward surveys for 27,357 people, including 1,810 male entrepreneurs, 13,939 male non-entrepreneurs, 404 female entrepreneurs, and 11,204 female non-entrepreneurs.

12. See Gimeno et al. (1997) for more details on the differences between formal and tacit human capital, and Aldrich et al. (2006, chap. 4) for a discussion of procedural memory, declarative memory, and the accumulation of the tacit knowledge of how and when to invoke each type of memory.

13. Building on Fiske et al. (1991), Aldrich et al. (2006:76) define schemata as "cognitive structures that represent organized knowledge about a

given concept or type of stimulus." They define three levels of schemata: *person schemata*, which affect how people assess new people they encounter, the personality traits they associate with them, and the groups of personality traits they associate with each other; *role schemata*, which affect the behaviors they expect of people in particular social positions (and which they expect of themselves when they are in those positions); and *event schemata*, which affect the sequences of events people expect in situations similar to ones they have experienced.

14. Other factors shaping people's schemata include advice from mentors and experts and the structure and actions of other organizations they have read or heard about (Aldrich et al., 2006).

15. (Beckes-Gellner et al., 2008) The authors use a sample of 2000 German university students from Cologne. "Willingness to become an entrepreneur" was measured on a 4-point scale in response to a single item on the questionnaire. Of the sample, 16% was identified as willing to become an entrepreneur. "Broad human capital portfolio" was measured as a count of the different types of work experiences and academic degrees an individual holds. This variable was associated with a 116% increase in willingness to become an entrepreneur.

16. (Shane, 2008:47, italics in original) Likewise, Davidsson et al. (2003) matched a group of 623 nascent entrepreneurs from Sweden with a group of 608 non-entrepreneurs. "Explicit human capital" was measured by the highest level of formal education completed. This variable was associated with a 16.7% increase in the likelihood of being sorted into the nascent entrepreneur group.

17. Across all of the startups in my dataset, 25% of founder-CEOs had pre-founding management experience: 27% for technology founder-CEOs and 19% for life sciences founder-CEOs.

18. Meyer et al. (1990) undertake a close study of 25 founder-CEOs of high-tech firms in Boulder, Colorado. They find that founders are predominantly technical in their skills and identify four aspects of this mindset that make technical founders averse to developing management skills: Technical CEOs (a) are detail-oriented to the exclusion of the big picture, (b) lack flexibility, (c) dislike formal, structured environments, and (d) are "elitist" and unwilling to seek expert management advice.

19. (Bhide, 2000:47)

20. In their groundbreaking theoretical study on the effects of an organization's top managers, Hambrick et al. (1984) propose that functional backgrounds often have an important influence on firm strategy.

21. (Shane 2008:38) Similarly, in a study of 100 companies from the *Inc. 500* list of the fastest-growing private companies in the United States, 40% of the founders had no prior experience in the industry in which they

founded their startups and many others had only shallow or narrow experience in the industry (Bhide, 2000).

22. Indeed, having a well-developed cognitive structure regarding a context can prevent a person from seeing disconfirming or novel evidence and can inhibit creative problem solving (Walsh, 1995).

23. Examining 1,849 founders who registered a new business in Germany between 1985 and 1986, Bruderl et al. (1992:237) found that industry-specific experience was associated with a 33.2% decrease in the rate of startup failure. Industry-specific experience was significantly and positively related to seed capital, legal incorporation, and employment growth, leading the authors to conclude that "starting a business without experience in the industry sharply increases the mortality rate."

24. (Higgins, 2005b)

25. Previous startup experience was associated with a 78% increase in the likelihood of being in the nascent entrepreneur group (Davidsson et al., 2003).

26. For more details, see Baron et al. (2006). People with more entrepreneurial experience evaluated opportunities using the following dimensions: solving a customer's problems, generating positive cash flow, manageable risk, speed of revenue generation, and the existence of others in their network with whom to develop the venture. People with little or no entrepreneurial experience used the following dimensions: how novel the idea was, whether it was based on new technology, superiority of product/service, potential to change the industry, and intuition or gut feel.

27. (Shane et al., 2000)

28. (Gompers et al., 2005)

29. In this study (Elfenbein et al., 2009), companies with 100 or fewer employees had fewer than 20% of all employees in the sample, but produced 64% of the founders. The researchers drew their data from the National Science Foundation's SESTAT and focused on data from 1995 to 2001. It should be noted that every individual in the sample had at least a bachelor's degree in a science or engineering field, and that the researchers included in their sample only men who worked full-time.

30. Using a sample of 2,692 MBA graduates of a U.S. business school, Dobrev et al. (2005) found that the size of the organization in each person-year is associated with an 8% decrease in likelihood of transitioning to entrepreneurship in the next person-year.

31. (Higgins, 2005b)

32. For broad coverage of the types and uses of social capital, see Kim et al. (2005).

33. Across a 1971–1981 sample of 1,443 white men, including 89 entrepreneurs, the average probability of being a financially constrained

entrepreneur was 3.75%, while the probability of being an unconstrained entrepreneur was 0.06% (Evans et al., 1989).

34. Blanchflower et al. (1998) used a sample from the National Child Development Study, a longitudinal birth-cohort study including all individuals in the United Kingdom born between March 3 and March 9, 1958. Data for the study were collected in 1981 (age 23) and 1991 (age 33).

35. In a sample of 275 high-potential startups that went public in 1996, for all levels of human resources (composite of industry experience, startup experience, and VC directors), social resources (composite of business network, personal network, and underwriter prestige) were associated with a 23% increase in financial capital (Florin et al., 2003).

36. Being involved in a business assistance network and having family and friends encourage the venture were associated with a faster pace of completing certain "gestation activities" (Davidsson et al., 2003).

37. This means that someone who started working at age 21 founded a startup 25 years later at age 46.

38. Bruderl et al. (1992) found a nonlinear relationship between years of work experience and rate of startup failure. The relationship was negative until 25 years of experience, after which it became positive.

39. In a sample of 5,000 respondents who were graduates of Stanford's MBA program, the likelihood that an employment spell is entrepreneurial is positively and strongly associated with the number of prior roles held by an individual at all of his or her past jobs combined (Lazear, 2004).

40. Interestingly, Elfenbein et al. (2009) suggest that having children in the household may be associated with an *increased* chance of making the leap into founderhood, a result that should be validated and whose underlying reasons should be explored. It is possible that, for potential founders, the arrival of an infant differs from having adolescent or teenage children in the household, or that having an initial child differs from already being an experienced parent.

41. This survey was of 549 founders from a wide variety of industries, including computer and electronics, healthcare, aerospace and defense, and services (Wadhwa et al., 2009).

42. Having an unemployed spouse had a small but significant negative effect on transition to entrepreneurship (Elfenbein et al., 2009).

43. In a study of 5,112 startups that had received VC funding from 1986 to 1999, Gompers et al. (2005) focused on the public companies that spawned spin-off startups and found that an increase in sales growth from the 25th percentile to the 75th percentile decreased spawning rates by 4.6%.

44. Elfenbein et al. (2009) used paid wage as a proxy for performance. Individuals from the 5th percentile of the wage distribution were 35%

more likely than individuals at the median to enter into entrepreneurship, while individuals at the 95th percentile were 28% more likely.

45. Respondents who had received £5,000 or more were twice as likely to become entrepreneurs than those who had received nothing (Blanchflower et al., 1998).

46. (Hart et al., 2003)

47. See Bhide (1994). A separate study of small businesses found that 56% of founders identified their new business ideas based on prior experience in the market or industry (Hills et al., 2004).

48. For the most influential of these, see Porter (1980).

49. (Bruderl et al., 1992)

50. Christensen et al. (1996) constructed a complete census of products and specifications for every model introduced in the computer disk-drive industry from 1975 to 1990. Based on interviews with 70 executives in 21 companies, they created a model of "sustaining" versus "disruptive" technological change. (Other researchers refer to these differences as "competence destroying" and "competence sustaining.") Aldrich et al. (2006) suggest that established firms succeeded in introducing sustaining technologies but failed to capitalize on disruptive technologies because their marketing focus groups could not find a use for them.

51. (Hannan et al., 1989)

52. Pennings (1982) compared data on new organizations in three industries with census data on major American cities. Cities with increased organizational birth rates had larger industry populations, residents who had more income and more savings to invest in business, above-average domestic immigration, and local colleges and universities.

53. Respondents' subjective assessment of the competitive intensity of the environment facing them was associated with a 20% decrease in organizational survival rates (Bruderl et al., 1992).

54. For an overview of network effects, including the sources of network effects and the characteristics of industries affected by them, see Economides (1996). For an examination of the two-sided markets in which network effects can be particularly strong, see Eisenmann et al. (2006).

55. (Hamermesh et al., 2008:3)

56. Cooper et al. (1988) surveyed 2,994 owner-managers (including founders and nonfounder-CEOs) in 1984 and 1985. The sample was drawn from the 1985 National Federation of Independent Businesses listing, covering all industries and all geographic regions of the United States.

57. The survey included six questions about death rates from diseases in the United States, along with follow-up questions that tested the confidence the respondent had in his or her answers. Overconfidence was measured by taking into account the mean confidence level respondents had

for all their answers, by subtracting the mean from the actual percentage of correct answers (Busenitz et al., 1997).

58. Bernardo et al. (2001) constructed a theoretical model of social populations in which entrepreneurs are individuals who will be more likely to act on their own private information as opposed to public information. As overconfidence increases, founders are more likely to act based on their own information.

59. In a study of 143 founders of high-growth printing and graphics firms, Baum et al. (2010) found that respondents' answers to questions about their confidence in their ability to perform business tasks was associated with a 33% increase in "swift action" in problem-solving scenarios.

60. Lovallo et al. (2003) outline the "planning fallacy" to which founders are susceptible because business plans are anchored in proposals meant to market the organization to resource providers and because entrepreneurs tend to focus on internal causes instead of external competitors. They recommend that entrepreneurs creating business plans should minimize the risk of succumbing to the planning fallacy by focusing on a reference group.

61. Hayward et al. (2006) propose that overconfident founders may attain smaller initial resource endowments and may be more committed to the initial opportunity, causing them to be less flexible and more prone to failure.

62. (Hmieleski et al., 2009; Malach-Pines et al., 2002)

63. Hmieleski et al. (2009) surveyed 201 founder-CEOs of U.S. businesses operating in 114 different industries.

64. (Kawasaki, 2006)

65. (Blank, 2009)

66. (Wasserman, 2008a)

CHAPTER THREE

1. (Stinchcombe, 1965)

2. These analyses used data on 1,531 core founders from my 2006–2009 CompStudy datasets. The effect of having prior management experience had a strongly significant impact on the decision to solo-found. The effects of (a) having been a serial entrepreneur and (b) having more years of prior work experience were much weaker, possibly because serial entrepreneurs and people with more work experience may have counterbalancing factors that lead them to cofound more often. For instance, they may have developed better networks with which to find stronger potential cofounders, making it more attractive to cofound.

3. (Awad et al., 2010:11)

4. In a study of 1,849 founders of German small businesses, Bruderl et al. (1992) found that having prior experience in the industry in which the business was founded (as did Barry Nalls) was associated with a 33.2% lower chance of business failure.

5. The Panel Study of Entrepreneurial Dynamics (PSED) is a research program, headquartered at the University of Michigan, consisting of two longitudinal projects designed to identify and interview "nascent entrepreneurs"—individuals involved in the early process of creating firms. PSED I began in 1998 with a cohort of 830 nascent entrepreneurs who were interviewed every 13–14 months in 1998–2000. PSED II was a revised and enhanced version of PSED I in which a cohort of 1,214 nascent entrepreneurs were interviewed every 12 months beginning in 2005.

6. It is interesting to note that, within the PSED small-business dataset, there are also some gender and ethnic effects on solo founderhood. Ruef et al. (2003) estimate that women are 1.2 times more likely than men to solo-found, which is consistent with the data presented in Chapter 1 on the gender differences in control motivations. Also, minority solo-founding is 1.2 times more likely than solo-founding by nonminorities.

7. (Stinchcombe, 1965)

8. (Hackman et al., 2000; Mosakowski, 1998)

9. (Eisenmann et al., 2006)

10. Among teams in the computer industry, Haleblian et al. (1993) found that larger teams were associated with a 49% increase in performance. They conclude that in turbulent environments, the information-processing benefits of a larger team outweigh the added coordination and communication costs.

11. (Aldrich et al., 2006; Eisenhardt et al., 1988; Keck, 1997; Virany et al., 1992)

12. (Haleblian et al., 1993)

13. (Bruderl et al., 1992; Eisenhardt et al., 1990; Singh et al., 1990) These findings have interesting implications for Stinchcombe's (1965) theory about the internal causes of the liability of newness, suggesting benefits of founding teams that may counterbalance the risks he highlights.

14. (Reynolds et al., 2008; Shane, 2008) Only 13% of PSED small businesses were founded by more than two people (Aldrich et al., 2004). In the *Inc. 500* list of the fastest-growing private companies in the United States, approximately 30% were started by solo founders (Bhide, 2000).

15. As we will see in subsequent chapters, such "founders" may also own significantly less of the startup's equity than their cofounders, or have less-central roles.

16. (Bussgang, 2010)

CHAPTER FOUR

1. (Ruef et al., 2003)

2. Baker et al. (2003) present a theoretical framework of founder improvisation or "bricolage," in which time-constrained entrepreneurs use the most readily available resources to construct their startups.

3. Aldrich et al. (2006) argue that hiring more strangers increases the difficulty of creating organizational boundaries between members and nonmembers, and propose that, in new organizations, hiring more strangers should be associated with higher turnover.

4. (Hambrick et al., 1984)

5. (Amason, 1996; Knight et al., 1999)

6. In a 1979 sample of 79 individuals from 20 work groups in franchises of a national chain, more heterogeneity in tenure at the organization and in age was associated with 54% and 25% decreases, respectively, in group-level social integration measures (O'Reilly et al., 1989).

7. For instance, teams with diverse experiences, such as having created comic books in a broader range of genres, are better suited to producing innovative products, though extremely high levels of diversity can be counterproductive (Taylor et al., 2006). In the founding-team context, see also Ucbasaran et al. (2003).

8. In turbulent contexts, functional heterogeneity is associated with increased returns (Keck, 1997; Wiersema et al., 1992).

9. (Beckman, 2006) Each additional diverse-employer relationship meant the firm was 1.2 times more likely to tend toward exploration; each additional common-employer relationship meant the firm was 1.4 times more likely to tend toward exploitation.

10. (Kim et al., 2005) The authors argue that founding teams with non-overlapping networks gain more rapid access to diverse information and opportunities. Similarly, homogeneous teams tend to have less collective social capital because the members' networks tend to overlap (Burt, 1992). The author presents a theoretical model of social capital that proposes that networks rich in structural holes (i.e., communication nodes that are not in contact with each other) should give the focal actor advantages from nonredundant information.

11. Beckes-Gellner et al. (2008) used the Cologne Founder Study, a dataset of German university students from five universities in metropolitan Cologne in 1999 and 2000, to estimate willingness to become an entrepreneur. Similarly, individuals with more ties to diverse contacts in nonoverlapping networks (indicated by involvement in multiple business networks such as trade associations and rotary clubs, seeking advice from

small-business assistance organizations, etc.) begin new companies more often (Davidsson et al., 2003). In the latter study, which compared 623 nascent entrepreneurs to 608 non-entrepreneurs, membership in multiple business networks was positively and significantly associated with nascent entrepreneurship.

12. Interestingly, homophilic tendencies may be exacerbated by student self-selection into schools and by school admission committees, both of which may serve as a strong homogenizing influence on classmates.

13. (Wozniak, 2006:279)

14. (Wozniak, 2006:12, 43, 147)

15. (Schaubroeck et al., 1998)

16. Genesis 2:18, Artscroll translation of the interpretation of Rabbi Shlomo Yitzchaki (aka Rashi).

17. (Ruef et al., 2003)

18. (Wasserman et al., 2008)

19. In Baron et al.'s (1996) sample of 172 high-technology startups in Silicon Valley, the commitment blueprint (for details, see Chapter 8) was adopted by 83% of firms in which family or friends of the founder were listed as key partners, compared to just 30% of the total sample.

20. (Eisenhardt et al., 1990; O'Reilly et al., 1989; Pennings et al., 2010; Ucbasaran et al., 2003) In the context of Wall Street analysts, teams of prior coworkers who moved together to a new firm performed better than analysts who moved alone (Groysberg, 2010).

21. (Wozniak, 2006:172)

22. The fear of conflict within the team causes artificial harmony (Lencioni, 2002).

23. (Wozniak, 2006:147)

CHAPTER FIVE

1. (Roberts et al., 2009)

2. A notable exception is professional-services firms, where small firms tend to be structured as "upside-down pyramids" until they grow older, bigger, and more formalized, at which point they become much more pyramidal (Wasserman, 2005). Another exception, closer to home, is the early-stage venture capital firms that invest in startups. For details about the performance implications for VC firms of adopting pyramidal versus upside-down pyramidal structures, see Wasserman (2008b).

3. These analyses included 952 idea and non-idea founders from technology and life sciences ventures surveyed in 2008–2009.

4. (Jehn, 1997)

5. In Weberian sociology, ideal types are formed from characteristics and elements of a phenomenon. Ideal types focus on elements found in many cases of the phenomenon, but may not correspond to all of the elements of any particular case. They enable the creation of "unified analytical constructs" for analyzing those cases and facilitate comparisons across cases (Weber, 1949/1997).

6. Weber provided the classic analysis of the value—and challenges—of hierarchy. His core example is the bureaucratic organization, which emphasizes technical expertise and the division of labor among the offices in a hierarchy. Such an organization has far greater efficiency, reliability, and stability than other forms of organization (Weber, 1946).

7. In a study by Haleblian et al. (1993), firm performance was measured as an aggregate of return on assets, return on sales, and return on equity. CEO dominance—an estimate of how unevenly power is concentrated in the company's CEO—was measured by averaging the coefficients of variation for each of 10 indicators of power—including compensation, titles, board membership, education, and expertise—within the top management team of each company.

8. Eisenhardt et al. (1988) focused on high-technology firms in "high-velocity" environments.

9. In a study of 26 large firms in the computer industry, CEO dominance was associated with a 19% decrease in firm performance, measured as an aggregate of return on assets, return on sales, and return on equity (Haleblian et al., 1993).

10. An in-depth study of eight teams in the microcomputer industry found that consensus-based approaches took too much time and caused slow decision making, leading firms to miss opportunities in the fast-moving industry (Eisenhardt, 1989).

11. (Rogers et al., 2006:56)

12. Panel at meeting of The Indus Entrepreneurs-Boston (TiE-Boston) group, November 2005, moderated by Noam Wasserman.

13. Venture capitalists also tend to disapprove of egalitarian teams, preferring instead to have a clear "buck stops here" CEO with whom they can interact. This antagonism toward egalitarianism in startups is particularly interesting because most early-stage VC firms are also run as egalitarian partnerships, with multiple general partners making decisions collectively (Wasserman, 2002, 2008b).

14. Blau (1970) showed that an increase in organizational size is usually accompanied by an increase in structural differentiation, resulting in greater heterogeneity of the work performed across the organization. This increased heterogeneity deepens the division of labor and introduces problems of coordination and integration.

15. (Hellman et al., 2002)

16. Eisenhardt (1989) examined this approach in her study and proposed that it would be an effective model for making fast decisions in high-velocity environments while still achieving universal buy-in.

17. In an in-depth study of strategic decisions from 45 teams in the food-processing industry, team size was associated with a 13.9% increase in affective conflict (Amason et al., 1997).

CHAPTER SIX

1. See Hall et al. (2010) for evidence of this in venture-backed startups, and Hamilton (2000) and Moskowitz et al. (2002) for evidence of this in small businesses. Cash and credit constraints can also force founders to accept lower pay or to take more deferred compensation than in alternate employment options.

2. (Northcraft et al., 1987)

3. For more on free riding and the double-sided moral hazards that can arise from "any type of joint production arrangement where two parties each contribute some unmarketed input to the production process," see Bhattacharyya et al. (1995:767).

4. (Young et al., 2004:34)

5. See Appendix B for the specific questions used.

6. The dependent variable in these ordinary least squares (OLS) models was the percentage of equity received by each founder. The core independent variable was a dummy variable that captured whether each founder had been an idea person. The control variables included controls for the founders' backgrounds (e.g., years of prior work experience, experience in the same industry, whether a founder was a serial entrepreneur), early contributions to the startup (e.g., capital contributed), initial position within the founding team, the number of founders, the startup's industry segment, and other variables.

7. The specific size of the idea premium varied slightly by industry and by the type of regression model, but always fell within the 10–15 percentage-point range. Variations within this range may also be due to the difference in ideas: Well-developed ideas that are new in a fundamental way should receive more of a premium than nascent ideas that are less groundbreaking. This estimate of the idea premium was also confirmed by my deeper analyses with Thomas Hellmann of my 2008–2009 dataset.

8. In the PSED dataset of small businesses, a cofounder's contribution of seed capital was associated with a 20.6% increase in that cofounder's equity stake (Ruef, 2009).

9. A study of 623 nascent entrepreneurs and a control group of 608 non-entrepreneurs found that previous startup experience was associated with a 77% increase in probability of being in the nascent entrepreneur group (Davidsson et al., 2003).

10. In the Panel Study of Entrepreneurial Dynamics dataset, differential seed capital contribution is associated with a 20.6% increase in founder equity stake.

11. See Wasserman et al. (2010a) for details. The analyses in this paper focused on the results from my 2008 and 2009 surveys, which included 1,476 founders from 511 private technology and life sciences ventures.

12. In these probit models, the dependent variable was a binary indicator of whether the split was equal or not. The models included the team's prior relationships, the team's average amount of these four variables, the team's coefficient of variation for each of the four team-level variables, founding-team size, and dummies for industry, location, and year of split.

13. Some types of equality are more equal than others. Our analysis found that the more similar the founders' initial capital contributions, the more likely the team was to split the equity equally. In fact, when we analyzed the different types of splits, of all of the factors in our regression analyses, the capital-contribution variables almost always had the strongest levels of statistical significance.

14. In these analyses, the dependent variable was the log transformation of the venture's pre-money valuation during its first round of outside financing. The core independent variable was the binary indicator of whether the team had split the equity equally, with an accompanying binary indicator for whether the equity split was quick or slow. Control variables included the same variables used in the equal-split probit analyses described above: the team's prior relationships, the team's average amount of each of the four background and early-contribution variables (prior founding experience, prior years of overall work experience, idea person, and seed capital contributed), the team's coefficient of variation for each of the four team-level variables, founding-team size, and dummies for industry, location, and year in which the round was raised. Given that some of our ventures had not raised an outside round of financing, $N = 298$ ventures for these OLS regression models.

15. (Bagley et al., 2003)

16. (Strasser et al., 1991)

17. Each state has its own governing body of law that will determine whether a contract existed, what its terms were, whether a breach occurred, and what remedies are available. However, the overall elements of a contract are (a) an offer, (b) acceptance, and (c) consideration. If these

three elements exist, a contract can be found to have been established under common law. At the same time, oral agreements are hard to enforce in situations in which negotiations have been drawn out or are complicated and ambiguous. Individual states have adopted statute-of-fraud laws that require certain types of contracts (including, interestingly, marital prenuptial agreements) to be put in writing. To avoid the possibility of having an agreement ruled unenforceable, parties should put in writing any contract that might take more than a year to perform (Bagley et al., 2003).

18. (Malhotra, 2009)

19. (Shane, 2008:69) In the high-tech realm, the SPEC study found that 15% of its startups had made major changes to their business strategies and a much higher percentage had made lesser but important strategic changes (Hannan et al., 1996). Scholars predict that strategic change in new ventures will become even more common as globalization increases (McDougall et al., 1996).

20. (Video accompanying Hart et al., 2003)

21. (Hegedus et al., 2001)

22. Press briefing by former U.S. Secretary of Defense Donald Rumsfeld on February 12, 2002.

23. (Coleman, 1988) The author argues that dense and redundant networks enforce mutual obligations and thus form the basis of social capital.

24. In "closed" teams or partnerships, free riding and other moral hazards can be solved by separating ownership from control and bringing in a principal to monitor the agents' inputs and behaviors. When the venture matures and takes in outside capital, such a shift eventually occurs, as discussed in Chapter 9. For more information, see Alchian et al. (1972) or Holmstrom (1982).

25. To get these descriptive data, I combined my annual cross-sectional datasets from the 2005–2009 surveys in both technology and life sciences and focused on the startups that had two or more cofounders still working. The resulting dataset included 2,815 cofounders from 1,148 startups. Initial analyses of potential survival biases indicated that it was not a problem, but subsequent research may want to take a longitudinal and multivariate approach to such analyses and assess whether the results are affected by differential survival rates within two-founder versus three-founder teams and other such differences.

26. (Jensen et al., 1976)

CHAPTER SEVEN

1. This is based on the SPEC sample of 172 high-tech firms from Silicon Valley (Baron et al., 1996).

2. (Ruef, 2009)

3. (Adams, 1965; Deutsch, 1975; Leventhal, 1976)

4. (Deutsch, 1975).

5. (Austin, 1980) Similarly, Kabanoff (1991) suggested that equality rules are consistent with social logics while equity rules are consistent with task logics.

6. (Deutsch, 1975; Leventhal, 1976; Leventhal et al., 1980)

7. (Wasserman et al., 2008)

8. (Lawler, 1971; Leventhal, 1976)

9. (Leventhal, 1976)

10. (Wasserman, 2006b)

11. (Sabherwal et al., 2001)

PART III: INTRODUCTION

1. This description of organizational evolution was heavily influenced and informed by multiple frameworks (e.g., Baron et al., 1996; Baron et al., 2001; Galbraith, 1982; Greiner, 1972).

2. This is the central message of exchange theory and resource-dependence theory. For more details on these theoretical foundations, see Blau et al. (1962), Emerson (1962), and Pfeffer et al. (1978).

CHAPTER EIGHT

1. Beginning in 1994, the SPEC study tracked 172 high-technology startups in Silicon Valley. Researchers conducted interviews with founders, CEOs, and HR directors and supplemented this information with public and private data on strategy, HR practices, business partners, financing, and other aspects of the business.

2. Of the sample, 50.9% did not change their blueprint at all, while 29.7% changed only along one dimension (Baron et al., 2001; Baron et al., 2002).

3. Baker et al. (2003) present a theoretical framework of founder improvisation or "bricolage," in which time-constrained entrepreneurs use the most readily available resources to construct their startups.

4. These data include 1,522 nonfounding executives from founder-CEO-led startups in the 2007, 2008, and 2009 annual surveys in technology and life sciences. More specifically, the data include 285 CFOs, 202 CTOs and CSOs, 121 COOs, and 914 VPs (heads of sales, marketing, business development, engineering, human resources, and—where relevant—professional services, manufacturing/operations, clinical research, and regulatory affairs).

5. (Aldrich et al., 2006; Waldinger et al., 2003)

6. Hsu's (2007) sample included 149 startups participating in a semester-long educational program at MIT known as the "entrepreneurship laboratory."

7. Use of a strong tie was associated with a 40% decrease in occupational status from first job and a 29% decrease in status of last job. The sample included 399 males, 20 to 64 years of age, in the tricity capital area of New York State in 1975 (Lin et al., 1981).

8. (Aldrich et al., 2006)

9. (Bhide, 2000:49)

10. (Sherer, 1995)

11. (Hitt et al., 2001; Wasserman, 2008b)

12. In an in-depth study of 14 startups in North Carolina's Research Triangle, Baker et al. (1994) constructed a punctuated-equilibrium model whereby organizations become more formalized over time as founders reach outside of their personal networks for more and more specialized employees.

13. In their analysis of the SPEC sample of high-tech startups, Burton et al. (2007) find that position successors (i.e., the second generation or more of employees at a company) with different functional backgrounds than the position creator have an 11% higher turnover rate. Successors who follow "atypical" position creators (defined as individuals with functional backgrounds that differ from the average functional background for their position in the sample) have 15% to 23% higher turnover rates.

14. (Baker et al., 1994) Early employees tended to be hired through informal or personal channels, tended to end up in the most senior jobs, and tended to be generalists with substantial experience who were willing to accept relatively undefined positions.

15. (Baker et al., 1994) In the early stages of startup evolution, senior-level employees were mainly differentiated along the lines of operational and technical functions; it was only after the depletion of seed capital that clear roles developed for senior marketing and sales executives.

16. (Baron et al., 2001)

17. (Hart et al., 2003:9)

18. (Baker et al., 1994) In contrast, startups that take on junior employees with a background in large companies may feel pressure to provide some of the same human resource management practices to which the new hires grew accustomed at their old jobs.

19. In early-stage startups, when roles are most likely to overlap, it is harder to measure individual performance and thus to tie compensation effectively to individual performance (Aldrich et al., 2006), possibly increasing the emphasis in startups on the equity side of the reward structure.

20. Carpenter et al. (2002) found, in their study of a five-year survey of executives conducted by a major compensation consulting company in the

early to mid-1980s (which included 34,500 executive-year observations from 90 public companies), that an executive's total compensation was significantly related to the similarity between the executive's function and the most critical strategic contingency facing the company.

21. In a diverse sample of 209 California companies, franchises, and subsidiaries, Baron et al. (1986) found evidence supporting the existence of a gender gap in compensation. For an examination of pre-hiring rather than post-hiring effects on gender segregation, see Fernandez et al. (2005).

22. The analyses described here are based on my 2008 data, when I added a gender question to my annual survey. The resulting dataset included 2,202 C-level and VP-level executives from 459 private technology and life sciences startups. The regression models controlled for differences in positions (15 C-level and VP-level position dummy variables), industry, geography, company maturity (both the number of rounds of financing raised and the number of employees), executive backgrounds (founder status, years of prior work experience, tenure in company, and educational background), and executive's equity stake.

23. (Jensen et al., 1976)

24. Using a sample of executive compensation data for 316 information technology firms, Anderson et al. (2000) found that employers substitute bonuses for options and vice versa.

CHAPTER NINE

1. (Gorman et al., 1989:241)

2. Gimeno et al. (1997) used a sample from the National Federation for Independent Businesses database that included more than 1,500 entrepreneurs whose businesses had been in operation for less than 18 months.

3. For a discussion of how contextual factors and growth goals affect financing choices in startups, see Sapienza et al. (2003).

4. More generally, *agency problems*—problems that arise from the separation of owners (the principals) and management (their agents), where the agents make self-interested decisions rather than decisions that the owners would make themselves—can be reduced by the use of tangible assets that can be used as collateral, opening up new financing options (Jensen et al., 1976).

5. In the Silicon Valley startups included in Stanford's SPEC project, the average startup required about $2.5 million in funding (Burton, 1995).

6. Analyses of the first round of SPEC companies, which included 100 high-tech firms in Silicon Valley, found that firms having received VC financing were 47.7% more likely to undertake a series of human resources management (HRM) policies that rationalized employment practices (Hellman et al., 2002).

7. In their book *The Venture Capital Cycle*, Paul Gompers and Josh Lerner classify seed/startup rounds as "early rounds"; first and early-stage rounds as "middle rounds"; and second, third, expansion, and bridge rounds as "late rounds," with VCs increasingly focusing on late-stage investments (Gompers et al., 1999:183–187). Similar three-stage models have been proposed by others (e.g., Prowse, 1998; Sohl, 2003).

8. For the A-round, these numbers vary slightly between the technology and life sciences industries, with 31% of founders investing in the A-round in technology startups and 36% in life sciences startups. For all subsequent rounds, the two industries are within two percentage points of each other.

9. For more details, see Aldrich et al. (1996). In contrast, regarding the other investors examined below, founders have a wide set of weaker ties that are of short duration, intermittent, and tapped when needed or for instrumental reasons.

10. See Nanda (2008) for a rigorous examination of how capital availability can lead founders to start marginal businesses that wouldn't be founded when capital is more constrained. He concludes that wealthy individuals can start businesses with lower growth potential because they do not face "the discipline of external finance."

11. http://www.hbs.edu/entrepreneurs/scottcook.html, accessed October 2010.

12. (Heskett, 1996:2)

13. (Cespedes, 2009:1)

14. Press release, University of New Hampshire, Center for Venture Research, June 11, 2003.

15. For more details, see Kerr et al. (2010).

16. (Prowse, 1998)

17. For more details, see Sohl (2001–2009).

18. (Kerr et al., 2010) Based on quantitative analyses of the investments made by the two angel forums.

19. For more details, see Sohl (2001–2009).

20. VC data are taken from Thomson Reuters's ThomsonOne Banker database, accessed September 20, 2010, for all venture capital deals in all industries.

21. For more details, see Sohl (2001–2009).

22. For more details, see Hall et al. (2010). In comparison, a 1995 study of 794 startups that had received VC financing between 1961 and 1992 found that 23.8% of the startups had merged or been acquired, 22.5% had gone public, 15.6% had been liquidated or had gone bankrupt, and 38.1% remained private (Gompers, 1995).

23. This study examined 246 offers to 149 startups in MIT's Entrepreneurship Laboratory (E-Lab). For more details, see Hsu (2004).

24. (Gompers et al., 1999)

25. The sample was taken from the VentureOne database from 1987 to 2000, including 16,613 financing rounds for 7,765 companies (Cochrane, 2004).

26. VC data are taken from Thomson Reuters's ThomsonOne Banker database, accessed September 20, 2010, for all venture capital deals in all industries.

27. (Stinchcombe, 1965)

28. In a sample of 62 VCs that self-reported the activities they undertook for their portfolio investments, equity financing averaged a score of 3.63 out of 5, and interfacing with other investors averaged 3.62 out of 5 (MacMillan et al., 1989).

29. Rosenstein et al.'s (1993) survey of CEOs of 162 high-tech companies included a list of 11 activity areas that was based on the survey used by MacMillan et al. (1989).

30. Corporate—or "strategic"—investors are usually larger corporations in the same or a related sector that invest in startups for strategic and/or financial reasons and may later become leading candidates to acquire the startup.

31. "Prominence" was measured as the proportion of all biotech alliances in the industry in which each investor had participated. For more details, see Stuart et al. (1999).

32. On a 5-point Likert-type scale, VCs reported they were most directly involved in "serving as a sounding board" to the top-team, with an average score of 3.77 out of 5 (MacMillan et al., 1989).

33. In a sample of 162 firms with VC financing, 38.3% of the sample rated serving as a sounding board as one of the top-three most helpful activities by their investors (Rosenstein et al., 1993).

34. (Hellman et al., 2002)

35. In a study of 246 offers to 149 startups in MIT's E-Lab, the average entrepreneur with multiple offers gave up $4.1 million in pre-money valuation in order to get a VC who would add value (Hsu, 2004).

36. (Bussgang, 2010:114)

37. As a proxy for the amount of time the board members informally spent on the startup's business, we used the number of hours per months that the board's nonexecutive chairman—the most active outside director—worked on the startup.

38. These findings parallel findings from the literature on mentor-protégé relationships, which suggest that inexperienced executives receive less mentorship than they need because they have lower readiness for mentorship (Healy et al., 1990), middle-experience executives get more mentorship (closer to the amount they need), and those with a lot of experience get less mentorship because they require less (Kram, 1985).

39. Chief executives with backgrounds in sales and other output functions may have more ability to grow the business beyond its earliest stages than do CEOs coming from throughput functions (Boeker et al., 2005).

40. (Bagley et al., 2003:112)

41. The sample included 307 private biotechnology startups that received VC financing between 1978 and 1989 (Lerner, 1995).

42. (Kaplan et al., 2004)

43. (Wilmerding, 2004)

44. This term actually has two parts. The "preference" governs whether investors recoup 100% of their investment, or a multiple thereof, before nonpreferred shareholders (e.g., the founders who own common stock) receive any proceeds. The second part is whether the new shares issued to the new investors are "participating" or not. Participation indicates whether or not investors participate in the back end of payouts, when the proceeds from the exit are divided among the common shareholders. The participation can also be capped at a certain level. For more details, see Wasserman et al. (2010b). In a representative sample of VC financing deals that was compiled by the law firm Wilson Sonsini Goodrich & Rosati, 21%–29% of the investments included capped participation, 30%–35% included uncapped participation, and 40%–44% did not include any back-end participation for VCs. For details, see Baudler (2009).

45. The more external risks the startup faces (e.g., the more uncertain its market size, expected customer adoption rate, competition, and financial market/exit condition risk), the more likely the VC will insist on terms that affect exit payoffs, such as redemption rights (Kaplan et al., 2004; Wilmerding, 2004).

46. The fact that taking investor money increases organizational survival while increasing team turnover might suggest that the turnover that occurs may be beneficial by helping increase survival, a testable proposition that deserves systematic attention from researchers.

47. Another 8% of seats were held by nonfounding executives, who may at times side with the founders and at other times side with the investors who helped hire them into the startup.

48. In their analyses of the first round of SPEC firms, the increased use of HRM techniques in VC-backed startups led Hellman et al. (2002) to conclude that VCs play a critical role in "professionalizing" startups.

49. VCs themselves often use the following line about the perils of having too many VCs on a startup's board: "VCs on your board are like martinis: One is good, two is better, three is a problem."

50. Interestingly, one of the few potential advantages of receiving a down round may be the chance to shrink the startup's board. Venture capitalist Scott Yaphe observed, "When a company has raised capital

through multiple rounds, and then undergoes a recapitalization or wash-out round, the board size tends to shrink. Investors often use the recap as a cleansing event and included in this cleansing is board composition. Non-participating or weak investor groups may be taken off the board and not replaced. The larger investors view a smaller board as a way to more efficiently control a bad situation that they are trying to improve."

51. In a random sample of 794 VC-backed firms from 1961 to 1992, Gompers (1995) found that VCs used smaller/shorter rounds for startups where there was more uncertainty.

52. Additional details about these secondary terms and how they affect both ownership and control can be found in Wasserman et al. (2010b).

53. Standard investment agreements assume that founders are agents whose actions have to be closely monitored and who need strong incentives to act in the interest of the startup. However, to the extent that founders may sometime act more like stewards (Donaldson et al., 1991)—for whom such incentive structures may be unnecessary or even counterproductive, not to mention costly—their investment agreements might need to have different incentive structures than those used with agents.

CHAPTER TEN

1. In 2008 and 2009, I enriched my annual survey to ask more detailed questions about founder-CEO succession. These surveys are the source of the data in this chapter regarding (a) triggers, (b) whether the replaced founder stayed on as an executive or a board member, and (c) the background of the successor-CEOs. These data include 169 founder-CEO succession events.

2. (Virany et al., 1986)

3. (Gompers et al., 1999; Stuart et al., 1999)

4. (Wasserman, 2003)

5. (Greiner, 1972; Kazanjian, 1988)

6. (Emerson, 1962; Pfeffer et al., 1978)

7. (Boeker et al., 2002)

8. (Agrawal et al., 2006)

9. This is true regarding stock returns (Fee et al., 2003) and operating performance (Agrawal et al., 2006); bad performance in either metric dramatically increases the chances that the board will hire an outside successor.

10. In analyses of the SPEC sample of high-tech startups, Burton et al. (2007) found that position successors (i.e., the second generation or more of employees at companies) who followed "atypical" position creators (defined as individuals with functional backgrounds that differ from the

average functional background for their position in the sample) had 15% to 23% higher turnover rates.

11. (Hamermesh, 2003:7)

12. (Hamermesh, 2003:7)

13. (Hamermesh, 2003:8)

14. (Kirsner, 2010)

CHAPTER ELEVEN

1. (Stevenson et al., 1990:23)

2. Evans et al. (1989:824) state that across their full population of entrepreneurs and non-entrepreneurs, "The average probability of being a constrained entrepreneur is 3.75 percent, and the average probability of being an unconstrained entrepreneur is 0.06 percent."

3. (Starr et al., 1990; Stevenson et al., 1990; Venkataraman, 1997)

4. (Romanelli, 1989:375)

5. (Stinchcombe, 1965)

6. (Peteraf, 1993)

7. (Pfeffer et al., 1978)

8. (e.g., Amit et al., 1990; Coff, 1999)

9. (Hellman, 1998; Wasserman, 2003)

10. (Lerner, 1995; Sahlman, 1990)

11. For more details, see Wasserman (2006a). Past studies often used ownership percentage as a proxy for decision-making control (e.g., Finkelstein et al., 1989; Gomez-Mejia et al., 1987; Salancik et al., 1980). However, the startup context is one in which ownership and decision-making control can diverge markedly (Kaplan et al., 2003). Therefore, in my analyses, control of decision making at the CEO and board levels was observed directly rather than inferred from ownership percentages.

12. (Miller, 2010)

13. Erick Schonfeld, http://techcrunch.com/2011/03/03/jack-dorsey-twitter-punched-stomach/, March 3, 2011.

14. (Miller, 2010)

15. (Bhide, 2000)

16. (Wasserman, 2003)

17. Brian Bell, chairman of Buffalo Angel Network, comments made March 1, 2006.

18. Or, "Queen-oriented."

19. (Baum et al., 2001) Likewise, large companies that do not pick a clear strategy—e.g., being best at cost leadership, product differentiation, or focus—are usually at a competitive disadvantage (Porter, 1980).

20. (Marlin et al., 1994; Porter, 1980)
21. (Hamermesh, 2003:9)
22. (Abetti, 2005)
23. (Hamermesh, 2003:4)
24. (Bhide, 2000:149)
25. For more details, see Sapienza et al. (2003).
26. However, three characteristics of a transaction—its frequency, uncertainty, and asset specificity (measured by the forgone economic benefits
of discontinuing a relationship)—are positively related to the likelihood
that a firm will bring the needed resource inside its own boundaries. This is
because the hierarchical relationships within firms are more effective than
market relationships at resolving potential disputes (Williamson, 1985).
Further insights come from the "incomplete contracts" approach to deciding which assets belong within the firm's boundaries (e.g., Grossman et al.,
1986; Hart et al., 1990).
27. (Agrawal et al., 1995; Lillis et al., 1976)
28. (Burt, 1997; Lin, 1999:35)
29. (Burt, 1997)
30. (Shane et al., 2002)
31. (Burt, 1997)
32. (Shane et al., 2002)
33. In a detailed study of the New York City garment-manufacturing industry, Uzzi (1997) concluded that mutual reciprocity and dense networks
allowed managers to enter into partnerships with suppliers without their
having to waste time on additional due diligence.
34. (Fredrickson et al., 1988)
35. (Tsai et al., 1998)
36. (Lippman et al., 2003)
37. (Evans et al., 1989)
38. (Holtz-Eakin et al., 1994)
39. (e.g., Spence, 2002)
40. In a sample of 8,753 startups from 1987 to 2000, Gompers et al.
(2010) found that previous startup experience was associated with a 3.8%
increase in successful IPO, and that previous experience leading a startup
to IPO was associated with a 7.8% increase in likelihood of taking the
current startup to IPO.
41. (e.g., Finkelstein, 1992)
42. (Mills, 1956:162)
43. (Jensen et al., 1976)
44. (e.g., Davis et al., 1997)
45. (e.g., Hamilton, 2000; Hurst et al., 2010b; Moskowitz et al., 2002)

46. (Stevenson et al., 1990)

47. Ostrander (1987) examined established, endowed, private social-service agencies that serve families in a large U.S. city and depend on private funds for discretionary income. The actions of the agency leaders were constrained by the elite board members who provided funding to the agency.

48. For more details on the GEM efforts and the reports they produce, see http://www3.babson.edu/eship/research-publications/gem.cfm.

49. The latter two exceptions were France, with a wealth/control breakdown of about 10%/90%, and Switzerland, with a breakdown of about 22%/78%.

50. For instance, see Gompers et al. (2010).

51. One example of such a partnership may be the franchising relationship, in which the founder of the franchisor decides not to grow by opening new company-owned stores (which often require a lot of capital) but instead to partner with franchisees who will provide the capital and personnel to run the new stores and who will give the franchisor a share (but certainly not all) of the financial gains. Using a "Rich vs. King" lens to examine franchising relationships may provide further insights into potential "75% Rich, 75% King" relationships with outside resource providers.

52. (Aldrich et al., 2006)

53. (Lerner, 1995)

54. See Broughman et al. (2010) on founders' exit issues.

55. (Livingston, 2007:123)

56. (Miller, 2010)

57. (Black et al., 1995)

58. (Chemmanur et al., 1999)

59. (Black et al., 1995)

60. (Lin et al., 1995)

61. (Delfassy et al., 2010:7)

APPENDIX A

1. (Jensen et al., 1990)

2. (Beatty et al., 1994)

3. (Deckop, 1988; Henderson et al., 1996)

4. (Wasserman, 2003, 2006a, 2006b; Wasserman et al., 2005; Wasserman et al., 2008; Wasserman et al., 2010a)

5. (Wasserman, 2003, 2006b)

6. (Wasserman, 2006b)

7. (Finkelstein, 1992; Waldman et al., 2001)

BIBLIOGRAPHY

Abetti PA. 2005. The creative evolution of Steria. *Creativity and Innovation Management* **14**(2): 191–204.

Adams JS. 1965. Inequity in social exchange. In L Berkowitz (Ed.), *Advances in Experimental Social Psychology*, Vol. 2: 267–299. Academic Press: New York.

Agrawal A, Knoeber CR, Tsoulouhas T. 2006. Are outsiders handicapped in CEO successions? *Journal of Corporate Finance* **12**(3): 619–644.

Agrawal D, Lal R. 1995. Contractual arrangements in franchising: An empirical investigation. *Journal of Marketing Research* **22**(May): 213–221.

Alchian AA, Demsetz H. 1972. Production, information costs and economic organization. *American Economic Review* **62**: 777–795.

Aldrich H. 2010. Beam me up, Scott(ie)! Institutional theorists' struggles with the emergent nature of entrepreneurship. In W Sine, R David (Eds.), *Research in the Sociology of Work, on Institutions and Entrepreneurship*, Vol. 21: 329–364. Emerald: Bradford, UK.

Aldrich H, Carter N, Ruef M. 2004. Teams. In WB Gartner, KG Shaver, P Reynolds (Eds.), *Handbook of Entrepreneurial Dynamics*: 299–324. Sage: Thousand Oaks, CA.

Aldrich H, Ruef M. 2006. *Organizations Evolving* (2nd ed.). Sage: Thousand Oaks, CA.

Aldrich HE, Elam AB, Reese PR. 1996. Strong ties, weak ties, and strangers. In S Birley, IC MacMillan (Eds.), *Entrepreneurship in a Global Context*: 1–25. Routledge: London.

Allen P. 2011. *Idea Man*. Portfolio/Penguin, New York.

Amason AC. 1996. Distinguishing the effects of functional and dysfunctional conflict on strategic decision making: Resolving a paradox for top management teams. *Academy of Management Journal* **39**: 123–149.

Amason AC, Sapienza HJ. 1997. The effects of top management team size and interaction norms on cognitive and affective conflict. *Journal of Management* **23**(4): 495–516.

Amit R, Glosten L, Muller E. 1990. Entrepreneurial ability, venture investments, and risk sharing. *Management Science* **36**(10): 1232–1245.

Amit R, MacCrimmon KR, Zietsma C, Oesch JM. 2000. Does money matter? Wealth attainment as the motive for initiating growth-oriented technology ventures. *Journal of Business Venturing* **16**: 119–143.

Anderson MC, Banker RD, Ravindran S. 2000. Executive compensation in the IT industry. *Management Science* **3**: 530–547.

Austin W. 1980. Friendship and fairness: Effects of type of relationship and task performance on choice of distribution rules. *Personality and Social Psychology Bulletin* **6**: 402–408.

Awad J, Perkins B, Neff M. 2010. Building a team and Rich vs. King in the context of functional beverage ventures. *Founders' Dilemmas Paper* (April).

Bagley CE, Dauchy CE. 2003. *The Entrepreneur's Guide to Business Law*. Thomson Learning: Ontario, Canada.

Baker T, Aldrich H. 1994. Friends and strangers: Early hiring practices and idiosyncratic jobs. *Frontiers of Entrepreneurship Research* **13**: 75–87.

Baker T, Miner AS, Eesley DT. 2003. Improvising firms: Bricolage, account-giving, and improvisational competencies in the founding process. *Research Policy* **32**: 255–276.

Baker T, Nelson RE. 2005. Creating something from nothing: Resource construction through entrepreneurial bricolage. *Administrative Science Quarterly* **50**: 329–366.

Baron J, Bielby T. 1986. Men and women at work: Sex segregation and statistical discrimination. *American Journal of Sociology* **91**(4): 759–799.

Baron JN, Burton MD, Hannan MT. 1996. The road taken: Origins and evolution of employment systems in emerging companies. *Industrial and Corporate Change* **5**(2): 239–275.

Baron JN, Hannan MT. 2002. Organizational blueprints for success in high-technology start-ups: Lessons from SPEC. *California Management Review* **44**(3): 8–36.

Baron JN, Hannan MT, Burton MD. 2001. Labor pains: Change in organizational models and employee turnover in young, high-tech firms. *American Journal of Sociology* **106**(4): 960–1012.

Baron RA. 1998. Cognitive mechanisms in entrepreneurship: Why and when entrepreneurs think differently than other people. *Journal of Business Venturing* **13**: 275–294.

Baron RA, Ensley MD. 2006. Opportunity recognition as the detection of meaningful patterns: Evidence from novice and experienced entrepreneurs. *Management Science* **52**(6): 1331–1344.

Baudler M. 2009. From the WSGR Database: Financing trends. In *The Entrepreneur's Report: Private Company Financing Trends*. http://www.wsgr.com/publications/PDFSearch/entreport/Summer2009/private-company-financing-trends.htm#3.

Baum JR, Bird BJ. 2010. The successful intelligence of high-growth entrepreneurs: Links to new venture growth. *Organization Science* **21**(2): 397–412.

Baum JR, Locke EA. 2004. The relationship of entrepreneurial traits, skill, and motivation to subsequent venture growth. *Journal of Applied Psychology* 89(4): 587–598.

Baum JR, Locke EA, Smith KG. 2001. A multidimensional model of venture growth. *Academy of Management Journal* 44(2): 292–303.

Beatty RP, Zajac EJ. 1994. Managerial incentives, monitoring, and risk bearing: A study of executive compensation, ownership, and board structure in initial public offerings. *Administrative Science Quarterly* 39(2): 313–335.

Beckes-Gellner U, Moog PM. 2008. Who chooses to become an entrepreneur? The jacks-of-all-trades in human and social capital. *University of Zurich Working Paper.*

Beckman C. 2006. The influence of founding team company affiliations on firm behavior. *Academy of Management Journal* 49(4): 741–758.

Bernardo AE, Welch I. 2001. On the evolution of overconfidence and entrepreneurs. *Yale International Center for Finance, Working Paper Series No. 137.*

Bhattacharyya S, Lafontaine F. 1995. Double-sided moral hazard and the nature of share contracts. *RAND Journal of Economics* 26(4): 761–781.

Bhide A. 1994. How entrepreneurs craft strategies that work. *Harvard Business Review* 72(2): 150–161.

Bhide A. 2000. *The Origin and Evolution of New Businesses.* Oxford University Press: Oxford.

Black BS, Gilson RJ. 1995. Venture capital and the structure of capital markets. *Journal of Financial Economics* 47(3): 243–277.

Blanchflower DG, Oswald AJ. 1998. What makes an entrepreneur? *Journal of Labor Economics* 1(1): 26–60.

Blank S. 2009. Lies entrepreneurs tell themselves. http://steveblank.com/2009/06/15/lies-entrepreneurs-tell-themselves/.

Blau P. 1970. A formal theory of differentiation in organizations. *American Sociological Review* 35: 201–218.

Blau PM, Scott WR. 1962. *Formal Organizations.* Chandler: San Francisco.

Boeker W. 1988. Organizational origins: Entrepreneurial and environmental imprinting at the time of founding. In GR Carroll (Ed.), *Ecological Models of Organizations: 33–51.* Ballinger: Cambridge, MA.

Boeker W. 1989. Strategic change: The effects of founding and history. *Academy of Management Journal* 32: 489–515.

Boeker W, Karichalil R. 2002. Entrepreneurial transitions: Factors influencing founder departure. *Academy of Management Journal* 45(3): 818–826.

Boeker W, Wiltbank R. 2005. New venture evolution and managerial capabilities. *Organization Science* 16(2): 123–133.

Broughman B, Fried J. 2010. Renegotiation of cash flow rights in the sale of VC-backed firms. *Journal of Financial Economics* **95**(3): 384–399.

Bruderl J, Preisendorfer P, Ziegler R. 1992. Survival chances of newly founded business organizations. *American Sociological Review* **57**(April): 227–242.

Burt RS. 1992. *Structural Holes: The Social Structure of Competition*. Harvard University Press: Cambridge, MA.

Burt RS. 1997. The contingent value of social capital. *Administrative Science Quarterly* **42**(2): 339–365.

Burton D. 1995. The evolution of employment systems in high technology firms. *Unpublished Ph.D. dissertation, Department of Sociology, Stanford University*.

Burton MD, Beckman C. 2007. Leaving a legacy: Position imprints and successor turnover in young firms. *American Review of Sociology* **72**: 239–266.

Busenitz LW, Barney JB. 1997. Differences between entrepreneurs and managers in large organizations: Biases and heuristics in strategic decision-making. *Journal of Business Venturing* **12**(1): 9–30.

Bussgang J. 2010. *Mastering the VC Game*. Portfolio hardcover.

Carland JW, Hoy F, Boulton W, Carland JAC. 1984. Differentiating entrepreneurs from small business owners: A conceptualization. *Academy of Management Review* **9**: 354–359.

Carpenter M, Wade J. 2002. Microlevel opportunity structures as determinants of non-CEO executive pay. *Academy of Management Journal* **45**(6): 1085–1103.

Cespedes FV. 2009. Intuit. *Harvard Business School Case No. 810-018*.

Chemmanur TJ, Fulghieri P. 1999. A theory of the going-public decision. *Review of Financial Studies* **12**(2): 249–279.

Christensen CM, Bower JL. 1996. Customer power, strategic investment, and the failure of leading firms. *Strategic Management Journal* **17**: 197–218.

Cochrane JH. 2004. *The Risk and Return of Venture Capital*. University of Chicago: Chicago.

Coff RW. 1999. When competitive advantage doesn't lead to performance: The resource-based view and stakeholder bargaining power. *Organization Science* **10**(2): 119–133.

Coleman JS. 1988. Social capital in the creation of human capital. *American Journal of Sociology* **94**: 95–120.

Cooper AC, Woo CY, Dunkelberg WC. 1988. Entrepreneurs' perceived chances for success. *Journal of Business Venturing* **3**: 97–108.

Davidsson P, Honig B. 2003. The role of social and human capital among nascent entrepreneurs. *Journal of Business Venturing* **18**: 301–331.

Davis JH, Schoorman FD, Donaldson L. 1997. Toward a stewardship theory of management. *Academy of Management Review* **22**(1): 20–47.

Deckop JR. 1988. Determinants of chief executive officer compensation. *Industrial and Labor Relations Review* **41**(2): 215–226.

Delfassy N, Price G. 2010. Entrepreneurial contradictions: Making sense of differences in theory and practice. *Founders' Dilemmas Paper* (April).

Deutsch M. 1975. Equity, equality and need: What determines which value will be used as the basis for distributive justice? *Journal of Social Issues* **31**: 137–149.

Dobrev SD, Barnett WP. 2005. Organizational roles and transition to entrepreneurship. *Academy of Management Journal* **48**(3): 433–449.

Donaldson L, Davis JH. 1991. Stewardship theory or agency theory: CEO governance and shareholder returns. *Australian Journal of Management* **16**(1): 49–64.

Economides N. 1996. The economics of networks. *International Journal of Industrial Organization* **14**(6): 673–699.

Edmondson AC, McManus SE. 2007. Methodological fit in management field research. *Academy of Management Review* **32**(4): 1155–1179.

Eisenhardt KM, Bourgeois III L. 1988. Politics of strategic decision making in high-velocity environments. *Academy of Management Journal* **31**: 143–159.

Eisenhardt KM. 1989. Making fast strategic decisions in high-velocity environments. *Academy of Management Journal* **32**(3): 543–576.

Eisenhardt KM, Schoonhoven CB. 1990. Organizational growth: Linking founding team, strategy, environment, and growth among U.S. semiconductor ventures, 1978–1988. *Administrative Science Quarterly* **35**: 504–529.

Eisenmann TR, Parker G, Alstyne MV. 2006. Strategies for two-sided markets. *Harvard Business Review* **84**(10): 92–101.

Elfenbein DW, Hamilton BH, Zenger TR. 2009. Entrepreneurial spawning of scientists and engineers: Stars, slugs and small firms. *Washington University, St. Louis Working Paper*.

Emerson RM. 1962. Power-dependence relations. *American Sociological Review* **27**: 31–40.

Evans DS, Jovanovic B. 1989. An estimated model of entrepreneurial choice under liquidity constraints. *Journal of Political Economy* **97**(4): 808–827.

Fama EF, Jensen ML. 1983. Separation of ownership and control. *Journal of Law and Economics* **26**: 301–325.

Fee CE, Hadlock C. 2003. Raids, rewards, and reputations in the market for managerial talent. *Review of Financial Studies* **16**(4): 1315–1357.

Fernandez R, Sosa ML. 2005. Gendering the job: Networks and recruitment at a call center. *American Journal of Sociology* **111**(3): 859–904.

Finkelstein S. 1992. Power in top management teams: Dimensions, measurement, and validation. *Academy of Management Journal* 35: 505–538.

Finkelstein S, Hambrick DC. 1989. Chief executive compensation: A study of the intersection of markets and political processes. *Strategic Management Journal* 10: 121–134.

Fiske ST, Taylor SE. 1991. *Social Cognition: From Brains to Culture.* McGraw-Hill: New York.

Florin J, Lubatkin M, Schulze W. 2003. A social capital model of high-growth ventures. *Academy of Management Journal* 46(3): 374–384.

Fredrickson JW, Hambrick DC, Baumrin S. 1988. A model of CEO dismissal. *Academy of Management Review* 13(2): 255–270.

Galbraith J. 1982. The stages of growth. *Journal of Business Strategy* (Summer): 70–79.

Gimeno J, Folta TB, Cooper AC, Woo CY. 1997. Survival of the fittest? Entrepreneurial human capital and the persistence of underperforming firms. *Administrative Science Quarterly* 42(4): 750–783.

Goldin C. 2008. Gender gap. In *Library of Economics and Liberty: The Concise Encyclopedia of Economics.* http://www.econlib.org/library/Enc/GenderGap.html.

Gomez-Mejia LR, Tosi HL, Hinken T. 1987. Managerial control, performance, and executive compensation. *Academy of Management Journal* 30: 51–70.

Gompers P. 1995. Optimal investment, monitoring, and the staging of venture capital. *Journal of Finance* 50: 1461–1489.

Gompers P, Lerner J. 1999. *The Venture Capital Cycle.* MIT Press: Boston.

Gompers P, Lerner J, Scharfstein D. 2005. Entrepreneurial spawning: Public corporations and the genesis of new ventures. *Journal of Finance* 60(2): 577–614.

Gompers P, Lerner J, Scharfstein D, Kovner AR. 2010. Performance persistence in entrepreneurship and venture capital. *Journal of Financial Economics* 96(1): 18–32.

Gorman M, Sahlman WA. 1989. What do venture capitalists do? *Journal of Business Venturing* 4(4): 231–248.

Granovetter M. 1973. The strength of weak ties. *American Journal of Sociology* 78: 1360–1380.

Greiner LE. 1972. Evolution and revolution as organizations grow. *Harvard Business Review* 50(4): 37–46.

Grossman SJ, Hart OD. 1986. The costs and benefits of ownership: A theory of vertical and lateral integration. *Journal of Political Economy* 94(4): 691–719.

Grossman SJ, Hart OD. 1988. One share-one vote and the market for corporate control. *Journal of Financial Economics* 20: 175–202.

Groysberg B. 2010. *Chasing Stars: The Myth of Talent and the Portability of Performance*. Princeton University Press: Princeton, NJ.

Hackman JR, Wageman R, Ruddy T, Ray CR. 2000. Team effectiveness in theory and practice. In E Locke (Ed.), *Industrial and Organizational Psychology: Linking Theory with Practice*: 275–294. Blackwell: London.

Haleblian J, Finkelstein S. 1993. Top management team size, CEO dominance, and firm performance: The moderating roles of environmental turbulence and discretion. *Academy of Management Journal* 38(4): 844–863.

Hall RE, Woodward SE. 2010. The burden of the nondiversifiable risk of entrepreneurship. *American Economic Review* 100(June): 1163–1194.

Hambrick DC, Mason PA. 1984. Upper echelons: The organization as a reflection of its top managers. *Academy of Management Review* 9: 193–206.

Hamermesh RG. 2003. Managing Segway's early development. *Harvard Business School Case No. 804-065.*

Hamermesh RG, Barley L, Graham G. 2008. Proteus Biomedical: Making pigs fly. *Harvard Business School Case No. 809-051.*

Hamilton BH. 2000. Does entrepreneurship pay? An empirical analysis of the returns to self-employment. *Journal of Political Economy* 108(3): 604–631.

Hannan MT, Burton D, Baron J. 1996. Inertia and change in the early years: Employment relations in young, high-tech firms. *Industrial and Corporate Change* 5(2): 239–275.

Hannan MT, Freeman J. 1989. *Organizational Ecology*. Harvard University Press: Cambridge, MA.

Hart MM, Roberts MJ, Stevens JD. 2003. Zipcar: Refining the business model. *Harvard Business School Case No. 803-096.*

Hart O, Moore J. 1990. Property rights and the nature of the firm. *Journal of Political Economy* 98(6): 1119–1158.

Hayward M, Shepherd DA, Griffin D. 2006. A hubris theory of entrepreneurship. *Management Science* 52(2): 160–172.

Healy CC, Welchart A. 1990. Mentoring relations: A definition to advance research and practice. *Educational Researcher* 19(9): 17–21.

Hegedus C, Noujaim J. 2001. *Startup.com* (Documentary). Live/Artisan: Santa Monica, CA.

Hellman T. 1998. The allocation of control rights in venture capital contracts. *RAND Journal of Economics* 29: 57–76.

Hellman T, Puri M. 2002. Venture capital and the professionalization of start-up firms: Empirical evidence. *Journal of Finance* 57(1): 169–197.

Henderson AD, Fredrickson JW. 1996. Information-processing demands as a determinant of CEO compensation. *Academy of Management Journal* 39(3): 575–606.

Heskett JL. 1996. Scott Cook and Intuit. *Harvard Business School Case No. 396-282.*

Higgins M. 2005a. Building career foundations: Humphrey Chen. *Harvard Business School Video Series No. 405-704.*

Higgins M. 2005b. *Career Imprints: Creating Leaders across an Industry.* Jossey-Bass: San Francisco.

Higgins M, Wasserman N. 2010. Humphrey and Cecilia. *Harvard Business School Video Series No. 810-702.*

Hills G, Singh R. 2004. Opportunity recognition. In WB Gartner, KG Shaver, P Reynolds (Eds.), *Handbook of Entrepreneurial Dynamics:* 259–272. Sage: Thousand Oaks, CA.

Hitt MA, Bierman L, Shimizu K, Kochhar R. 2001. Direct and moderating effects of human capital on strategy and performance in professional service firms: A resource-based perspective. *Academy of Management Journal* 44(1): 13–28.

Hmieleski KM, Baron RA. 2009. Entrepreneurs' optimism and new venture performance: A social cognitive perspective. *Academy of Management Journal* 52(3): 473–488.

Holmstrom B. 1982. Moral hazard in teams. *Bell Journal of Economics* 13: 324–340.

Holtz-Eakin D, Joulfaian D, Rosen HS. 1994. Entrepreneurial decisions and liquidity constraints. *RAND Journal of Economics* 25(2): 334–347.

Hsu D. 2004. What do entrepreneurs pay for venture capital affiliation? *Journal of Finance* 59(4): 1805–1844.

Hsu D. 2007. Experienced entrepreneurs, capital and VC funding. *Research Policy* 36: 722–741.

Hsu D, Roberts DR, Eesley D. 2007. Entrepreneurs from technology-based universities: Evidence from MIT. *Organization Science* 6(3): 768–788.

Hurst E, Li G, Pugsley B. 2010a. Using expenditures to estimate missing self employed income. *University of Chicago Working Paper.*

Hurst EG, Pugsley BW. 2010b. Non pecuniary benefits of small business ownership. *University of Chicago Working Paper.*

Jehn KA. 1997. Affective and cognitive conflict in work groups: Increasing performance through value-based intragroup conflict. In CKW De Dreu, E Van de Vliert (Eds.), *Using Conflict in Organizations:* 87–100. Sage: Thousand Oaks, CA.

Jensen M, Meckling W. 1976. Theory of the firm: Managerial behavior, agency costs and ownership structure. *Journal of Financial Economics* 3: 305–360.

Jensen M, Murphy K. 1990. Performance pay and top management incentives. *Journal of Political Economy* 98: 225–264.

Kabanoff B. 1991. Equity, equality, power and conflict. *Academy of Management Review* **16**: 416–441.

Kaplan SN, Stromberg P. 2003. Financial contracting theory meets the real world: An empirical analysis of venture capital contracts. *Review of Economic Studies* **70**: 281–315.

Kaplan SN, Stromberg P. 2004. Characteristics, contracts, and actions: Evidence from venture capitalist analyses. *Journal of Finance* **59**: 2173–2206.

Kawasaki G. 2006. Top ten lies of entrepreneurs. http://blog.guykawasaki .com/2006/01/the_top_ten_lie_1.html.

Kazanjian RK. 1988. Relation of dominant problems to stages of growth in technology-based new ventures. *Academy of Management Journal* **31**(2): 257–279.

Keck SL. 1997. Top management team structure: Differential effects by environmental context. *Organization Science* **8**(2): 143–156.

Kerr W, Lerner J, Schoar A. 2010. The consequences of entrepreneurial finance: A regression discontinuity analysis. *NBER Working Paper*. Harvard Business School, MIT.

Kim PH, Aldrich HE. 2005. Social capital and entrepreneurship. In *Foundations and Trends in Entrepreneurship:* Vol. 1, Issue 2. NOW: Hanover, MA.

Kirsner S. 2010. Legendary Hub venture investor, musician works on his next hit. *Boston Globe*. http://www.boston.com/business/articles/2010/07/18/ legendary_hub_venture_investor_musician_works_on_his_next_hit/.

Kirzner IM. 1973. *Competition and Entrepreneurship*. University of Chicago Press: Chicago.

Knight D, Pearce C, Smith KG, Olian JD, Sims HP, Smith KA, Flood P. 1999. Top management team diversity, group process and strategic consensus. *Strategic Management Journal* **20**: 445–465.

Kram KE. 1985. *Mentoring at Work: Developing Relationships in Organizational Life*. Scott, Foresman: Glenview, IL.

Lawler EEI. 1971. *Pay and Organizational Effectiveness: A Psychological View*. McGraw-Hill: New York.

Lazear EP. 2004. Balanced skills and entrepreneurship. *American Economic Review* **94**: 208–211.

Lease RC, McConnell JJ, Mikkelson WH. 1983. The market value of control in publicly-traded corporations. *Journal of Financial Economics* **11**: 439–471.

Lencioni P. 2002. *The Five Dysfunctions of a Team*. Jossey-Bass: San Francisco.

Lerner J. 1995. Venture capitalists and the oversight of private firms. *Journal of Finance* **50**: 301–318.

Leventhal GS. 1976. The distribution of rewards and resources in groups and organizations. In L Berkowitz, E Walster (Eds.), *Equity Theory: Toward a General Theory of Social Interaction*: 92–133. Academic Press: New York.

Leventhal GS, Karuza J, Fry WR. 1980. Beyond fairness: A theory of allocation preferences. In G Mikula (Ed.), *Justice and Social Interaction: Experimental and Theoretical Contributions from Psychological Research*: 167–208. Springer-Verlag: New York.

Lillis C, Chem N, Gilman J. 1976. Competitive advantage variation over the life cycle of a franchise. *Journal of Marketing* 40(4): 77–80.

Lin N. 1999. Building a network theory of social capital. *Connections* 22(1): 28–51.

Lin N, Ensel W, Vaughn JC. 1981. Social resources and strength of ties: Structural factors in occupational status attainment. *American Sociological Review* 46(August): 393–405.

Lin TH, Smith RL. 1995. Insider reputation and selling decisions: The unwinding of venture capital investments during equity IPOs. *Claremont College Working Paper.*

Lippman SA, Rumelt RP. 2003. A bargaining perspective on resource advantage. *Strategic Management Journal* 24: 1069–1086.

Livingston J. 2007. *Founders at Work*. Apress: New York.

Lovallo D, Kahneman D. 2003. Delusions of success: How optimism undermines executives' decisions. *Harvard Business Review* 81(7): 56–67.

MacMillan IC, Kulow DM, Khoylian R. 1989. Venture capitalists' involvement in their investment: Extent and performance. *Journal of Business Venturing* 4(1): 27–47.

Malach-Pines A, Sadeh A, Dvir A, Yafe-Yanai O. 2002. Entrepreneurs and managers: Similar yet different. *International Journal of Organizational Analysis* 10(2): 172–190.

Malhotra D. 2009. When contracts destroy trust. *Harvard Business Review* 87(5): 25.

Marlin D, Lamont BT, Hoffman JJ. 1994. Choice situation, strategy, and performance: A reexamination. *Strategic Management Journal* 15: 229–239.

McCall MW. 1998. *High Flyers: Developing the Next Generation of Leaders*. Harvard Business School Press: Boston.

McDougall P, Oviatt B. 1996. New venture internationalization, strategic change, and performance: A follow-up study. *Journal of Business Venturing* 11(1): 23–40.

Meyer GD, Dean TJ. 1990. Upper echelons perspective on transformational leadership problems in high-technology firms. *Journal of High Technology Management Research* 1(2): 223–242.

Miller CC. 2010. Why Twitter's C.E.O. demoted himself. *New York Times*, October 30, 2010.

Mills CW. 1956. *The Power Elite*. Oxford University Press: New York.

Miner JB, Raju NS. 2004. Risk propensity differences between managers and entrepreneurs and between low- and high-growth entrepreneurs: A reply in a more conservative vein. *Journal of Applied Psychology* 89(1): 3–13.

Moore GA. 2002. *Crossing the Chasm* (3rd ed.). HarperCollins: New York.

Mosakowski E. 1998. Entrepreneurial resources, organizational choices, and competitive outcomes. *Organization Science* 9(6): 625–643.

Moskowitz TJ, Vissing-Jorgensen A. 2002. The returns to entrepreneurial investment: A private equity premium puzzle? *American Economic Review* 92(4): 745–778.

Nanda R. 2008. Entrepreneurship and the discipline of external finance. *Harvard Business School Working Paper No. 08-047.*

Northcraft GB, Neale MA. 1987. Experts, amateurs, and real estate: An anchoring-and-adjustment perspective on property pricing decisions. *Organizational Behavior and Human Decision Processes* 39(1): 84–97.

O'Reilly CA, Caldwell D, Barnett WP. 1989. Work group demography, social integration, and turnover. *Administrative Science Quarterly* 34: 21–37.

Ostrander SA. 1987. Elite domination in private social agencies. In GW Domhoff, TR Dye (Eds.), *Power Elites in Organizations*: 85–102. Sage: Thousand Oaks, CA.

Pennings JM. 1982. Organizational birth frequencies: An empirical investigation. *Administrative Science Quarterly* 29(1): 120–144.

Pennings JM, Wezel FC. 2010. Faraway, yet so close: Organizations in demographic flux. *Organization Science* 21(2): 451–468.

Peteraf MA. 1993. The cornerstones of competitive advantage: A resource-based view. *Strategic Management Journal* 14(3): 179–191.

Pfeffer J, Salancik GR. 1978. *The External Control of Organizations: A Resource Dependence Perspective*. Harper and Row: New York.

Porter ME. 1980. *Competitive Strategy*. Free Press: New York.

Prowse S. 1998. Angel investors and the market for angel investments. *Journal of Banking and Finance* 22(6–8): 785–792.

Reynolds PD, Curtin RT. 2008. *Business Creation in the United States*. NOW: Hanover, MA.

Roberts P, Khaire M. 2009. Getting known by the company you keep: Publicizing the qualifications and former associations of skilled employees. *Industrial and Corporate Change* 18(1): 77–106.

Rogers P, Blenko M. 2006. Who has the D? How clear decision roles enhance organization performance. *Harvard Business Review* 84(1): 52–61.

Romanelli E. 1989. Environments and strategies of organization start-up: Effect on early survival. *Administrative Science Quarterly* **34**(3): 369–387.

Rosenstein J, Bruno AV, Bygrave WD, Taylor NT. 1993. The CEO, venture capitalists, and the board. *Journal of Business Venturing* **8**(2): 99–113.

Ruef M. 2009. Economic inequality among entrepreneurs. In LA Keister (Ed.), *Economic Sociology of Work*, Vol. 18: 57–71. Emerald: Bradford, UK.

Ruef M. 2010. *The Entrepreneurial Group: Social Identities, Relations, and Collective Action*. Princeton University Press: Princeton, NJ.

Ruef M, Aldrich HE, Carter N. 2003. The structure of founding teams: Homophily, strong ties, and isolation among U.S. entrepreneurs. *American Sociological Review* **68**: 195–222.

Sabherwal R, Hirschheim R, Goles T. 2001. The dynamics of alignment: Insights from a punctuated equilibrium model. *Organization Science* **12**(2): 179–197.

Sahlman W. 1990. The structure and governance of venture-capital organizations. *Journal of Financial Economics* **27**: 473–521.

Salancik GR, Pfeffer J. 1980. Effects of ownership and performance on executive tenure in U.S. corporations. *Academy of Management Journal* **23**(4): 653–664.

Sapienza HJ, Korsgaard MA, Forbes DP. 2003. The self-determination motive and entrepreneurs' choice of financing. In JA Katz, D Shepherd (Eds.), *Cognitive Approaches to Entrepreneurship Research*, Vol. 6: 105–138. Elsevier: Burlington, MA.

Sarasvathy S. 2008. *Effectuation: Elements of Entrepreneurial Expertise*. Edward Elgar: Northampton, MA.

Schaubroeck J, Ganster DC, Jones JR. 1998. Organization and occupational influences in the attraction-selection-attribution process. *Journal of Applied Psychology* **83**: 869–891.

Schumpeter J. 1934. *Theory of Economic Development*. Harper and Row: New York.

Schumpeter J. 1942. *Capitalist, Socialism, and Democracy*. Harper & Brothers: New York.

Scitovszky TD. 1943. A note on profit maximization and its implications. *Review of Economic Studies* **11**(1): 57–60.

Shane S. 2008. *Illusions of Entrepreneurship*. Yale University Press: New Haven, CT.

Shane S, Stuart T. 2002. Organizational endowments and the performance of university start-ups. *Management Science* **48**(1): 154–170.

Shane S, Venkataraman S. 2000. The promise of entrepreneurship as a field of research. *Academy of Management Review* **25**: 217–226.

Sherer PD. 1995. Leveraging human assets in law firms: Human capital structures and organizational capabilities. *Industrial and Labor Relations Review* **48**: 671–691.

Singh JV, Lumsden CJ. 1990. Theory and research in organizational ecology. *Annual Review of Sociology* **16**: 161–195.

Sohl J. 2001–2009. Annual report: The angel investor market. *Center for Venture Research, University of New Hampshire.*

Sohl JE. 2003. The U.S. angel and venture capital market recent trends and developments. *Journal of Private Equity* **6**(2): 7–17.

Spence M. 2002. Signaling in retrospect and the informational structure of markets. *American Economic Review* **92**(3): 434–459.

Spolsky J. 2003. Fixing venture capital. *Joel on Software blog*, June 3, 2003. http://www.joelonsoftware.com/articles/VC.html.

Stam E, Thurik R, Van der Zwan P. 2008. Entrepreneurial exit in real and imagined markets. *Tinbergen Institute Discussion Paper No. 08-031/3.*

Starr JA, MacMillan IC. 1990. Resource cooptation via social contracting: Resource acquisition strategies for new ventures. *Strategic Management Journal* **11**: 79–92.

Stevenson HH, Jarillo JC. 1990. A paradigm of entrepreneurship: Entrepreneurial management. *Strategic Management Journal* **11**(1): 17–27.

Stewart WH, Roth PL. 2001. Risk propensity differences between entrepreneurs and managers: A meta-analytic review. *Journal of Applied Psychology* **86**(1): 145–153.

Stinchcombe AL. 1965. Organizations and social structure. In JG March (Ed.), *Handbook of Organizations*: 153–193. Rand McNally: Chicago.

Strasser JB, Becklund L. 1991. *Swoosh: The Unauthorized Story of Nike and the Men Who Played There.* Harcourt Brace Jovanovich: New York.

Stuart T, Hoang H, Hybels R. 1999. Interorganizational endorsements and the performance of entrepreneurial ventures. *Administrative Science Quarterly* **44**: 315–349.

Taylor A, Greve HR. 2006. Superman or Fantastic Four? Knowledge combination and experience in innovative teams. *Academy of Management Journal* **49**(4): 723–740.

Tsai W, Ghoshal S. 1998. Social capital and value creation: The role of intrafirm networks. *Academy of Management Journal* **41**(4): 464–476.

Ucbasaran D, Lockett A, Wright M, Westhead P. 2003. Entrepreneurial founding teams: Factors associated with member entry and exit. *Entrepreneurship Theory and Practice* **28**: 107–128.

Uzzi B. 1997. Social structures and competition in interfirm networks: The paradox of embeddedness. *Administrative Science Quarterly* **42**(1): 35–67.

Venkataraman S. 1997. The distinctive domain of entrepreneurship research. In *Advances in Entrepreneurship, Firm Emergence, and Growth*, Vol. 3: 119–138. JAI: Greenwich, CT.

Virany B, Tushman ML. 1986. Top management teams and corporate success in an emerging industry. *Journal of Business Venturing* 1(3): 261–274.

Virany B, Tushman ML, Romanelli E. 1992. Executive succession and organization outcomes in turbulent environments: An organization learning approach. *Organization Science* 3(1): 72–91.

Wadhwa V, Aggarwal R, Holly K, Salkever A. 2009. The anatomy of an entrepreneur: Family background and motivation. *Kauffman Foundation Research Paper* (July).

Waldinger RD, Lichter MI. 2003. *How the Other Half Works: Immigration and the Social Organization of Labor*. University of California Press: Berkeley.

Waldman DA, Ramirez GG, House RJ, Puranam P. 2001. Does leadership matter? CEO leadership attributes and profitability under conditions of perceived environmental uncertainty. *Academy of Management Journal* 44(1): 134–143.

Walsh JP. 1995. Managerial and organizational cognition: A trip down memory lane. *Organization Science* 6(3): 280–321.

Walton RE, McKersie RB. 1965. *A Behavioral Theory of Labor Negotiations: An Analysis of a Social Interaction System*. McGraw-Hill: New York.

Wasserman N. 2002. The venture capitalist as entrepreneur: Characteristics and dynamics within VC firms. *Unpublished Ph.D. thesis, Harvard University*.

Wasserman N. 2003. Founder-CEO succession and the paradox of entrepreneurial success. *Organization Science* 14(2): 149–172.

Wasserman N. 2005. Upside-down venture capitalists and the transition toward pyramidal firms. In L Keister (Ed.), *Research in the Sociology of Work: Entrepreneurship*: 151–208. JAI: Greenwich, CT.

Wasserman N. 2006a. Rich vs. King: The entrepreneur's dilemma. *Best Paper Proceedings, Academy of Management*.

Wasserman N. 2006b. Stewards, agents, and the founder discount: Executive compensation in new ventures. *Academy of Management Journal* 49: 960–976.

Wasserman N. 2008a. Don't wait too long to become an entrepreneur. *Harvard Business Review Blogs*, September 9, 2008. http://blogs.hbr.org/cs/2008/09/dont_wait_too_long_to_become_a.html.

Wasserman N. 2008b. Revisiting the strategy-structure-performance paradigm: The case of venture capital. *Organization Science* 19(2): 241–259.

Wasserman N, Barley L. 2009. A note on the legal and tax implications of founders' equity splits. *Harvard Business School Note No. 809-110*, 1–15.

Wasserman N, Boeker W. 2005. Mentoring and monitoring: The evolution of boards of directors in new ventures. *Best Paper Proceedings, Babson Research Conference.*

Wasserman N, Hellman T. 2010a. The first deal: The division of founder equity in new ventures. *Academy of Management Annual Meeting.*

Wasserman N, Marx M. 2008. Split decisions: How social and economic choices affect the stability of founding. *Academy of Management Annual Meeting.*

Wasserman N, Nazeeri F, Anderson K. 2010b. A "Rich-vs.-King" approach to term sheet negotiations. *Harvard Business School Note No. 810-119.*

Weber M. 1946. *From Max Weber: Essays in Sociology.* Oxford University Press: New York.

Weber M. 1949/1997. *The Methodology of the Social Sciences* (EA Shils, HA Finch, Trans.). Free Press: New York.

Wiersema MF, Bantel KA. 1992. Top management team demography and corporate strategic change. *Academy of Management Journal* 35(1): 91–121.

Williamson OE. 1985. *The Economic Institutions of Capitalism: Firms, Markets, Relational Contracting.* Free Press: New York.

Wilmerding A. 2004. *Term Sheets & Valuations.* Aspatore: Boston.

Wozniak S. 2006. *iWoz: Computer Geek to Cult Icon: How I Invented the Personal Computer, Co-Founded Apple, and Had Fun Doing It.* Norton: New York.

Young JS, Simon WL. 2004. *iCon: Steve Jobs, the Greatest Second Act in the History of Business.* John Wiley: San Francisco.

Zaleznik A, Kets de Vries MFR. 1975. *Power and the Corporate Mind.* Houghton Mifflin: Boston.

INDEX

Abbott Labs, 45
accountability and role assignments, 128
acquisition route, exit decisions, 376–83
Adams, Tim, 320, 346
Addante, Frank: decision-making approach, 191; entrepreneurial motivations, 33, 119, 355; equity split decisions, 150, 151, 162, 197; financing decisions, 252, 271–72; hiring decisions, 228–29, 230, 343–44; IPO decision-making, 383, 384, 385
Adnet, 150
age factor, entrepreneurship decision, 27–29, 34–35, 427nn3–5
agency theory, 180–82, 362–63, 447n53
Aldrich, H., 6n, 428n13, 432n50, 435n3
The Alexander Group (TAG), 49–50
alignment, decision-making. *See* Three Rs equilibrium
Allen, Paul, 166
altruism motivation, entrepreneurship, 32, 33, 35
Anderson, M. C., 443n24
angel investors: overview, 255, 262–67; and entrepreneurship timing, 66; financial capital statistics, 20, 270, 427n31; social capital benefits, 271. *See also* financing approaches; venture capitalists
Antje, at Zipcar, 167
Apple Computer. *See* Jobs, Steve *and* Wozniak, Steve

autocracy blueprint, hiring decisions, 210n
autocratic model, decision-making approach, 129–30, 134–38, 437nn6, 9
autonomy motivation, 33

Bagley, C. E., 277
Baker, T., 435n2, 441n3, 442n12
Balsillie, James, 132n
Baron, J, 443n22
Baron, J. N., 436n19
Baum, J. R., 433n59
Baxter company, 44–45
Beckes-Gellner, U., 435n11
Ben and Jerry's, 131n
Bergen, Chris, 384
Bernardo, A. E., 433n58
Bhide, Amar, 3, 425n3
Biblical wisdom, 99, 307n
Blanchflower, D. G., 48
Blank, Steve, 65
Blau, P., 437n14
Blogger. *See* Williams, Evan
blueprint study, hiring decisions, 210–11, 441nn1–2 (ch 8)
Blumberg, Matt, 287
board of directors: angel investor participation, 263–64; and founder backgrounds, 45–46; founder participation numbers, 138–40, 143–44, 285; solo approach correlations, 340; venture capitalist impact, 273–78, 284–93, 446nn48–50, 447n51. *See also* succession process, founder-CEOs